378.1664 SAT verbal workbook.
SAT

$16.00

3400

DATE			

Other Kaplan Books for College-Bound Students

College Admissions and Financial Aid

Guide to the Best Colleges in the U.S.

Kaplan/Newsweek College Catalog

Parent's Guide to College Admissions

Scholarships

What to Study: 101 Fields in a Flash

You Can Afford College

The Yale Daily News Guide to Succeeding in College

Test Preparation

SAT & PSAT

SAT Math Workbook

SAT Verbal Velocity

SAT II: Biology

SAT II: Chemistry

SAT II: Mathematics

SAT II: Writing

SAT or ACT? Test Your Best

ACT

SAT*
Verbal Workbook

BY THE STAFF OF KAPLAN EDUCATIONAL CENTERS

Simon & Schuster

NEW YORK · LONDON · SINGAPORE · SYDNEY · TORONTO

*SAT is a registered trademark of the College Entrance Examination Board,
which was not involved in the production of, and does not endorse, this product.

Kaplan Publishing
Published by Simon & Schuster
1230 Avenue of the Americas
New York, NY 10020

"Brightening the City" by Juan Carlos Langlois, *The Unesco Courier*, April 1992. Reprinted by permission of UNESCO.
"Earth's Ozone Shield Under Threat" by France Bequette, *The Unesco Courier*, June 1990. Reprinted by permission of UNESCO.
From *Life Itself* by Francis Crick. Copyright © 1981 by Francis Crick. Reproduced with the permission of Felicity Bryan Literary Agency.

Project Editor: Megan Duffy

Cover Design: Cheung Tai

Interior Page Layout: Martha Arango

Production Editor: Maude Spekes

Desktop Publishing Manager: Michael Shevlin

Managing Editor: Dave Chipps

Executive Editor: Del Franz

Special thanks to: Laura Barnes, Maureen Blair, Michael Cader, Gerard Capistrano, Joanna Cohen, Gordon Drummond, Kate Foster, Amparo Graf, Jay Johnson, Liza Kleinman, Kiernan McGuire, Marie Mockett, Krista Pfeiffer, John Polstein, and Donna Ratajczak.

The material in this book is up-to-date at the time of publication. The College Entrance Examination Board may have instituted changes after this book was published. Please read all materials you receive regarding the SAT carefully.

October 2000

10 9 8 7 6 5 4 3 2 1

Manufactured in the United States of America

Published simultaneously in Canada

ISBN 0-7432-0182-5

Table of Contents

↗ + Short Comprehension

How to Use This Book

Since a great way to prepare yourself for the SAT is to practice answering testlike questions, this workbook gives you hundreds of sample Verbal problems to work on.

Practice Sets

Most of this workbook is divided into practice sets corresponding to the three Verbal question types you'll get on the SAT: Analogies, Sentence Completions, and Critical Reading. There's an introduction for each of these question types that briefly goes over the key strategies you need to effectively answer each question type. Write your answers directly in the book on the answer ovals provided.

Order of Difficulty

With the exception of Critical Reading, questions within each practice set are arranged by order of difficulty—just like on the real SAT. You should practice with all three question types, paying attention to the recommended time for each practice test. Scorecards are provided to help you track your progress.

Explanations

We've included explanations for every question in this workbook. Use these explanations to figure out why you got questions wrong and how to avoid making the same mistakes in the future. You should also look at the explanations for questions that you got right—especially if you weren't sure and guessed—to find out the best way to answer questions. You'll also notice intervals where we give you words and their definitions—use these helpful sidebars to learn new words and flex your vocabulary muscles on the SAT.

Kaplan's Word List and Root List

This workbook contains a reference section that gives you a Word List and Root List to help you build your SAT-level vocabulary for Test Day.

Sample Tests

Finally, there are Verbal sections of two sample SAT tests—for a total of six Verbal sections. You should take these under timed, testlike conditions.

NOTE: *For more tips on the verbal portion of the SAT, pick up Kaplan's* SAT & PSAT. *For a last-minute, well-organized practice, look for Kaplan's* SAT & PSAT Essential Review. *If you have any questions about the SAT, or want more information about Kaplan, call us at 1–800–KAP–TEST, or visit our Web site at kaptest.com.*

A Special Note for International Students

If you are an international student considering attending an American university, you are not alone. Approximately 500,000 international students pursued academic degrees at the undergraduate, graduate, or professional school level at U.S. universities during the 1998–1999 academic year, according to the Institute of International Education's *Open Doors* report. Almost 50 percent of these students were studying for a bachelor's or first university degree. This number of international students pursuing higher education in the United States is expected to continue to grow. Business, management, engineering, and the physical and life sciences are particularly popular majors for students coming to the United States from other countries.

If you are not a U.S. citizen and you are interested in attending college or university in the United States, here is what you'll need to get started.

- If English is not your first language, you'll probably need to take the TOEFL (Test of English as a Foreign Language) or provide some other evidence that you are proficient in English in order to complete an academic degree program. Colleges and universities in the United States will differ on what they consider to be an acceptable TOEFL score. A minimum TOEFL score of 213 (550 on the paper-based TOEFL) or better is often required by more prestigious and competitive institutions. Because American undergraduate programs require all students to take a certain number of general education courses, all students—even math and computer science students—need to be able to communicate well in spoken and written English.

- You may also need to take the SAT or the ACT. Many undergraduate institutions in the United States require both the SAT and TOEFL of international students.

- There are over 2,700 accredited colleges and universities in the United States, so selecting the correct undergraduate school can be a confusing task for anyone. You will need to get help from a good adviser or at least a good college guide that gives you detailed information on the different schools available. Since admission to many undergraduate programs is quite competitive, you may want to select three or four colleges and complete applications for each school.

- You should begin the application process at least a year in advance. An increasing number of schools accept applications year round. In any case, find out the application deadlines and plan accordingly. Although September (the fall semester) is the traditional time to begin university study in the United States, you can begin your studies at many schools in January (the spring semester).

- In addition, you will need to obtain an I-20 Certificate of Eligibility from the school you plan to attend if you intend to apply for an F-1 Student Visa to study in the United States.

Kaplan International Programs

If you need more help with the complex process of university admissions, assistance preparing for the SAT, ACT, or TOEFL, or help building your English language skills in general, you may be interested in Kaplan's programs for international students.

Kaplan International Programs were designed to help students and professionals from outside the United States meet their educational and career goals. At locations throughout the United States, international students take advantage of Kaplan's programs to help them improve their academic and conversational English skills, raise their scores on the TOEFL, SAT, ACT, and other standardized exams, and gain admission to the schools of their choice. Our staff and instructors give international students the individualized attention they need to succeed. Here is a brief description of some of Kaplan's programs for international students:

General Intensive English

Kaplan's General Intensive English classes are designed to help you improve your skills in all areas of English and to increase your fluency in spoken and written English. Classes are available for beginning to advanced students, and the average class size is 12 students.

English for TOEFL and University Preparation

This course provides you with the skills you need to improve your TOEFL score and succeed in a U.S. university or graduate program. It includes advanced reading, writing, listening, grammar, and conversational English, plus university admissions counseling. You will also receive training for the TOEFL using Kaplan's exclusive computer-based practice materials.

SAT Test Preparation Course

The SAT is an important admission criterion for U.S. colleges and universities. A high score can help you stand out from other applicants. This course includes the skills you need to succeed on each section of the SAT, as well as access to Kaplan's exclusive practice materials.

English & SAT

This course includes a combination of English instruction and SAT test preparation. Our English & SAT course is for students who need to boost their English skills while preparing for the SAT and admission into an American university.

KAPLAN

Other Kaplan Programs

Since 1938, more than 3 million students have come to Kaplan to advance their studies, prepare for entry to American universities, and further their careers. In addition to the above programs, Kaplan offers courses to prepare for the ACT, GMAT, GRE, MCAT, DAT, USMLE, NCLEX, and other standardized exams at locations throughout the United States.

Applying to Kaplan International Programs

To get more information, or to apply for admission to any of Kaplan's programs for international students and professionals, contact us at:

Kaplan International Programs
888 Seventh Avenue, New York, NY 10106 USA
Telephone: (212) 492-5990 Fax: (212) 957-1654
E-mail: world@kaplan.com
Web: www.studyusa.kaplan.com

Kaplan is authorized under federal law to enroll nonimmigrant alien students.
Kaplan is authorized to issue Form IAP-66 needed for a J-1 (Exchange Visitor) visa.
Kaplan is accredited by ACCET (Accrediting Council for Continuing Education and Training).
Test names are registered trademarks of their respective owners.

SAT
Analogies

INTRODUCTION TO SAT ANALOGIES

Analogies test your ability to define relationships between words. Analogies also test your knowledge of college-level vocabulary.

The Structure

You'll probably see thirteen Analogies in one of the two 30-minute Verbal sections and six Analogies in the other. Both sections also include Sentence Completions and Critical Reading.

Analogies are arranged in order of difficulty. The hardest questions are at the end of each set.

The Format

The instructions for Analogies appear at the top of the questions. They look something like this:

Choose the lettered pair of words that is related in the same way as the pair in capital letters.

EXAMPLE

FLAKE : SNOW ::

(A) storm : hail

(B) drop : rain

(C) field : wheat

(D) stack : hay

(E) cloud : fog

Kaplan's Method

Here's our simple Three-Step Method for doing Analogies:

- Build a bridge.
- Plug the bridge into the answer choices.
- Adjust the bridge if you need to.

1. Build a bridge.

First, build a bridge between the two words in capital letters, the *stem words*. In the example above, your bridge might be: SNOW, by definition, is made of FLAKE(S).

HINT: *A good bridge is a sentence that makes a strong, definite connection, such as "Snow is always made of flakes."*

2. Plug the answer choices into the bridge.

Take your bridge and plug in answer choices (A) through (E). The two words in the correct answer relate in the same way as the stem words.

(A)   *Hail* is made of *storm(s)*? No.

(B)   *Rain* is made of *drop(s)*? Yes.

(C)   *Wheat* is made of *field(s)*? No.

(D)   *Hay* is made of *stack(s)*? No.

(E)   *Cloud* is made of *sky*? No.

3. Adjust the bridge if you need to.

If more than one answer fits your bridge, try building a different bridge. Here the only correct answer is (B), so there's no need for adjustments.

HINT: *If more than one answer choice works, make your bridge more specific.*

Pacing

You need to leave plenty of time for Critical Reading, so work systematically.

- Do the early, more basic Analogies quickly.

- Take no more than 40 seconds on any Analogy.

HINT: *Stumped? Circle the question in your test book and skip it on your answer sheet. Come back if there's time after you've finished the whole section.*

What If a Stem Word Could Be Two Parts of Speech?

If a stem word could be either a noun or a verb, how can you build a bridge? Look down the column below the word, and see what all the other words are.

HINT: *In the same column, every word will be the same part of speech.*

In the Analogy that follows, how do you know whether *peel* is a noun (a banana peel) or a verb (to peel a banana)?

BANANA : PEEL ::

(A) egg : crack

(B) carrot : uproot

(C) apple : core

(D) bread : slice

(E) corn : husk

HINT: *Look at the answer choice words under* PEEL. *Four words—crack, core, slice, and husk—can be nouns or verbs. But answer choice (B)* **uproot** *must be a verb. Since all the words in the same column must be the same part of speech, you know* peel *is being used as a verb. So your bridge could be: When you peel a banana, you take off the skin.*

What If You Don't Know a Stem Word?

In addition to testing your thinking skills, Analogies test your vocabulary. That's why it's important to study Kaplan's Word List and Root List, found at the back of this book.

Regardless of how hard you study, sometimes you won't know one or both stem words. If that happens, don't give up. Instead, focus on the answer choices and use the following strategies.

Analogy Strategy 1: Eliminate Answer Choices with Weak Bridges

Even without understanding the stem pair on an Analogy question, you can often tell which answer choices are likely to be right and which are probably wrong. Think of it this way: The stem pair in an SAT Analogy almost always has a strong bridge. The correct answer must have the same bridge, so it will have a strong bridge, too. By a "strong bridge" we mean a specific, definite connection. For example, the pair **STABLE : HORSE** has a strong bridge: "A **stable** is, by definition, where you keep a **horse.**" On the other hand, **STABLE : OATS** has a weak bridge. You may or may not find **oats** in a **stable.** As you do Analogy questions, you can safely eliminate such pairs with weak bridges because they can't be correct. Don't waste time thinking about them. Cross them out. Then focus on the answer choices that are more likely to be correct.

Analogy Strategy 2: Eliminate Pairs with Identical Bridges

There's another way of eliminating some wrong choices that's so obvious you might not think of it. If two choices have the same bridge, it follows that neither one can be more right than the other. And since they can't both be right, they must both be wrong.

Analogy Strategy 3: Look for a Strong Bridge

Since the correct answer has to have the same strong bridge as the stem pair, after you've eliminated choices with distinctly weak bridges, and after you've eliminated choices with identical bridges, it's a good guessing strategy to pick the choice with the strongest bridge.

Analogy Strategy 4: Work Backwards from the Answer Choices

Even if you're not sure what one of the stem words means, you always know that the two stem words are related to each other in some way. The five answer choices provide you with five ways in which the stem words *might* be related to each other. Work out bridges for the answer choices, then compare these with the stem pair. Some of the answer choices will seem unlikely given the stem word that you already know—these can be rejected.

Keep in mind that you may not always be able to eliminate *all* the wrong answer choices. However, if you can eliminate any choices at all, it is worth your while to guess.

Checklist

Analogies:

❑ Use Kaplan's Three-Step Method: Build a bridge, plug it in, and adjust it if you need to.

❑ Spend no more than 40 seconds on even the hardest Analogy.

❑ If you don't know a stem word, try Analogy Strategies:

  • Eliminate answer choices with weak bridges.

  • Eliminate pairs with identical bridges.

  • Look for a strong bridge.

  • Work backwards from the answer choices.

❑ If all else fails, guess—as long as you can eliminate at least one wrong answer choice.

6. VOID : EMPTY ::

(A) glut : prosperous
(B) system : organized
(C) answer : questioning
(D) ration : scarce
(E) intent : clear   Ⓐ Ⓑ Ⓒ Ⓓ Ⓔ

7. EVADE : STRAIGHTFORWARD ::

(A) leave : inviting
(B) enliven : animated
(C) flatten : smooth
(D) boast : modest
(E) assist : helpful   Ⓐ Ⓑ Ⓒ Ⓓ Ⓔ

8. FICKLE : INCONSISTENCY ::

(A) cloudy : warmth
(B) innate : capability
(C) worthy : heroism
(D) placid : calmness
(E) solid : order   Ⓐ Ⓑ Ⓒ Ⓓ Ⓔ

9. IMMATURE : DEVELOP ::

(A) tempestuous : explode
(B) unready : prepare
(C) superstitious : believe
(D) unfeasible : originate
(E) fortuitous : plan   Ⓐ Ⓑ Ⓒ Ⓓ Ⓔ

10. INDOLENT : SLOTH ::

(A) fertile : fecundity
(B) presumptuous : deviation
(C) miserable : tragedy
(D) appealing : delineation
(E) destructive : progress   Ⓐ Ⓑ Ⓒ Ⓓ Ⓔ

Suggested Time: 7 minutes

Directions—Choose the lettered pair of words that is related in the same way as the pair in capital letters.

Example:
FLAKE : SNOW ::

(A) storm : hail
(B) drop : rain
(C) field : wheat
(D) stack : hay
(E) cloud : fog   Ⓐ ● Ⓒ Ⓓ Ⓔ

1. TREE : FOREST ::

(A) bird : sky
(B) fish : sea
(C) star : galaxy
(D) mammal : land
(E) lake : river   Ⓐ Ⓑ Ⓒ Ⓓ Ⓔ

2. MARE : HORSE ::

(A) cat : dog
(B) shark : fish
(C) worm : snake
(D) lion : tiger
(E) ewe : sheep   Ⓐ Ⓑ Ⓒ Ⓓ Ⓔ

3. CEASE-FIRE : HOSTILITIES ::

(A) reckoning : probabilities
(B) truce : belligerents
(C) artillery : tanks
(D) campaign : strategies
(E) adjournment : proceedings   Ⓐ Ⓑ Ⓒ Ⓓ Ⓔ

4. FLORAL : FLOWERS ::

(A) perennial : plants
(B) morbid : cemeteries
(C) emotional : feelings
(D) moral : stories
(E) maniacal : men   Ⓐ Ⓑ Ⓒ Ⓓ Ⓔ

5. SEQUESTER : JUROR ::

(A) quarantine : patient
(B) cloister : convent
(C) parole : prisoner
(D) graduate : pupil
(E) elect : mayor   Ⓐ Ⓑ Ⓒ Ⓓ Ⓔ

SCORECARD	
Number of Questions Right:	
Number of Questions Wrong:	
Number of Questions Omitted:	
Number of Correct Guesses:	
Number of Wrong Guesses:	
Time Used:	

ANSWERS AND EXPLANATIONS

1. C

A strong bridge here might be: *A* **FOREST** *is made up of many* **TREES.**

When you plug it in to the answer choices, only (C) makes sense. A **galaxy** is made up of many **stars.**

There may be **birds** in the **sky, fish** in the **sea,** and **mammals** on **land,** but the sky, seas, and land aren't made up of these creatures. Finally, a **lake** and a **river** are two different kinds of bodies of water.

2. E

Bridge: *A* **MARE,** *by definition, is a female* **HORSE.** The only answer choice that makes sense is (E)—A **ewe** is a female **sheep.**

If you knew that a **MARE** is a female **HORSE,** but you didn't know that a **ewe** is a female **sheep,** you could still have picked (E) by process of elimination. No other answer choice has the bridge "X is a female Y."

If you knew that a **MARE** is some type of **HORSE,** but you didn't know that it was a female horse, you could still have eliminated (A), (C), and (D), where the word pairs don't refer to the same kind of animal. Then you would guess between (B) and (E).

3. E

Bridge: *A* **CEASE-FIRE** *marks the end of* **HOSTILITIES.**

(B) is tempting, but the bridge doesn't fit. A **truce** marks the end of **belligerents**—no. A **truce** marks the end of fighting, but **belligerents** are the warring parties, and they don't disappear when you make a **truce.**

In (E), an **adjournment** marks the end of **proceedings.** The answer choice fits.

> *cease-fire: temporary end to fighting*
> *hostilities: warlike activities*
> *adjournment: a temporary suspension*
> *proceedings: activities or events*
> *belligerents: warring parties or sides*
> *reckoning: estimation or calculation*
> *artillery: large-caliber firearms*

4. C

Bridge: **FLORAL** *means "having to do with* **FLOWERS."**

In (A), **perennial** means having to do with special kinds of **plants,** but not with plants as a whole. In (B), **morbid** has to do with death, but not specifically with **cemeteries.** In (C), **emotional** means having to do with **feelings.** A good definition, but continue to plug the bridge into the other choices.

(D) **Moral** means ethical, relating to principles of right and wrong, not having to do with **stories.** This connection is weak.

(E) **Maniacal** means having to do with **men**—no. Although the words look similar, "maniacal" has no relation to men. It's related to "mania."

> *perennial: coming back every year, as with perennial plants*
> *morbid: referring to death or disease*
> *maniacal: frantic or characterized by madness*

5. A

The first bridge you thought of might have been: **JURORS** *get* **SEQUESTERED.** But that's a weak bridge because it's so general. So think again.

A strong bridge might be: *By definition, to* **SEQUESTER JURORS** *means to isolate them.* When you plug the bridge into the answer choices, (A) fits. To **quarantine patients** is to isolate them. This could be the answer, but check the other choices.

In (B), **cloister** might be tempting, but to **cloister** isn't to isolate a **convent.**

sequester: to set apart or segregate
quarantine: to isolate
cloister: to cut off from the world
convent: a place where nuns live
parole: to release a prisoner
*   conditionally, before a sentence is*
*   fully served*

6. B

To make your bridge you need to know that **VOID** is a noun and **EMPTY** is an adjective. Remember the rule: All the words in the same column must be the same part of speech.

Since **system** and **intent** in column one can only be nouns, all words in the first column must be nouns. Since **prosperous** and **scarce** in column two can only be adjectives, all the words in the second column are adjectives.

Bridge: *Something* **EMPTY** *is a* **VOID.** Plug it into the answer choices:

(A) Something **prosperous** is a **glut**—doesn't make sense.

(B) Something **organized** is a **system**—yes.

(C) Something **questioning** is an **answer**—no.

(D) Something **scarce** is a **ration**—no.

(E) Something **clear** is an **intent**—no.

(B) is the only possible answer.

prosperous: flourishing or wealthy
glut: oversupply
ration: allotment or share

7. D

Bridge: *Someone who* **EVADES** *is, by definition, not* **STRAIGHTFORWARD.**

When you plug it into all the answer choices, the only one that makes sense is (D): Someone who **boasts** is not **modest**.

evade: to avoid or go around something
animated: lively

8. D

Bridge: *To be* **FICKLE** *is to show* **INCONSISTENCY.**

Now plug the bridge into the answer choices.

(A) To be **cloudy** is to show **warmth**—no.

(B) To be **innate** is to show **capability**—no.

(C) To be **worthy** is to show **heroism.** Not necessarily. You can be worthy without displaying heroism.

(D) To be **placid** is to show **calmness**—definitely.

(E) To be **solid** is to show **order**—no.

So (C) is a possibility, but (D) is the stronger choice. Pick (D).

innate: essential or inborn
placid: calm

9. B

This bridge is: *Someone (or something)* **IMMATURE** *hasn't* **DEVELOPED.**

When you plug it in:

(A) Someone **tempestuous** hasn't **exploded.** Maybe or maybe not.

(B) Someone **unready** hasn't **prepared**—a possibility.

(C) Someone **superstitious** hasn't **believed**—no. Superstitious people *do* believe.

(D) Something **unfeasible** hasn't **originated**—no.

(E) Something **fortuitous** hasn't been **planned**—true. Here's another possibility.

To choose between (B) and (E), define the stem bridge

a little more carefully. Someone who's **IMMATURE** hasn't **DEVELOPED** *yet,* but should.

(B) fits that bridge; someone who's **unready**—for the SAT, for example—hasn't **prepared** yet, but should.

But (E) doesn't work. It doesn't make sense to say: Something **fortuitous** hasn't **planned** yet.

So (B) is correct.

immature: not mature or developed
tempestuous: stormy
superstitious: believing in magic or
*   chance*
unfeasible: impossible
fortuitous: fortunate, lucky, occurring
*   by chance*

10. A

The bridge is a definition: **SLOTH** *is the quality of being* **INDOLENT.**

Now plug the bridge into the answer choices.

(A) **Fecundity** is the quality of being **fertile.** True, so (A) has the same relationship as the stem pair.

(B) **Deviation** is the quality of being **presumptuous**—no. They have nothing to do with each other.

(C) **Tragedy** is the quality of being **miserable**—not quite. *Misery* is the quality of being miserable. Still, you might think (C) is a possibility.

(D) **Delineation** is the quality of being **appealing**—not so.

(E) **Progress** is the quality of being **destructive**—nonsense.

Even if you thought (C) was a possible answer, (A) is the stronger, clearer match.

HINT: *Sometimes a stem word has two meanings.*

In this case, a **SLOTH** is also a lazy, slow-moving mammal. If your original stem bridge doesn't fit any answer choice, build a new bridge using the second meaning.

indolent: lazy
sloth: laziness; also a type of tree-
*   dwelling, slow-moving animal*
fecundity: the ability to reproduce or be
*   fruitful*
fertile: fruitful
tragedy: a disastrous event, a calamity
presumptuous: taking liberties or over-
*   stepping boundaries*
deviation: departure from the norm
delineation: outline or sketch

KAPLAN

Example:
FLAKE : SNOW ::

(A) storm : hail
(B) drop : rain
(C) field : wheat
(D) stack : hay
(E) cloud : fog

Ⓐ ⬤ Ⓒ Ⓓ Ⓔ

1. PILOT : AIRPLANE ::

(A) team : players ✕
(B) helmsman : ship
(C) horse : cart ✕
(D) passenger : train
(E) army : country

Ⓐ Ⓑ Ⓒ Ⓓ Ⓔ

2. BANANA : PEEL ::

(A) egg : crack
(B) carrot : uproot
(C) apple : core
(D) bread : slice
(E) corn : husk

Ⓐ Ⓑ Ⓒ Ⓓ Ⓔ

3. BONE : BODY ::

(A) floor : house ✕
(B) motor : boat
(C) driver : car ✕
(D) knob : door
(E) beam : building

Ⓐ Ⓑ Ⓒ Ⓓ Ⓔ

4. WHIP : LASH ::

(A) mitt : throw
(B) shoe : walk
(C) baton : defy
(D) paddle : play
(E) club : beat

Ⓐ Ⓑ Ⓒ Ⓓ Ⓔ

5. MIGRATION : SWALLOW ::

(A) hibernation : groundhog
(B) dissection : frog
(C) predation : elk
(D) diversity : finch
(E) mimicry : ape

Ⓐ Ⓑ Ⓒ Ⓓ Ⓔ

6. TOUCH : TACTILE ::

(A) sound : noisy
(B) smell : olfactory
(C) mouth : verbal
(D) vision : beautiful
(E) taste : critical

Ⓐ Ⓑ Ⓒ Ⓓ Ⓔ

7. CURIOSITY : KNOW ::

(A) chattiness : listen
(B) talent : develop
(C) greediness : possess
(D) deception : disclose
(E) boredom : entertain

Ⓐ Ⓑ Ⓒ Ⓓ Ⓔ

8. ARTICULATENESS : SPEECH ::

(A) behavior : society
(B) music : note
(C) ballet : form
(D) legibility : handwriting
(E) painting : palette

Ⓐ Ⓑ Ⓒ Ⓓ Ⓔ

9. ATTENTIVENESS : RAPT ::

(A) loyalty : unscrupulous
(B) diatribe : derisive
(C) creativity : innovative
(D) jealousy : indolent
(E) impudence : polite

Ⓐ Ⓑ Ⓒ Ⓓ Ⓔ

10. DISPUTANT : ALTERCATION ::

(A) interlocutor : conversation
(B) lecturer : dialogue
(C) deliverer : message
(D) chatterbox : refutation
(E) orator : language

Ⓐ Ⓑ Ⓒ Ⓓ Ⓔ

SCORECARD	
Number of Questions Right:	9
Number of Questions Wrong:	1
Number of Questions Omitted:	—
Number of Correct Guesses:	1
Number of Wrong Guesses:	
Time Used:	

ANSWERS AND EXPLANATIONS

1. B

The first bridge you think of might be: A **PILOT** flies an **AIRPLANE.** But a quick trip through the answer choices will tell you that bridge doesn't fit. So try another: *A **PILOT**, by definition, is someone who operates or steers an **AIRPLANE.***

A **team** is not the person who operates **players.** But a **helmsman** does operate or steer a **ship.** If you don't know a **helmsman** from a helmet, see if you can rule out any more wrong answers. **Horses** pull **carts,** but they don't operate or steer them; drivers do. And **passengers** ride in **trains,** but they don't run them. Finally, although the **army** runs some **countries,** operating or steering a **country** is not part of the definition of an **army.** So even if you didn't know what **helmsman** means, you could have chosen (B) by the process of elimination.

2. E

To build this bridge you have to know whether **PEEL** is a noun (the skin of a banana) or a verb (to peel a banana). Remember our rule: All words in the same column are the same part of speech. In the answer choices below **PEEL,** four words (**crack, core, slice, husk**) can be either verbs or nouns. But **uproot** can be used only as a verb. That means **PEEL** and all words beneath **PEEL** are verbs. So the bridge is: *To **PEEL** a **BANANA** means to remove its outer covering.*

(C) means almost the opposite: To **core** an **apple** means to remove the center portion. **Uprooting** a **carrot** means to dig it up. The only two choices that involve removing an outer covering are (A) and (E). **Cracking** an **egg** doesn't necessarily remove the eggshell. But **husking** means removing the covering from an ear of **corn,** so (E) fits the stem bridge.

3. E

The obvious stem bridge here is: *A **BONE** is part of a **BODY,*** but that would fit too many answer choices. So try working backwards. Define bridges for each answer choice, and see which one also fits the stem pair.

The **floor** of a **house** is a horizontal surface. That doesn't work for the stem pair. A **motor** provides power to make a **boat** move, but a **BONE** doesn't make a **BODY** move. Nor does a **BONE** steer a **BODY** as a **driver** steers a **car.** And you don't use a **BONE** to open a **BODY,** as you would use a **knob** to open a **door.** So it looks like (E) is correct, by process of elimination. A **beam** is part of the structural support of a **building.** Sure enough, a **BONE** is part of the structural support of a **BODY.**

4. E

To make your bridge, you need to know whether **WHIP** and **LASH** are verbs or nouns. Again, apply our rule: The answer choices below each column are all the same part of speech. In the first column, **mitt** can only be a noun (you can't **mitt** someone), so **WHIP** is also a noun. In column two, **defy** can't be a noun, so all the words must be verbs, including **LASH.**

Now you can build your stem bridge: *You **LASH** someone with a **WHIP.***

The only tempting choices are (D) and (E). You can't **paddle** someone with a **play**—a **paddle** is used to **play** a game. But you can **beat** someone with a **club.**

5. A

Your bridge might be: *By definition, **MIGRATION** is something **SWALLOWS** do every year.* **Hibernation** is something **groundhogs** do every year, so (A) looks like a winner. Check out the other choices, though.

Choices (B) through (E)—**dissection, predation, diversity,** and **mimicry**—have nothing to do with seasonal activities of the animals or birds paired with these words, so stay with (A).

migration: *movement from one area to*
    another; seasonal change of location
hibernation: *sleeplike state many*
    animals go through each winter
dissection: *process of surgical cutting to*
    expose parts for scientific
    examination
predation: *the act of preying on*
diversity: *variety*
mimicry: *the practice or art of*
    imitation

6. B

Here you really have to know what the stem words mean to create the bridge: **TACTILE** *means pertaining to the sense of* **TOUCH.** In the same way, **olfactory** means pertaining to the sense of **smell.**

Check the other answers; in (A), **noisy** doesn't mean pertaining to the sense of **sound. Noisy** means loud. In (C), **verbal** doesn't mean pertaining to the sense of **mouth.** In (D), **beautiful** doesn't mean pertaining to the sense of **vision.** In (E), **critical** doesn't mean pertaining to the sense of **taste.**

7. C

A strong bridge would be: **CURIOSITY,** *by definition, is the urge to* **KNOW** *things.* In the same way, **greediness** is the urge to **possess** things.

In (A), **chattiness** is not an urge to **listen.** In (D), **deception** has more to do with an urge to hide something than with an urge to **disclose.** In (B), **talent** does not imply an urge to **develop.** Now look at answer choice (E). **Boredom** and **entertain** relate, but not in the same way as the stem words. **Boredom** is not the urge to **entertain.** It might prompt an urge to be entertained (by others), but that's another story.

disclose: *to reveal*
deception: *fraud, double-dealing,*
    trickery

8. D

If you know what **ARTICULATENESS** means, finding the answer is easy. Your bridge is: **ARTICULATENESS** *is clarity of* **SPEECH.** Since **legibility** is clarity of **handwriting,** (D) is the right answer.

If you're not sure how **ARTICULATENESS** relates to **SPEECH,** you can still find the answer by working backwards from the answer choices. There's no obvious bridge between **behavior** and **society,** so rule out (A). In (B), you could say **music** is made up of **notes,** but it's unlikely that **ARTICULATENESS** is made up of **SPEECH,** so (B) is probably wrong.

In (C), **form** has no direct relationship to **ballet,** so it's probably wrong. In (D), **legibility** means clarity of **handwriting. ARTICULATENESS** could be clarity of **SPEECH,** so (D) could be right. Checking out (E), a **palette** for mixing colors when **painting** has nothing in common with the stem words.

(D) sounds the best, and in fact, is right.

articulateness: *the quality of clear and*
    effective speech
legibility: *the quality of being readable*
    or decipherable
palette: *small, handheld board for*
    mixing paint colors; range of colors

9. C

Your bridge: *Someone who's* **RAPT** *is, by definition,* super**ATTENTIVE.** Similarly, an **innovative** person is super**creative,** choice (C).

Pairs (A) and (E) are both almost opposites: If you're **unscrupulous,** you're certainly not **loyal.** If you're **polite,** you're not **impudent.** Keep in mind that when two pairs have the same bridge, they must both be wrong. After all, they can't both be right! As for (B), a **diatribe** may or may not be **derisive.** And in (D), **indolent** has no connection whatsoever with **jealousy.**

rapt: fascinated, wholly absorbed
unscrupulous: having no morals or
   ethics
diatribe: a long, bitter speech
derisive: mocking
innovative: highly original, novel
indolent: lazy
impudence: insolence, cockiness

10. A

The stem bridge is: *A* **DISPUTANT** *takes part in an* **ALTERCATION.** An **interlocutor** takes part in a **conversation,** so the relationship in (A) is the same.

HINT: *Our Root List (near the back of the book) clues you in to the meanings of words like* **interlocutor.** *It comes from* **INTER-** *(between) and* **LOC** *(speech, talk).*

Checking out the other answers, a **lecturer** (B) doesn't participate in a **dialogue** with others; he gives a speech. In (C), a **deliverer** doesn't exactly take part in a **message.** In (D), **chatterbox** has no clear relationship to **refutation.** And in (E), an **orator** uses **language** masterfully, but a **DISPUTANT** doesn't use an **ALTERCATION.**

disputant: someone who disputes or
   argues
altercation: noisy, angry argument
interlocutor: someone who takes part in
   a conversation
deliverer: savior, rescuer, someone who
   delivers others from danger or
   hardship
refutation: act of proving something
   wrong
orator: public speaker

Suggested Time: 7 minutes

Directions—Choose the lettered pair of words that is related in the same way as the pair in capital letters.

Example:
FLAKE : SNOW ::

(A) storm : hail
(B) drop : rain
(C) field : wheat
(D) stack : hay
(E) cloud : fog

Ⓐ ● Ⓒ Ⓓ Ⓔ

1. RINK : SKATE ::

(A) escalator : turn
(B) track : run
(C) boat : swim
(D) airplane : fly
(E) office : drive

Ⓐ Ⓑ Ⓒ Ⓓ Ⓔ

2. GENERAL : ARMY ::

(A) officer : uniform
(B) rifle : bullet
(C) soldier : barracks
(D) quarterback : team
(E) manager : profit

Ⓐ Ⓑ Ⓒ Ⓓ Ⓔ

3. SODA : BEVERAGE ::

(A) hat : coat
(B) sand : desert
(C) coffee : milk
(D) cat : animal
(E) cup : handle

Ⓐ Ⓑ Ⓒ Ⓓ Ⓔ

4. DENOUNCE : DISAPPROVAL ::

(A) enfeeble : weakness
(B) pass : legislation
(C) rant : anger
(D) condemn : building
(E) award : gift

Ⓐ Ⓑ Ⓒ Ⓓ Ⓔ

5. FLURRY : BLIZZARD ::

(A) dew : meadow
(B) warmth : coolness
(C) moisture : sponge
(D) coat : protection
(E) glance : stare

Ⓐ Ⓑ Ⓒ Ⓓ Ⓔ

6. COLLABORATE : WORK ::

(A) question : borrow
(B) clot : bleed
(C) cohabit : live
(D) synchronize : watch
(E) cooperate : please

Ⓐ Ⓑ Ⓒ Ⓓ Ⓔ

7. CHRONICLE : EVENTS ::

(A) transcribe : statements
(B) heal : medicine
(C) remove : predicaments
(D) flatter : compliments
(E) review : documents

Ⓐ Ⓑ Ⓒ Ⓓ Ⓔ

8. CONTENTMENT : PURR ::

(A) irrationality : growl
(B) terror : scream
(C) hatred : yelp
(D) distress : whisper
(E) entanglement : snarl

Ⓐ Ⓑ Ⓒ Ⓓ Ⓔ

9. ERADICATE : DISEASE ::

(A) complicate : tangle
(B) elaborate : theme
(C) lengthen : dimension
(D) symbolize : model
(E) exterminate : species

Ⓐ Ⓑ Ⓒ Ⓓ Ⓔ

10. PUTREFACTION : FRESH ::

(A) cohesion : disjointed
(B) delectation : pungent
(C) contraction : complex
(D) excoriation : proud
(E) emendation : flawed

Ⓐ Ⓑ Ⓒ Ⓓ Ⓔ

SCORECARD	
Number of Questions Right:	9
Number of Questions Wrong:	1
Number of Questions Omitted:	
Number of Correct Guesses:	0
Number of Wrong Guesses:	1
Time Used:	

ANSWERS AND EXPLANATIONS

1. B

A simple bridge is: *You* **SKATE** *on a structure called a* **RINK**. The only answer choice that fits is (B): You **run** on a structure called a **track.**

The only other answer choice that might tempt you is (D): You can **fly** in an **airplane,** but the **airplane** does the **fly**ing, not you. However, you do **run** on a **track** or **SKATE** on a **RINK,** so pick (B).

2. D

Your bridge is: *A* **GENERAL** *commands an* **ARMY.** An **officer** doesn't command a **uniform,** so (A) is wrong, and a **rifle** doesn't command a **bullet,** so (B) is wrong. And (C) a **soldier** doesn't command a **barracks.** That leaves (D) and (E).

When you can't decide between two or three answer choices, do one of two things: Rephrase your stem bridge, or define a bridge for each remaining answer choice and see which one also fits the stem pair. Let's try the the latter.

In (D), a **quarterback** leads a **team,** the same way a **GENERAL** leads an **ARMY.** In (E), **profit** is the goal for a **manager,** but an **ARMY** isn't a goal for a **GENERAL.** So (D) is correct.

---
barracks: living quarters for soldiers
---

3. D

The test makers try to distract you with **coffee, milk,** and **cup**—words that remind you of **BEVERAGE.** But your bridge is: *By definition, a* **SODA** *is a type of* **BEVERAGE.** The only answer choice whose first word is a type of its second word is (D): A **cat** is a type of **animal.**

4. C

Bridge: *You show strong* **DISAPPROVAL** *when you* **DENOUNCE** *someone.* Similarly, you show strong **anger** when you **rant** at someone.

At first glance (A) looks possible, but check out the bridge: You don't show **weakness** when you **enfeeble** someone.

---
enfeeble: to weaken
rant: to be in a rage, to talk noisily and excitedly
---

5. E

The stem pair refers to different types of snow activity. A good bridge would be: *A* **FLURRY** *is much less intense than a* **BLIZZARD.** Similarly, a **glance** is much less intense than a **stare.** A **glance** is a quick, surface look; a **stare** is a prolonged, intense look.

HINT: *Don't pick answer choices just because they refer to the same topic as the stem words. Look for the one that the stem bridge fits.*

---
flurry: quick, surface sprinkling of snow
blizzard: prolonged, intense snowstorm
glance: quick, casual look
stare: prolonged, intense look
---

6. C

The bridge is: *By definition, to* **COLLABORATE** *is to* **WORK** *together.* In the same way, to **cohabit** is to **live** together, so (C) is correct.

If you didn't know what **COLLABORATE** meant, you might have figured it out: the prefix **CO-** means "with" or "together," and the root **LABOR** means "work."

Plugging your bridge into the other choices, (A) and (B) make no sense. In (D), you might think: When watches are **synchronized,** they work together. But **watch** in choice (D) isn't a noun, it's a verb—to watch.

HINT: *Remember, the parts of speech in corresponding words of an analogy question are always consistent. You'll never find a verb : noun combination in the stem and a noun : verb combination in the correct answer.*

collaborate: to work together
clot: to become semisolid; to coagulate
cohabit: to live or reside together
synchronize: to cause to operate at the same time or rate

irrationality: the quality of being illogical
yelp: a quick, high-pitched sound
distress: discomfort or trouble

7. A

A quick glance at the first words in the answer choices tells you **CHRONICLE** is being used as a verb. So build a bridge: *To* **CHRONICLE EVENTS** *means to record them, usually in writing.* When you **transcribe** you also write down or record. A court stenographer **transcribes** the proceedings of a trial, including all **statements** made by the witnesses. To **transcribe statements** is to record them, so (A) is correct.

Choice (E) might have attracted you because of associations called up by the words **CHRONICLE, EVENTS, review,** and **documents.** But when you **review documents,** you don't write them down—you just reread them.

predicaments: difficult or perplexing situations, dilemmas

8. B

All the second words here can act as either nouns or verbs. So the stem bridge could be phrased one of two ways. If **PURR** is a verb: *To* **PURR** *means to utter sounds of* **CONTENTMENT.** If **PURR** is a noun: *A* **PURR** *is a sound of* **CONTENTMENT.** Either way, the only answer that matches is choice (B).

In (C), a **yelp** is more often associated with pain than with **hatred.** In (E), a **snarl** is a growl or tangle; it is not a sound of **entanglement.**

9. E

The bridge: *By definition, to* **ERADICATE** *a* **DISEASE** *is to wipe it out,* as smallpox was **ERADICATED** earlier in the twentieth century. Similarly, to **exterminate** a **species** is to wipe it out.

In choice (B), **elaborate,** like all the other first words here, is a verb; a composer **elaborates** on a **theme** by ornamenting and varying the original motif.

exterminate: to destroy completely

10. A

PUTREFACTION is related to the simpler words putrid and putrefy. The stem bridge is: *Something characterized by* **PUTREFACTION** *is not* **FRESH.**

HINT: *PUTREFACTION comes from the roots* **PUTER** *(rotten), and* **FAC** *(to make or do). See our Root List.*

Here you need to know the hard words in the answer choices. In (A), something—a speech, for example—characterized by **cohesion** displays unity and is *not* **disjointed.** That's true. But check out the other choices.

The stem bridge doesn't make sense in (B). In (C), something that contains no **contraction** is not necessarily **complex.** In (D), the stem bridge doesn't fit. You wouldn't say: Something that contains no **excoriation** is considered **proud.**

In (E), it's not necessarily true that something—like a document—characterized by **emendations** is not **flawed.**

putrefaction: state of decay, process of rotting

cohesion: sticking together, displaying physical, logical, or political unity

disjointed: separate and unconnected

delectation: delight or enjoyment

pungent: having a sharp smell or taste, like vinegar

contraction: shortening, as of a muscle or word (won't is a contraction for will not)

excoriation: a bitter denunciation

emendation: a correction

Suggested Time: 7 minutes

Directions—Choose the lettered pair of words that is related in the same way as the pair in capital letters.

Example:
FLAKE : SNOW ::

(A) storm : hail
(B) drop : rain
(C) field : wheat
(D) stack : hay
(E) cloud : fog   Ⓐ ● Ⓒ Ⓓ Ⓔ

1. FEATHER : BIRD ::

(A) scale : fish
(B) hair : braid
(C) wing : flight
(D) fang : snake
(E) antenna : insect   Ⓐ Ⓑ Ⓒ Ⓓ Ⓔ

2. CHALK : BLACKBOARD ::

(A) eraser : mistake
(B) needle : thread
(C) brush : paint
(D) pen : paper
(E) crayon : drawing   Ⓐ Ⓑ Ⓒ Ⓓ Ⓔ

3. FOOT : LENGTH ::

(A) hour : watch
(B) height : growth
(C) teaspoon : recipe
(D) canyon : depth
(E) acre : area   Ⓐ Ⓑ Ⓒ Ⓓ Ⓔ

4. DEAFENING : LOUD ::

(A) believable : dramatic
(B) penurious : sad
(C) mysterious : quiet
(D) hilarious : amusing
(E) desirous : pathetic   Ⓐ Ⓑ Ⓒ Ⓓ Ⓔ

5. BOTANIST : PLANTS ::

(A) zoologist : animals
(B) linguist : verbs
(C) philologist : stamps
(D) physicist : experiments
(E) chemist : laboratories   Ⓐ Ⓑ Ⓒ Ⓓ Ⓔ

6. STETHOSCOPE : LISTEN ::

(A) microscope : record
(B) needle : inject
(C) bandage : cut
(D) scale : reduce
(E) cough : breathe   Ⓐ Ⓑ Ⓒ Ⓓ Ⓔ

7. INCITE : ACTION ::

(A) control : crowd
(B) conserve : fuel
(C) kindle : fire
(D) start : end
(E) become : thing   Ⓐ Ⓑ Ⓒ Ⓓ Ⓔ

8. WATERLOGGED : MOISTURE ::

(A) buoyant : balloon
(B) extroverted : personality
(C) overinflated : air
(D) windblown : pollen
(E) coarse : steam   Ⓐ Ⓑ Ⓒ Ⓓ Ⓔ

9. REPREHENSIBLE : BLAME ::

(A) incomprehensible : knowledge
(B) treasonable : invasion
(C) relevant : information
(D) difficult : evasion
(E) admirable : praise   Ⓐ Ⓑ Ⓒ Ⓓ Ⓔ

10. DISCIPLINARIAN : STRICTNESS ::

(A) curmudgeon : sadness
(B) miser : stinginess
(C) boor : heartiness
(D) innovator : forgetfulness
(E) soldier : wariness   Ⓐ Ⓑ Ⓒ Ⓓ Ⓔ

SCORECARD	
Number of Questions Right:	10
Number of Questions Wrong:	0
Number of Questions Omitted:	✗
Number of Correct Guesses:	2
Number of Wrong Guesses:	0
Time Used:	

ANSWERS AND EXPLANATIONS

1. A

If you simply say: *A* **BIRD** *has* **FEATHERS,** you won't know whether to pick (A), (D), or (E). You'll have to restate the stem bridge more specifically: *A* **BIRD** *is covered with* **FEATHERS;** a **fish,** with **scales.**

2. D

With years of school behind you, this stem bridge should come easily: *You use* **CHALK** *to write on a* **BLACKBOARD,** just as you use a **pen** to write on **paper.**

Again, don't be misled by associations that the stem words and answer choices evoke for you. Many of the other answer choices may make you think about grade school, but the only pair that fits the stem bridge is (D).

3. E

Your bridge is: *A* **FOOT** *is a measurement of* **LENGTH.**

(E) is the only answer choice that fits: An **acre** is a measurement of **area.** Some of the wrong answers have strong bridges, but they're not the same as the stem bridge. A **watch** can be used to measure an **hour,** but an **hour** isn't a measurement of **watch. Growth** is a change in dimension, most commonly in **height.**

4. D

A strong bridge would be: *Something that's* **DEAFENING** *is, by definition, extremely* **LOUD.** In (D), something that's **hilarious** is extremely **amusing,** but check the other choices.

In (B), **penurious** has no direct relationship to **sad.** Choice (E) is a good example of a word pair with a weak bridge. Someone who is **desirous,** that is, whose actions are ruled by desire, may or may not be **pathetic.** There's no definite connection between the two words.

penurious: stingy; poor
pathetic: worthy of pity

5. A

The bridge is: *A* **BOTANIST** *is someone who studies* **PLANTS.** A **zoologist** is someone who studies **animals.** In (B), a **linguist** studies language in general, not **verbs** in particular.

Incidentally, a **philologist** is someone who loves words and studies their history, not to be confused with a philatelist, who collects or studies **stamps.**

6. B

Try this bridge: *A* **STETHOSCOPE** *is a medical device that's used to* **LISTEN.** Look for a first word that's a device, preferably medical. That rules out (E) immediately, because a **cough** isn't a device, medical or otherwise. The second word of the correct answer should tell us what the device is used for. Only choice (B) does that: A **needle** is a medical device that's used to **inject.**

7. C

You can incite a riot, or an action, so a good bridge would be: *To* **INCITE** *is to provoke or start an* **ACTION.** That's certainly not the same bridge as (A), (B), (D), or (E). But it's close to the connection between **kindle** and **fire.** To **kindle** means to light or start a **fire.**

HINT: *Don't reject an answer choice just because it's not a perfect match for your bridge. Pick the one choice that is the best fit.*

Since none of the other answer choices fits the stem bridge at all, (C) must be correct.

incite: provoke to action; stir up

8. C

Your bridge is: *Something that contains way too much* **MOISTURE** *is, by definition,* **WATERLOGGED.** In (A), something **buoyant** doesn't contain way too much **balloon.** And (E) makes no sense at all. (B) and (C) seem like good possibilities. But **extroverted** doesn't mean having too much **personality.** On the other hand, something that contains way too much **air** is **overinflated,** so (C) is correct.

> *buoyant: floating or capable of floating*
> *extroverted: having an outgoing*
>   *personality*

9. E

The bridge is: *A person or action that is* **REPREHENSI-BLE** *is deserving of* **BLAME.** The only answer choice that fits the bridge is (E): Something **admirable** is worthy of **praise.**

If you didn't know what **REPREHENSIBLE** meant, you could have tried working backwards from the answer choices. It's hard to build a strong bridge between the words of most of the answer choices. For instance, **treasonable** means "relating to or involving treason." There's no strong link with **invasion,** so (B) is out. **Information** that's **relevant** is pertinent or significant; it doesn't seem likely that **BLAME** that is **REPREHENSIBLE** is pertinent or significant. But something that's **admirable** is worthy of **praise,** and **REPREHENSIBLE** could (and does) mean "worthy of **BLAME**"; therefore, (E) is correct.

> *reprehensible: deserving of blame*
> *incomprehensible: impossible to*
>   *understand*
> *treasonable: relating to or involving*
>   *betrayal, especially of one's country*
> *relevant: pertinent or significant*
> *admirable: worthy of praise*

10. B

Your bridge: *A* **DISCIPLINARIAN** *is characterized by* **STRICTNESS.**

In (A), a **curmudgeon** isn't necessarily characterized by **sadness.** In (B), a **miser** is indeed characterized by **stinginess.** But check out the other answer choices, just to make sure.

Look for an answer choice whose first word is a person or thing, and whose second word characterizes the first word.

In (C), a **boor** doesn't have to be **hearty.** In (D), an **innovator** has nothing to do with **forgetfulness.** The root **NOV** means "new." Finally, in (E), **wariness** is not necessarily a characteristic of **soldiers.** It has nothing to do with the word **war.**

> *disciplinarian: someone who enforces*
>   *order*
> *miser: someone who lives miserably in*
>   *order to hoard his wealth; extremely*
>   *stingy person*
> *boor: rude or insensitive person*
> *innovator: someone who produces new*
>   *ideas or inventions*
> *wariness: caution or carefulness*
> *curmudgeon: grouch, ill-tempered*
>   *person*

Suggested Time: 7 minutes

Directions—Choose the lettered pair of words that is related in the same way as the pair in capital letters.

Example:
FLAKE : SNOW ::

(A) storm : hail
(B) drop : rain
(C) field : wheat
(D) stack : hay
(E) cloud : fog   (A) ● (C) (D) (E)

1. SKUNK : SCENT ::

(A) fur : cat
(B) porcupine : quill
(C) prey : animal
(D) gland : odor
(E) leaf : shrub   (A) (B) (C) (D) (E)

2. RECESS : SCHOOL ::

(A) intermission : play
(B) pause : reflection
(C) vacation : time
(D) score : game
(E) dining : restaurant   (A) (B) (C) (D) (E)

3. DISMANTLE : APPARATUS ::

to strip apart

(A) dismay : emotion
(B) distend : stomach
(C) distort : static
(D) disband : group
(E) display : window   (A) (B) (C) (D) (E)

4. BIPED : HUMAN ::

(A) tentacle : octopus
(B) quadruped : horse
(C) foot : centipede
(D) kingdom : animal
(E) pouch : kangaroo   (A) (B) (C) (D) (E)

5. CALM : COMPOSURE ::

(A) scared : trouble
(B) cold : sickness
(C) congested : traffic
(D) sad : melancholy
(E) bored : gladness   (A) (B) (C) (D) (E)

6. ILLICIT : LEGALITY ::

(A) grateful : thanklessness
(B) innocent : punishment
(C) hardy : graciousness
(D) guilty : uncertainty
(E) wicked : evil   (A) (B) (C) (D) (E)

7. ANNOYED : RAGE ::

(A) glad : euphoria
(B) useless : necessity
(C) humorous : attentiveness
(D) aggressive : hopefulness
(E) nasty : amusement   (A) (B) (C) (D) (E)

8. ABDICATE : THRONE ::

(A) rule : nation
(B) revolt : government
(C) defeat : candidate
(D) impeach : official
(E) resign : job   (A) (B) (C) (D) (E)

9. LUCRATIVE : PROFIT ::

(A) valuable : price
(B) fictitious : hero
(C) fertile : offspring
(D) commanding : chaos
(E) episodic : publicity   (A) (B) (C) (D) (E)

10. MISANTHROPE : HUMANKIND ::

(A) cynic : kindness
(B) martyr : punishment
(C) xenophobe : foreigners
(D) optimist : hope
(E) derelict : officers   (A) (B) (C) (D) (E)

SCORECARD	
Number of Questions Right:	10
Number of Questions Wrong:	
Number of Questions Omitted:	
Number of Correct Guesses:	
Number of Wrong Guesses:	
Time Used:	

ANSWERS AND EXPLANATIONS

1. B

Your bridge could be: *A* **SKUNK** *uses a* **SCENT** *to repel its enemies.* You'll probably see right away that a **porcupine** uses **quills** to repel its enemies.

2. A

Your bridge is: *A* **RECESS,** *by definition, is a short break in the middle of* **SCHOOL,** just as an **intermission** is a short break in the middle of a **play.**

In (B), a **pause** is also a short break, but not in the middle of a **reflection.** Similarly, in (C) a **vacation** is a break, but not in the middle of **time.**

3. D

A good bridge might be: *To* **DISMANTLE** *an* **APPARATUS** *is to take it apart.* Similarly, to **disband** a **group** is to break it up or dissolve it. No other answer choice involves the idea of taking some collective unit apart.

In choice (B), if you eat too much, your **stomach** becomes **distended.** In (C), if you **distort** an audio signal by turning up the volume past what your speakers can handle, you may get what sounds like radio **static.**

> dismantle: to take apart piece by piece
> apparatus: a piece of equipment made
>   of different parts and used for some
>   particular function
> distend: to swell or extend
> distort: to deform or twist out of shape

4. B

A clear bridge would be: **HUMANS** *are* **BIPEDS,** *i.e., they have two legs.*

In (A) and (E), a **tentacle** or **pouch** is something an **octopus** or **kangaroo** has, not something it is. You can use the same logic to eliminate (C). The bridge doesn't fit (D) at all. But a **horse** is a **quadruped,** a four-legged animal, so (B) is correct.

HINT: *BIPED comes from the prefix BI- meaning "two" (as in bicycle), and the root PED meaning "foot" or "leg" (as in pedal). Quadruped has the prefix QUAD-, meaning "four."*

5. D

A good bridge would be: *When you're* **CALM,** *you are in a state of* **COMPOSURE.** In the same way, when you're **sad,** you are in a state of **melancholy.** No other answer choice fits.

> composure: self-possession or calmness
>   of mind
> melancholy: depression, gloominess
> congested: clogged

6. A

There's a suggestion of opposites in the stem pair, so your bridge could be: *By definition, something* **ILLICIT** *is not characterized by* **LEGALITY.**

Now look for a similar contrast in the answer pairs. (A) comes closest: Someone **grateful** is not characterized by **thanklessness.** In (B), it doesn't make sense to say: Someone **innocent** is not characterized by **punishment.**

> legality: the quality of being legal
> illicit: illegal
> hardy: strong, robust, capable of with-
>   standing hardships

7. A

These two stem words represent different degrees of the same emotion. Bridge: *Someone who becomes extremely* **ANNOYED** *feels* **RAGE.**

Since (B), (C), (D), and (E) don't fit that bridge, you might have been able to choose (A) without even knowing what **euphoria** meant. Someone extremely **glad** feels **euphoria,** so (A)'s right.

> *euphoria: an overwhelming feeling of elation or happiness*

8. E

A strong bridge is: *When you* **ABDICATE** *a* **THRONE,** *you give it up.* The only choice that fits this bridge is (E): When you **resign** from a **job,** you give it up.

> *abdicate: to withdraw from or give up a high office or function*

9. C

A strong bridge would be: *Something,* like a business, *that's* **LUCRATIVE** *produces* **PROFIT.** The only answer choice that fits the bridge is (C): Something **fertile,** like an animal, produces **offspring,** or children.

> *lucrative: profitable*
> *fictitious: made-up*
> *fertile: capable of producing offspring, fruitful*
> *episodic: temporary, occasional, made up of separate episodes*

10. C

Your stem bridge is: *A* **MISANTHROPE** *is, by definition, a person who hates all* **HUMANKIND.** In (C), a **xenophobe** is a person who hates **foreigners,** so that's probably the right answer, but check the other choices.

HINT: *If you didn't know what a* **MISANTHROPE** *was, our Root List could help you. The prefix* **MIS-** *is negative, and the root* **ANTHROP** *(also found in* **anthropology** *and* **philanthropy***) means "human beings."*

In (A), a **cynic** sees ulterior motives behind all good deeds, but doesn't necessarily hate all **kindness.** In (B), **martyrs** don't hate **punishment;** they willingly suffer **punishment** for their beliefs. In (D), an **optimist** certainly doesn't hate **hope.** Finally, in (E), **derelict** is being used as a noun to mean "a vagrant," and there's no direct connection between **derelict** and **officers.**

> *misanthrope: someone who hates other people*
> *cynic: one who believes only selfishness motivates human actions*
> *martyr: someone willing to suffer or die for a cause or religion*
> *optimist: one who looks on the bright side of things*
> *xenophobe: someone who hates and fears foreigners*
> *derelict (noun): a vagrant*
> *derelict (adjective): negligent or neglectful*

Suggested Time: 7 minutes

Directions—Choose the lettered pair of words that is related in the same way as the pair in capital letters.

Example:
FLAKE : SNOW ::

(A) storm : hail
(B) drop : rain
(C) field : wheat
(D) stack : hay
(E) cloud : fog   Ⓐ ● Ⓒ Ⓓ Ⓔ

1. IRON : WRINKLE ::

(A) bleach : color
(B) mow : lawn
(C) sweep : broom
(D) cook : food
(E) build : model   Ⓐ Ⓑ Ⓒ Ⓓ Ⓔ

2. WRITER : NOVELIST ::

(A) scientist : astronomer
(B) teacher : student
(C) physician : patient
(D) poet : researcher
(E) worker : exertion   Ⓐ Ⓑ Ⓒ Ⓓ Ⓔ

3. COW : CALF ::

(A) hog : pork
(B) horse : mule
(C) sheep : lamb
(D) tiger : stripe
(E) ram : ewe   Ⓐ Ⓑ Ⓒ Ⓓ Ⓔ

4. STAR : STELLAR ::

(A) space : spherical
(B) comet : planetary
(C) vapor : solid
(D) earth : terrestrial
(E) ship : orbital   Ⓐ Ⓑ Ⓒ Ⓓ Ⓔ

5. BAY : WOLVES ::

(A) canter : horses
(B) parley : people
(C) low : cattle
(D) molt : lizards
(E) root : swine   Ⓐ Ⓑ Ⓒ Ⓓ Ⓔ

6. MOVEMENT : SYMPHONY ::

(A) note : piano
(B) frame : film
(C) canvas : painting
(D) rhythm : poem
(E) act : play   Ⓐ Ⓑ Ⓒ Ⓓ Ⓔ

7. SLAKE : THIRST ::

(A) stoke : fire
(B) starve : hunger
(C) assuage : pain
(D) endure : discomfort
(E) induce : sleep   Ⓐ Ⓑ Ⓒ Ⓓ Ⓔ

8. REBEL : AUTHORITY ::

(A) solver : problem
(B) anarchist : change
(C) farmer : urbanity
(D) pacifist : serenity
(E) nonconformist : convention   Ⓐ Ⓑ Ⓒ Ⓓ Ⓔ

9. PHILANTHROPIST : GENEROSITY ::

(A) teacher : pedantry
(B) swindler : deceitfulness
(C) novice : intelligence
(D) editor : validation
(E) coward : tenacity   Ⓐ Ⓑ Ⓒ Ⓓ Ⓔ

10. RUTHLESS : MERCY ::

(A) judgmental : theory
(B) unmarred : blemish
(C) arresting : evidence
(D) vicious : circle
(E) avaricious : selfishness   Ⓐ Ⓑ Ⓒ Ⓓ Ⓔ

SCORECARD	
Number of Questions Right:	9
Number of Questions Wrong:	1
Number of Questions Omitted:	
Number of Correct Guesses:	
Number of Wrong Guesses:	
Time Used:	

ANSWERS AND EXPLANATIONS

1. A

In case you had doubts, a quick look at the answer choices will tell you that **IRON** is being used as a verb (**mow** can't be either a noun or adjective) and **WRIN-KLE** as a noun (**lawn, broom,** and **food** can't be used as verbs).

So make your bridge: *You* **IRON** *to remove a* **WRIN-KLE.**

At first glance, you might think two answer choices fit that bridge: You **bleach** to remove **color,** and you **mow** to remove a **lawn.** But when you **mow** the grass, you don't remove a **lawn;** you simply cut it back. **IRON**ing and **bleaching,** on the other hand, take out **WRIN-KLES** and **color,** respectively.

2. A

This bridge should come easily: *A* **NOVELIST,** *by definition, is a type of* **WRITER.** Look for the answer choice pair with the same relationship.

Don't pick an answer just because the two words are closely related, as in choices (B) and (C). A **student** is not a type of **teacher.** And a **patient** is not a type of **physician.** But an **astronomer** is a type of **scientist,** so (A) is correct.

exertion: effort or labor

3. C

You know this bridge: *A* **CALF** *is a young* **COW.** Look for an answer choice whose second word is a young animal. The only one is (C): A **lamb** is a young **sheep.** In choice (E), **rams** and **ewes** are male and female sheep, respectively.

4. D

The bridge is: **STELLAR** *means coming from or having to do with* **STARS.**

In (D), **terrestrial** means coming from or having to do with the **earth.** In science fiction, alien creatures from other planets are often called extra**terrestrials,** indi-

cating that they come from beyond (**EXTRA-**) the earth (**TERR**).

5. C

Here, all the words in the first column are verbs, so you need to know what **BAY** means as a verb. **WOLVES,** coyotes, and dogs are all said to **BAY** at the moon.

Your bridge might be: **WOLVES** *make a sound called* **BAY***ing.*

The only answer choice that fits the bridge is: **cattle** make a sound called **low**ing, so (C) is correct.

bay (verb): to bark or howl
canter: of horses, an easy gallop
parley: to speak with, consult with
low (verb): to moo
molt: to shed feathers, fur, or scales
root (verb): of pigs, to dig in the dirt
   looking for food

6. E

If you phrased your stem bridge as "a **MOVEMENT** is a piece of a **SYMPHONY,**" you probably had trouble choosing between (A), (B), (E), and maybe even (D). The problem was that your bridge wasn't specific enough.

A better bridge would be *A* **SYMPHONY** *is divided into three or four long sections, called* **MOVEMENTS.** Only in (E) is the first word a long section or division of the second word.

7. C

Try this bridge: *By definition, to* **SLAKE** *is to relieve your* **THIRST.**

Look for a first word in the answer choices that also means "relieve." The only one is **assuage.** You **assuage,** or relieve, **pain,** so the bridge fits, and (C) is correct.

> *slake: to quench or satisfy*
> *assuage: to relieve, ease*
> *stoke: to feed a fire*
> *induce: to cause something to occur*

8. E

The stem bridge could be: *A* **REBEL** *defies* **AUTHORITY.** The only answer choice that fits the bridge is (E): A **nonconformist** defies **convention.**

> *anarchist: one who believes that the*
> *best government is no government at*
> *all*
> *urbanity: smoothness or sophistication*
> *pacifist: someone who embraces peace*
> *and seeks to avoid physical conflict*
> *nonconformist: someone who doesn't*
> *abide by society's expectations or*
> *conventions*

9. B

Bridge: *A* **PHILANTHROPIST,** *by definition, always shows* **GENEROSITY.** In (A), a **teacher** doesn't always show **pedantry.** But **deceitfulness** is a fundamental, defining characteristic of a **swindler.** None of the other choices has the same relationship as the stem words, so (B) is right.

> *philanthropist: someone who donates*
> *money to socially useful purposes*
> *pedantry: narrow-minded or overly*
> *detailed teaching*
> *novice: someone who is new to a given*
> *position or activity*
> *validation: the act or process of*
> *confirming something*
> *tenacity: dogged persistence,*
> *stubbornness*

10. B

Bridge: *Someone who's* **RUTHLESS** *has or shows no* **MERCY.** Something that's **unmarred** has or shows no **blemish.**

HINT: *Answers like choice (D), in which the two words combine to form a common phrase, can be very attractive but are rarely correct. If the relationship between the two words doesn't match the relationship between the stem words, eliminate the choice.*

> *marred: spoiled by a flaw*
> *arresting (adjective): striking,*
> *impressive*
> *avaricious: greedy*

Suggested Time: 7 minutes

Directions—Choose the lettered pair of words that is related in the same way as the pair in capital letters.

Example:
FLAKE : SNOW ::

(A) storm : hail
(B) drop : rain
(C) field : wheat
(D) stack : hay
(E) cloud : fog

Ⓐ ⬤ Ⓒ Ⓓ Ⓔ

1. ILLNESS : MEASLES ::

(A) beverage : meal
(B) insect : creature
(C) reptile : mammal
(D) flower : tree
(E) bird : sparrow

Ⓐ Ⓑ Ⓒ Ⓓ Ⓔ

2. GLASSBLOWER : VASE ::

(A) stonecutter : monument
(B) lumberjack : tree
(C) gentleman : manners
(D) landlord : building
(E) storekeeper : merchandise

Ⓐ Ⓑ Ⓒ Ⓓ Ⓔ

3. GROCER : FOOD ::

(A) bureaucrat : paper
(B) locksmith : jewels
(C) librarian : books
(D) writer : pens
(E) apothecary : medicine

Ⓐ Ⓑ Ⓒ Ⓓ Ⓔ

4. BRIGAND : BAND ::

(A) gourmand : crew
(B) despot : retinue
(C) performer : troupe
(D) musician : instrument
(E) organizer : union

Ⓐ Ⓑ Ⓒ Ⓓ Ⓔ

5. GLOBAL : WORLD ::

(A) national : security
(B) tropical : jungle
(C) municipal : city
(D) internal : medicine
(E) regional : state

Ⓐ Ⓑ Ⓒ Ⓓ Ⓔ

6. VAGUE : DEFINE ::

(A) sterile : produce
(B) disguised : recognize
(C) tough : strengthen
(D) precious : save
(E) modest : hide

Ⓐ Ⓑ Ⓒ Ⓓ Ⓔ

7. LITIGATION : COURT ::

(A) population : room
(B) experimentation : laboratory
(C) gesture : motion
(D) accusation : jury
(E) competition : promotion

Ⓐ Ⓑ Ⓒ Ⓓ Ⓔ

8. ABUNDANT : ADEQUATE ::

(A) arid : moist
(B) peaceful : boisterous
(C) timid : illegitimate
(D) overflowing : full
(E) bold : fearless

Ⓐ Ⓑ Ⓒ Ⓓ Ⓔ

9. PERTURBED : TRANQUILITY ::

(A) joyous : pleasure
(B) impudent : dissension
(C) consoled : weeping
(D) reassured : anxiety
(E) admiring : awe

Ⓐ Ⓑ Ⓒ Ⓓ Ⓔ

10. PLATITUDE : TRITE ::

(A) riddle : cryptic
(B) axiom : geometric
(C) attitude : sinister
(D) syllogism : wise
(E) circumlocution : concise

Ⓐ Ⓑ Ⓒ Ⓓ Ⓔ

SCORECARD	
Number of Questions Right:	
Number of Questions Wrong:	
Number of Questions Omitted:	
Number of Correct Guesses:	
Number of Wrong Guesses:	
Time Used:	

ANSWERS AND EXPLANATIONS

1. E

The stem bridge is: **MEASLES** *is a type of* **ILLNESS.**

As you scan the answer choices, look for one whose second word is a type of its first word. A **meal** isn't a type of **beverage;** a **creature** isn't a type of **insect;** a **mammal** isn't a type of **reptile;** and a **tree** isn't a type of **flower.** But a **sparrow** is a type of **bird,** so (E) is correct.

2. A

A **GLASSBLOWER** is a person who makes objects from molten glass by blowing air through a hollow rod.

Your bridge is: *A* **VASE** *would be created by a* **GLASSBLOWER.**

Similarly, a **monument** would be created by a **stonecutter.** None of the other answer choices has as its first word a person who creates its second word. **Lumberjacks** don't create **trees;** they cut them down. A **gentleman** displays or is known for having good **manners;** a **landlord** owns a **building;** and a **storekeeper** sells **merchandise.**

3. E

Bridge: *A* **GROCER** *is, by definition, someone who sells* **FOOD.**

Bureaucrats are often called **paper** shufflers, but a **bureaucrat** doesn't sell **paper.** A **locksmith** has no direct connection with **jewels.** A **librarian** catalogues, sorts, and lends **books,** but doesn't sell them. And, of course, **writers** don't sell **pens.** But an **apothecary** is someone who sells drugs or **medicine.**

HINT: *If you didn't know what* apothecary *meant, you could still have found the answer by eliminating the choices that did* **not** *make sense.*

> bureaucrat: government or corporate
>   employee who works within narrow
>   channels of authority and follows a
>   rigid routine
> locksmith: someone who makes and
>   installs locks and keys
> apothecary: a pharmacist

4. C

Your bridge is: *A group of* **BRIGANDS** *is called a* **BAND.** Looking quickly through the choices, the only two that have a similar relationship are (C) and (E).

The words in choice (A) have nothing to do with each other. A group of **gourmands** is not a **crew.** In (B), **despots** may or may not *have* a **retinue,** but they would not be *part* of a **retinue.** In (C) a group of **performers** is called a **troupe.** In (D), a group of **musicians** is not an **instrument.** In (E) an **organizer** tries to start a **union,** but a group of organizers is not a **union,** so (C) is the best available answer.

> brigand: someone who robs people,
>   usually as part of a group or band
> gourmand: a glutton, someone who
>   eats a lot of fine food
> despot: tyrant
> retinue: a group of attendants serving
>   an important person
> troupe: a group of theatrical performers

5. C

Your bridge is: *Something* **GLOBAL** *pertains to the* **WORLD.** In the same way something **municipal** pertains to a **city.**

In (A), **national** doesn't necessarily pertain to **security,** though it can. In (B), **tropical** doesn't necessarily pertain just to a **jungle;** it relates to the tropics in general, i.e., the latitudes around the equator. In (D), **internal** just means "inner"; it doesn't necessarily have anything to do with **medicine.** And something that's **regional** pertains to an area that may be smaller, or broader, than one **state.**

> global: characteristic of or pertaining to
>   the world
> municipal: characteristic of or
>   pertaining to the city

6. B

At least two bridges seem to fit this stem pair. *Something that's* **VAGUE** *can be either hard to* **DEFINE** *or poorly* **DEFINED.**

(B) seems the best bet. Something that's **disguised** can be hard to **recognize.** That's certainly true. (B) is probably right, but check the other choices, just to make sure.

In (A), something that's **sterile** isn't hard to **produce** or poorly **produced;** it can't **produce** offspring, but that's something else. The other choices don't fit either, so (B) is correct.

7. B

If you know what **LITIGATION** means, you can build your bridge: **LITIGATION** *is a process that takes place in* **COURT.**

Look for an answer choice whose first word describes a process, and whose second describes the place where the process goes on. In (B), **experimentation** is a process that takes place in a **laboratory. Room** in choice (A) also describes a place, but **population** doesn't take place in a **room,** so choice (B) is correct.

> litigation: a lawsuit

8. D

Here the two words reflect different amounts. So you can build a bridge: *By definition, something* **ABUNDANT** *is much more than* **ADEQUATE.**

Look for an answer choice whose the first word means *more than* the second word.

The bridge doesn't fit in (A), where **arid** and **moist** are almost opposites. **Peaceful** and **boisterous** are also opposites, so (B) is also wrong. The stem words in (C) have no clear connection. In (E), **bold** and **fearless** are

almost synonyms; **bold** doesn't mean "more than **fearless.**" The only choice in which the first word means *more than* the second word is (D): **Overflowing** means "more than **full.**"

> abundant: extremely plentiful
> adequate: enough to fulfill
>   requirements
> arid: very dry
> boisterous: rough and noisy
> illegitimate: unlawful, illegal, born out
>   of wedlock
> overflowing: more than full

9. D

Again, the stem words feel like opposites. Your bridge might be: *Someone who feels* **PERTURBED** *does not feel* **TRANQUILITY.**

Look for an answer whose two words describe opposite states.

You can reject (A) and (E), in which both pairs are positive. In (B), the words have a weak connection, and they're both negative. In both (C) and (D), the relationships between the words seem to involve opposites. To choose between them, plug the word pairs into the stem bridge. Which sounds right: Someone who feels **consoled** does not feel **weeping**? Or: Someone who feels **reassured** does not feel **anxiety**? Since both **TRANQUILITY** and **anxiety** are states of mind, while **weeping** is an action, (D) is a better fit.

> perturbed: upset
> tranquility: calmness
> impudent: cocky or insolent
> dissension: disagreement or quarreling
>   with in a group

10. A

To do well on this one, you need to know the meaning of some hard words. A strong bridge is: *A* **PLATITUDE** *is a* **TRITE** *saying.* The second word describes the first.

(A) fits the stem bridge and is probably right: A **riddle** is a **cryptic** saying. But check the other choices. Although you probably memorized **axioms** in geometry class, **axioms** are not **geometric** sayings, so (B) doesn't fit. In (C), an **attitude** is not a saying, though it sounds like **PLATITUDE.** In (D), a **syllogism** is a form of deductive logic (e.g., all dogs are mammals; this animal is a dog; therefore, this animal is a mammal), not a **wise** saying. Finally, in (E), both meanings of **circumlocution** imply beating around the bush rather than coming to the point, so a **circumlocution** is definitely not a **concise** saying.

platitude: a cliché, usually with a moral
trite: stale, ordinary, commonplace
cryptic: obscure or secret
axiom: statement that is self-evident or doesn't require proof
syllogism: a form of deductive logic
circumlocution: using more words than necessary, or speaking evasively

Suggested Time: 7 minutes

Directions—Choose the lettered pair of words that is related in the same way as the pair in capital letters.

Example:
FLAKE : SNOW ::

(A) storm : hail
(B) drop : rain
(C) field : wheat
(D) stack : hay
(E) cloud : fog   Ⓐ ● Ⓒ Ⓓ Ⓔ

1. BAKER : BREAD ::

(A) artist : studio
(B) weaver : cloth
(C) factory : clearance
(D) florist : flowers
(E) druggist : illness   Ⓐ Ⓑ Ⓒ Ⓓ Ⓔ

2. SHIP : FLEET ::

(A) grass : field
(B) container : milk
(C) cow : herd
(D) beak : bird
(E) swamp : glade   Ⓐ Ⓑ Ⓒ Ⓓ Ⓔ

3. HYPOCRITE : INSINCERITY ::

(A) braggart : modesty
(B) criminal : sympathy
(C) liar : dishonesty
(D) patriot : disloyalty
(E) witness : truthfulness   Ⓐ Ⓑ Ⓒ Ⓓ Ⓔ

4. ANCHOR : BOAT ::

(A) sink : ship
(B) launch : pier
(C) propel : rocket
(D) tether : horse
(E) waddle : duck   Ⓐ Ⓑ Ⓒ Ⓓ Ⓔ

5. CRUTCH : SUPPORT ::

(A) needle : measurement
(B) thermometer : fever
(C) drill : numbness
(D) bandage : protection
(E) hospital : gravity   Ⓐ Ⓑ Ⓒ Ⓓ Ⓔ

6. FUNNEL : CONICAL ::

(A) pipe : cylindrical
(B) solid : spherical
(C) hose : spiral
(D) line : parallel
(E) hive : hexagonal   Ⓐ Ⓑ Ⓒ Ⓓ Ⓔ

7. REND : TATTERS ::

(A) fry : onions
(B) burn : ashes
(C) donate : beggars
(D) irrigate : clods
(E) water : plants   Ⓐ Ⓑ Ⓒ Ⓓ Ⓔ

8. DOUBLE-CROSSER : BETRAY ::

(A) slowpoke : lag
(B) watchdog : dread
(C) trendsetter : pace
(D) sweetheart : hug
(E) pessimist : cooperate   Ⓐ Ⓑ Ⓒ Ⓓ Ⓔ

9. SUBMISSION : KNEEL ::

(A) equilibrium : stand
(B) leisure : sit
(C) mutiny : lie
(D) disrespect : bow
(E) assent : nod   Ⓐ Ⓑ Ⓒ Ⓓ Ⓔ

10. CONCORD : AGREEMENT ::

(A) insurrection : calm
(B) chaos : order
(C) promise : peace
(D) revolution : army
(E) flux : change   Ⓐ Ⓑ Ⓒ Ⓓ Ⓔ

SCORECARD	
Number of Questions Right:	
Number of Questions Wrong:	
Number of Questions Omitted:	
Number of Correct Guesses:	
Number of Wrong Guesses:	
Time Used:	

ANSWERS AND EXPLANATIONS

1. B

Your bridge links the person with the product he or she makes: *A BAKER makes BREAD.*

A **weaver** makes **cloth,** so (B) is probably correct. But check out the other answers.

(C) is clearly wrong. A **factory** doesn't make a **clearance.** In (A), a **studio** is a place where an **artist** works; an **artist** doesn't make a **studio.** In (D), **flowers** are sold, but not made, by **florists.** In (E), **druggists** don't make **illness;** they sell products that treat and cure **illnesses.**

2. C

A strong bridge is: *A group of SHIPS is called a FLEET.*

The only answer choice in which the second word obviously describes a group is (C). So check whether it fits the stem bridge. It does: A group of **cows** is called a **herd.**

> glade: an open space surrounded by
> woods.

3. C

If you know how a hypocrite behaves, you have your bridge: *A HYPOCRITE is someone who displays INSINCERITY.*

In (E), a **witness** doesn't necessarily display **truthfulness,** so (E) is a weak possibility at best. But a **liar** displays **dishonesty,** so (C) is the best answer.

If you make your bridge more specific, the choice between (C) and (E) becomes clearer. Try the bridge: *A HYPOCRITE is someone who is guilty of INSINCERITY.* A **witness** is not guilty of **truthfulness,** but a **liar** is certainly guilty of **dishonesty.**

> braggart: someone who boasts
> hypocrite: a deceiver, a dissembler,
> someone who pretends to be what he
> or she is not

4. D

If you tried to build a bridge that linked an **ANCHOR** and a **BOAT,** you were slightly off track. A quick look at the answer choices indicates that all the first words are verbs, including **ANCHOR.**

Your bridge could be: *To ANCHOR a BOAT means to secure it so that it doesn't drift away.* Similarly, to **tether** a **horse** means to tie it to some fixed point so it doesn't wander off. No other answer choice fits the stem bridge.

5. D

Bridge: *By definition, a CRUTCH provides SUPPORT.*

The answer choices all contain words associated with injuries or medicine. Don't be tempted by these associations. You'll have to plug each word pair into the stem bridge and see which fits best. The only one that fits at all is (D): A **bandage** provides **protection.**

> gravity: the attractive force that makes
> objects fall towards the earth; also
> seriousness, e.g., the gravity of the
> situation.

6. A

Bridge: *A FUNNEL looks like a cone; it's CONICAL in shape.* A **pipe** looks like a cylinder; it's **cylindrical** in shape.

Checking out the other choices, in (B), something **spherical** can be either **solid** or hollow. In (C), a **hose** isn't necessarily a **spiral** in shape, only when it's wound up. In (D), two **lines** may be **parallel,** but a **line** is not **parallel** in shape. (E) is tricky. The cells of a honeycomb are **hexagonal** in shape, but the **hive** that contains them is generally not.

> *spherical: globular, shaped like a sphere*
>   *or ball*
> *hive: colony of bees; place swarming*
>   *with occupants*

7. B

A good bridge is: **RENDING** *fabric thoroughly will reduce it to* **TATTERS,** or rags.

So look for an answer choice whose first word describes an action that reduces something to an unusable state. Only **burn** in answer choice (B) fits that description, so plug in your stem bridge: **Burning** something thoroughly will reduce it to **ashes.** That's true, so (B) is correct.

> *rend: to tear*
> *irrigate: to supply with water*
> *clods: lumps of earth*

8. A

Your bridge is: *A* **DOUBLE-CROSSER** *is someone who, by definition,* **BETRAYS.**

(A) works quite well. A **slowpoke** is someone who **lags,** or falls behind.

(D) doesn't quite fit the stem bridge. By definition, **DOUBLE-CROSSERS BETRAY** and **slowpokes lag;** but while it's very common for **sweethearts** to **hug,** the definition of a **sweetheart** isn't someone who **hugs.**

9. E

SUBMISSION has several meanings, but the one most closely connected with **KNEEL** has to do with being humble. With that in mind, you can phrase this stem bridge as: *One* **KNEELS** *to express* **SUBMISSION.**

In (A), your sense of **equilibrium** allows you to stand, but you don't **stand** to express **equilibrium.** If you have **leisure,** or free time, you may choose to **sit** for a while, but you don't **sit** in order to express **leisure.** In fact, none of the answer choices fits the stem bridge until you get to the last one: You **nod** to express **assent,** or agreement.

> *submission: condition of being humble;*
>   *something submitted, like an*
>   *application*
> *equilibrium: balance*

10. E

To build a stem bridge you need to know what **CONCORD** means: **CONCORD** *is a state of* **AGREEMENT.** The two words are almost synonymous. The only answer choice whose words mean almost the same thing is (E), **flux** and **change.** So plug in your bridge: **Flux** is a state of **change.** It fits.

In (A) and (B), the word pairs are almost opposites. In (C), a **promise** is not a state of **peace.** In (D), a **revolution** is fought by an **army,** but **revolution** is not a state of **army.**

> *insurrection: rebellion*
> *chaos: total disorder*

Suggested Time: 7 minutes

Directions—Choose the lettered pair of words that is related in the same way as the pair in capital letters.

Example:
FLAKE : SNOW ::

(A) storm : hail
(B) drop : rain
(C) field : wheat
(D) stack : hay
(E) cloud : fog

Ⓐ ● Ⓒ Ⓓ Ⓔ

1. WATCH : TIME ::

(A) tape : measurement
(B) ruler : length
(C) meter : measurement
(D) barometer : gauge
(E) hour : minute

Ⓐ Ⓑ Ⓒ Ⓓ Ⓔ

2. ARBOREAL : TREES ::

(A) national : government
(B) chemical : solution
(C) urban : city
(D) botanical : garden
(E) lunar : eclipse

Ⓐ Ⓑ Ⓒ Ⓓ Ⓔ

3. ARCHIPELAGO : ISLANDS ::

(A) ocean : fish
(B) constellation : stars
(C) universe : comets
(D) zoo : bears
(E) delta : rivers

Ⓐ Ⓑ Ⓒ Ⓓ Ⓔ

4. PREAMBLE : DOCUMENT ::

(A) overture : opera
(B) exit : door
(C) paragraph : line
(D) stanza : poem
(E) score : music

Ⓐ Ⓑ Ⓒ Ⓓ Ⓔ

5. ENTICING : ATTRACT ::

(A) welcome : warm
(B) elusive : allure
(C) withering : shock
(D) glittery : engross
(E) repugnant : repulse

Ⓐ Ⓑ Ⓒ Ⓓ Ⓔ

6. PUERILE : IMMATURITY ::

(A) hardworking : dexterity
(B) sly : craftiness
(C) unscrupulous : honesty
(D) boorish : politeness
(E) loquacious : oratory

Ⓐ Ⓑ Ⓒ Ⓓ Ⓔ

7. KINETIC : MOTION ::

(A) insipid : taste
(B) extinct : species
(C) frenetic : speed
(D) fictional : literature
(E) scholastic : education

Ⓐ Ⓑ Ⓒ Ⓓ Ⓔ

8. PUTRID : DECAY ::

(A) compelling : fear
(B) tortuous : pain
(C) old : rusty
(D) decrepit : age
(E) superficial : depth

Ⓐ Ⓑ Ⓒ Ⓓ Ⓔ

9 CONFLAGRATION : FIRE ::

(A) match : tinder
(B) sanctuary : church
(C) ice : storm
(D) bees : swarm
(E) deluge : flood

Ⓐ Ⓑ Ⓒ Ⓓ Ⓔ

10. SACROSANCT : CRITICISM ::

(A) quiescent : calm
(B) precise : time
(C) therapeutic : relaxation
(D) unmanageable : control
(E) subversive : law

Ⓐ Ⓑ Ⓒ Ⓓ Ⓔ

SCORECARD	
Number of Questions Right:	
Number of Questions Wrong:	
Number of Questions Omitted:	
Number of Correct Guesses:	
Number of Wrong Guesses:	
Time Used:	

ANSWERS AND EXPLANATIONS

1. B

The bridge is clear: *The function of a* **WATCH** *is, by definition, to measure* **TIME.** The correct answer is (B)—the function of a **ruler** is to measure **length.**

> *gauge: standard measure, an*
> *instrument for measuring*

2. C

ARBOREAL *means having to do with* **TREES.** In (C), the word **urban** means having to do with the **city.**

The other answer choices are wrong; either the words within each pair are connected only loosely, or their relationship doesn't have anything to do with the relationship between the stem words. For example, in (A), a **national government** is the **government** of a particular nation. **ARBOREAL TREES** aren't the **TREES** of a particular **ARBOR,** or shelter of vines and branches, so (A) can't work. In (B), a **chemical** substance may or may not be a **solution**—this word pair has a weak bridge. A **botanical garden** (D) is a place where plants and trees are grown for scientific study. Again, that bridge does not sound right when used with the stem words.

> *arboreal: having to do with trees*
> *urban: having to do with the city*

3. B

An **ARCHIPELAGO** *is a group of* **ISLANDS;** a **constellation** is a group of **stars.**

The **universe** consists of all matter known to exist; it's not a group of **comets.**

4. A

The prefix *pre-* in the word **PREAMBLE** should suggest to you that it has something to do with "going before." In fact, *a* **PREAMBLE** *is a preliminary statement, or introduction to a* **DOCUMENT.**

Now let's check through the answer choices and see which one fits this bridge. In (A), an **overture** is, by definition, an orchestral composition that forms the prelude or introduction to an **opera,** or ballet. So (A) is correct.

You should always run through the other choices just to be sure. In (B), an **exit** does not come before a **door.** In (C), a **paragraph** contains **lines,** but a **paragraph** isn't the introduction to a **line.** In choice (D), a **stanza** is a subdivision of a **poem,** not the introduction to a **poem.** In (E), the **score** is the written copy of a piece of **music.**

> *preamble: a preliminary statement, or*
> *introduction to a document*
> *overture: an orchestral composition*
> *that forms the prelude to an opera or*
> *ballet*

5. E

Bridge: *Things that are* **ENTICING** *tend to* **ATTRACT.** Things that are **repugnant** tend to **repulse,** or repel.

6. B

PUERILE means childish, so the bridge is: *Someone* **PUERILE** *shows* **IMMATURITY.** (B) is right—someone **sly** shows **craftiness.**

Choices (A) and (E) can be eliminated because they have weak bridges; someone **hardworking** is not necessarily gifted with **dexterity,** or nimbleness. Similarly, someone **loquacious** does not necessarily practice **oratory.** Because choices (C) and (D) have the same bridge, they can both be eliminated. Someone **unscrupulous** lacks **honesty,** as someone **boorish** lacks **politeness.** So (B) is the correct answer, by process of elimination.

> *unscrupulous: lacking principles;*
> *unethical*
> *puerile: childish*
> *loquacious: talkative*
> *boorish: ill-mannered and rude*
> *oratory: the art of public speaking*

> *putrid: decomposed, rotting, foul-*
> *smelling*
> *decrepit: made weak by hard use, or old*
> *age*
> *tortuous: twisted, crooked, or winding*

7. E

KINETIC *means having to do with* **MOTION.** In (E), **scholastic** means having to do with **education.**

> *kinetic: having to do with motion*
> *scholastic: having to do with education*
> *insipid: tasteless, dull, lacking in flavor*
> *extinct: no longer active or existing*
> *frenetic: frantic, wildly exciting*
> *fictional: invented, imagined*

8. D

By definition, something **PUTRID** *shows signs of* **DECAY,** just as something **decrepit** shows signs of **age.**

If you did not understand the meaning of **PUTRID,** how could you proceed? Well, you know **PUTRID** is an adjective, since the first word in each of the answer choices is an adjective. Also, **PUTRID** sounds negative. You could reason that the words in the correct answer choice will also be similar in meaning to each other. Choices (A), (B), and (C) can be ruled out, because they all have weak bridges. (E) has a strong bridge: Something that is **superficial,** or shallow, lacks **depth.** However, since we've already decided that we are looking for two words that have the same "charge," this bridge does not fit. Either way, (D) must be the correct answer.

9. E

A **CONFLAGRATION** *is an enormous* **FIRE.** A **deluge** is an enormous **flood.**

> *sanctuary: a place of refuge or*
> *protection; or the most sacred part of*
> *a religious building*

10. D

Bridge: **SACROSANCT** *means beyond* **CRITICISM.** (D) is correct, because something **unmanageable** is beyond **control.**

Could you arrive at the right answer without understanding the meaning of **SACROSANCT?** Yes, if you work backwards. (A), (B), (C), and (E) have bridges that are either weak, or unworkable with the stem words, so they can all be ruled out. (C) has a weak bridge—the purpose of something **therapeutic** is not necessarily to induce **relaxation,** but to remedy an ailment. In (E), a **subversive** act—one that is designed to weaken authority—may or may not be against the **law;** (E) is also weak.

> *sacrosanct: accorded the highest*
> *reverence and respect, beyond*
> *criticism*
> *quiescent: calm*

Suggested Time: 7 minutes

Directions—Choose the lettered pair of words that is related in the same way as the pair in capital letters.

Example:
FLAKE : SNOW ::

(A) storm : hail
(B) drop : rain
(C) field : wheat
(D) stack : hay
(E) cloud : fog

Ⓐ ● Ⓒ Ⓓ Ⓔ

1. PLAYWRIGHT : PLAY ::

(A) painter : canvas
(B) critic : literature
(C) composer : score
(D) announcer : radio
(E) musician : instrument

Ⓐ Ⓑ Ⓒ Ⓓ Ⓔ

2. CLOG : SHOE ::

(A) boot : mud
(B) drain : liquid
(C) sombrero : hat
(D) gold : jewelry
(E) wig : head

Ⓐ Ⓑ Ⓒ Ⓓ Ⓔ

3. SWILL : DRINK ::

(A) consume : digest
(B) gossip : talk
(C) risk : gamble
(D) gorge : eat
(E) swallow : sip

Ⓐ Ⓑ Ⓒ Ⓓ Ⓔ

4. THRIFTY : PARSIMONIOUS ::

(A) inquisitive : prying
(B) brave : timid
(C) aggressive : alert
(D) timorous : gentle
(E) stern : yielding

Ⓐ Ⓑ Ⓒ Ⓓ Ⓔ

5. PLANE : SMOOTH ::

(A) embellish : expensive
(B) burnish : shiny
(C) merge : complex
(D) pulverize : dusty
(E) flatten : small

Ⓐ Ⓑ Ⓒ Ⓓ Ⓔ

6. WHIFF : SMELL ::

(A) pain : sensation
(B) food : taste
(C) tinge : color
(D) fall : accident
(E) answer : solution

Ⓐ Ⓑ Ⓒ Ⓓ Ⓔ

7. PHARMACY : DRUGS ::

(A) nursery : florists
(B) terrarium : sod
(C) seminary : textbooks
(D) auditorium : plays
(E) haberdashery : clothing

Ⓐ Ⓑ Ⓒ Ⓓ Ⓔ

8. IMPROVIDENT : FORESIGHT ::

(A) fortunate : opportunity
(B) ill-tempered : prudence
(C) incapacitated : wisdom
(D) ambitious : success
(E) skeptical : belief

Ⓐ Ⓑ Ⓒ Ⓓ Ⓔ

9. BOMBASTIC : GRANDILOQUENCE ::

(A) unyielding : resolution
(B) finicky : variety
(C) timid : confidence
(D) retiring : age
(E) calm : excitement

Ⓐ Ⓑ Ⓒ Ⓓ Ⓔ

10. APOSTATE : RELIGION ::

(A) pedant : erudition
(B) benefactor : largess
(C) politician : sovereignty
(D) defector : cause
(E) reprobate : crime

Ⓐ Ⓑ Ⓒ Ⓓ Ⓔ

SCORECARD	
Number of Questions Right:	
Number of Questions Wrong:	
Number of Questions Omitted:	
Number of Correct Guesses:	
Number of Wrong Guesses:	
Time Used:	

ANSWERS AND EXPLANATIONS

1. C

A **PLAYWRIGHT** *is the author of a* **PLAY** just as a **composer** is the author of a **score.**

A **painter** is not really the author of a **canvas,** since a **canvas** is a piece of cloth framed and backed so as to be a surface for painting.

2. C

A **CLOG** *is a type of* **SHOE,** just as a **sombrero** is a type of **hat.**

(A) might have tempted you, since **boot** and **SHOE** are similar. But a **boot** isn't a type of **mud.** In (B), a **drain** is a means by which **liquid** is drawn off or emptied; a **drain** isn't a type of **liquid.**

3. D

Bridge: *To* **SWILL** *is to* **DRINK** *in a greedy manner or to excess.* To **gorge** is to **eat** in a greedy manner or to excess.

Choice (A), **consume: digest,** may remind you of the stem pair, but that's not enough to make it the right answer. If you plug (A) into the bridge, you get: To **consume** is to **digest** in a greedy manner. That makes no sense, so (A) can't be right.

4. A

The bridge is: *Someone who is overly* **THRIFTY** *is by definition* **PARSIMONIOUS.** Someone overly **inquisitive** is **prying.**

In (D), someone **timorous** is probably also **gentle,** but you wouldn't say that someone overly **timorous** is **gentle** by definition.

timorous: meek

5. B

The challenge here is to think of the right meaning of **PLANE. PLANE** is being used as a verb here, so your bridge is: *To* **PLANE** *is to make something* **SMOOTH.** In the same way, to **burnish** is to make something **shiny.**

plane: to make smooth or level
burnish: to polish until shiny
pulverize: to crush into powder

6. C

Bridge: A **WHIFF** *is a slight trace of* **SMELL.** A **tinge** is a slight trace of **color.**

7. E

The bridge is: *You buy* **DRUGS** *at a* **PHARMACY,** just as you buy **clothing** at a **haberdashery.** In (A), a **nursery** is where plants are grown or sold. **Florists** might go to a **nursery,** but **florists** aren't bought there.

terrarium: a glass container for raising
    plants or animals indoors
seminary: an institution of higher
    education, especially one that trains
    people to be priests, ministers, or
    rabbis
haberdashery: clothing store

8. E

The bridge is: *Someone* **IMPROVIDENT** *lacks* **FORESIGHT** the same way someone **skeptical** lacks **belief.**

improvident: thoughtless, unwary,
    neglecting to provide for future needs

9. A

BOMBASTIC *means characterized by* **GRANDILOQUENCE. Unyielding** means characterized by **resolution,** or firmness.

KAPLAN

If you were not able to define these words, the only effective strategy open to you was elimination of wrong answers. Let's see how it works here. As we've already seen, (A) has a strong bridge: **Unyielding** means characterized by **resolution.** In (B), someone **finicky** may or may not like **variety.** The two words in (B) have a weak relationship, so (B) can be eliminated. (C) is pretty strong: Someone who is **timid** does not exhibit **confidence.** It's a possible right answer, so keep it in mind for the moment. In (D), **retiring** has nothing to with **age.** (E) has a strong bridge: Someone who is **calm** does not exhibit **excitement.** However, since (C) and (E) have the same bridge, they must both be wrong. After all, there can be only one answer choice that has the same bridge as the stem words. By process of elimination, (A) is the correct answer.

---

grandiloquence: extravagant, pompous language
bombastic: using pompous language
unyielding: characterized by resolution
retiring: reserved or shy

---

10. D

Bridge: *By definition, an* **APOSTATE** *is someone who has renounced a particular* **RELIGION.** In (D), a **defector** is someone who has renounced a particular **cause.**

---

apostate: someone who has renounced a particular religion
pedant: someone overly concerned with small, insignificant details of knowledge
erudition: learning
benefactor: a donor, one who makes a large gift
largess: generosity
sovereignty: supreme power or freedom from external controls
reprobate: a scoundrel, an immoral or wicked person

SAT
Sentence
Completions

INTRODUCTION TO SAT SENTENCE COMPLETIONS

Sentence Completions test your ability to read carefully and think logically. Sentence Completions also test your knowledge of college-level vocabulary.

The Structure

You'll probably see nine Sentence Completions at the beginning of one 30-minute Verbal section, and ten at the beginning of the other. The rest of those sections will consist of Analogies and Critical Reading.

The Format

The directions for Sentence Completions appear at the top of the questions. They look something like this:

Select the lettered word or set of words that best completes the sentence.

> EXAMPLE
>
> Today's small, portable computers contrast markedly with the earliest electronic computers, which were ----.
>
> (A) effective
>
> (B) invented
>
> (C) useful
>
> (D) destructive
>
> (E) enormous

In the example, the new computers, which are small and portable, are contrasted with old computers. You can infer that the old computers must be the opposite of small and portable, so (E) **enormous** is right.

Though the real SAT directions and sample question will look slightly different, they'll mean the same thing. Now you know what to do when you open your booklet to Sentence Completions. So don't waste time reading the directions on Test Day.

Sentence Completions are arranged in order of difficulty. The hardest questions are at the end of each set, so pace yourself accordingly. Take no more than 40 seconds on each Sentence Completion. Save the bulk of your 30 minutes for Critical Reading questions.

If a question stumps you, mark it in your test booklet, skip it on your answer sheet, and come back to it later if you have time. But first finish all the other questions in Sentence Completions, Analogies, and Critical Reading.

HINT: *Don't get hung up on any one question. Your goal is to answer correctly as many questions as possible.*

Like everything else on the SAT, Sentence Completions come in a standard format. Once you get used to solving them, they can be quite easy. So if you're having trouble, practice.

Kaplan's Method

Kaplan has a tested method for solving Sentence Completions. It works whether your sentence deals with tarantulas, stained glass windows, or Native American dance forms. Here's what to do:

- Read the sentence carefully, searching for clue words or phrases.

HINT: *Words or phrases like* and, but, although, *and* such as *are clues because they indicate contrast or similarity. Clues like these can tell you where a sentence is headed and what kind of word goes in the blank or blanks.*

- Predict what should go into the blank or blanks. Do this before you glance at the answer choices.

HINT: *Your prediction doesn't have to be exact. A rough idea of what goes in the blanks will do.*

- Compare your prediction to the answer choices. Pick the choice that best matches your prediction.
- Scan the other choices to make sure you've picked the best answer.
- Read the sentence with your answer choice in the blank. If it sounds right, you're done.

Dealing with Hard Words

You'll find hard words in the sentences and the answer choices. That's why it's important to study our Word and Root Lists. But what if you still don't know some words? Don't give up. Try these suggestions for working around unknown words:

- Look in the sentence itself for clues to a word's meaning.
- Think about where you might have heard the word before.
- Try to spot familiar roots or prefixes that can help you understand the word's meaning.
- If all else fails, eliminate answers you think are wrong and guess.

Dealing with Hard Sentences

It's important to read the sentences and answer choices carefully, especially near the end of the set. Follow the twists and turns of the sentence, and be sure you understand what it says. Then you won't get caught by tricky answers that the test makers like to include.

- Don't pick an answer just because it sounds hard. Be sure the answer you choose makes sense.

- Don't choose an answer choice that is the opposite of the correct answer. Read the sentence carefully.

Dealing with Two-Blank Sentences

Two-blank sentences can be easier than one-blankers. In two-blankers you can:

- Scan the sentence and start with the easier blank.

- Eliminate all answer choices that won't work for that blank.

- Try only the remaining choices in the second blank.

HINT: *In two-blankers, don't pick a choice that fits one blank but not the other.*

Checklist

Sentence Completions:

❑ Use Kaplan's Method: Read carefully, predict an answer, find a match for your prediction, and check your answer.

❑ Work systematically, but quickly.

❑ Spend no more than 40 seconds on each question.

❑ Search the sentence for clue words and phrases.

❑ To figure out what a hard word means, figure out how it's used in the sentence, think where you may have heard it before, and look for familiar prefixes and roots. If all else fails, eliminate wrong answers and guess.

❑ On two-blankers, do the easier blank first. Then make sure the answer choice you pick fits both blanks.

❑ On the last few questions, don't pick answers just because they sound hard. Watch out for wrong answer choices that are opposites of right answers.

678 485 1261

Suggested Time: 7 minutes

Directions: Select the lettered word or set of words that best completes the sentence.

Example:

Today's small, portable computers contrast markedly with the earliest electronic computers, which were ----.

(A) effective
(B) invented
(C) useful
(D) destructive
(E) enormous

1. Joseph's employees were ---- by the ---- manner in which he dealt with them.

(A) repulsed . . placid
(B) irritated . . curt
(C) incensed . . droll
(D) perturbed . . amiable
(E) weakened . . sullen

2. It is sometimes customary to view rain as ---- sign; many believe that if it rains on the day of your wedding, you will enjoy financial prosperity.

(A) an inopportune
(B) a meager
(C) an auspicious
(D) an untimely
(E) a modest

3. Once a ---- population center, the city gradually lost residents to the factory towns of the North.

(A) bustling
(B) manufactured
(C) rural
(D) seedy
(E) deserted

4. The scene was even ---- than Rebecca had ----; dead trees and patchy brown grass seemed to stretch on forever under a leaden sky.

(A) uglier . . feigned
(B) drearier . . envisioned
(C) lazier . . divulged
(D) scantier . . desired
(E) keener . . perceived

5. Proponents of a bill requiring each home to keep a firearm and ammunition sought to placate their opponents by including ---- for those who did not ---- gun possession.

(A) a penalty . . frown upon
(B) an exemption . . support
(C) a theory . . relish
(D) an addendum . . continue
(E) a waiver . . abolish

6. Otis ---- agreed to ---- his partner's decision, misguided though he thought it was.

(A) gracefully . . rail at
(B) maliciously . . compromise on
(C) wistfully . . bargain with
(D) grudgingly . . abide by
(E) cynically . . reign over

7. The name of the housing development is a ----; although it is called "Forest Hills," it is located in a ---- valley.

(A) dilution . . river
(B) fallacy . . neglected
(C) misnomer . . treeless
(D) retelling . . contented
(E) fault . . barren

8. Far from being ----, today's television advertising, with its constant barrage of last-minute sales and new-and-improved products, practically ---- the viewer.

(A) subtle . . assaults
(B) engaging . . titillates
(C) utilitarian . . assists
(D) obtuse . . ridicules
(E) informative . . ignores

9. Unfortunately, the treasurer's plan to get the company out of debt ---- gaining access to certain funds that may never become available.

(A) speaks to
(B) treats with
(C) delves into
(D) metes out
(E) hinges on

10. A true ascetic, Jorge ---- luxuries and other worldly pleasures in an effort to ---- his spiritual side.

    (A) spurns . . fortify
    (B) embraces . . emulate
    (C) relishes . . assist
    (D) condones . . reclaim
    (E) lambastes . . interpret

    Ⓐ Ⓑ ⓒ ⓓ Ⓔ

SCORECARD	
Number of Questions Right:	
Number of Questions Wrong:	
Number of Questions Omitted:	
Number of Correct Guesses:	
Number of Wrong Guesses:	
Time Used:	

ANSWERS AND EXPLANATIONS

1. B

In this sentence, you can figure out the relation between the two words. Either the employees were "pleased" by the "nice" manner in which he dealt with them, or they were "displeased" by the "not nice" manner in which he dealt with them. In other words, the two words must reinforce each other.

In (A), **placid** and **repulsed** have nothing to do with each other. In (B), it makes sense that employees would be **irritated** by their employer's **curt** manner, so (B) is probably right. But check out the other answers.

In (C) and (D), the words are almost opposites. In (E), they have little connection. So go with (B).

repulsed: repelled
placid: calm
curt: rudely brief in speech

2. C

Financial prosperity is a strong clue. Since it's a good thing, *rain* must be a sign of good fortune. Scanning the answer choices, the closest match is (C) **auspicious**.

inopportune: inconvenient
auspicious: foretelling good fortune

3. A

Clue words here are *once* and *lost residents.* Since it *lost residents,* the city once must have been a large *population center.* That sense is conveyed by (A) **bustling**. It certainly is not conveyed by **deserted, seedy, manufactured,** or **rural.**

bustling: crowded and busy
seedy: rundown

4. B

The semicolon offers a clue. The words that go in the blanks must fit the gloomy description after the semicolon. Your phrase might be: *The scene was even "worse" than Rebecca had "imagined."* In the first blank, **lazier, keener,** and **scantier** aren't close to "worse," and they don't fit, so you are left with (A) and (B). Since either **uglier** or **drearier** would fit the first blank, you have to decide between (A) and (B) based on their second words. **Feigned** doesn't make sense in this context. But **envisioned** works fine.

feigned: pretended
envisioned: imagined
scantier: scarcer

5. B

This one's tough if you don't know the vocabulary (see below). The *proponents* were trying to get the bill passed by the legislature. They wanted firearm possession to be mandatory. Presumably *their opponents* didn't favor keeping guns, so the second blank should be filled by something that means "supported."

The first blank might be filled by something like "a loophole," a way for people who don't want to obey the law to avoid its requirements.

(A) is out because **penalty** doesn't fit the first blank, and **frown upon** is the opposite of what we want for the second blank. In (C), it doesn't make sense for **a theory** to be included in *a bill.* Moreover, **relish** is totally at odds with our description for the second blank. **An addendum** is usually "attached to" something, rather than *included* in it. And since **continue** doesn't make any sense in the second blank, (D) must be wrong. In (E), **a waiver** precisely matches our word "loophole" for the first blank, but it doesn't make sense to talk about exempting those who do not **abolish** *gun possession.* (B), the only remaining choice, fits both blanks.

proponents: supporters
placate: soothe or appease
exemption: waiver or exception from a
*   requirement*
relish: enjoy greatly
addendum: addition

6. D

Your clue here is *misguided*. Since Otis thought his partner's decision was *misguided*, he obviously "reluctantly" *agreed to* "go along with it." (D) fits both descriptions. *Otis* **grudgingly** *agreed to* **abide by** *his partner's decision.*

Checking the other choices, (A) **gracefully,** (B) **maliciously,** and (C) **wistfully** don't make sense. In (E), **cynically** could possibly fit, but **reign over** is clearly wrong.

maliciously: spitefully
grudgingly: unwillingly or reluctantly
abide by: act according to
cynically: pessimistically, distrustfully

7. C

The sentence suggests that the housing development's name is misleading. It may have been called *Forest Hills,* but it was actually constructed *in a ---- valley,* not in the *Hills.* So you need a word like "mistake," or even "fraud," for the first blank. And for the second blank, you're looking for something that contrasts with *Forest.*

Start with the first blank. (B) **fallacy** and (C) **misnomer** are the only two possible choices. So rule out the others and check the second words for (B) and (C). In (B), **neglected** doesn't fit. In (C), **treeless** does fit the second blank. Since both the words in choice (C) match the predicted meanings, (C) is correct.

fallacy: logical error
misnomer: a wrong name

8. A

The clue here is *far from being*. It tells you that you are dealing with two contrasting sentence parts. *Far from being ----, today's television ---- the viewer.* We're also told that *today's television advertising* consists of a *constant barrage* of information. The implication is that today's television advertising "attacks" the viewer. So you need to look for a second word that's similar to "attacks," and a first word that contrasts with it.

The only second word that means "attacks" is **assaults,** in (A). The *advertising practically* **assaults** *the viewer* in a heavy-handed way. **Subtle** is a good opposite, so this fits.

In (B), **engaging** and **titillates** are not opposites; **engaging** commercials might very well **titillate** the viewer. (C) **utilitarian** makes no sense. (D) **obtuse** has little to do with **ridicules.** In (E), **informative** might be right, but the *barrage* of television advertising certainly doesn't **ignore** the viewer.

barrage: rapid, concentrated
*   outpouring*
subtle: indirect, delicate
engaging: attractive
titillates: arouses or stimulates
utilitarian: functional
obtuse: dull or stupid

9. E

Your clue is *unfortunately. The treasurer's plan unfortunately* may not work because it *---- gaining access to certain funds that may never become available.* To fill the blank, look for a phrase like "relies on" or is "based on." The closest choice is (E) **hinges on.**

The other four familiar phrases don't make sense in this sentence.

> *speaks to: addresses (an issue or a*
> *point)*
> *treats with: negotiates with*
> *delves into: digs or searches deeply and*
> *carefully*
> *metes out: gives out small rations or*
> *allotments*
> *hinges on: depends on*

10. A

Since *Jorge* is a *true ascetic,* the word in the first blank must support that description. You could say: A true ascetic "gives up" luxuries. To make sense, the second blank has to reinforce that. He "gives up" *luxuries* in order to "strengthen" *his spiritual side.*

Checking the first words in the answer choices, you'll see (A) **spurns** works best. Now check out the second word. A true ascetic **spurns** luxuries in an effort to **fortify** his spiritual side. That makes sense.

Later on in a set, answer choices often contain some difficult words. If you don't know them all, eliminate choices when one word doesn't make sense. In this case, you probably knew that **embraces** and **relishes** mean almost the opposite of "gives up," so you could eliminate (B) and (C). You might also have guessed that **interpret** has nothing to do with "strengthen," so you could eliminate (E). Then you could guess between (A) and (D).

> *ascetic: one who practices self-denial*
> *spurns: rejects*
> *fortify: strengthen*
> *embraces: clasps in one's arms, accepts*
> *wholeheartedly*
> *emulate: imitate or strive to equal*
> *relishes: enjoys*
> *condones: pardons*
> *reclaim: rescue*
> *lambaste: whip verbally or censure*
> *interpret: explain or give the meaning*
> *of*

Suggested Time: 7 minutes

Directions: Select the lettered word or set of words that best completes the sentence.

Example:

Today's small, portable computers contrast markedly with the earliest electronic computers, which were ----.

(A) effective
(B) invented
(C) useful
(D) destructive
(E) enormous

Ⓐ ● Ⓒ Ⓓ Ⓔ

1. Barbara Walters distinguished herself as a journalist by asking famous people the kinds of ---- questions that other reporters shied away from.

(A) discreet
(B) intriguing
(C) pointed
(D) gentle
(E) indirect

Ⓐ Ⓑ Ⓒ Ⓓ Ⓔ

2. Ozone in the upper layers of Earth's atmosphere is beneficial, ---- animal and plant life from dangerous ultraviolet radiation.

(A) reflecting
(B) withdrawing
(C) displacing
(D) thwarting
(E) protecting

Ⓐ Ⓑ Ⓒ Ⓓ Ⓔ

3. All of today's navel oranges are ---- of a single mutant tree that began producing seedless fruit nearly 200 years ago.

(A) progenitors
(B) hybrids
(C) descendants
(D) conglomerations
(E) spores

Ⓐ Ⓑ Ⓒ Ⓓ Ⓔ

4. So ---- was the saleswoman's pitch about the value of the used car that Hallie nearly missed the ---- in its logic.

(A) convincing . . fallacy
(B) inept . . liability
(C) relieving . . reason
(D) tired . . persuasiveness
(E) sarcastic . . rejoinder

Ⓐ Ⓑ Ⓒ Ⓓ Ⓔ

5. Certain members of the pack viciously ---- others, ---- the hierarchical structure of the group.

(A) venerate . . destroying
(B) bully . . reinforcing
(C) coax . . subsidizing
(D) terrorize . . memorizing
(E) pass . . reacting

Ⓐ Ⓑ Ⓒ Ⓓ Ⓔ

6. After inventing a sign language for the deaf in the mid-1700s, Giacobbo Rodriguez Pereira ---- his business activities in order to ---- all his energies to humanitarian work.

(A) shouldered . . donate
(B) elicited . . transmit
(C) abandoned . . devote
(D) ceased . . attach
(E) ceded . . sell

Ⓐ Ⓑ Ⓒ Ⓓ Ⓔ

7. Investigators are trying to determine whether the recent rash of fires is the work of ---- or simply a ---- of unfortunate accidents.

(A) a pyromaniac . . source
(B) an accomplice . . consequence
(C) a criminal . . premonition
(D) an arsonist . . series
(E) an assortment . . string

Ⓐ Ⓑ Ⓒ Ⓓ Ⓔ

8. Despite his physical disability, the soccer player was ---- in helping his country's team capture the World Cup.

(A) ungainly
(B) accessible
(C) rampant
(D) instrumental
(E) unvarying

Ⓐ Ⓑ Ⓒ Ⓓ Ⓔ

9. Doing much more than was expected of her, Henrietta ---- the responsibilities of a department supervisor's position for eight months before she finally received the title.

    (A) undertook
    (B) procured
    (C) entreated
    (D) bestowed
    (E) precipitated

    Ⓐ Ⓑ Ⓒ Ⓓ Ⓔ

10. The poet received room, board, and ---- from the university in return for leading two seminars.

    (A) an impetus
    (B) an amulet
    (C) a writ
    (D) a niche
    (E) a stipend

SCORECARD	
Number of Questions Right:	
Number of Questions Wrong:	
Number of Questions Omitted:	
Number of Correct Guesses:	
Number of Wrong Guesses:	
Time Used:	

ANSWERS AND EXPLANATIONS

1. C

The sentence says that *Barbara Walters* earned a reputation for *herself as a journalist by* doing what *other reporters shied away from* or "avoided." The clue lies in *the kinds of questions* she asked—the kind *others shied away from.* You can predict that Ms. Walters asked personal, probing questions about controversial subjects. The only answer that describes such questions is (C) **pointed**.

A journalist wouldn't *shy away from* (D) **gentle** and (E) **indirect** questions. So (D) and (E) are thus eliminated. As for (B), all reporters try to make their questions **intriguing**.

> *discreet: prudently quiet or circumspect*
> *intriguing: exciting interest or curiosity*

2. E

In the upper layers of the Earth's atmosphere, ozone is said to be beneficial or "helpful," so it must do something good for animal and plant life. (E) **protecting** fits the bill.

> *thwart: to hinder, obstruct, or frustrate*

3. C

You have to predict a relationship between *all of today's navel oranges* and *a single mutant tree that* produced *seedless fruit* a long time ago. *Today's navel oranges* are (C) **descendants** or offspring of that first tree.

Mutant may confuse the hasty reader into selecting (B) **hybrids,** but the sentence does not suggest that *today's navel oranges* are offspring of two different species. (A) **Progenitors** describe a *mutant tree,* but not *today's navel oranges.* Likewise, in (D), **conglomeration** does not describe *navel oranges.* Finally, **spores** have to do with reproductive methods that are not discussed here, so (E) is not a good choice.

> *progenitors: ancestors, forebears*
> *conglomeration: mixture of various things*
> *spores: reproductive bodies released by certain primitive plants*

4. A

The saleswoman's pitch is her sales talk. We need a word like "persuasive" for the first blank and something like "flaw" for the second. Choice (A) is the only one that matches either prediction.

> *fallacy: error in logic*
> *inept: incompetent*
> *rejoinder: reply or "comeback"*

5. B

Suppose you didn't know some of the difficult words in this question. You could still eliminate wrong choices and guess. The only two choices whose first words can reasonably be modified by *viciously* are (B) **bully** and (D) **terrorize.** Choices (A) **venerate,** (C) **coax,** and (E) **pass** don't fit at all.

Checking the second blank, (B) makes sense and (D) doesn't. The aggressive behavior of these pack animals was **reinforcing** the *structure of the group* rather than **memorizing** it. So you could arrive at (B) by process of elimination.

Had you known the vocabulary words, you could have reached the same conclusion more quickly and with more certainty. The first part of the sentence indicates that some *members of the pack* get away with *viciously* attacking *others.* The second part implies that these attacks have something to do with the group's *hierarchical structure.* (B) best fits the meaning of the sentence, since the aggressive members of the pack control the weaker members.

hierarchical: having grades or ranks of
    authority or status
venerate: worship, esteem highly
coax: persuade gently

6. C

You can find the correct answer by examining the main clause alone: *Pereira ---- his business activities in order to ---- all his energies to humanitarian work.* In other words, he wanted to spend less time on *business activities* and more on *humanitarian work.* In the second blank, (A) **donate** and (C) **devote** are the only choices that fit. You can't **transmit, attach,** or **sell** your *energies* to a project.

So the only options you need to consider for the first blank are (A) **shouldered** and (C) **abandoned.** Since he wanted to spend less time on business activities, he probably abandoned them, so (C) is the right answer. He **abandoned** *his business activities in order to* **devote** *all his energies to humanitarian work.*

shoulder: to take on a burden or
    responsibility
abandoned: gave up, relinquished
elicited: evoked or produced
ceded: gave over or granted

7. D

In this context, a *rash* is not a skin irritation but a large number of instances within a short period of time. Here we're talking about a recent series of fires. For the first blank, we'll need a person or thing that might have caused the *fires.* The best options for the first blank are (A) **a pyromaniac** and (D) **an arsonist.** Although (C) **a criminal** might have started the fires, **a criminal** does not have as specific a connection with *fires.* And (B) **an accomplice** would by definition have helped set the *fires,* rather than setting them himself or herself.

Now look at the words that (A) and (D) offer for the second blank. *The recent rash of fires* could not have been *a* **source** *of unfortunate accidents* unless it caused

accidents, which we are not told. But **series** *of accidents* fits well with the idea of a *rash of fires.*

pyromaniac: someone who has an
    irresistible impulse to set fires
arsonist: someone who burns property
    for spite or profit
premonition: a hunch or feeling of
    foreboding

8. D

Despite is the clue word. It allows you to predict that in spite of *his physical disability, the soccer player* was important to his team. The only answer choice that comes close to that prediction is (D) **instrumental,** or helpful. In other words, the *team* won *the World Cup* because of the disabled player's efforts.

instrumental: serving as a means,
    agent, or tool
ungainly: awkward
accessible: open, capable of being
    reached
rampant: widespread
unvarying: unchanging

9. A

A long time elapsed between when *Henrietta ---- the responsibilities of a department supervisor's position* and when *she finally received the title.* You might predict a word like "assumed" or "shouldered" for the blank. The closest choice is (A) **undertook.** As for (B), Henrietta eventually **procured** *the title,* but first she **undertook** *the responsibilities.*

*procured: obtained or achieved by some
    effort*
entreated: pleaded with, begged
bestowed: presented as a gift
precipitated: brought about suddenly

*stipend: wage or other form of
    compensation to defray expenses*
impetus: stimulus or driving force
amulet: good luck charm
writ: formal legal document
niche: small opening or space

10. E

What might the university have given *the poet* as compensation *for leading two seminars?* We know that *the poet received room* and *board,* or living quarters and meals. The other obvious form of compensation would be money. The only answer choice that has anything to do with monetary compensation is (E) **a stipend.**

Suggested Time: 7 minutes

Directions: Select the lettered word or set of words that best completes the sentence.

Example:

Today's small, portable computers contrast markedly with the earliest electronic computers, which were ----.

(A) effective
(B) invented
(C) useful
(D) destructive
(E) enormous

Ⓐ ● Ⓒ Ⓓ Ⓔ

1. The first primitive fish had lungs; in most of their descendants, these ---- have ----- into swim bladders.

(A) animals . . merged
(B) organs . . evolved
(C) ancients . . combined
(D) organisms . . stretched
(E) functions . . barged

Ⓐ Ⓑ Ⓒ Ⓓ Ⓔ

2. Martha's wardrobe looked as though it had been ---- from a rag bin; her expensive boots were her sole ---- fashion.

(A) swiped . . agreement with
(B) compartmentalized . . return to
(C) beguiled . . contribution to
(D) salvaged . . concession to
(E) bought . . interruption from

Ⓐ Ⓑ Ⓒ Ⓓ Ⓔ

3. John Price was ---- from the slave-hunters who had abducted him by the citizens of Oberlin and the neighboring towns; 37 of these citizens were then ---- under the Fugitive Slave Act.

(A) kidnapped . . legislated
(B) recovered . . deemed
(C) rescued . . indicted
(D) serenaded . . jailed
(E) pressured . . penalized

Ⓐ Ⓑ Ⓒ Ⓓ Ⓔ

4. The 150-year-old church had been ---- for demolition until architects and neighborhood residents ---- to have it declared an historic landmark.

(A) scheduled . . declined
(B) excommunicated . . prayed
(C) slated . . rallied
(D) exchanged . . paid
(E) repaired . . sought

Ⓐ Ⓑ Ⓒ Ⓓ Ⓔ

5. In 1883, ---- eruption of Mount Krakatoa killed many thousands of people and ---- havoc on the coasts of Java and Sumatra.

(A) a fateful . . diminished
(B) an inoffensive . . spawned
(C) an immoral . . reigned
(D) a blistering . . authorized
(E) a disastrous . . wreaked

Ⓐ Ⓑ Ⓒ Ⓓ Ⓔ

6. The contractor first quoted an outrageous figure to repair the roof but appeared willing to ---- when Ben ---- at the price.

(A) negotiate . . balked
(B) bargain . . floundered
(C) participate . . recoiled
(D) reconsider . . waived
(E) intensify . . fainted

Ⓐ Ⓑ Ⓒ Ⓓ Ⓔ

7. Because the ancient Egyptians ---- the hour as one-twelfth of the time from dawn to dusk, its length varied during the ---- of the year.

(A) measured . . remainder
(B) revered . . occurrence
(C) imagined . . dates
(D) defined . . course
(E) idealized . . seasons

Ⓐ Ⓑ Ⓒ Ⓓ Ⓔ

8. The candidate answered tough questions with ---- candor, winning over many viewers who had previously supported her rival.

(A) presumptuous
(B) impatient
(C) unintentional
(D) dogmatic
(E) disarming

Ⓐ Ⓑ Ⓒ Ⓓ Ⓔ

9. Henry Louis Gates Jr. believes that Frederick Douglass ---- patterned his 1845 autobiography after the ---- of former slave Olaudah Equiano, whose life story was published in 1789.

   (A) patronizingly . . reminder
   (B) consciously . . narrative
   (C) anxiously . . capture
   (D) expectantly . . epitaph
   (E) belatedly . . antiquity

   Ⓐ Ⓑ Ⓒ Ⓓ Ⓔ

10. It was difficult to imagine George, ---- man, as a psychiatrist; listening while others talked was not his style.

   (A) a voluble
   (B) an insensitive
   (C) a pessimistic
   (D) a truculent
   (E) a depressed

   Ⓐ Ⓑ Ⓒ Ⓓ Ⓔ

SCORECARD	
Number of Questions Right:	
Number of Questions Wrong:	
Number of Questions Omitted:	
Number of Correct Guesses:	
Number of Wrong Guesses:	
Time Used:	

ANSWERS AND EXPLANATIONS

1. B

You don't need a science background to complete this sentence correctly. You just need to understand the logic of the sentence. For the first blank, the phrase *these ----* must refer to lungs. Apparently the lungs have developed into *swim bladders* in most of today's fish. So you might predict a word like "structures" for the first blank, and something like "developed" for the second blank. The choice that comes closest to those predictions is (B): the **organs** *have* **evolved** *into swim bladders*.

> *organs: parts of an organism (e.g., brain, heart, eye) that perform a specific function*
> *organisms: individual life forms, such as plants or animals*
> *merged: combined or joined into one unit*
> *barge: to intrude or move clumsily*

2. D

The word that goes in the first blank has to mean something like "taken." (B) **compartmentalized** and (C) **beguiled** don't make sense. You might **beguile,** or try to win over, someone in order to take something from him or her, but **beguiled** doesn't mean "taken." The remaining three choices have first words that mean "taken," but only one of them matches up with *a bin* that contains worthless rags and clothes. (A) and (E) won't work, because no one would have **swiped** or **bought** anything from a rag bin. But **salvaged** makes perfect sense. It also makes sense to say that *her expensive boots were her sole* **concession to** *fashion*. The only acknowledgment to fashion in Martha's wardrobe were her *expensive boots.*

> *compartmentalized: separated into compartments or categories*
> *beguiled: cheated, charmed*
> *salvaged: rescued from scrap or demolition*
> *concession: acknowledgment or admission*

3. C

Since the citizens must have "taken" *John Price* away from *the slave-hunters,* choices (A), (B), and (C) might fit the first blank. (D) and (E) are out, because **serenaded** and **pressured** have no meaning in this context.

Now check the second blanks of (A), (B), and (C). You have to decide between three relatively tough second words. In (A), one can **legislate** behavior, but not people, so it doesn't make sense to say that the *citizens were then* **legislated.** (B) **deemed** doesn't work either, since the word has to be followed by an adjective or noun. *These citizens* might have been "judged" or "tried" *under the Fugitive Slave Act;* they might even have been **deemed** "guilty," but they could not simply have been **deemed.** However, they could have been **indicted** for helping a runaway slave, so (C) is correct.

> *serenaded: sang love songs to*
> *legislated: governed by passing and enforcing laws*
> *deemed: judged or believed*
> *indicted: charged with or accused of a crime*

4. C

Your clue is the conjunction *until,* which divides this sentence into two time periods. In the first period, you can predict that the *church* was scheduled *for demolition;* in the second, people banded together to *have it declared an historic landmark.* You can rule out (B) immediately. People can be **excommunicated;** an old *church* cannot. (D) and (E) are also wrong, since the *church* couldn't have been **exchanged** or **repaired** *for demolition.*

On the other hand, **scheduled** matches our prediction, and so does **slated,** so (A) and (C) would both fit the first blank. But in (A), **declined** doesn't fit the second blank. If people had **declined** or refused *to have it declared an historic landmark,* the *church* would presumably still have been demolished. Instead, they must have **rallied** on its behalf.

---

demolition: tearing down or destroying by explosion
excommunicated: excluded from the church or from a group
slated: put on the schedule
rallied: banded together for action

---

5. E

An eruption that kills *many thousands of people* must be "bad" or "severe." (E) **disastrous** is the obvious choice for the first blank, although **fateful** and **blistering** are possible. (B) **inoffensive** is clearly wrong, and it doesn't make sense to describe a natural disaster as (C) **immoral.**

For the second blank, check out (A), (D), and (E). It makes no sense to say the *eruption* **diminished** or **authorized** *havoc.* Clearly, (E) **wreaked** is our best answer.

---

spawned: sired, gave birth to, or (figuratively) caused
diminished: reduced
authorized: granted authority, gave permission
wreaked: inflicted

---

6. A

The clue word *but* suggests that the contractor was willing to lower his price because of Ben's response, so the word that goes in the first blank should mean something like "lower his price" or "bargain." The second blank probably has to do with Ben's refusing to pay or being shocked.

(A) **negotiate,** (B) **bargain,** and (D) **reconsider** would all work in the first blank, but (C) and (E) don't fit the prediction at all.

Now try the second blanks for (A), (B), and (D). The second words in most of the answer choices are relatively difficult. (B) doesn't work well. Why would Ben have **floundered** *at the price?* In (D), **waived** makes no sense because it should be *the contractor* who **waived** *the price,* not *Ben.* But (A) **balked** makes sense here: The *outrageous figure* stopped *Ben* cold, and he refused to complete the transaction unless *the contractor* was *willing to* **negotiate.**

---

balked: stopped short, failed to complete a motion or activity
floundered: struggled to move, proceeded clumsily
recoiled: pulled back in horror or fear
waived: voluntarily gave up a claim or right

---

7. D

This one's hard to predict, but we need a word that describes an *hour.* Looking at the first word in each answer choice, **measured** and **defined** seem more likely than **revered, imagined,** or **idealized.** So ignore (B), (C), and (E), and examine the second words in (A) and (D).

The only one that makes sense in this context is **course.** If you plug (D) into the blanks, the logic of the sentence becomes clear. A summer's day is longer than a winter's day; therefore, *one-twelfth of the time from dawn to dusk* is not constant through the year. So the *length* of an ancient Egyptian hour *varied during the* **course** *of the year because* it was **defined** in terms of the total length of a day.

---

revered: honored or worshipped

---

8. E

To figure out which answer choice best modifies *candor* in this sentence, you don't even have to know the meaning of *candor*. The fact that *the candidate's candor* earned her many new supporters suggests that it was a good trait, so the word that fills the blank should be positive.

Presumptuous, impatient, and **dogmatic** are all negative. **Unintentional** isn't inherently negative, but it certainly isn't positive. The only positive word here is (E) **disarming.** *The candidate's candor* **disarmed** or won over voters *who had previously supported her rival.*

> *candor: frankness, honesty, and openness*
> *presumptuous: taking liberties, overstepping the bounds of one's position*
> *dogmatic: dictatorial, insisting on one's own beliefs*
> *disarming: easing or neutralizing criticism or hostility*

9. B

If *Frederick Douglass ... patterned his ... autobiography after* something, he must have modeled it on another literary work. The type of work should go in the second blank. Of the second words in the answer choices, only **narrative** and **epitaph** are in any sense literary works. It would be hard to model an entire *autobiography* on a simple **epitaph,** so you can pick (B) as the correct answer on the basis of the second blank alone. But in any two-blank sentence, you should check to make sure that both words fit the respective blanks. **Consciously** fits fine in the first blank, so (B) is indeed correct.

> *narrative: story or account of events*
> *epitaph: tombstone inscription, brief saying that commemorates the dead*
> *patronizingly: with a smug or superior air*
> *expectantly: with anticipation*
> *consciously: with full awareness*

10. A

Ignore the phrase *as a psychiatrist.* The main hint lies in the contrast between the two halves of the sentence: *George was ----;* **listening** *while others talked was not his style.* Look for a word that means "noisy" or "talkative." The only choice that has anything to do with talking or not talking is (A) **voluble.**

> *voluble: talkative*
> *truculent: cruel, fierce*

1. Happy ---- have replaced the ---- outcomes of some stories in the updated English translations of Hans Christian Andersen's fairy tales.

   (A) plots . . silly
   (B) endings . . gloomy
   (C) characters . . mythical
   (D) results . . lanky
   (E) moods . . historic

2. A report that the corporation was precariously close to the ---- of bankruptcy caused panic among its creditors and stockholders.

   (A) cessation
   (B) deficit
   (C) brink
   (D) absorption
   (E) absence

3. Gary was ---- about the ---- of his family heirlooms and personal mementos in the fire.

   (A) depressed . . meaning
   (B) noncommittal . . eradication
   (C) incensed . . recovery
   (D) mournful . . insurance
   (E) distraught . . destruction

4. Julio's good mood was ----; within minutes, his normally ---- partners were grinning and choking back laughter.

   (A) promiscuous . . glum
   (B) genial . . famished
   (C) ghastly . . intolerable
   (D) pretentious . . forlorn
   (E) infectious . . stolid

5. Many novels by the Brontë sisters and other nineteenth-century female authors were initially published under masculine ---- in the belief that works by ---- authors would meet more favorable reception.

   (A) monikers . . patriarchal
   (B) aliases . . established
   (C) rubrics . . famous
   (D) pseudonyms . . male
   (E) criteria . . talented

6. Moira forced herself to eat every morsel on her plate; although she found the food practically ----, she wanted to avoid offending her kind hosts.

   (A) egregious
   (B) nourishing
   (C) inedible
   (D) overheated
   (E) sodden

   Ⓐ Ⓑ Ⓒ Ⓓ Ⓔ

7. Architect Tadao Ando's penchant for placing ---- concerns above technical practicalities sometimes ---- unsettling, even precarious, structures.

   (A) artistic . . results in
   (B) monetary . . clashes with
   (C) mundane . . replaces
   (D) lofty . . cuts down
   (E) social . . supports

   Ⓐ Ⓑ Ⓒ Ⓓ Ⓔ

8. With his army already ---- in the snow, Napoleon's retreat from the outskirts of Moscow turned into a rout after Russian troops began to ---- his soldiers.

   (A) vacillating . . ravage
   (B) jangling . . harass
   (C) plummeting . . insinuate
   (D) foundering . . assault
   (E) tottering . . upbraid

9. Traditionally, any citizen is entitled to be tried by a jury of her peers; however, the law does not ---- how or to what extent the jurors must ---- the defendant.

   (A) monitor . . assess
   (B) specify . . resemble
   (C) indicate . . charge
   (D) necessitate . . enable
   (E) predict . . mirror

   Ⓐ Ⓑ Ⓒ Ⓓ Ⓔ

10. The features of Noh, the oldest form of Japanese drama, are highly ----; verse sections must be sung, and the vocal style in the prose passages has to be based on the chanting of specific Buddhist prayers.

    (A) prescribed
    (B) undertaken
    (C) ineffectual
    (D) frugal
    (E) absolute

    Ⓐ Ⓑ Ⓒ Ⓓ Ⓔ

SCORECARD	
Number of Questions Right:	
Number of Questions Wrong:	
Number of Questions Omitted:	
Number of Correct Guesses:	
Number of Wrong Guesses:	
Time Used:	

ANSWERS AND EXPLANATIONS

1. B

The first blank must have something to do with *outcomes*, because you can't replace *outcomes* with a word that serves an entirely different function. The second blank seems to refer to mood: If happy *outcomes* replaced the original *outcomes,* the original *outcomes* were probably sad.

Either (B) **endings** or (D) **results** would match the prediction for the first blank, but only **gloomy** matches the prediction for the second.

> *lanky: tall and thin, ungraceful*

2. C

You don't really need to know what *precariously* means to find the right answer here. The word that fills the blank must be something like "point" or "edge." A (C) **brink** is the edge of a steep place such as a cliff or a river bank, so it's the best answer.

> *precariously: characterized by*
> *   instability or uncertainty*
> *cessation: stopping*
> *deficit: shortage or shortfall*

3. E

Gary must have been upset because *his family heirlooms and personal mementos* had been lost or destroyed *in the fire.* So look for a first word that means "upset" and a second word that means "loss." (A) **depressed,** (E) **distraught,** and (D) **mournful** work best for the first blank. Since **destruction** fits the second blank best, (E) is correct.

In (B), **eradication** is related to **destruction** but isn't usually applied to objects, such as *personal mementos.* Besides, Gary certainly wasn't **noncommittal** about the loss, so the first blank for (B) does not fit.

> *distraught: extremely upset or agitated*
> *mournful: sorrowful*
> *noncommittal: giving no clear sign of*
> *   how one feels*
> *eradication: extermination*
> *incensed: outraged, extremely angry*

4. E

It sounds as though *Julio's* colleagues don't usually go around *grinning and choking back laughter,* so we can predict that the second blank might be filled by something like "stern" or "glum." To explain why they suddenly found themselves in such a good mood, we can predict a word like "catching" or "contagious" to fill the first blank. **Infectious** is a good synonym for "contagious," and **stolid** means "unemotional," so (E) matches the predictions well.

> *infectious: contagious*
> *stolid: unemotional*
> *genial: kindly*
> *famished: starving*
> *ghastly: frightening, horrible*
> *forlorn: alone, isolated, miserable*

5. D

The major contrast in this sentence is one of gender: *female authors* versus *masculine* pen names. The second blank will almost certainly be filled by something like "masculine." The only answer choices whose second words have anything to do with "masculine" are (A) and (D). **Patriarchal** seems a bit overspecialized in this context, but check the first words to make sure that (D) **male** is the better choice.

Pseudonyms are used by people who don't want their work published under their real names. When you plug (A) and (D) into the sentence, (D) makes the internal logic tighter: The *novels* written by *female authors were initially published under masculine* **pseudonyms** because *works by* **male** *authors* generally received more favorable reviews.

> *patriarchal: ruled by men*
> *rubrics: category headings*
> *monikers: nicknames*
> *pseudonyms: fictitious names, pen*
>   *names*

6. C

Moira didn't want to eat *the food,* but she also didn't want to offend her *hosts.* The word *practically* tells us she must have disliked the food very much, so the correct answer will be a very negative word like "revolting." (B) **nourishing** is positive, and (D) **overheated** doesn't seem negative enough. (A) **egregious** describes bad mistakes but not bad *food.* In (E), **sodden** *food* isn't necessarily bad; a rum cake, for example, tastes good when saturated with rum. So the best answer is (C) **inedible,** which means "uneatable."

> *egregious: conspicuously bad*
> *sodden: soaked, saturated*

7. A

If Ando places (A) **artistic,** or (B) **monetary,** or any other interests *above technical practicalities,* the building he designs could be *precarious.* So most choices would fit in the first blank. But only choice (A) provides a suitable answer for the second blank: If Ando places **artistic** interests above *technical practicalities,* it **results in** *precarious structures.*

> *penchant: tendency*
> *mundane: ordinary, everyday*
> *monetary: relating to money*
> *precarious: unstable*

8. D

We can predict that *Napoleon's army* was stuck *in the snow* and "doing badly" as they tried to *retreat* from Moscow. As a result, the retreat became a *rout.* (D) **foundering** and (E) **tottering** are the best options. (A) **vacillating** means the army was wavering, which does-

n't fit the context. For the second blank, it makes sense to say the *Russian troops began to* **assault** the *soldiers,* so (D) is the logical choice.

> *rout: hasty, humiliating retreat*
> *foundering: stumbling*
> *vacillating: failing to make up one's*
>   *mind*
> *assault: to attack physically*
> *upbraid: to criticize verbally*

9. B

The *citizen* who is *tried,* or brought to court on criminal charges, is the *defendant.* A jury of your *peers* is a jury of your equals. So it sounds as though *the law does not* dictate the exact way in which *the jurors* should be the equals of *the defendant.*

In (A), **monitor** is not quite what we had predicted, but it might still fit. However, **assess** doesn't match the predicted meaning at all. If we plug it into the second blank, the two halves of the sentence no longer connect to each other. An SAT Sentence Completion generally has tight internal logic, but choice (A) doesn't. Choice (C) has the same problem. (D) just doesn't make sense when you plug it into the blanks. That leaves (B) and (E).

(B) works better; the function of *the law* is to (B) **specify,** not to (E) **predict.** (B) explains that, although tradition dictates that a *defendant* be judged by *a jury of her peers,* the law doesn't **specify** in what way *the jurors* should **resemble,** or be *peers* of, *the defendant.*

> *peer: equal*
> *monitor: watch closely*
> *assess: evaluate or estimate*

10. A

At first glance, you might think that the blank should be filled by a word like "musical" or "vocal." But no such word appears in the answer choices. The only choice that tightens up the internal logic of the sentence when you plug it in is (A) **prescribed**. The words *must be* and *has to be* indicate that aspects of *Noh* are strictly dictated or **prescribed.**

prescribed: ordered or dictated
ineffectual: not effective, futile
frugal: thrifty

Suggested Time: 7 minutes

Directions: Select the lettered word or set of words that best completes the sentence.

Example:

Today's small, portable computers contrast markedly with the earliest electronic computers, which were ----.

(A) effective
(B) invented
(C) useful
(D) destructive
(E) enormous

Ⓐ ● Ⓒ Ⓓ Ⓔ

1. Because of the ---- and prolonged nature of the ----, water must be carefully conserved and rationed.

(A) arid . . reservoir
(B) dire . . forecast
(C) severe . . drought
(D) negligible . . emergency
(E) miserly . . supply

2. The spectacular ---- of the Grand Canyon cannot be fully captured by a two-dimensional ---- such as a photograph.

(A) periphery . . benchmark
(B) vista . . opportunity
(C) foliage . . screening
(D) topography . . representation
(E) graphics . . likeness

3. Until his defeat by the newcomer, the veteran boxer won most of his bouts by knockouts and had achieved an ---- series of wins.

(A) inconsequential
(B) exaggerated
(C) able-bodied
(D) unbroken
(E) observable

4. Although the whale shark is found in equatorial waters around the world, it is ---- encountered by divers because of its low numbers and ---- nature.

(A) persistently . . reluctant
(B) successfully . . aggressive
(C) anxiously . . unfortunate
(D) constantly . . indifferent
(E) rarely . . solitary

5. Some of the paintings formerly ---- the Italian Renaissance artist are now thought to have been created by one of his students.

(A) exhibited with
(B) submitted to
(C) adapted from
(D) attributed to
(E) denied by

6. Although both plants control soil erosion, kudzu disrupts the local ecology by displacing native fauna, while vetiver has no ---- effects.

(A) foreseeable
(B) adverse
(C) domestic
(D) permanent
(E) advantageous

Ⓐ Ⓑ Ⓒ Ⓓ Ⓔ

7. Because its bookkeepers altered some figures and completely fabricated others, the company's financial records were entirely ----.

(A) spurious
(B) disseminated
(C) singular
(D) concealed
(E) cursory

Ⓐ Ⓑ Ⓒ Ⓓ Ⓔ

8. The journalist's ---- to accurately describe events in the region was not attributable to a lack of effort, but to a dearth of ---- and unbiased information.

(A) willingness . . prevalent
(B) failure . . reliable
(C) training . . universal
(C) hesitation . . dominant
(E) incentive . . clear

9. As ---- as she is original, choreographer Twyla Tharp has created dances for mainstream ballet, Hollywood films, and commercial theater, as well as more offbeat venues.

   (A) charming
   (B) redundant
   (C) versatile
   (D) polished
   (E) rarefied

   Ⓐ Ⓑ Ⓒ Ⓓ Ⓔ

10. Peach pits, which contain small amounts of the poisonous compound cyanide, are not usually harmful, but, if consumed in sufficient quantities, can be ----.

    (A) acerbic
    (B) superfluous
    (C) virulent
    (D) unpalatable
    (E) multifarious

    Ⓐ Ⓑ Ⓒ Ⓓ Ⓔ

SCORECARD

Number of Questions Right:	
Number of Questions Wrong:	
Number of Questions Omitted:	
Number of Correct Guesses:	
Number of Wrong Guesses:	
Time Used:	

ANSWERS AND EXPLANATIONS

1. C

You're told that *water must be carefully conserved and rationed because of the prolonged nature of the ----*, so you can predict that the word in the second blank will be something like *water shortage*. Choice (C) **drought** seems like a perfect match. Choice (D) **emergency** would also be a possibility, so check out the first blank for (C) and (D).

The word in the first blank is connected by *and* to the phrase *prolonged nature*. So the word for this blank should be consistent with *prolonged*. You need a word like "serious." The first word in choice (C), **severe,** means the same thing as "serious." Our other contender, choice (D), has **negligible** in the first blank. **Negligible** means "not serious," so (C) is correct.

If you checked out the first blanks in the other choices, you might have been tempted by (A) and (B), **arid** and **dire.** But these two choices don't make sense when you plug the second blank into the sentence. (A) is not logical because if a **reservoir** were **arid,** or completely dry, there would be no water to ration. (B) doesn't explain why water must be rationed. A **dire forecast** isn't necessarily a **forecast** of **drought**—a **forecast** of a violent thunderstorm would also be **dire.** Always look for the choice that fits best.

> negligible: unimportant, not serious
> dire: terrible
> miserly: stingy

2. D

What could be *spectacular* about the Grand Canyon? Three choices seem possible for the first blank: the **vista** in (B), the **foliage** in (C), and the **topography** in (D). You can eliminate two unlikely choices: (A) **periphery** and (E) **graphics.**

In the second blank, you want a word that could apply to photography, which the sentence calls *a two-dimensional ----.* **Opportunity** and **screening** clearly don't fit, so eliminate (B) and (C). That leaves (D) **representation,** which means "a presentation or depiction." You can say that a two-dimensional **representation** can't capture the spectacular **topography.**

> vista: view
> foliage: the leaves of a tree, or plant life
> topography: physical contours and
>   features
> periphery: outer boundary
> representation: presentation, depiction

3. D

Since *the veteran boxer* had *won most of his bouts by knockouts,* you can assume that he was pretty successful. (D) **unbroken** is the only choice that describes his *series of wins* in a way that suggests success; an **unbroken** series of victories would be a winning streak with no losses.

(A) **inconsequential** and (B) **exaggerated** are contradicted by information in the sentence itself. Choice (C) **able-bodied** may seem to fit in a sentence about a boxer, but what's an **able-bodied** *series of wins?* (E) **observable** makes some sense, since you could watch someone win lots of fights, but we have to reject it because the sentence is about a boxer who, after winning many fights, finally loses to a newcomer. In Sentence Completions, the correct answer is the one that makes the whole sentence cohere, and that would be choice (D).

> inconsequential: of slight importance
> observable: visible

4. E

The clue word *although* sets up a contrast between the whale shark's appearance all over the world and the way that it's *encountered by divers.* A word like *seldom* would set up the needed contrast. (E) **rarely** is the best fit.

For the second blank, look for a word that explains why the shark's *nature* makes it hard for humans to spot. "Shy" or "tending to avoid people" would work well. (E) **solitary** fits the bill. **Reluctant,** in (A), could be a longshot to fill the second blank, but we don't need to spend time thinking about the other choices, since only (E) fits the first blank.

equatorial: relating to the region of the earth halfway between the north and south poles

5. D

This sentence tests your understanding of the word **attributed,** a word often followed by *to.* A painting that's **attributed to** a Renaissance painter is one "credited to" him, or generally thought to have been painted by him.

The sentence contains a virtual definition of **attributed** in the phrase *thought to have been created by.* The clue words *formerly* and *now* in the sentence signal a contrast between the past and present: The paintings were *formerly* **attributed to** the artist, but *now* they're thought to have been painted by one of his students.

attributed: assigned or credited to

6. B

Although sets up a contrast between *kudzu,* which *disrupts the local ecology,* and *vetiver,* which *has no ----effects.* The sentence is comparing the consequences of the two plants. The missing word refers to kudzu's disruptive ecological effects. Look for a word like "bad" or "negative." (B) **adverse** most closely matches this prediction.

(E) **advantageous** is the opposite of what's needed. **Foreseeable** and **permanent,** choices (A) and (D), don't make sense because nothing else in the sentence refers to the predictability or lasting effect of the two plants. (C) is wrong because nothing in the sentence refers to either foreign or **domestic** origins.

HINT: *You don't have to know the meaning of every exotic word in the sentence to pick the right answer. To see what fits in the blank(s), figure out how the parts of the sentence relate.*

vetiver: a grass with long roots
kudzu: a kind of vine
adverse: unfavorable

7. A

A good vocabulary will help you figure out this one. The bookkeepers *altered some financial records and completely fabricated others,* so you need a word like "altered," "falsified," or "fictitious" for the blank. (A) **spurious** is the only choice that matches.

It makes no sense to say the financial records were entirely **disseminated** or entirely **singular,** so rule out (B) and (C). (D) can be eliminated because the sentence doesn't say the records have been **concealed.** (E) **cursory** doesn't fit either. The sentence doesn't say the records were hastily thrown together; it says they were faked.

fabricated: made up
spurious: false, lacking authenticity
concealed: hidden
cursory: hastily done
disseminated: distributed widely
singular: unique

8. B

The second blank may be easier to fill here, so start with that. The clue word *and* tells you that the missing word in the phrase *---- and unbiased information* will be consistent with *unbiased.* So you can predict that the missing word will have a meaning similar to *unbiased,* like "impartial." (B) **reliable** and (E) **clear** are both pretty close to *unbiased,* so let's try them in the first blank.

For the first blank, *the journalist's ---- to accurately describe events* results from a *dearth* or "lack" of good information. A lack of good information might prevent someone from describing a situation accurately.

We can predict a word like "inability" for this blank. The first word in (E), **incentive,** means "motivation," which doesn't match. The first word in (B), **failure,** matches perfectly.

---

unbiased: impartial, unprejudiced
dearth: lack

---

9. C

Since *Twyla Tharp has created* a wide range of *dances* ranging from movies and *mainstream ballet* to *more offbeat* forms, she's a (C) **versatile** *choreographer.* Though her work may also be **polished,** the sentence concerns the range of her activities, not their quality, so (D) is wrong. Someone who works in several *mainstream* areas wouldn't be termed **rarefied,** so (E) is out. Even though several kinds of dance production are mentioned, nothing suggests that they are **redundant,** so (B) is wrong, too; moreover, **redundant** is a negative term, but the sentence is positive—it praises Tharp's work. Choice (A)'s **charming** sounds okay with the word *original,* but the sentence talks about Tharp's accomplishments as a choreographer, not about her personality.

---

rarefied: understood only by a select
group; rarer and more refined
redundant: repetitive

---

10. C

The sentence hinges on knowing what (C) **virulent** means. You're told that certain *poisonous compounds* in *peach pits* are *usually not harmful. But,* the sentence continues, if you eat enough of them, they are ----. So you need a word that means *poisonous* or *harmful* for the blank. **Virulent** fits that definition.

If you couldn't figure that out, you could have tried eliminating answer choices. (A) **acerbic** and (D) **unpalatable** relate to things that taste bad, but neither word means *poisonous.* Neither (B) nor (E) makes sense in the blank.

HINT: *Knowing related words can help here. If you didn't know* **virulent,** *you might have known the related word virus, a disease-causing agent. Then you could have figured out* **virulent** *has something to do with disease and harm.*

---

acerbic: sour, harsh
unpalatable: distasteful, unpleasant
superfluous: unnecessary
multifarious: diverse
virulent: intensely poisonous

Suggested Time: 7 minutes

Directions: Select the lettered word or set of words that best completes the sentence.

Example:

Today's small, portable computers contrast markedly with the earliest electronic computers, which were ----.

(A) effective
(B) invented
(C) useful
(D) destructive
(E) enormous

1. Once ----, wolves have been hunted almost to extinction.

(A) nonexistent
(B) numerous
(C) garrulous
(D) captive
(E) natural   Ⓐ Ⓑ Ⓒ Ⓓ Ⓔ

2. The benefits of the exchange program are ----, with both countries acquiring new technical insights and manufacturing techniques.

(A) promised
(B) inclusive
(C) blatant
(D) mutual
(E) applicable   Ⓐ Ⓑ Ⓒ Ⓓ Ⓔ

3. The author monotonously catalogues the ---- points of fashion history, while omitting the details that might ---- the reader's interest.

(A) vital . . acquire
(B) trivial . . enhance
(C) salient . . offend
(D) undisputed . . limit
(E) essential . . rescind   Ⓐ Ⓑ Ⓒ Ⓓ Ⓔ

4. The Morgan Library in New York provides a ---- environment in which scholars work amidst tapestries, paintings, stained-glass windows, and handcrafted furniture.

(A) realistic
(B) frugal
(C) sumptuous
(D) friendly
(E) practical   Ⓐ Ⓑ Ⓒ Ⓓ Ⓔ

5. The eruption ---- tons of mineral-rich volcanic ash, restoring to the soil nutrients long since ---- by decades of farming.

(A) deposited . . depleted
(B) clumped . . harvested
(C) removed . . secreted
(D) displaced . . entrenched
(E) regained . . fertilized   Ⓐ Ⓑ Ⓒ Ⓓ Ⓔ

6. The fullest edition of the letters of H. P. Lovecraft consists of five volumes; however, only a small fraction of Lovecraft's ---- correspondence has ever been published.

(A) laconic
(B) unknown
(C) voluminous
(D) verbal
(E) popular   Ⓐ Ⓑ Ⓒ Ⓓ Ⓔ

7. The candidate denounced as ---- his rival's solution to the problem of unemployment, but offered no ---- alternative.

(A) arbitrary . . altruistic
(B) elitist . . virulent
(C) salutary . . absolute
(D) convoluted . . provincial
(E) unworkable . . viable   Ⓐ Ⓑ Ⓒ Ⓓ Ⓔ

8. The government decided against ---- assemblies and strikes organized by the opposition, fearing that such a measure might ---- armed conflict.

(A) continuing . . multiply
(B) intimidating . . interrupt
(C) banning . . precipitate
(D) granting . . reapportion
(E) welcoming . . voice   Ⓐ Ⓑ Ⓒ Ⓓ Ⓔ

9. Prime Minister Neville Chamberlain of Great Britain adopted a ---- approach to Hitler, even accepting Germany's annexation of Austria.

   (A) hasty
   (B) precarious
   (C) haughty
   (D) conciliatory
   (E) dependent

   Ⓐ Ⓑ Ⓒ Ⓓ Ⓔ

10. Medieval kings customarily gave away valuables and property, expecting that their ---- would ensure the ---- of their vassals.

    (A) imprudence . . probity
    (B) largess . . fidelity
    (C) adaptation . . integrity
    (D) formality . . sophistry
    (E) haste . . mirth

    Ⓐ Ⓑ Ⓒ Ⓓ Ⓔ

SCORECARD	
Number of Questions Right:	
Number of Questions Wrong:	
Number of Questions Omitted:	
Number of Correct Guesses:	
Number of Wrong Guesses:	
Time Used:	

ANSWERS AND EXPLANATIONS

1. B

Once, the first word in the sentence, is an important structural clue. It signals that there's a contrast between the status of wolves at an earlier time (before excessive hunting) and the status of wolves now (almost extinct). To set up the contrast, the word in the blank has to mean something like "abundant." Choice (B) **numerous** is the most logical option.

2. D

Since *both* countries are *acquiring new technical insights and manufacturing techniques* in their exchange program, they are benefiting from each other. We can predict that the word in the blank will mean something like "shared" or "reciprocal," since the benefits go both ways. Choice (D) **mutual** matches this prediction perfectly.

Don't be fooled by choice (E) **applicable.** The *technical insights and techniques* may very well be **applicable** somewhere, but we're being asked to describe the success of *the exchange program,* not the status of the *manufacturing techniques.*

3. B

The important clue word here is *monotonously.* If the author is *monotonously cataloguing the ---- points of fashion history,* we can safely predict that those points are going to be "boring" or another such negative word. Choice (B) **trivial** best fits the description.

In the second part of the sentence, *while,* which follows the comma, is another clue. It signals a contrast between the boring *cataloguing* and the omitted details that *might* have ---- *the reader's interest.* Look for a second-blank word that means something like "increased." Choice (B) again makes the most sense: *The author monotonously catalogues the* **trivial** *points while omitting the details that might* **enhance** *the reader's interest.*

---

monotonously: without variety or variation
enhance: to increase
salient: striking, prominent
rescind: to disavow, take back

---

4. C

What word would you use to describe an environment that's full of *tapestries, paintings, stained-glass windows, and hand-crafted furniture?* Probably something like "fancy" or "elegant." The closest choice to this prediction is (C) **sumptuous.**

It doesn't make sense to describe such an environment as (A) **realistic** or (B) **frugal.** And, while the library's atmosphere may very well be (D) **friendly** or (E) **practical,** those choices don't make sense in the context, which mentions only the elegant surroundings.

---

sumptuous: luxurious, elegant, stately
frugal: thrifty, not wasteful

---

5. A

When a volcano erupts, it ejects lava, ash, and other material. Therefore, it's unlikely that the volcano (B) **clumped** or (C) **removed** tons of volcanic ash. Choice (E) **regained** means the volcano was sucking ash into itself instead of spewing it out—a very unlikely situation. This leaves choices (A) and (D).

Choice (A) sounds good—*the eruption* **deposited** *mineral-rich ash, restoring to the soil nutrients long since* **depleted** *by decades of farming.* In (D), the eruption could conceivably **displace** ash, but the second-blank word doesn't make sense in the sentence. If nutrients were long since **entrenched** in the ground, there would be no need to restore them to the soil. Choice (A) is the best answer.

clumped: assembled, bundled
depleted: exhausted, used up
displaced: pushed out
entrenched: established, settled

denounced: condemned
viable: workable, achievable
virulent: severe, poisonous
salutary: healthful
convoluted: complicated, involved

6. C

The clue word *however* sets up a contrast between *the fullest edition* and the *small fraction of correspondence* that's *been published*. This tells us that a great deal of *Lovecraft's ---- correspondence* remains unpublished, so fill the blank with a word like "abundant." Choice (C) **voluminous** best completes the sentence's meaning. Choice (E) **popular** is a weak second best.

voluminous: abundant
laconic: restrained, uncommunicative

7. E

If *the candidate denounced his rival's solution as ----*, the word in the first blank will be negative. Since four of the five answer choices have negative first words, you'll find it hard to eliminate possibilities. So start with the second blank.

HINT: *In a sentence with two blanks, you can choose which blank to do first. Start with the blank that's easier to fill.*

If the candidate *offered no ---- alternative*, we can infer that the candidate offered no good or workable alternative. Choice (E)'s **viable** best matches this prediction.

Plugging the first word of (E) into the sentence, we see that it makes sense too—*the candidate denounced as* **unworkable** *his rival's solution, but offered no* **viable** *alternative himself.* None of the other choices makes as much sense.

8. C

The second half of this sentence follows directly from the first: *The government decided against* doing something *to assemblies and strikes* because they feared *armed conflict.* Choice (C) best completes the logic of the sentence: *The government decided against* **banning** *assemblies and strikes because they feared such a move would* **precipitate** *armed conflict.*

intimidating: threatening
banning: prohibiting, especially by
   official decree
precipitate: instigate, bring about
reapportion: distribute anew

9. D

Since *Chamberlain even accepted Germany's annexation of Austria*, his approach to German aggression was certainly not tough or militant. He probably adopted a nonaggressive, accepting approach to Hitler. The choice that comes closest to this prediction is (D) **conciliatory.**

conciliatory: tending to pacify or
   accommodate
precarious: uncertain, dangerous
haughty: arrogant, snobby

10. B

The *kings gave away valuables and property, expecting* something back from their subjects. The first blank relates to the action of giving away all these nice things, so we can predict a word like "generosity." As for what they expected in return, we might predict something like "respect," "happiness," or "loyalty." Therefore, the two blanks have to be filled by two positive words.

Looking through the answer choices, we see that choice (B) has two distinctly positive words—**largess** and **fidelity.** Plugging (B) into the sentence, we see it makes perfect sense: *The kings gave away property, expecting that their **largess** would ensure the **fidelity** of their subjects.*

You may have been tempted by (D) **formality,** since the kings' generosity could be seen as a formal exercise. But this kind of thinking is stretching the sentence's meaning. Besides, if you check out the second blank, **sophistry** doesn't make sense.

largess: generosity
fidelity: faithfulness, loyalty
sophistry: misleading argumentative
   style

Suggested Time: 7 minutes

Directions: Select the lettered word or set of words that best completes the sentence.

Example:

Today's small, portable computers contrast markedly with the earliest electronic computers, which were ----.

(A) effective
(B) invented
(C) useful
(D) destructive
(E) enormous

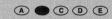

1. Unlike her first novel, which received kudos for its ----, her second effort was widely criticized as uninventive and predictable.

   (A) monotony
   (B) originality
   (C) conventionality
   (D) prudence
   (E) literacy

2. Medieval alchemists tried to attain wealth by ---- lead and other base metals into gold.

   (A) transforming
   (B) encouraging
   (C) replicating
   (D) displacing
   (E) copying

3. The dance critic was ---- in her praise of the company, describing the choreography in glowing terms and ---- the poise and elegance of every dancer.

   (A) agreeable . . insulting
   (B) vague . . demonstrating
   (C) conciliatory . . relating
   (D) timorous . . describing
   (E) effusive . . extolling

4. The British social philosopher Thomas Malthus predicted that population growth would eventually ---- world food production, resulting in massive famine and political unrest.

   (A) pressure
   (B) forbid
   (C) resist
   (D) surpass
   (E) confront

5. Bird species ---- to this island were exterminated by feral cats, ---- of pets abandoned here decades ago by sailors.

   (A) provincial . . competitors
   (B) harmless . . liberators
   (C) indigenous . . descendants
   (D) unusual . . signals
   (E) benign . . ancestors

6. Soon after adopting a syllabic system of writing, the Greeks made the final step to a phonetic alphabet, dividing the consonants from the vowels and writing each ----.

   (A) formally
   (B) abstractly
   (C) separately
   (D) mysteriously
   (E) accurately

7. In the early nineteenth century, some British agricultural workers felt that newly invented farm machinery threatened their jobs, and they ---- their fear of ---- by smashing machines.

   (A) lessened . . injustice
   (B) aggravated . . landlords
   (C) displayed . . technology
   (D) accommodated . . equipment
   (E) magnified . . exploitation

8. The restaurant manager, who had ---- provided crayons and paper tablecloths for the amusement of small children, found that adult patrons were equally ---- the opportunity to express themselves.

   (A) aggressively . . delighted by
   (B) impulsively . . anxious about
   (C) warily . . shrewd about
   (D) initially . . enthralled with
   (E) imaginatively . . alarmed by

9. Before it became involved in the Second World War, the United States held to a policy of neutrality, setting up legislation explicitly ---- the sale of weapons to ---- nations.

    (A) repealing . . expatriate
    (B) forbidding . . belligerent
    (C) enacting . . dependent
    (D) prompting . . arbitrary
    (E) defending . . isolated

    Ⓐ Ⓑ Ⓒ Ⓓ Ⓔ

10. By 1918, the painter André Derain had ---- both Cubism and the new abstract art in favor of a more ---- approach based on the example of the old masters.

    (A) compiled . . reticent
    (B) vexed . . indulgent
    (C) thwarted . . expressive
    (D) discarded . . tentative
    (E) repudiated . . traditional

    Ⓐ Ⓑ Ⓒ Ⓓ Ⓔ

SCORECARD	
Number of Questions Right:	
Number of Questions Wrong:	
Number of Questions Omitted:	
Number of Correct Guesses:	
Number of Wrong Guesses:	
Time Used:	

ANSWERS AND EXPLANATIONS

1. B

This sentence contains the word *kudos,* which might have thrown you off. But, as in most Sentence Completions, you can get the answer if you focus on the logic of the sentence. Notice the clue word *unlike; unlike* signals a contrast. If her first novel is *unlike* her *uninventive and predictable* second novel, her first novel must be the opposite. It must have had (B) **originality.**

> *kudos: praise, honor*

2. A

Again you've got a difficult word in the sentence. And again, you can work around it. If you don't know what *alchemists* are, keep reading. The *alchemists tried to attain wealth by ---- lead into gold.* (C) and (E) won't work because you don't **replicate** or **copy** *lead into gold,* you transform it. The only logical answer is (A) **transforming.**

> *replicating: duplicating, copying*
> *alchemists: in the Middle Ages,*
>   *practitioners of a study combining*
>   *chemistry and philosophy who tried*
>   *to turn base metals into gold*

3. E

The important clue here is the word *glowing.* Since *the critic described the choreography in glowing terms,* she was ---- *in her praise.* Look for a positive word in the first blank that means "enthusiastic." You can quickly eliminate (B) **vague,** (C) **conciliatory,** and (D) **timorous.** That leaves (A) **agreeable** and (E) **effusive,** so let's try (A) and (E) in the second blank.

In the second part of the sentence, the connecting word *and* indicates consistency, so the second blank must also be positive. Look for an answer choice that means she praised the poise and elegance of the dancers. Remember, we've already eliminated (B), (C),

and (D). (A) **insulting** is obviously wrong. A critic wouldn't *describe the choreography in glowing terms,* and then **insult** *the poise of the dancers.* But **extolling** is a positive word, so (E) is correct.

> *glowing: enthusiastic; shining*
> *conciliatory: appeasing*
> *timorous: meek*
> *effusive: excessively demonstrative,*
>   *gushing*
> *extolling: praising highly*

4. D

Don't be intimidated by the serious subject matter. Just take the sentence apart and look for clues. The biggest clue is the word *famine.* The sentence says: When the relationship between *population growth* and *world food production* changes in some way, the result is *famine.* You know that *famine* happens when there's not enough food for a large number of people to live on. Or, as the sentence puts it, *population growth would eventually* exceed *food production, resulting in massive famine.* The answer choice that best matches this prediction is (D) **surpass.**

> *surpass: exceed*

5. C

Don't give up if you don't know the word *feral.* Instead, read this two-blank sentence looking for one blank that leaps out as predictable. Start working with that one, and use it to rule out choices for the second blank.

If the second blank looks easier, start with that. You're told that *bird species were exterminated by cats.* These cats had something to do with *pets abandoned here decades ago by sailors.* That probably means the cats were (C) **descendants** of pets. But check out the other choices.

Since the pets were abandoned on the island decades ago, the cats couldn't logically be (B) **liberators** of pets, (D) **signals** of pets, or (E) **ancestors** of pets. And it's unlikely they'd be (A) **competitors** of pets, either. (C) makes the most sense in the second blank.

Now try the first blank. Bird species **indigenous** to the island were exterminated by the descendants of abandoned pets—that seems to make sense. A quick glance at the other choices confirms that (C) is right.

> *exterminated: killed off*
> *feral: wild*
> *provincial: unsophisticated, narrow-
>   minded*
> *benign: harmless*
> *indigenous: native*

6. C

This fairly easy sentence contains the clue word *and*. Since the phrase *dividing the consonants from the vowels* is joined to *writing each* with the word *and*, the two phrases must agree with each other. So whatever goes in the blank must go along with the idea of dividing consonants and vowels. The choice that makes sense is (C) **separately:** *The Greeks divided consonants from vowels and wrote each* **separately.** The rest of the choices don't fit the context. For instance, (E) **accurately** might have seemed sensible, but the whole point is that the Greeks divided up their letters, not that they wrote precisely.

7. C

Again the clue word *and* indicates consistency throughout the sentence: The workers felt threatened, *and* their fear led them to smash machines. Their fear of what? Probably a fear of (C) **technology.** (C)'s first blank works well, too—the farm *workers* **displayed** *their fear of* **technology** *by smashing machines.* So (C) looks correct. Check the other answers just to make sure they don't work.

(A) **injustice** and (E) **exploitation** might seem to go along with the subject. But there's nothing in the sentence to indicate the workers *fear* those things. Besides, in both cases the first blanks don't fit. (C) works best.

8. D

Since this is a two-blank sentence, pick one blank to work on—whichever strikes you as more predictable—and use that blank to rule out possibilities

for the other blank. In the first half, you read that *the crayons and paper tablecloths* had been *provided for the amusement of small children.* In the last half, you read that adults were *equally ---- about the opportunity to express themselves.* The clue word *equally* tells you the adults felt the same way as the kids. So the adults must have been equally (A) **delighted by** the opportunity, or (D) **enthralled with** the opportunity.

Now all you have to do is try (A) and (D)'s first words in the first blank. In (A), **aggressively** doesn't fit with the rest of the sentence. Why would a restaurant **aggressively** provide crayons and paper to kids? But (D) **initially** works fine. The restaurant, which had **initially** *provided crayons and paper* just for kids, *found that adults were equally* **enthralled with** *the opportunity to express themselves.*

> *enthralled: enchanted, captivated, held
>   spellbound*
> *initially: at first*

9. B

If the United States is practicing *neutrality*, you can predict it will forbid *the sale of weapons* to *nations* taking part in the war. The answer choice that matches that prediction is (B): *Holding to its policy of neutrality, the United States* set up legislation **forbidding** *the sale of weapons to* **belligerent** *nations.*

(C) **enacting**, (D) **prompting**, and (E) **defending** suggest that the United States was encouraging the sale of weapons. (A) **repealing** implies that legislation already existed and was being overturned.

> *neutrality: the policy of not favoring
>   either side in a dispute or a war;
>   impartiality*
> *belligerent: waging war, hostile*
> *expatriate: exiled*

10. E

Two important phrases clue you in to the sentence's meaning: *in favor of* and *based on the example of the old masters.* The second blank looks easier, so let's deal with it first.

If Derain's new approach is *based on the example of the old masters,* you can predict it must be old-fashioned. The answer choice that fits this prediction is (E) **traditional.** (C) **expressive** might also seem like a good word to describe a painting style. But you're not told that the old masters were expressive—you just know they were old. Let's try (C) and (E) in the first blank just to make sure.

(C) **thwarted** clearly doesn't fit. It's not clear how Derain was hindering or obstructing Cubism and abstract art, and it's not correct English to say he hindered one style of art *in favor of* another. Looking at (E), **repudiated** makes much more sense. Derain rejected abstract art *in favor of* a more traditional approach. (E) fits well in both blanks, so it's our answer.

> *thwarted: hindered or obstructed*
> *repudiated: rejected*
> *vexed: annoyed, aggravated*

Suggested Time: 7 minutes

Directions: Select the lettered word or set of words that best completes the sentence.

Example:

Today's small, portable computers contrast markedly with the earliest electronic computers, which were ----.

(A) effective
(B) invented
(C) useful
(D) destructive
(E) enormous   Ⓐ ⬤ Ⓒ Ⓓ Ⓔ

1. Rosa embarked on a ---- of strenuous exercise to build up the ---- to complete a marathon.

(A) program . . lethargy
(B) regimen . . endurance
(C) pursuit . . stamina
(D) commitment . . strength
(E) complex . . rhythm   

2. An editorial praised the generosity of an anonymous ----, who had donated over a million dollars and several priceless paintings to the college.

(A) mercenary
(B) agnostic
(C) curmudgeon
(D) benefactor
(E) harbinger   

3. Some historians claim that the concept of courtly love is a ---- that dates from the age of chivalry, while others believe it has more ---- origins.

(A) relic . . simultaneous
(B) notion . . ancient
(C) memento . . discovered
(D) period . . documented
(E) suitor . . amorous   

4. The general was ---- of low morale among his troops, but still refused to ---- his command.

(A) informed . . bequeath
(B) appreciative . . subvert
(C) fearful . . proscribe
(D) wary . . deprecate
(E) cognizant . . relinquish   Ⓐ Ⓑ Ⓒ Ⓓ Ⓔ

5. In the wake of several tragic accidents caused by wind shear, major airports installed new radar systems ---- enough to ---- this complex atmospheric phenomenon.

(A) generalized . . track
(B) lamentable . . honor
(C) flimsy . . withstand
(D) sophisticated . . detect
(E) sturdy . . demolish   

6. Although marine engineers claimed that its hull was ----, the Titanic sank after hitting an iceberg.

(A) amorphous
(B) equivocal
(C) preeminent
(D) impenetrable
(E) viscous   Ⓐ Ⓑ Ⓒ Ⓓ Ⓔ

7. Based on factual ---- rather than conjecture, Dr. Singh's report will ---- previously held views about the nesting habits of the rare species.

(A) conjecture . . ignore
(B) evidence . . refute
(C) theory . . negate
(D) projections . . corroborate
(E) documentation . . inspire   

8. As they helped the community recover from the storm's devastation, the apparently ---- relief workers worked around the clock with an energy that never seemed to wane.

(A) dexterous
(B) indefatigable
(C) obsequious
(D) syncopated
(E) transcendent   Ⓐ Ⓑ Ⓒ Ⓓ Ⓔ

9. Although others found them impressive, Lewis found Senator Gantry's speeches ---- and believed that they ---- the real issues with elaborate but meaningless rhetoric.

(A) bombastic . . obscured
(B) verbose . . clarified
(C) captivating . . defined
(D) exuberant . . misconstrued
(E) persuasive . . illuminated   

10. The characters in Jane Austen's novels never argue; rather, they employ more subtle verbal weapons: irony and ----.

    (A) candor
    (B) humility
    (C) innuendo
    (D) farce
    (E) pantomime

    Ⓐ Ⓑ Ⓒ Ⓓ Ⓔ

SCORECARD	
Number of Questions Right:	
Number of Questions Wrong:	
Number of Questions Omitted:	
Number of Correct Guesses:	
Number of Wrong Guesses:	
Time Used:	

ANSWERS AND EXPLANATIONS

1. B

Let's concentrate on the second blank first. What do you need *to complete a marathon,* a very long race? You need **endurance, stamina,** or **strength,** so (B), (C), and (D) are all possibilities. **Lethargy** would slow you down in a race, so you can definitely eliminate (A). **Rhythm** might be of some value in running a marathon, but it's not the most important thing, so eliminate (E). As for the first blank, you embark on a **regimen** of exercise, but you don't embark on a (C) **pursuit** or a (D) **commitment** of exercise. So (B) is the best answer.

> *lethargy: extreme sleepiness or sluggishness*

2. D

You're looking for a very positive word, since this anonymous person is being praised for his or her very generous donations. The most positive answer choice is (D) **benefactor.** None of the other answer choices make sense.

HINT: *Benefactor contains the roots* **BENE,** *"good," and* **FAC,** *"make or do." A benefactor is someone who does good things for someone else's sake.*

> *mercenary: professional soldier who serves a foreign army*
> *agnostic: doubter, one who doubts the existence of God*
> *curmudgeon: cranky or grumpy person*
> *harbinger: herald or omen*

3. B

The word *while* signals contrast. If *some historians claim that the concept of courtly love dates from* a specific period—*the age of chivalry*—the others must be saying that it has either earlier origins or more recent origins. Only **ancient** in choice (B) relates to time and provides the necessary contrast. As for the first blank,

the concept of courtly love can't be a (A) **relic,** (C) **memento,** (D) **period,** or (E) **suitor;** it can only be a **notion.** (B) is the answer.

4. E

But is a signal of contrast. If *morale was low among his troops,* what should the general have done about *his command?* He might have **relinquished** it, as choice (E) suggests; none of the alternatives makes sense. Checking out the first blank, if *the general was* **cognizant** *of low morale among his troops,* that would have been reason to do something about it. (E) is the answer.

> *cognizant: aware*
> *relinquish: to give up*

5. D

Since *wind shear* is a *complex atmospheric phenomenon,* which caused *several tragic accidents,* the radar systems installed by the airports need to be technologically advanced. They're certainly not (B) **lamentable,** (C) **flimsy,** or (A) **generalized.** They're probably (D) **sophisticated.** But they could also be (E) **sturdy.**

So check out the second word for these two choices. (E)'s second word doesn't work; a radar system can't **demolish** wind shear. Rather, you'd expect it to **detect** *wind shear,* so the correct answer is (D).

6. D

Although signals contrast; we want a word that suggests why *marine engineers* would not have expected the *Titanic* to *sink.* The best answer is (D) **impenetrable.**

*impenetrable: incapable of being
    penetrated*
amorphous: shapeless
equivocal: ambiguous, doubtful
preeminent: outstanding
viscous: thick, as applied to a liquid

7. B

In the first blank, something *factual* is contrasted with *conjecture;* (B) **evidence** and (E) **documentation** are both possible answers. In the second blank, it doesn't make sense to say that something could **inspire** *previously held views,* but something could certainly **refute** *previously held views,* so choice (B) is the correct answer.

*conjecture: speculation, opinion based
    on incomplete evidence*
refute: to prove to be false or erroneous
negate: to nullify or invalidate
corroborate: confirm

8. B

The definition of the missing word is implicit in the sentence; we're looking for a word that means able to *work around the clock with an energy that never seems to wane.* That's the meaning of (B) **indefatigable.** (E) **transcendent** is too vague here. So (B) is the answer.

indefatigable: tireless
dexterous: nimble, adroit
obsequious: submissive
*syncopated: in music, stressing
    normally unaccented beats*
transcendent: supreme

9. A

Although indicates a contrast with *impressive.* We want negative words for both blanks. For the first blank, (A) **bombastic** and (B) **verbose** are negative. For the second, (A) **obscured** and (D) **misconstrued** are negative. Only choice (A) provides suitable negative answers for both blanks, so it's correct.

bombastic: inflated, pretentious
obscured: hid
verbose: overly wordy
clarified: made clear or intelligible
*exuberant: lavish, overflowing, full of
    unrestrained enthusiasm*
*misconstrued: misunderstood,
    misinterpreted*

10. C

The key word is *subtle.* (D) **farce** is not *subtle,* it's a form of obvious humor. (A) **candor,** or complete honesty, isn't *subtle* either. (B) **humility** isn't a *verbal weapon,* and it's not a subtle alternative to arguing. And (E) **pantomime** isn't verbal at all, it's an art form consisting of silent gestures and movements. The answer is choice (C) **innuendo.**

candor: complete honesty
innuendo: hinting, indirect statement

1. The famous movie star regarded her mountain cabin as ----; she felt safe there from the annoying ---- of reporters and photographers.

    (A) a retreat . . writings
    (B) a liability . . prying
    (C) an excuse . . adulation
    (D) a haven . . intrusions
    (E) an occupation . . attentions

    Ⓐ Ⓑ Ⓒ Ⓓ Ⓔ

2. The congressman promised that he would consider all viewpoints and that he was willing, not only to discuss his proposal, but to ---- it.

    (A) amend
    (B) state
    (C) silence
    (D) accept
    (E) approve

    Ⓐ Ⓑ Ⓒ Ⓓ Ⓔ

3. The ombudsman was critical of the city's law enforcement agencies for the ---- of their efforts to stem the increase in criminal activity.

    (A) renewal
    (B) inadequacy
    (C) rejection
    (D) ratification
    (E) model

    Ⓐ Ⓑ Ⓒ Ⓓ Ⓔ

4. The review board ruled that the intern's behavior had been ----; he had violated the high standards required of members of the profession.

    (A) usual
    (B) exemplary
    (C) laudatory
    (D) unethical
    (E) ineffective

    Ⓐ Ⓑ Ⓒ Ⓓ Ⓔ

5. Critics ---- the play and described the playwright as prolific, brilliant, and ----.

    (A) acclaimed . . incisive
    (B) berated . . entertaining
    (C) praised . . prosaic
    (D) welcomed . . derivative
    (E) censured . . imaginative

    Ⓐ Ⓑ Ⓒ Ⓓ Ⓔ

6. Because of her ---- views, the professor frequently found herself defending traditional values and the status quo in arguments with her more radical students.

    (A) liberal
    (B) extreme
    (C) conservative
    (D) unorthodox
    (E) economic

    Ⓐ Ⓑ Ⓒ Ⓓ Ⓔ

7. The dramatist lived ---- life and his fame was achieved ----; few people had ever heard of him, or his works, until several years after his death.

    (A) a hapless . . effortlessly
    (B) an obscure . . posthumously
    (C) an infamous . . gradually
    (D) a monastic . . publicly
    (E) an eventful . . prematurely

    Ⓐ Ⓑ Ⓒ Ⓓ Ⓔ

8. Despite his usual sensitivity to criticism, the commissioner did not ---- his position on the issue, even after he was ---- in the press.

    (A) develop . . approached
    (B) abandon . . ridiculed
    (C) alter . . acclaimed
    (D) explain . . covered
    (E) relinquish . . substituted

    Ⓐ Ⓑ Ⓒ Ⓓ Ⓔ

9. In his later work, the artist finally attained a maturity of style utterly ---- his early, amateurish pieces.

    (A) descriptive of
    (B) superseded by
    (C) absent from
    (D) celebrated in
    (E) featured in   Ⓐ Ⓑ Ⓒ Ⓓ Ⓔ

10. The ambitions of tyrants are not ----, but excited, by partial concessions; that is why we must be ---- in opposing their demands.

    (A) realized . . clement
    (B) stimulated . . adamant
    (C) satisfied . . yielding
    (D) appeased . . resolute
    (E) inhibited . . generous   Ⓐ Ⓑ Ⓒ Ⓓ Ⓔ

SCORECARD	
Number of Questions Right:	
Number of Questions Wrong:	
Number of Questions Omitted:	
Number of Correct Guesses:	
Number of Wrong Guesses:	
Time Used:	

ANSWERS AND EXPLANATIONS

1. D

The semicolon is important in this sentence. The part of the sentence that follows the semicolon will elaborate on, and possibly help define, what has gone before. The real clue to filling both blanks lies in the phrase *she felt safe there*. It is clear that the first blank means a "safe place," while the second will refer to something negative that the movie star wishes to avoid. (D) should have jumped out as the correct answer. The cabin is **a haven** from the **intrusions** of reporters and photographers. In (A), **retreat** is good, but the second blank doesn't make sense. Choice (B) is wrong because **liability** does not fit the meaning of the sentence. Both words in choice (C) are way off. (E)'s second word, **attentions,** is fine, but **an occupation** is wrong in this context. So (D) is the correct answer.

> *haven: safe place*
> *retreat: a place for withdrawal*
> *liability: a disadvantage or handicap*
> *adulation: excessive flattery*

2. A

The structural clue in this sentence is the expression *not only . . . but*. The congressman *was willing, not only to discuss his proposal, but* to do something else consistent with his promise to consider all viewpoints. Choice (A) **amend** is right. Choice (B) is incorrect; **state** is too close in meaning to *discuss*.

> *amend: to correct or change*

3. B

You don't need to know what an *ombudsman* is to answer this one. What would *law enforcement* officials be criticized for? Probably their failure to do enough to fight crime. Or, as (B) puts it, *the* **inadequacy** *of their efforts to stem the increase in criminal activity*. (A) **renewal** contradicts the meaning of the sentence.

Choices (C), (D), and (E) do not make sense when plugged into the sentence, so you can eliminate them.

> *ombudsman: someone who settles people's complaints against a government, agency, or public institution*
> *ratification: formal approval*

4. D

The semicolon is the clue here. Again, what follows the semicolon will elaborate on what comes before. Clearly, the intern's behavior was very bad; the word *violated* tells you that. You can eliminate (A) because **usual** behavior is not in violation of standards. Eliminate (B) and (C) also. Being **ineffective** is bad, but it's not necessarily violating any standards, so (E) is wrong. Choice (D) is correct.

> *exemplary: deserving imitation*
> *laudatory: praiseworthy*
> *ineffective: not achieving any results*
> *unethical: not conforming to accepted or professional standards of behavior*

5. A

If you noticed the clue word *and*, you might have found it easier to work with the second blank first. *And* tells you that the word in the second blank has to be positive, to go along with *prolific* and *brilliant*. Once you've established that, you can eliminate (C) **prosaic** and (D) **derivative**. The second words in (A), (B), and (E) will work, so let's try their first-blank words. Clearly, the critics liked the play, so we need a positive word here. **Acclaimed,** in (A), is the only positive first-blank choice, and the only one that works when plugged in, so it's correct.

prosaic: dull and unimaginative,
  ordinary
derivative: taken from some original
  source
incisive: perceptive
acclaimed: enthusiastically applauded
berated: harshly criticized

6. C

Radical in the political sense means "desiring radical reforms." If the *professor* defended tradition in arguments with *radical students,* her views must be the opposite of radical. They must be **conservative**. So (C) is the correct answer. (A) **liberal** is not sufficiently different from *radical* to be the answer. (B) and (D) don't make logical sense either; a person with **extreme** or **unorthodox** (unconventional) views may or may not defend tradition. Finally, saying that the professor's views were **economic** in choice (E) does not explain why she would defend *the status quo.*

conservative: traditional or opposing
  change
liberal: tolerant, open-minded

7. B

In sentences whose clauses are separated by a semicolon, you should always very carefully read the part that does not contain the blanks. Often the clue to filling the blanks lies there. Since *few had heard* of the dramatist, you can predict that he lived a quiet or secluded life. The word in the second blank describes how his fame was achieved, so it will mean something like "after his death." (B) is the correct answer. *The dramatist lived* **an obscure** *life and his fame was achieved* **posthumously**. (A) makes no sense. You wouldn't say that *the dramatist lived a* **hapless** *life and that his fame was achieved* **effortlessly**. When you plug the other choices in, you'll find them equally unworkable.

obscure: not well known
posthumously: after one's death
hapless: unlucky
infamous: having a bad reputation
monastic: secluded

8. B

The word *despite* jumps right out here as a clue to the direction that the sentence will take. You can predict that this time the commissioner wasn't so sensitive to criticism. He did not change his position on the issue just because of the censure it brought him. For the first blank, we need a word like "change." Choices (B), (C), and (E) look good: **abandon**, **alter**, and **relinquish** might all work.

Now that we've narrowed the choices to three, let's try to fill the second blank. We're looking here for something like "criticized." (C) **acclaimed** means "praised," so eliminate it. (E) **substituted** doesn't mean "criticized." By process of elimination, (B) is right. It makes sense to say, *he did not* **abandon** *his position, even after he was* **ridiculed** *in the press.* So (B) is the correct answer.

acclaimed: praised
ridiculed: scorned, criticized

9. C

The opening phrase of the sentence—*in his later work*—and the concluding words—*his early, amateurish pieces*—tell us that a comparison is being drawn between the two stages of the artist's career. We are told that he attained a *maturity of style*—something that we might expect to come with age and therefore not to have been present in his early work. Choice (C), **absent from**, is consistent with this idea. (A) is wrong because it contradicts the sense of the sentence: A mature style wouldn't be **descriptive of** early, amateurish works. In (B), **superseded by** is clearly wrong. You'd expect more mature art to supersede amateur art, not the other way around. (D) is similarly illogical; so is (E).

superseded: replaced

10. D

The word *not* is an important clue in filling the first blank. It suggests that the missing word will be the opposite of *excited*. So you can predict a word like "calmed" for the blank. That eliminates answer choice (B) at once. (A) and (E) can also be ruled out since their first words aren't anywhere near "calmed." That leaves (C) **satisfied** and (D) **appeased** as possible right answers.

Now let's try (C) and (D)'s second-blank choices. **Yielding** is wrong. The idea is that since *partial concessions* encourage tyrants to push for more, we must be strong *in opposing their demands*. (D)'s **resolute** is the only answer that makes sense in this context.

clement: merciful
adamant: uncompromising, unyielding
inhibited: repressed or restrained

Suggested Time: 7 minutes

Directions: Select the lettered word or set of words that best completes the sentence.

Example:

Today's small, portable computers contrast markedly with the earliest electronic computers, which were ----.

(A) effective
(B) invented
(C) useful
(D) destructive
(E) enormous

1. Generally, fund-raising parties are quite labor-intensive and not very cost-effective; in other words, putting in a great deal of ---- doesn't mean you'll ---- a great deal of income.

(A) restraint . . obtain
(B) effort . . generate
(C) management . . spend
(D) reception . . limit
(E) materials . . lose

2. The leader of the task force on food quality deplored the fact that her efforts at investigation were ----, largely because of a lack of ---- between task force members and the health departments under investigation.

(A) final . . disagreement
(B) persistent . . energy
(C) successful . . resistance
(D) challenged . . discussion
(E) futile . . cooperation

3. Scientists had incorrectly assumed that parasites were primitive and ---- life forms; further research has revealed that parasites are actually quite ----.

(A) uncomplicated . . complex
(B) viable . . unproven
(C) mobile . . remote
(D) vigorous . . unscientific
(E) humorous . . inaccurate

4. Though people often think of them as ---- carnivores, many species of piranha are vegetarian.

(A) nomadic
(B) lugubrious
(C) voracious
(D) covetous
(E) exotic

5. On the Serengeti Plain, gazelles ---- from place to place in search of food until forced to run from hungry ---- like lions.

(A) migrate . . reprobates
(B) saunter . . predators
(C) ramble . . insurgents
(D) falter . . carnivores
(E) meander . . tyrants

6. Inflation has made the cost of consumer goods so ---- that most people can barely afford to buy basic food items.

(A) insignificant
(B) dubious
(C) coercive
(D) exorbitant
(E) repugnant

7. In the 19th century, a number of ---- farming communities were founded in the United States by groups of people who sought to create ideal societies.

(A) utopian
(B) mawkish
(C) decorous
(D) venerable
(E) surreptitious

8. Although the applicant was well qualified, she wasn't even considered for the job because the ---- way in which she boasted of her past accomplishments seemed ---- to the interviewer.

(A) awkward . . haughty
(B) candid . . optimistic
(C) exemplary . . antagonistic
(D) pompous . . excessive
(E) effusive . . frugal

9. Yeats's poetry became steadily more elaborate and more ---- during the 1890s; his audience found his poems increasingly difficult to interpret.

    (A) laconic
    (B) inscrutable
    (C) effusive
    (D) lyrical
    (E) euphonious   Ⓐ Ⓑ Ⓒ Ⓓ Ⓔ

10. Even if ---- life exists elsewhere in the universe, we humans may never know it, since it may be impossible for us to ---- with these alien beings.

    (A) avaricious . . confer
    (B) prodigal . . reside
    (C) sentient . . communicate
    (D) lachrymose . . traipse
    (E) extraneous . . exit   Ⓐ Ⓑ Ⓒ Ⓓ Ⓔ

SCORECARD	
Number of Questions Right:	
Number of Questions Wrong:	
Number of Questions Omitted:	
Number of Correct Guesses:	
Number of Wrong Guesses:	
Time Used:	

ANSWERS AND EXPLANATIONS

1. B

The suggestion made in this sentence is quite straightforward: The energy expended on fund-raising parties does not always match the income that results from them. If you have trouble, simply plug in the answer choices one at a time and listen to the logic of the sentence. Try choice (A): *Putting in* **restraint** *doesn't mean you'll* **obtain** *income.* That doesn't make any sense. Move on to (B): *Putting in* **effort** *doesn't mean you'll* **generate** *income.* That sounds perfectly sensible, and it follows through on the idea expressed in the first part of the sentence. (B) is the correct answer.

Continue to check the others just to make sure. In (C), *putting in* **management** *and* **spend**ing income sounds funny and doesn't make sense. In (D), **reception** has nothing to do with **limit**ing income. And in (E), why would you put in **materials** in order to **lose** income?

2. E

In the first part of the sentence, the verb *deplored* lets us know that the first blank will be a negative word. So, we can predict that the task force leader must have regretted that her efforts were "disregarded," "useless," or some other negative quality. Looking at the answer choices, we can rule out (A), (B), and (C).

That leaves us with (D) and (E), so let's try out (D) and (E)'s second words. (D) is too vague: Why would the leader's efforts be **challenged** because of a lack of **discussion**? (E) makes more sense. *Efforts at investigation were* **futile** *because of a lack of* **cooperation** *between task force members and those under investigation.*

> *deplored: regretted deeply or disapproved of*
> *futile: useless*

3. A

You know that the parasites were assumed to be *primitive and ---- life forms.* So whatever goes in the first blank must go along with the word *primitive.* The first word will be something like "simple." In the second

blank, the parasites are *actually quite ----.* So we are looking for a word like "complex" for the second blank. That means (A) is right. *Life forms* first thought to be *primitive* and **uncomplicated** have been *revealed* to be quite **complex**.

4. C

The clue is the word *although.* We need a word that is consistent with the *piranha's* image as a *carnivore,* yet contrasts with the reality that many piranhas eat only plants. (C) **voracious** works best. None of the other choices makes sense. If you knew that piranhas were tropical fish, you might have fallen for (E), but piranhas' exotic nature has nothing to do with their diet.

> *voracious: greedy, having a huge appetite*
> *nomadic: wandering from place to place*
> *lugubrious: mournful*
> *covetous: eagerly desiring something belonging to someone else*
> *exotic: foreign*

5. B

A number of the first-blank words look possible here, so it's easiest to start on the second blank. Of the second words, only two are real possibilities. The *lions* are either (B) **predators** or (D) **carnivores**. Checking (B) and (D)'s first words, we see that only (B) works for the first blank, since *gazelles* wouldn't **falter** *from place to place*.

6. D

Since *most people can barely afford to buy basic food items,* we can predict that inflation has made the cost of consumer goods extremely expensive. The best choice is (D) **exorbitant**.

exorbitant: excessive or costly
dubious: doubtful
coercive: forceful, threatening, bullying
repugnant: offensive, repulsive

7. A

A virtual definition of the word in the blank is found in the sentence. *People who sought to create ideal societies* would set up (A) **utopian** *farming communities.*

utopian: idealistic or visionary
mawkish: sickeningly sentimental
decorous: dignified or proper
venerable: deserving of respect because of great age or character
surreptitious: secret or clandestine

8. D

Although implies contrast. Even though *the applicant was well qualified,* there was definitely something wrong with the way she *boasted* about her *accomplishments.* So the first blank must be filled by a negative word, and looking at the first-position answer choices, the only ones we have are (A) **awkward** and (D) **pompous.**

Trying (A) and (D) in the second blank, we see that only (D) makes sense. If she had boasted **awkward**ly, that probably wouldn't have seemed **haughty** to the interviewer. But if she had boasted **pompously**, that could indeed seem **excessive.**

9. B

There are two significant clues in this sentence. The first is the word *and,* which tells us that the word in the blank will continue the idea expressed by the adjective *elaborate,* that *Yeats's poetry* became more complex. Secondly, the semicolon suggests that an explanation of the missing word will follow in the second part of the sentence—which goes on to tell us that people had difficulty interpreting his poems. We should look, therefore, for a word that means "difficult to understand." (B) **inscrutable** is the correct answer. None of

the three words in (A), (C), and (E) would make Yeats's poetry difficult to understand, so they are wrong.

inscrutable: difficult or impossible to understand or interpret
laconic: using few words
effusive: expressing emotions in an unrestrained way
euphonious: pleasant-sounding
lyrical: having the quality of a song

10. C

Assuming some alien intelligence exists, why might humans never know it? Logically, it must be because we can't (C) **communicate** with the alien life forms. (C) works: *If* **sentient,** *or conscious, life exists, we humans might never know because we could be unable to* **communicate** *with that life.* In (A), **confer** might be possible, but **avaricious** won't fit.

sentient: conscious, characterized by sensation
avaricious: greedy
prodigal: extravagant
lachrymose: tearful, mournful
traipse: walk aimlessly
extraneous: external; not relevant

SAT
Critical
Reading

INTRODUCTION TO SAT CRITICAL READING

The Critical Reading section tests your ability to read long passages quickly and perceptively. It also tests your understanding of how words are used in context. You'll be asked questions about the overall point of the passage, the author's point of view, the details, and what's implied. You'll also need to compare and contrast related passages.

The Structure

Critical Reading passages and questions appear in all the Verbal sections of the SAT. Each section contains either one long passage (or a paired passage) with 12–13 questions or two separate, shorter passages with a total of 15–16 questions.

The Format

Although the Critical Reading directions you'll see on the actual test will be worded slightly differently than the following sentence, they'll be basically the same. Get familiar with the directions now, so you won't waste precious time on Test Day:

Answer the questions below based on the information in the accompanying passages.

After the directions, you'll see four long (400- to 850-word) reading passages. One "paired passage" requires you to read and compare two related passages whose views oppose, support, or otherwise complement each other.

Critical Reading passages cover a wide variety of subjects, including the humanities, the arts, the social sciences, and the natural sciences. One reading selection will be narrative or fiction.

HINT: *A brief introduction precedes each passage. It often contains valuable information about the author and the passage that will help you earn points. Never skip it.*

Each passage is followed by five to thirteen questions. The questions are ordered: The first few ask about the beginning of the passage, the last few about the end of the passage. With paired passages, some questions will ask you about individual passages; others will ask you to compare and contrast the pair.

HINT: *Most unfamiliar words will be defined. You don't need any outside knowledge to answer the Critical Reading questions.*

Reading Tips

One Verbal section has two reading selections. You can start with either one. Scan both introductions, and do the passage you find easier first.

- Don't read the passage thoroughly—that's a waste of time.

- Do *skim* the passage to get the drift. If you miss the details, don't worry. The questions will direct you back to important points in the passage.

HINT: *The less time you spend reading the passages, the more time you'll have to answer questions, and that's where you score points.*

Answering the Questions

There are three kinds of Critical Reading questions: Big Picture, Little Picture, and Vocabulary-in-Context. All three are worth the same number of points. So don't get hung up on any one question.

Big Picture questions ask about the overall focus of the passage and the main points. To answer them accurately, you need to read *actively*, asking yourself, "Why did the author write this? What's the point of this?"

Little Picture questions are usually keyed: They give you a line reference, or refer you to a particular paragraph—a strong clue to where in the passage you'll find your answer. If you're given a line reference, don't read only that line. Read a few lines before and after to get an idea of the *context* in which that line appears.

Vocabulary-in-Context questions don't test your ability to define hard words. Instead, they ask how a word is used in the passage. The most common meaning of the word is probably not the correct answer. *Always* look back to the passage to see how the word is used in context.

Paired Passages

With paired passages, the first few questions relate to the first passage, the next few to the second passage, and the final questions ask about the passages as a pair. The best way to do paired passages is:

- Skim the first passage, and do the questions about it.

- Skim the second passage, thinking about how it relates to the first.

- Do the questions about the second passage.

- Do the questions about the relationship between the two passages.

Checklist

Critical Reading:

❏ Learn the instructions now.

❏ Always read the brief introductions.

❏ In the section with two passages, do the passage you find easier first.

❏ Read actively, searching for important points.

❏ Don't sweat the details.

❏ Read the lines before and after a line reference.

❏ Don't spend too much time on any one question. If you come across a hard one, move on and come back to it later.

❏ Avoid the "obvious" choice in Vocabulary-in-Context questions.

❏ In a paired passage, do all the questions about the first passage before you read the second passage.

Suggested Time: 7 Minutes

Directions: Answer the questions below based on the information in the accompanying passage.

Practice Passage 1: Willa Cather

The following passage analyzes one of Willa Cather's (1873–1947) novels.

Sapphira and the Slave Girl was the last novel of Willa Cather's illustrious literary career. Begun in the late summer of 1937 and finally completed in 1941, it
Line is often regarded by critics as one of her most personal
(5) works. Although the story takes place in 1856, well before her own birth, she drew heavily on both vivid childhood memories and tales handed down by older relatives to describe life in rural northern Virginia in the middle of the 19th century. She even went on an
(10) extended journey to the area to give the story a further ring of authenticity.

Of all of Cather's many novels, *Sapphira and the Slave Girl* is the one most concerned with providing an overall picture of day-to-day life in a specific era. A
(15) number of the novel's characters, it would seem, are included in the story only because they are representative of the types of people to be found in 19th-century rural Virginia; indeed, a few of them play no part whatsoever in the unfolding of the plot. For
(20) instance, we are introduced to a poor white woman, Mandy Ringer, who is portrayed as intelligent and content, despite the fact that she has no formal education and must toil constantly in the fields. And we meet Dr. Clevenger, a country doctor who, with his
(25) patrician manners, evokes a strong image of the pre-Civil War South.

The title, however, accurately suggests that the novel is mainly about slavery. Cather's attitude toward this institution may best be summed up as somewhat
(30) ambiguous. On the one hand, she displays almost total indifference to the legal and political aspects of slavery when she misidentifies certain crucial dates in its growth and development. Nor does she ever really offer a direct condemnation of slavery. Yet, on the other
(35) hand, the evil that was slavery gets through to us, albeit in typically subtle ways. Those characters, like Mrs. Blake, who oppose the institution are portrayed in a sympathetic light. Furthermore, the suffering of the slaves themselves and the petty, nasty, often cruel,
(40) behavior of the slaveowners are painted in stark terms.

Although *Sapphira and the Slave Girl* was certainly not meant to be a political tract, the novel is

sometimes considered to be a denunciation of bygone days. Nothing could be further from the truth. In spite
(45) of her willingness to acknowledge that particular aspects of the past were far from ideal, Willa Cather was, if anything, a bit of a romantic. Especially in the final years of her life, an increasing note of anger about the emptiness of the present crept into her writings.
(50) Earlier generations, she concluded, had been the real heroes, the real creators of all that was good in America.

1. The word *extended* in line 10 most nearly means

   (A) enlarged
   (B) increased
   (C) postponed
   (D) stretched
   (E) prolonged

2. In the discussion of Willa Cather's *Sapphira and the Slave Girl,* the author refers to the book primarily as a

   (A) heroic tale of the Civil War
   (B) sweeping epic of the old South
   (C) story based on personal material
   (D) political treatise on slavery
   (E) veiled condemnation of 1930s America

   Ⓐ Ⓑ Ⓒ Ⓓ Ⓔ

3. In the second paragraph, the author mentions Mandy Ringer and Dr. Clevenger in order to emphasize which point about *Sapphira and the Slave Girl*?

   (A) A number of the characters in the novel are based on people Cather knew in her childhood.
   (B) The novel displays Cather's mixed feelings about slavery.
   (C) Cather took four years to complete the novel because she carefully researched her characters.
   (D) One of Cather's purposes in writing the novel was to paint a full portrait of life in rural Virginia in the years before the Civil War.
   (E) The characters in the novel are portrayed in a positive light since Cather was a great admirer of the old South.

4. According to the author, why is Willa Cather's attitude toward slavery "somewhat ambiguous" (lines 29–30)?

   (A) She was ignorant of the legal and political aspects of slavery even though she was a keen observer of history.
   (B) She did not denounce slavery directly but criticized it in more roundabout ways.
   (C) She sympathized equally with both slaves and slaveowners.
   (D) She was an enemy of slavery but refrained from getting involved in political issues.
   (E) She disliked the treatment of slaves yet never tried to help improve their lot in life.

   Ⓐ Ⓑ Ⓒ Ⓓ Ⓔ

5. In context, "a bit of a romantic" (line 47) suggests that Willa Cather

   (A) condemned the evils of slavery
   (B) favored the past over the present
   (C) disliked writing about life in the 1930s
   (D) denounced certain aspects of 19th-century life
   (E) exaggerated the evils of earlier generations

   Ⓐ Ⓑ Ⓒ Ⓓ Ⓔ

SCORECARD	
Number of Questions Right:	
Number of Questions Wrong:	
Number of Questions Omitted:	
Number of Correct Guesses:	
Number of Wrong Guesses:	
Time Used:	

ANSWERS AND EXPLANATIONS

Practice Passage 1: Willa Cather

After your first reading, you should know roughly what the passage as a whole is about, and what each paragraph is about. The first paragraph tells us *Sapphira and the Slave Girl* is one of Cather's most authentic and personal works. The second paragraph tells us that *Sapphira and the Slave Girl* sets out to provide a picture of everyday life in the pre–Civil War South. Paragraph three tells us that while the novel is mainly about slavery, Cather's attitude towards slavery is ambiguous. The final paragraph says that although some consider *Sapphira* a denunciation of the past, the author feels the opposite is true. You'd be wasting time to go into further depth before looking at the questions. The only points you need to spend time with are the ones you're asked about.

1. E

This is a Vocabulary-in-Context question. If an answer choice has already grabbed your eye, try it in context. If not, check out each choice. (A) **enlarged** might seem related to a long trip, but it doesn't sound right. Definitely check the rest of the choices. (B) **increased** doesn't make sense; increased from what? (C) **postponed** is easy to eliminate; Cather's trip was not put off till a future time. (D) **stretched** is a definition of *extended*, but not one that works here. Finally, (E) **prolonged** makes sense. The line, "She went on an extended journey," keeps its meaning if you substituted **prolonged** for *extended*. Both words give the idea of an extensive trip, one where Cather could get a real feel for the places she would later describe in her novel.

HINT: *Always turn to the cited line to see how the word is used before you pick an answer.*

2. C

Look in the first paragraph for the answer to this question. The first paragraph tells us that *Sapphira* is one of Cather's most personal works and drew heavily on her childhood memories. The answer is almost certainly (C).

If you doubt it, check out the other choices. In paragraph two we learn that the novel is largely a portrait of the pre–Civil War South, and in paragraph three that *Sapphira* is mainly about slavery—so choice (A) is out. There's nothing in the passage to suggest that *Sapphira* is a **sweeping epic**—choice (B). If anything, it's the opposite, a very personal novel. (D) can't be right, because the first line in paragraph four says *Sapphira* is "not meant to be a political tract." Choice (E) is less obviously wrong, but is still wrong. Also in paragraph four, the author tells us Cather was dissatisfied with the present, but this is not the focus of her novel.

3. D

Go back to paragraph two and see what's going on. The author mentions two characters who are included mainly to help complete Cather's portrait of rural Virginia. Choice (D) states this nicely and is the right answer.

Other answer choices might agree with points the author makes elsewhere in the passage, but this question asks specifically about paragraph two. Choice (A) is discussed in paragraph one. Choice (B) is discussed in paragraph three. And choice (C) is discussed in paragraph one. Choice (E) overstates the content in paragraph four.

4. B

This question sends us to the third paragraph. There, the author says Cather's attitude towards slavery is "somewhat ambiguous," and offers several bits of evidence. On the one hand, Cather never comes out and directly condemns slavery, and she displays ignorance of and indifference to its legal and political aspects. On the other hand, she sympathetically portrays characters opposed to slavery and clearly portrays the suffering of slaves and the cruelty of slave owners. Choice (A) captures only part of this evidence and is therefore wrong. Choice (B) sums the evidence up and is the right answer.

The author never says that Cather **sympathizes** with slave owners, so choice (C) is out. The passage says Cather's attitude towards slavery was "ambiguous," not that she was **an enemy of slavery,** so choice (D) is wrong. And finally, choice (E) is out because the author is talking about Cather's attitude towards slavery as expressed in *Sapphira,* not in terms of what she did or did not do in her life.

5. B

Again, go back to the text. In the last paragraph the author refers to Cather as "a bit of a romantic" who cherished past creativity over the present emptiness. Choice (B) is a nice paraphrase of this, and is the right answer.

(A) can't be right, because the passage says Cather's views of slavery are "ambiguous." Nothing suggests Cather **disliked writing about the 1930s,** so choice (C) is wrong. Cather did dislike certain aspects of mid-19th-century life, but that's the opposite of romanticizing those times, so eliminate choice (D). Finally, Cather didn't **exaggerate the evils** of the past; if anything, she underestimated them. So choice (E) is wrong.

ambiguous: not clear; capable of being understood in two or more ways

Practice Passage 2: Sweet Track

The following passage is excerpted from a popular journal of archeology.

About fifty miles west of Stonehenge, buried in the peat bogs of the Somerset flatlands in southwestern England, lies the oldest road known to humanity.
Line Dubbed the "Sweet Track" after its discoverer,
(5) Raymond Sweet, this painstakingly constructed 1,800-meter road dates back to the early Neolithic period, some 6,000 years ago. Thanks primarily to the overlying layer of acidic peat, which has kept the wood moist, inhibited the growth of decay bacteria, and
(10) discouraged the curiosity of animal life, the road is remarkably well preserved. Examination of its remains has provided extensive information about the people who constructed it.

The design of the Sweet Track indicates that its
(15) builders possessed extraordinary engineering skills. In constructing the road, they first hammered pegs into the soil in the form of upright X's. Single rails were slid beneath the pegs, so that the rails rested firmly on the soft surface of the bog. Then planks were placed in
(20) the V-shaped space formed by the upper arms of the pegs. This method of construction—allowing the underlying rail to distribute the weight of the plank above and thereby prevent the pegs from sinking into the marsh—is remarkably sophisticated, testifying to a
(25) surprisingly advanced level of technology.

Furthermore, in order to procure the materials for the road, several different species of tree had to be felled, debarked, and split. This suggests that the builders possessed high quality tools, and that they
(30) knew the differing properties of various roundwoods. It appears also that the builders were privy to the finer points of lumbering, maximizing the amount of wood extracted from a given tree by slicing logs of large diameter radially and logs of small diameter
(35) tangentially.

Studies of the Sweet Track further indicate a high level of social organization among its builders. This is supported by the observation that the road seems to have been completed in a very short time; tree-ring
(40) analysis confirms that the components of the Sweet Track were probably all felled within a single year. Moreover, the fact that such an involved engineering effort could be orchestrated in the first place hints at a complex social structure.

(45) Finally, excavation of the Sweet Track has provided evidence that the people who built it comprised a community devoted to land cultivation. It appears that the road was built to serve as a footpath linking two islands—islands that provided a source of
(50) timber, cropland, and pastures for the community that settled the hills to the south. Furthermore, the quality of the pegs indicates that the workers knew enough to fell trees in such a way as to encourage the rapid growth of long, straight, rodlike shoots from the
(55) remaining stumps, to be used as pegs. This method is called coppicing and its practice by the settlers is the earliest known example of woodland management.

Undoubtedly, the discovery of the Sweet Track in 1970 added much to our knowledge of Neolithic
(60) technology. But while study of the remains has revealed unexpectedly high levels of engineering and social organization, it must be remembered that the Sweet Track represents the work of a single isolated community. One must be careful not to extrapolate
(65) sweeping generalizations from the achievements of such a small sample of Neolithic humanity.

1. In the first paragraph, the author claims that which of the following was primarily responsible for the preservation of the Sweet Track until modern times?

   (A) It was located in an area containing very few animals.
   (B) Its components were buried beneath the peat bog.
   (C) It was only lightly traveled during its period of use.
   (D) Local authorities prohibited development in the surrounding area.
   (E) It was protected from excessive humidity.
   Ⓐ Ⓑ Ⓒ Ⓓ Ⓔ

2. The author's reference to the peat bog as "acidic" (line 8) primarily serves to

(A) indicate the importance of protecting ancient ruins from the effects of modern pollution
(B) emphasize that the Sweet Track was constructed of noncorrosive materials
(C) distinguish between the effects of acidic and basic conditions on ancient ruins
(D) suggest that acidic conditions were important in inhibiting decay
(E) prove the relevance of knowledge of chemical properties to archaeological concerns

Ⓐ Ⓑ Ⓒ Ⓓ Ⓔ

3. In lines 15–25, the author describes the construction of the Sweet Track primarily in order to

(A) explain the unusual strength of the structure
(B) show how it could withstand 6,000 years buried underground
(C) prove that its builders cooperated efficiently
(D) indicate its builders' advanced level of technological expertise
(E) emphasize the importance of careful construction techniques

Ⓐ Ⓑ Ⓒ Ⓓ Ⓔ

4. The primary focus of the passage is on

(A) the high degree of social organization exhibited by earlier cultures
(B) the complex construction and composition of the Sweet Track
(C) an explanation for the survival of the Sweet Track over 6,000 years
(D) ways in which the Sweet Track reveals aspects of a particular Neolithic society
(E) the innovative methods of woodland management practiced by early builders

Ⓐ Ⓑ Ⓒ Ⓓ Ⓔ

5. In line 31, the phrase *privy to* means

(A) close to
(B) expert at
(C) concealed from
(D) likely to
(E) familiar with

Ⓐ Ⓑ Ⓒ Ⓓ Ⓔ

6. In her discussion of social organization in paragraph four, the author mentions ring analysis primarily as evidence that

(A) the road is at least 6,000 years old
(B) the Sweet Track was constructed quickly
(C) the techniques used in building the road were quite sophisticated
(D) the builders knew enough to split thick trees radially and thin trees tangentially
(E) the builders felled a large variety of trees

 Ⓐ Ⓑ Ⓒ Ⓓ Ⓔ

7. The cited example of "woodland management" (line 57) is best described as a system in which trees are

(A) lumbered in controlled quantities
(B) planted only among trees of their own species
(C) cultivated in specialized ways for specific purposes
(D) felled only as they are needed
(E) harvested for use in construction only

 Ⓐ Ⓑ Ⓒ Ⓓ Ⓔ

8. In the last paragraph, the author cautions that the Sweet Track

(A) is not as technologically advanced as is generally believed
(B) should not necessarily be regarded as representative of its time
(C) has not been studied extensively enough to support generalized conclusions
(D) is probably not the earliest road in existence
(E) will force historians to reevaluate their assumptions about the Neolithic technology

Ⓐ Ⓑ Ⓒ Ⓓ Ⓔ

SCORECARD	
Number of Questions Right:	7
Number of Questions Wrong:	1
Number of Questions Omitted:	\
Number of Correct Guesses:	\
Number of Wrong Guesses:	\
Time Used:	10 mins

ANSWERS AND EXPLANATIONS

Practice Passage 2: Sweet Track

The next passage, which comes from "a popular journal of archeology," is about the "oldest road known to humanity," also known as the Sweet Track after its discoverer. The last sentence of the first paragraph makes the main point—that examination of the remains of the Sweet Track has revealed lots of information about the people who built it. The next four paragraphs provide examples and insights about the builders, revealed by studying the remains. Do you have to sweat the details of each example? No way. Don't waste time trying to understand the specific construction techniques, materials, tools, etcetera.

In the second paragraph, for instance, we hope you skimmed over all that description about wooden X-shaped pegs and the upper and lower rails. All you need to know is that the builders of the Sweet Track had a "surprisingly advanced level of technology."

The passage concludes with a little warning: Although the Sweet Track shows X, Y, and Z about the builders, this small group of people does not represent Neolithic peoples in general. You can't assume that all people in those long-ago days were as advanced as the builders of the Sweet Track.

1. B

This Little Picture question about the Sweet Track's preservation sends you back to the first paragraph. Right there in the third sentence you get the information you need. What accounts for the road's being so well preserved? The remains were **buried** under a layer of acidic peat, which kept the wood moist, prevented decay from bacteria, and kept nosy animals away. That should have led you to answer choice (B).

(A) may have given you pause, since a lack of interfering **animals** is mentioned in paragraph one. But it wasn't the location of the road that kept animals away; it was the fact that the road was **buried,** so the animals couldn't get to it. (C) and (D) might seem to offer reasonable explanations for the road's good condition, but the passage never mentions **light travel** patterns or **development prohibitions.** Finally, (E) gets it dead

wrong; the road was kept "moist," according to the author, so it was hardly **protected from excessive humidity.**

2. D

Reread the sentence in which "acidic" is mentioned. It says that the "acidic peat" allowed for three conditions that caused the road to be preserved: It kept it moist, relatively free of bacteria, and free from animal interference. So the fact that the bog was "acidic" must have something to do with causing those conditions. When you check the answer choices, only (D) mentions one of those conditions, so it's the right answer. Incorrect choices (A) and (C) bring in unmentioned issues; (A) **modern pollution** and (C) **acidic** versus **basic conditions** are never discussed in the passage. You know (B) is wrong because the author never mentions **noncorrosive materials** as a factor that kept the road in such good shape. And (E) is too general; the author is not making a big point about **chemicals** and **archeology.**

3. D

The line reference directs you to the second paragraph. You're asked why the author describes the construction of the Sweet Track. Don't read all the details; just look to see what the author concludes. In the last sentence of the paragraph, the author claims the method of construction "is remarkably sophisticated, testifying to a surprisingly advanced level of technology"—(D).

Incorrect choices (B) and (C) point to conclusions the author makes elsewhere in the passage, not in the lines specified in question 3. (A) talks about the **unusual strength** of the road, which the author never discusses in any paragraph. (E)'s sweeping reference to the **importance of careful construction techniques** is too general, since the author is only drawing conclusions about this one specific culture.

4. D

The key to this Big Picture question is in the last sentence of the first paragraph. The author says she's going to discuss how Sweet Track's remains tell us a great deal about the Neolithic people who built it—a focus best summed up by correct choice (D).

Choice (B) is probably the closest wrong choice, but it's only half of the main focus. The author does focus on the **complex construction and composition** of the road, but for a purpose—to discuss what that **construction and composition** tells us about the builders of the road. Choice (A) is too broad. The passage only discusses the **social organization** of one isolated community. (C) and (E) are too narrow. The **survival** of the road **over 6,000 years** (C) is the purpose of just the end of the first paragraph. And (E) is too narrow because **woodland management** is the topic of paragraph five only.

5. E

This is a Vocabulary-in-Context question, so go back and examine how *privy to* is used in the sentence *before* you try to answer.

The sentence says "the builders were *privy to* the finer points of lumbering" because they knew how to maximize the amount of wood extracted from a log by slicing it in different ways. That shows they were (E) **familiar with** the finer points of lumbering.

HINT: *You should look at the sentences around the word to figure out how the word is used.*

If you plug choices (A), (C), and (D) into that sentence, they don't make sense. How can somebody be **close to, concealed from,** or **likely to** the finer points of lumbering? Choice (B) sounds possible, but **familiar with** is a more moderate choice, so it's a better bet. Remember, you're looking for the "best" answer. So (E) is correct.

6. B

To find out why the author brings up *ring analysis,* reread paragraph four. The author writes that the road "seems to have been completed in a very short time." How do we know? Because "tree-ring analysis," the topic of this question, confirms that the trees used to build the road were all felled within a single year. So tree-ring analysis offers evidence to support the claim that the Sweet Track was built **quickly;** choice (B).

Choice (A) may seem plausible, because we usually count tree-rings to find out how **old** trees are. But in paragraph four of this passage, tree-ring analysis was used for another purpose. The other choices raise issues discussed elsewhere. Those **sophisticated** building **techniques,** choice (C), were the subject of paragraph two, while the fancy lumbering technique men-

tioned in choice (D), as well as the **large variety** of felled trees mentioned in choice (E), were brought up in paragraph three and have nothing to do with the tree-ring analysis mentioned in paragraph four.

7. C

What's *the cited example of "woodland management"* the question refers to? When you go to the line reference given, you'll find it's called "coppicing." Coppicing is described as the process of felling trees "in such a way as to encourage the rapid growth of long, straight, rodlike shoots from the remaining stumps, to be used as pegs." In other words, trees are grown in a special way in order to yield special materials—that is, *the rodlike shoots.* Choice (C) best paraphrases that process.

Choices (A) and (D) have nothing to do with the paragraph; nowhere does the author talk about lumbering (A) **controlled quantities** of trees or cutting down trees (D) **only as they are needed.** (B) may sound plausible, but the process described here focuses not on the *kind* of trees being planted, but rather the *way* they are planted. And (E) may have been tempting, because the lumber in question *was* harvested for **use in construction,** but again, the point is how the trees were planted, not what they were used for.

8. B

This question directs you to that interesting last paragraph we discussed above—the one that cautions not to generalize too much from the Sweet Track. The author says the Sweet Track represents "the work of a single isolated community," and that therefore we shouldn't use it to make conclusions about all Neolithic communities. That's best paraphrased by choice (B).

Choices (A) and (D) are not the subject of the last paragraph; besides, they're just plain wrong. (C) is a distortion. The reason we shouldn't draw **generalized conclusions** from the Sweet Track is because it is the work of just one small community, not because the road has been studied too little. And (E) implies that the study of the Sweet Track will bring about a fundamental revolution in historical thought about the whole Neolithic period—just the kind of general conclusions that the author explicitly warns against.

Suggested Time: 9 Minutes

Directions: Answer the questions below based on the information in the accompanying passage.

Practice Passage 3: Fallingwater

The following passage is excerpted from a study of modern architecture.

Fallingwater, a small country house constructed in 1936, stands as perhaps the greatest residential building achievement of the American architect Frank
Line Lloyd Wright. In designing the dwelling for the
(5) Pittsburgh millionaire Edgar J. Kaufmann, Wright was confronted with an unusually challenging site, beside a waterfall deep in a Pennsylvania ravine. However, Wright viewed this difficult location not as an obstacle, but as a unique opportunity to put his architectural
(10) ideals into concrete form. In the end, Wright was able to turn Fallingwater into an artistic link between untamed nature and domestic tranquility, and a masterpiece in his brilliant career.

Edgar J. Kaufmann had originally planned for his
(15) house to sit at the bottom of the waterfall, where there was ample flat land on which to build. But Wright proposed a more daring response to the site. The architect convinced Kaufmann to build his house at the top of the waterfall on a small stone precipice. Further,
(20) Wright proposed extending the living room of the house out over the rushing water, and making use of modern building techniques so that no vertical supports would be needed to hold up the room. Rather than allowing the environment to determine the
(25) placement and shape of the house, Wright sought to construct a home that actually confronted and interacted with the landscape.

In one sense, Fallingwater can be viewed as a showcase for unconventional building tactics. In
(30) designing the living room, for example, Wright made brilliant use of a technique called the cantilever, in which steel rods are laid inside a shelf of concrete, eliminating the need for external supports. But Fallingwater also contains a great many traditional and
(35) natural building materials. The boulders which form the foundation for the house also extend up through the floor and form part of the fireplace. A staircase in the living room extends down to an enclosed bathing pool at the top of the waterfall. To Wright, the ideal
(40) dwelling in this spot was not simply a modern extravaganza or a direct extension of natural surroundings; rather, it was a little of both.

Critics have taken a wide range of approaches to understanding this unique building. Some have
(45) postulated that the house exalts the artist's triumph over untamed nature. Others have compared Wright's building to a cave, providing a psychological and physical safe haven from a harsh, violent world. Edgar Kaufmann, Jr., the patron's son, may have summed up
(50) Fallingwater best when he said, "Wright understood that people were creatures of nature; hence an architecture which conformed to nature would conform to what was basic in people . . . . Sociability and privacy are both available, as are the comforts of
(55) home and the adventures of the seasons." This, then, is Frank Lloyd Wright's achievement in Fallingwater, a home which connects the human and the natural, for the invigoration and exaltation of both.

1. The primary purpose of the passage is to

    (A) showcase Wright's use of unconventional building tactics and techniques
    (B) describe the relationship between Wright and Edgar J. Kaufmann
    (C) judge the place of Fallingwater in the history of architecture
    (D) describe Fallingwater as Wright's response to a challenging building site
    (E) evaluate various critical responses to Fallingwater

2. The word *concrete* in line 10 could best be replaced by

    (A) dense
    (B) hard
    (C) substantial
    (D) durable
    (E) reinforced

Practice Set 3

3. The passage suggests that Edgar J. Kaufmann's original plans for the site were

(A) conservative
(B) inexpensive
(C) daring
(D) idealistic
(E) architecturally unsound

4. The author includes a description of a cantilever (lines 29–33) in order to explain

(A) the technique used to create the fireplace in Fallingwater
(B) the use of traditional engineering techniques in Fallingwater
(C) an unusual design feature of Fallingwater
(D) modern technological advances in the use of concrete
(E) how Fallingwater conforms to nature

5. The end of paragraph three indicates that, above all else, Wright wanted Kaufmann's home to be

(A) representative of its owner's wealth and position
(B) as durable as current construction techniques would allow
(C) a landmark in 20th century American architecture
(D) impressive yet in harmony with its surroundings
(E) a symbol of man's triumph over the natural landscape

6. Critics' comparison of Fallingwater to a cave (lines 46–48) suggests that the house conveys a sense of

(A) warmth
(B) darkness
(C) simplicity
(D) claustrophobia
(E) security

7. In context, the phrase "for the invigoration and exaltation of both" (lines 57–58) suggests that Fallingwater

(A) encourages visitors to appreciate the change of seasons
(B) benefits the environment as well as its occupants
(C) stands out as the most beautiful feature in the local landscape
(D) enables its owners to entertain in an impressive setting
(E) typifies Wright's efforts to infuse modern architecture with spirituality

Ⓐ Ⓑ Ⓒ Ⓓ Ⓔ

SCORECARD	
Number of Questions Right:	4
Number of Questions Wrong:	3
Number of Questions Omitted:	
Number of Correct Guesses:	
Number of Wrong Guesses:	
Time Used:	

ANSWERS AND EXPLANATIONS

Practice Passage 3: Fallingwater

This short passage is about Fallingwater, a house designed by the famous American architect Frank Lloyd Wright. Your initial quick skim should have told you that Fallingwater is regarded as a bold architectural statement, both because of its dramatic location atop a waterfall and because of various unconventional building techniques Wright used in the design. One running theme is the relationship of the house to the natural setting around it. Throughout the passage, the author comments on that relationship, indicating that Fallingwater "confronted and interacted with the landscape," so that the house was in part an extension of nature, but also an impressive "modern extravaganza."

1. D

This Big Picture question asks for the primary purpose of the passage. Your initial response might have been a general statement, such as "to describe the design of the Fallingwater house." But the correct answer should incorporate the running theme mentioned above—the relationship of the house to the natural setting. That's why choice (D) is correct.

Choice (A) is too broad. The author discusses Wright's **tactics and techniques** only in the design of one specific building, Fallingwater, which this choice does not specify. (B) is a distortion; although Kaufmann and Wright had different ideas about the ideal location for the house, describing the **relationship** between the two men is not *the purpose of* the passage. In (C), though the author says Fallingwater is unique, she never discusses its place in architectural **history.** And finally, (E) is the focus of the last paragraph only, where **critical responses** are discussed.

2. C

Next is a Vocabulary-in-Context question. To find a synonym for *concrete* that fits the context, go back to the actual sentence. You'll see *concrete* is used figuratively. Wright, the author says, regarded Fallingwater's site as an "opportunity to put his architectural ideals into *concrete* form"—out of the realm of ideals, in other words, and into the realm of real, tangible things.

So (C) **substantial** is the best replacement word; Wright wanted to give substance to his ideals by incorporating them in an actual building.

Choices (A), (B), and (E) are all too literal. We talk about **reinforced** concrete, about something being **hard** or **dense** as *concrete,* but that's not the meaning of *concrete* here. Choice (D) **durable** doesn't work either; although *concrete* is a **durable** substance, durable isn't a synonym for this figurative sense of the word.

3. A

Kaufmann's original plans for the house are discussed only at the beginning of the second paragraph, so go back to that spot. The author writes that Kaufmann had originally planned to put the house on a flat place near the bottom of the waterfall, but Wright convinced him to accept the "more daring" response of building the house right over the waterfall. While she doesn't say so directly, the author implies that Kaufmann's original plans were less daring, less risky, or, as correct choice (A) has it, more **conservative.**

As for the wrong choices, (C) is the opposite of what you want, since it was Wright who had the **daring** plan for the house. Similarly, (D) better describes Wright's plan than Kaufmann's, since the author claims that Wright's plan "put his architectural ideals into concrete form." (B) may be true, but the cost of the two plans are never discussed in the passage. And nowhere is Kaufmann's plan criticized as (E) **architecturally unsound;** in fact, it was almost certainly regarded as *more* sound than Wright's daring idea.

4. C

Don't worry if you can't tell a cantilever from a cantaloupe. To answer this question, you don't have to know what a cantilever is. You just have to know *why* the author described the technique.

As always, go to the place in the passage specified in the line reference, where the cantilever process is explained. We're told it's an example of the "unconventional building tactics" mentioned in the sentence before. "Unconventional" translates nicely to **unusual,** so (C) is the best answer here.

The construction of the **fireplace,** choice (A), is mentioned as an example of the traditional elements used in the house; it has nothing to do with cantilevers. (B) is the opposite of what you want, since "unconventional" and **traditional** are virtual antonyms. (D) might seem logical, but it's not in the paragraph; the author isn't talking broadly about **modern technological advances** in **concrete;** she only describes the advances used in the Fallingwater house. Finally, (E) is off base since there's nothing particularly natural about a cantilever; the discussion about **nature** comes later in the same paragraph and is not directly related.

5. D

At the end of the third paragraph, we learn that Wright's ideal dwelling for the waterfall site "was not simply a modern extravaganza or a direct extension of natural surroundings, [but] a little bit of both." So your answer has to incorporate both elements. And that makes (D) correct; Wright wanted the house to be **impressive** but still **harmonious.**

(A) is wrong because the passage offers no evidence that Kaufmann's **money and position** influenced Wright's thinking. (B)'s focus on **durability** makes it inappropriate; the end of paragraph three doesn't deal with Fallingwater's ability to survive over time. Nor does it deal with Wright's desire for the house to be considered an architectural **landmark,** so (C) is wrong. And (E) is a distortion; Wright wanted Fallingwater to be an "extension of [the] natural surroundings"—not a **triumph** over them.

6. E

The absolutely wrong way of approaching this question is to use your own impression of "cave[s]" as your guide. It's the critics' idea of a "cave" that's important here. According to the cited sentence, critics compared Fallingwater to a "cave" because the house provided "a psychological and physical safe haven from a harsh, violent world." So it's the quality of safety that's being equated here, leading you to correct choice (E) **security.**

(A) seems a possible choice, since **warmth** conveys a sense of refuge from the cold, but compare it with (E). Since security is more directly related to the mention of "safe haven," (A) is only second-best and will earn you no SAT points. (B) **darkness** and (D) **claustrophobia** are qualities that you personally may associate with "cave[s]," but they're not the qualities these "critics" had in mind. Finally, choice (C) **simplicity** is way off base; first, there's nothing particularly simple about a cave, and second, the "safe haven" is not from a complex world, but a "harsh, violent" world.

7. B

The line reference refers you to the very end of the passage. To answer correctly, you need to see that "both" refers to both "the human and the natural." This underlines the running theme we mentioned earlier— the interaction between the human, as represented by the house, and the natural, as represented by the natural setting. Wright wants to do justice to both, and so (B) best answers the question. It talks about **benefits to the environment** (the natural) as well as to the **occupants** (the human).

(A) and (D) miss half the message; they show how humans are "invigorated and exalted" by the natural setting, but not how nature benefits. (C) does the opposite, emphasizing how the house beautifies the setting but failing to mention how the setting beautifies the house. And (E) is an inference that goes too far. (B) is a better answer, and you need to go with the best choice.

Suggested Time: 13 Minutes

Directions: Answer the questions below based on the information in the accompanying passages.

Practice Passage 4: Paired Parks

The following passages present two views of the city. Passage 1 focuses on the decline of the city park system. Passage 2 describes the decline of the city as a work of art.

Passage 1

City parks were originally created to provide the local populace with a convenient refuge from the crowding and chaos of its surroundings. Until quite
Line recently, these parks served their purpose admirably.
(5) Whether city dwellers wanted to sit under a shady tree to think or take a vigorous stroll to get some exercise, they looked forward to visiting these nearby oases. Filled with trees, shrubs, flowers, meadows, and ponds, city parks were a tranquil spot in which to
(10) unwind from the daily pressures of urban life. They were places where people met their friends for picnics or sporting events. And they were also places to get some sun and fresh air in the midst of an often dark and dreary environment, with its seemingly endless rows
(15) of steel, glass, and concrete buildings.

For more than a century, the importance of these parks to the quality of life in cities has been recognized by urban planners. Yet city parks around the world have been allowed to deteriorate to an alarming extent
(20) in recent decades. In many cases, they have become centers of crime; some city parks are now so dangerous that local residents are afraid even to enter them. And the great natural beauty which was once their hallmark has been severely damaged. Trees, shrubs, flowers, and
(25) meadows have withered under the impact of intense air pollution and littering, and ponds have been fouled by untreated sewage.

This process of decline, however, is not inevitable. A few changes can turn the situation around. First,
(30) special police units, whose only responsibility would be to patrol city parks, should be created to ensure that they remain safe for those who wish to enjoy them. Second, more caretakers should be hired to care for the grounds and, in particular, to collect trash. Beyond the
(35) increased staffing requirements, it will also be necessary to insulate city parks from their surroundings. Total isolation is, of course, impossible; but many beneficial measures in that direction could be implemented without too much trouble. Vehicles, for
(40) instance, should be banned from city parks to cut down on air pollution. And sewage pipes should be rerouted away from park areas to prevent the contamination of land and water. If urban planners are willing to make these changes, city parks can be restored to their
(45) former glory for the benefit of all.

Passage 2

With the rise of the great metropolis in the industrial era, city planning in the West passed out of the hands of the architect and into the hands of the technocrat.* Unlike the architect who thought of the
(50) city as a work of art to be built up with an eye toward beauty, the technocrat has always taken a purely functional approach to city planning; the city exists for the sole purpose of serving the needs of its inhabitants. Its outward appearance has no intrinsic value.

(55) Over the span of a few centuries, this new breed of urban planner has succeeded in forever changing the face of the Western city. A brief visit to any large metropolis is enough to confirm this grim fact. Even a casual observer could not fail to notice that the typical
(60) urban landscape is arranged along the lines of the tedious chessboard pattern, with its four-cornered intersections and long, straight and dull streets. Strict building codes have resulted in an overabundance of unsightly neighborhoods in which there is only slight
(65) variation among structures. Rows of squat concrete apartment houses and files of gigantic steel and glass skyscrapers have almost completely replaced older, more personal buildings. Moreover, the lovely natural surroundings of many cities are no longer a part of the
(70) urban landscape. For the most part, the hills and rivers which were once so much a part of so many metropolitan settings have now been blotted out by thoughtless construction.

The lone bright spot amidst all of this urban blight
(75) has been the local park system, which is to be found in most Western cities. Large, centrally-located parks— for example, New York's Central Park or London's Hyde Park—and smaller, outlying parks bring a measure of beauty to Western cities by breaking up the
(80) man-made monotony. With their green pastures, dense woods, and pleasant ponds, streams and waterfalls, local park systems also offer a vast array of opportunities for city dwellers to rest or recreate, free of the intense burdens of urban life. If they have
(85) understood nothing else about the quality of life in urban areas, technocrats have at least had the good sense to recognize that people need a quiet refuge from the chaotic bustle of the city.

*technocrat: technical expert

1. The author of Passage 1 uses the phrase "convenient refuge" in line 2 to suggest that parks were

   (A) built in order to preserve plant life in cities
   (B) designed with the needs of city residents in mind
   (C) meant to end the unpleasantness of city life
   (D) supposed to help people make new friends
   (E) intended to allow natural light to filter into cities

2. By mentioning crime and pollution (lines 20–27), the author of Passage 1 primarily emphasizes

   (A) how rapidly the city parks have deteriorated
   (B) how city parks can once again be made safe and clean
   (C) why people can no longer rest and relax in city parks
   (D) why urban planners should not be in charge of city parks
   (E) who is responsible for damaging the quality of life in cities

3. In line 26, the word *intense* most nearly means

   (A) severe
   (B) fervent
   (C) piercing
   (D) strenuous
   (E) meticulous

4. In the last paragraph of Passage 1, the author acknowledges which problem in restoring city parks?

   (A) The constant need to collect trash
   (B) The difficulty in rerouting sewage pipes
   (C) The congestion caused by banning vehicular traffic
   (D) The lack of total separation from the surrounding city
   (E) The expense of creating additional police patrol units

5. In Passage 2, the reference to "a purely functional approach to city planning" (lines 52–53) serves to

   (A) demonstrate that architects and technocrats should cooperate
   (B) imply that architects are unconcerned about human comfort
   (C) indicate that architects are obsolete in an industrial era
   (D) stress that architects and technocrats have different priorities
   (E) show that technocrats have destroyed the natural beauty of cities

6. The word *face* in line 58 means

   (A) reputation
   (B) expression
   (C) value
   (D) dignity
   (E) appearance

7. In lines 59–74, the author's description of cities is

   (A) tolerant
   (B) surprised
   (C) derogatory
   (D) nostalgic
   (E) bewildered

8. In context, "the good sense to recognize" (lines 87–88) suggests that technocrats

   (A) want to get rid of urban blight
   (B) are aware of the stress of city life
   (C) support nature conservation programs
   (D) favor large city parks over smaller ones
   (E) think that greenery makes cities more attractive

9. Both passages focus primarily on

(A) criticizing certain aspects of the city
(B) romanticizing city life in a bygone era
(C) exploring the origins of urban decay
(D) blaming urban problems on city residents
(E) pointing out how city life could be improved

10. The author of Passage 1 would most likely react to the characterization of city parks presented in lines 81–85 by pointing out that

(A) this characterization is confirmed by the evidence
(B) future reforms will render this characterization false
(C) urban planners would reject this characterization
(D) this characterization is in bad taste
(E) recent developments have made this characterization obsolete

11. How would the author of Passage 1 respond to the way the author of Passage 2 uses the phrase "urban blight" (line 75) to describe the current state of cities?

(A) This phrase is not supported by the facts.
(B) It is being used to denounce what is best about cities.
(C) It is an accurate description of the situation.
(D) Choosing this phrase demonstrates very poor taste.
(E) New studies show that this phrase will soon be outdated.

SCORECARD	
Number of Questions Right:	
Number of Questions Wrong:	
Number of Questions Omitted:	
Number of Correct Guesses:	
Number of Wrong Guesses:	
Time Used:	

ANSWERS AND EXPLANATIONS

Practice Passage 4: Paired Parks

Always read the introduction to paired passages first, because it will indicate how the two passages relate. Do the questions keyed to Passage 1 after you read it. Then read the second passage and answer the rest of the questions. That way, you'll be answering questions while the general impressions from each passage are fresh in your mind.

Passage 1, on the decline of the city park system, is not wholly pessimistic. After depicting the parks as a once-ideal place for people to escape from the city, the author describes city parks around the world as ruined by crime and pollution. But the final paragraph expresses hope that the parks can be restored and offers suggestions for accomplishing this.

In contrast, Passage 2 sees parks as the "lone bright spot" amid cities marred by technocrats' "purely functional approach" to city planning. Technocrats get blamed for the ugly, unnatural, and impersonal look of the urban landscape of Western cities. The only good thing the technocrats have done is recognize that people need a park system as a refuge from city life.

1. B

The question stem directs you back to the first sentence of Passage 1. The author says parks were created to give people a "refuge" from the city. Scanning quickly through the answer choices, (B) jumps out because it fits the opening statement: Parks were **designed with the needs of city residents in mind.**

Choices (A), (D), and (E) are misleading bits of information from the rest of the first paragraph. Although parks may house **plant life, allow natural light into cities,** and provide a place to meet or **make friends,** that's not what "convenient refuge" means. As for (C), the author never suggests that parks are supposed to **end the unpleasantness of city life.** They merely provide a "refuge."

2. C

To answer this question, you have to understand the context in which crime and pollution are mentioned in the second paragraph. The author describes the deterioration of parks, including the effects of crime and pollution, to show that people can no longer use the parks as they were meant to be used. In other words, the author is talking about (C) **why people can no longer rest and relax** in the parks.

The author mentions that parks have deteriorated in recent decades, but the information on *crime and pollution* doesn't emphasize how **rapidly,** so (A) is out. Making parks **cleaner and safer** is the topic of the third paragraph, not the second, so (B) is wrong. The passage says nothing negative about **urban planners,** nor does it blame anyone in particular for **damaging the quality of life in cities,** so eliminate (D) and (E).

3. A

This is a Vocabulary-in-Context question. Since all the answer choices except (E) **meticulous** are possible synonyms for *intense,* you have to figure out how the word is used in the sentence. The author says greenery in the parks has been destroyed by *intense* pollution and littering. Pollution and littering clearly can't be (B) **fervent,** (C) **piercing,** or (D) **strenuous,** so (A) **severe** is the right choice.

4. D

The last paragraph of Passage 1 offers suggestions for reversing the decline of the parks: adding more police units and caretakers, banning vehicles, and rerouting sewage pipes. It is also necessary, the author says, to "insulate city parks from their surroundings," but the problem here is that "total isolation" is "impossible." This is paraphrased in the right choice, (D).

Choices (A), (B), (C), and (E) all twist information from the author's suggestions. Trash does need to be collected, but the author never says that (A) **the constant need to collect trash** would be a problem. Nor does the paragraph say that (B) **rerouting sewage pipes** will be difficult, (C) **banning traffic** will cause congestion, or (E) **additional police units** will be expensive.

5. D

This is the first question about Passage 2. Look again at the sentence that describes "a purely functional approach to city planning." The author contrasts architects, who view building a city as an artistic endeavor, to technocrats, who focus only on "serving the needs of . . . inhabitants." In other words, the author is (D) **stressing that architects and technocrats have different priorities.**

The author does not imply here that (A) **architects and technocrats should cooperate** or that architects do not care (B) **about human comfort.** Certainly, the author does not think (C) **architects are obsolete;** if anything, he regrets they no longer do city planning. As for (E), the author does think **technocrats have destroyed the natural beauty of the cities,** but this point comes up in the second and third paragraphs, not the first. In keyed questions like this, concentrate on the few sentences around the quoted phrase.

6. E

Once again, before you answer a Vocabulary-in-Context question, reread the sentence that contains the line reference. If you didn't do that here, several answer choices may have looked tempting. The author is talking about how the *face,* or **appearance,** of the Western city has been changed forever, so (E) is the only choice that fits.

7. C

Skim quickly over the sentence referred to in the second paragraph of Passage 2. You'll see phrases like "tedious chessboard pattern," "straight and dull streets," and "an overabundance of unsightly neighborhoods." Clearly, the author has a low opinion of modern cities; the tone is disparaging, or (C) **derogatory.** (A) **tolerant,** (B) **surprised,** and (E) **bewildered** are clearly wrong. Nor are the comments (D) **nostalgic,** or wistful. Although the author states that older, more personal buildings and lovely natural surroundings can no longer be found in cities, the tone is critical, rather than yearning.

8. B

Passage 2 concludes by saying that technocrats "have at least had the good sense to recognize that people need a quiet refuge" from the chaos of the city. The inference is that technocrats (B) **are aware of the stress of city life.**

The author certainly doesn't believe technocrats (A) **want to get rid of urban blight;** according to him, the technocrats caused it all. Nor does the final sentence indicate that technocrats (C) **support nature conservation programs,** or (D) **favor large city parks over smaller ones,** or (E) **think that greenery makes cities more attractive.**

9. A

The last three questions ask you to compare and contrast the two passages. To answer this one, look for the choice that accurately covers the subject matter of *both* passages, not just one.

Both passages certainly **criticize aspects of the city,** so (A) seems the right answer, but check out the other choices. (B) is wrong because it doesn't fit *both* passages: Although Passage 1 may **romanticize** parks of a bygone era, Passage 2 focuses on the present. (C) can be eliminated because it's not the primary focus of either passage; besides, only Passage 2 discusses **the origins of urban decay;** Passage 1 talks about the decline of parks. Passage 2 blames **urban problems** on technocrats, not **city residents,** so (D) is out. Finally, (E) doesn't fit because only Passage 1 points out **how city life can be improved.**

10. E

The final paragraph of Passage 2 offers a vision of a beautiful park system, very similar to the description in Passage 1 of the way parks used to be. But Passage 1 says parks have deteriorated considerably in recent decades. So the author of Passage 1 would probably point out that (E) **recent developments have made this [idealized] characterization obsolete.**

(A) is contrary to the evidence of Passage 1. (B) is wrong because **reforms** would improve parks, so the **characterization** in Passage 2 might be true, not **false.** Finally, since the parks in Passage 2 are presented as delightful places, the author of Passage 1 would be foolish to think that (C) **urban planners would reject this characterization** or that (D) **this characterization is in bad taste.**

11. C

The phrase *this urban blight* refers back to the bleak landscape described in the paragraph just above: "rows of squat concrete apartments" and "files of gigantic steel and glass skyscrapers." The author of Passage 1 portrays cities, aside from the parks, as "dark and dreary" environments, with "seemingly endless rows of steel, glass, and concrete buildings." The two pictures are very similar, so the author of Passage 1 would probably find *urban blight* to be (C) **an accurate description of the situation.**

Since the two authors agree on this point, choices (A), (B), and (D) can be eliminated. Finally, neither passage mentions any **new studies,** so (E) is wrong.

Practice Passage 5: Life on Mars

The following passage discusses the possibility that there is life on Mars. Interest in the subject reached a peak when the National Aeronautics and Space Administration sent two unmanned spacecraft to Mars in 1975. After ten months, Vikings 1 and 2 entered orbits around the red planet and released landers.

When the first of the two Viking landers touched down on Martian soil on July 20, 1976, and began to send camera images back to Earth, the scientists at the
Line Jet Propulsion Laboratory could not suppress a certain
(5) nervous anticipation, like people who hold a ticket to a lottery they have a one-in-a-million chance of winning. The first photographs that arrived, however, did not contain any evidence of life. What revealed itself to them was merely a barren landscape littered with rocks
(10) and boulders. The view resembled nothing so much as a flat section of desert—in fact, the winning entry in a contest at J.P.L. for the photograph most accurately predicting what Mars would look like was a snapshot taken in a particularly arid section of the Mojave
(15) Desert.

The scientists were soon ready to turn their attention from visible life to microorganisms. The twin Viking landers carried three experiments designed to detect current biological activity and one to detect
(20) organic compounds, because researchers thought it possible that life had developed on early Mars just as it is thought to have developed on Earth, through the gradual chemical evolution of complex organic molecules. To detect biological activity, Martian soil
(25) samples were treated with various nutrients that would produce characteristic by-products if life forms were active in the soil. The results from all three experiments were inconclusive. The fourth experiment heated a soil sample to look for signs of organic
(30) material but found none, an unexpected result because at least organic compounds from the steady bombardment of the Martian surface by meteorites were thought to have been present.

The absence of organic materials, some scientists
(35) speculated, was the result of intense ultraviolet radiation penetrating the atmosphere of Mars and destroying organic compounds in the soil. Although

Mars' atmosphere was at one time rich in carbon dioxide and thus thick enough to protect its surface
(40) from the harmful rays of the Sun, the carbon dioxide had gradually left the atmosphere and been converted into rocks. This means that even if life had gotten a start on early Mars, it could not have survived the exposure to ultraviolet radiation when the atmosphere
(45) thinned. Mars never developed a protective layer of ozone as Earth did.

Despite the disappointing Viking results, there are those who still keep open the possibility of life on Mars. They point out that the Viking data cannot be
(50) considered the final word on Martian life because the two landers only sampled two limited—and uninteresting—sites. The Viking landing sites were not chosen for what they might tell of the planet's biology. They were chosen primarily because they appeared to
(55) be safe for landing a spacecraft. The landing sites were on parts of the Martian plains that appeared relatively featureless from orbital photographs.

The type of Martian terrain that these researchers suggest may be a possible hiding place for active life
(60) has an Earthly parallel: the ice-free region of southern Victoria Land, Antarctica, where the temperatures in some dry valleys average below zero. Organisms known as endoliths, a form of blue-green algae that has adapted to this harsh environment, were found living
(65) inside certain translucent, porous rocks in these Antarctic valleys. The argument based on this discovery is that if life did exist on early Mars, it is possible that it escaped worsening conditions by similarly seeking refuge in rocks. Skeptics object,
(70) however, that Mars in its present state is simply too dry, even compared with Antarctic valleys, to sustain any life whatsoever.

Should Mars eventually prove to be completely barren of life, as some suspect, then this would have a
(75) significant impact on the current view of the chemical origin of life. It could be much more difficult to get life started on a planet than scientists thought before the Viking landings.

1. The major purpose of the passage is to

    (A) relate an account of an extraordinary scientific achievement
    (B) undermine the prevailing belief that life may exist on Mars
    (C) discuss the efforts of scientists to determine whether Martian life exists
    (D) show the limitations of the scientific investigation of other planets
    (E) examine the relationship between theories about Martian life and evolutionary theory
    Ⓐ Ⓑ Ⓒ Ⓓ Ⓔ

2. In line 4, the word *suppress* most nearly means

    (A) oppose
    (B) vanquish
    (C) prohibit
    (D) stifle
    (E) disguise
    Ⓐ Ⓑ Ⓒ Ⓓ Ⓔ

3. The reference to "people who hold a ticket to a lottery" (lines 5–6) serves to

    (A) point out the human facet of a scientific enterprise
    (B) indicate the expected likelihood of visible Martian life
    (C) show that there was doubt as to whether the camera would function
    (D) imply that any mission to another planet is a risky venture
    (E) reveal how the success of the Viking mission depended largely on chance
    Ⓐ Ⓑ Ⓒ Ⓓ Ⓔ

4. The author uses the evidence from the four Viking experiments (lines 24–33) to establish that

    (A) meteorites do not strike the surface of Mars as often as scientists had thought
    (B) current theory as to how life developed on Earth is probably flawed
    (C) there was no experimental confirmation of the theory that life exists on Mars
    (D) biological activity has been shown to be absent from the surface of Mars
    (E) the experiments were more fruitful than was examination of camera images
    Ⓐ Ⓑ Ⓒ Ⓓ Ⓔ

5. The third paragraph of the passage provides

    (A) an analysis of a theory proposed earlier
    (B) evidence supporting a statement made earlier
    (C) a theory about findings presented earlier
    (D) criticism of experiments discussed earlier
    (E) a synthesis of facts reviewed earlier

6. The author suggests that an important difference between Mars and Earth is that, unlike Earth, Mars

    (A) accumulated organic compounds from the steady bombardment of meteorites
    (B) possessed at one time an atmosphere rich in carbon dioxide
    (C) is in the path of the harmful rays of ultraviolet radiation
    (D) has an atmospheric layer that protects organic compounds
    (E) could not have sustained any life that developed

7. In the fourth paragraph, the author mentions the Viking landing sites (lines 52–55) in order to emphasize which point?

    (A) Although evidence of life was not found by the landers, this does not mean that Mars is devoid of life.
    (B) Although the landing sites were uninteresting, they could have harbored Martian life.
    (C) The Viking mission was unsuccessful largely due to poor selection of the landing sites.
    (D) The detection of life on Mars was not a primary objective of the scientists who sent the Viking landers.
    (E) Scientists were not expecting to discover life on the Martian plains.
    Ⓐ Ⓑ Ⓒ Ⓓ Ⓔ

8. In lines 66–69, the researchers' argument that life may exist in Martian rocks rests on the idea that

   (A) organisms may adopt identical survival strategies in comparable environments
   (B) life developed in the form of blue-green algae on Mars
   (C) life evolved in the same way on two different planets
   (D) endoliths are capable of living in the harsh environment of Mars
   (E) organisms that have survived in Antarctica could survive the Martian environment

   Ⓐ Ⓑ Ⓒ Ⓓ Ⓔ

SCORECARD	
Number of Questions Right:	
Number of Questions Wrong:	
Number of Questions Omitted:	
Number of Correct Guesses:	
Number of Wrong Guesses:	
Time Used:	

ANSWERS AND EXPLANATIONS

Practice Passage 5: Life on Mars

The subject of this science passage is the possibility that life exists, or has existed, on Mars. The first paragraph begins with a description of the scene at the Jet Propulsion Lab when pictures first arrived from the Viking landers on Mars. The second paragraph discusses the Viking experiments designed to detect microscopic signs of life on Mars, and the inconclusive or negative results of these experiments. The theory that some scientists have advanced to explain the negative results is discussed in the third paragraph: Organic materials on Mars might have been destroyed by the lack of protection from ultraviolet radiation.

The topic of the fourth paragraph is the possibility that there is life on Mars, and the two landers simply missed it. The fifth paragraph discusses the suggestion that if life can survive in Antarctica by living inside rocks, maybe life does the same thing on Mars. The author concludes the passage in the sixth paragraph by remarking that the evidence we have from Mars influences scientific theory regarding the chemical origin of life on Earth.

Some of this may have seemed difficult to wade through if you tried to get all of it the first time around, but remember, it isn't necessary to do that. The questions tell you where to go back to get the information you need.

1. C

For this Big Picture question, the answer has to be broad enough to cover the entire passage. We just reviewed the topics of the individual paragraphs; scientists get pictures, scientists run experiments, scientists propose theories and make suggestions throughout the passage. Clearly, the author is discussing the (C) **efforts of scientists.**

Although the Viking mission may have been **an extraordinary scientific achievement,** the author does much more than relate an account of the mission, so (A) is wrong. (B) is out, because the passage presents a balanced view on the question of life on Mars. (D) is wrong, because the only time the author discusses **limitations of the scientific investigation** of Mars is

in the fourth paragraph. (E) is wrong for a similar reason: The **relationship between** life on Mars and **evolutionary theory** is mentioned only in the second and sixth paragraphs.

2. D

This Vocabulary-in-Context question refers to the first sentence of the passage. Go back and read it to understand how *suppress* is being used. The scientists are trying in vain to *suppress,* or (D) **stifle,** their nervous anticipation. (A), (B), and (C) can all be synonyms of *suppress,* but none of them works in the context of the sentence. (E) **disguise** is not a synonym for *suppress.*

3. B

This question focuses on the same sentence as the last did, but you have to read a little further to figure it out. The word *however* in the next sentence indicates that what the scientists hardly dared to hope for (and didn't get) was some visible sign of Martian life. Therefore, the reference to "people who hold a ticket to the lottery" is there to show how **likely** it was that the photographs would show **Martian life** (B).

Although the first paragraph does give you a glimpse of scientists as **humans,** this is not why the author uses the lottery-ticket analogy, so (A) is wrong. (C) is a misreading of the first two sentences; there is nothing there to suggest that the scientists thought the **camera** might not **function.** (D) and (E) miss the mark completely by being far too broad.

4. C

You know by the end of the second paragraph that the experiments designed to detect biological life were inconclusive, and that no organic materials were found, either. There was, therefore, (C) **no experimental confirmation of the theory that life exists on Mars,** and that is all that the author is establishing here.

Several of the other choices may have tempted you, but they all involve making unsupported inferences. Just because there weren't organic materials from meteorites on Mars doesn't mean that (A) **meteorites do not strike the surface of Mars as often as scientists thought.** The author never implies that the (B) **theory**

as to how life developed on Earth is probably flawed. (D) is off because it is too sweeping. These four experiments were not the evidence to prove or disprove the existence of life on Mars. Finally, (E) can be eliminated because the experiments certainly didn't tell scientists much more than the photographs did.

5.   C

Here you need an understanding of the role the third paragraph plays in the context of the passage as a whole. Reread the end of the second paragraph and the beginning of the third. In the second paragraph, the author states that a Viking experiment turned up no trace of organic material on the Martian surface. The third paragraph presents the theory that UV radiation may have destroyed any organic materials once present in the Martian soil. So the third paragraph provides (C) **a theory about findings presented earlier.**

The **theory** is not **proposed earlier** in the passage, so (A) is out. The third paragraph does not give (B) **evidence supporting a statement made earlier,** nor does it (D) **criticize** anything. Finally, there is nothing like **facts reviewed earlier** in the third paragraph, so (E) can be eliminated.

6.   E

The author mentions Earth in the passage at the end of the third paragraph, where he says that Mars "never developed a protective layer of ozone as Earth did." Since it is life that the ozone layer protected on Earth, you can infer that Mars was not able to support life, (E), as Earth was.

(A) is wrong because it contradicts information from the passage that says that no organic compounds were found on Mars. (B) is out, because although Mars **possessed at one time an atmosphere rich in carbon dioxide,** the author never suggests that Earth *didn't.* Mars and Earth are both **in the path of the ultraviolet radiation** of the Sun, so (C) is out. Finally, (D) reverses Mars and Earth: Earth is the planet with **an atmospheric layer that protects organic compounds** from UV radiation, not Mars.

7.   A

Reread the sentences surrounding the reference to Viking landing sites, and look for a paraphrase among the answer choices. Those who still think that there might be life on Mars point out that there were only two Viking landers, that the experimental sites were limited and uninteresting, and that scientists were not concerned about finding life when they chose the landing spots. In other words, they are saying that (A) **although evidence of life was not found by the landers, this does not mean that Mars is devoid of life.**

Forget about choice (B); although the statement is true, this isn't why the author mentions the landing sites. The author never says that the Viking mission was **unsuccessful** or that the **selection** of landing sites was **poor,** so (C) is wrong. Choices (D) and (E) focus on the intentions and expectations of the scientists. All you know is that they wanted to land the spacecrafts safely, not whether they thought detection of life was a (D) **primary objective** or whether they (E) **expected to discover life on the Martian plains.**

8.   A

The argument of the researchers in the fifth paragraph is that, if endoliths could adapt to the harsh conditions of Antarctica by living in rocks, maybe some form of life did the same thing to survive on early Mars. The idea here is that Mars and Antarctica are (A) **comparable environments** and that life may adapt in the same way, or **adopt identical strategies,** to survive.

All of the wrong choices are based on distortions of the argument. Choices (B) and (D) are both wrong because the argument never states that **endoliths** or **blue-green algae** have anything to do with Mars; they were found in Antarctica and merely became the subject of speculation for the researchers. Choice (C) is too broad: Scientists think that organisms may have adapted to similar environments in similar ways, but this doesn't mean that all of **life evolved in the same way** on the two planets. That idea comes into play in the second paragraph, not in the fifth. As for (E), the author never suggests that the endoliths or any other type of organism **that has survived in Antarctica could survive** on Mars.

Practice Passage 6: TV in Courts

The role of television in the courtroom has been debated by members of the judicial system for the last two decades. Those who favor its presence are of the opinion that broadcasting courtroom proceedings is fully consistent with the ideal of the "public's right to know." Others believe that television distorts the judicial process by creating a theatrical atmosphere in the courtroom.

The following are excerpts from a speech about this issue given by a retired Chief Judge of New York State at a Pre-law Association meeting.

Justice is the most profound aspiration of men and women on earth; it is the allotment to each person of that to which he or she is entitled; it exists only when
Line there has been adherence to principles of honesty and
(5) fairness and disregard of other considerations.

Down through the centuries, the character of a particular government or civilization could be measured best by the sort of justice meted out to its citizens. In the more advanced and more humane
(10) governances, trials have taken place in courtrooms to which the public has been admitted. On the other hand, secret trials have almost invariably been the telltale sign of oppressive and autocratic regimes. Indeed, the grant of a fair trial is the greatest contribution of any
(15) jurisprudence.

The difference in openness is not without significance. It is not a matter of mere entertainment. It is far more serious than that. First, and foremost, unobstructed courtrooms are a guarantee of fairness
(20) and justice. Furthermore, the public officials functioning therein can be observed so that those performing well may be retained and those not may be replaced.

Courtrooms with "open doors" have always been
(25) a fetish for me. I stood here in this city sixteen years ago and in an interview announced that I favored cameras in the courts. Broadcasting from courtrooms was unpopular then and there were only four states in the Union permitting television of judicial
(30) proceedings. My response shocked many in this state. When the Chief Judgeship came my way, a rule was adopted permitting television and still cameras in the appellate courts of our jurisdiction and it was a

success. I worked long and hard in favor of an
(35) amendment of the Civil Rights Law to allow photography in the trial courts. I am pleased that that is now reality.

However, I am worried. I am worried about what seems to be an increasing antipathy toward the media
(40) and concurrent attempts to narrow the doors leading into courtrooms by distinguishing ancillary or supplemental proceedings from trials themselves. Freedom of the press and open courtrooms go together.

I believe in the First Amendment. I believe with
(45) might and main in the constitutional guarantee of freedom of the press, not merely to curry favor with those of the "Fourth Estate," not merely as an aid to the media in its varied shapes and forms, but more as a benefit for all the people. A broadly defined freedom of
(50) the press assures the maintenance of our political system of democracy, social equality, and public exposure. Indeed, the strength of America, different from any nation in the world, lies in its openness.

1. In line 16, the word *openness* most probably means

   (A) candor
   (B) tolerance
   (C) receptivity
   (D) friendliness
   (E) accessibility

   Ⓐ Ⓑ Ⓒ Ⓓ Ⓔ

2. The information in lines 38–43 suggests that the judge is very concerned about

   (A) restrictions being placed upon people opposed to media participation in the judicial process
   (B) undermining the rights of the accused by giving the media too much access to the judicial process
   (C) media abuse of the First Amendment to distort the judicial process
   (D) harm being caused to the judicial process by a distaste for the media
   (E) encouraging those who favor a narrow definition of civil rights by allowing the media to participate in the judicial process

   Ⓐ Ⓑ Ⓒ Ⓓ Ⓔ

3. The judge's point about the role of the media in the judicial process is made mainly through

    (A) general statements
    (B) specific examples
    (C) statistical data
    (D) long citations
    (E) scientific evidence

    Ⓐ Ⓑ Ⓒ Ⓓ Ⓔ

4. In lines 44–53, the judge reflects on the

    (A) strengths and weaknesses of the judicial system
    (B) attitude of the judicial system toward the media
    (C) role of a free press in maintaining a democratic society
    (D) ability of the media to function effectively in the courtroom
    (E) connection between the First Amendment and the Civil Rights Law

    Ⓐ Ⓑ Ⓒ Ⓓ Ⓔ

5. Which best describes the judge's view of cameras in the courtroom?

    (A) Cameras do not play a useful part in determining which members of the judicial system are competent and which members are incompetent.
    (B) While the First Amendment gives the media the right to bring cameras into the courtroom, their use has impaired the proper functioning of the judicial system.
    (C) Judicial systems that allow cameras into the courtroom are no more likely to be fair than judicial systems which do not admit them.
    (D) Regardless of the fact that many members of the judicial system do not approve of their presence, cameras should be permitted in every courtroom.
    (E) Oppressive and autocratic regimes are likely to place cameras in the courtroom to deter their subjects from committing criminal acts.

    Ⓐ Ⓑ Ⓒ Ⓓ Ⓔ

SCORECARD	
Number of Questions Right:	
Number of Questions Wrong:	
Number of Questions Omitted:	
Number of Correct Guesses:	
Number of Wrong Guesses:	
Time Used:	

ANSWERS AND EXPLANATIONS

Practice Passage 6: TV in Courts

This is a strong statement of an individual point of view. You may naturally respond by taking a stand yourself, for or against the author. But the questions never ask for your personal point of view. They ask only about the author's opinion.

In reading, skim over the first few paragraphs. Look for a definite statement of the author's opinion, which you get in paragraph four—the author favors cameras in court. This puts the rest of the passage in perspective. Don't worry about the details of the argument. Questions about details will be easy to answer based on specific context.

1.   E

This is another Vocabulary-in-Context question. As used in paragraph three, *openness* refers to the discussion in paragraph two about whether the public can be admitted to the courtroom. (E) **accessibility** best defines this sense of *openness*.

The other choices are all possible meanings of *openness*, but none fits the context. (A) **candor,** or frankness, refers to openness of one's own opinions; (B) **tolerance** is openness to other people or their views; (C) **receptivity** implies a willingness to be convinced. (D) **friendliness** suggests an outgoing nature, which doesn't match what the author is saying here.

2.   D

In paragraph five the author worries over "antipathy," or dislike, towards the media. This is paraphrased as **distaste** in (D). The **harm . . . to the judicial process** in this answer choice arises from the author's strong belief that media access is good for the judicial process, as expressed earlier.

If you know the author favors cameras, or *media participation,* you're likely to pick the right answer. The other four choices, in different ways, say the author worries about too *much* media participation; they contradict the author's point of view.

3.   A

Paragraphs one through three and paragraph six all contain broad arguments about the nature of justice, the need for public trials, and the importance of freedom of the press—(A) **general statements.** The author gives no (B) **specific examples** of how courtroom openness works, though there is one example of the author's own activity (paragraph four). The passage never uses (C) **statistics** or (E) **scientific** findings, and never refers to judicial decisions or other writings or speeches (D).

4.   C

This question asks about paragraph six, which discusses freedom of the press and its importance in upholding democracy, equality, and other American values (C).

Since the passage as a whole discusses **the attitude of the judicial system** to **the media,** you might be tempted to choose (B). But this is not a Big Picture question; you're asked to focus here only on certain lines from paragraph six. Similarly, (A) **strengths and weaknesses of the judicial system**—or strong and weak judicial systems—get discussed only in paragraph two. And while paragraph six mentions (E) **the First Amendment,** it never mentions the **Civil Rights Law.** Finally, (D) how **the media function in the courtroom** is never discussed.

5.   D

Here's a Big Picture question. You're looking for the answer choice that *best describes* the overall point of view. Since the author strongly supports cameras in the courts (paragraph four) and the whole passage defends this view, your answer must be (D), the only pro-camera choice. (D) acknowledges the opposition to cameras that the author notes in paragraph five, but says this opposition should be disregarded—as the author implies, too (paragraph six).

Choice (A) contradicts a minor point the author raises in the last part of paragraph three. (B) distorts what paragraph six says about the **First Amendment,** as well as the author's pro-media position. (C) contradicts the general sense of paragraph two, though **cameras** are not specifically discussed there. (E) refers to the discussion of **oppressive regimes** in this same paragraph, but the author never raises this point.

Suggested Time: 9 Minutes

Directions: Answer the questions below based on the information in the accompanying passage.

Practice Passage 7: Rosemary

In the following excerpt from a novella, Rosemary, an elderly woman, reminisces about her childhood as she waits for her grandson to wake up.

Rosemary sat at her kitchen table, working a crossword puzzle. Crosswords were nice; they filled the time, and kept the mind active. She needed just one
Line word to complete this morning's puzzle; the clue was
(5) "a Swiss river," and the first of its three letters was "A." Unfortunately, Rosemary had no idea what the name of the river was, and could not look it up. Her atlas was on her desk, and the desk was in the guest room, currently being occupied by her grandson Victor. Looking up
(10) over the tops of her bifocals, Rosemary glanced at the kitchen clock: it was almost 10 a.m. *Land sakes!* Did the boy intend to sleep all day? She noticed that the arthritis in her wrist was throbbing, and put down her pen. At eighty-seven years of age, she was glad she
(15) could still write at all. She had decided long ago that growing old was like slowly turning to stone; you couldn't take anything for granted. She stood up slowly, painfully, and started walking to the guest room.
(20) The trip, though only a distance of about twenty-five feet, seemed to take a long while. Late in her ninth decade now, Rosemary often experienced an expanded sense of time, with present and past tense intermingling in her mind. One minute she was
(25) padding in her slippers across the living room carpet, the next she was back on the farm where she'd grown up, a sturdy little girl treading the path behind the barn just before dawn. In her mind's eye, she could still pick her way among the stones in the darkness, more than
(30) seventy years later . . . . Rosemary arrived at the door to the guest room. It stood slightly ajar, and she peered through the opening. Victor lay sleeping on his side, his arms bent, his expression slightly pained. *Get up, lazy bones,* she wanted to say. Even in childhood,
(35) Rosemary had never slept past 4 a.m.; there were too many chores to do. How different things were for Victor's generation! Her youngest grandson behaved as if he had never done a chore in his life. Twenty-one years old, he had driven down to Florida to visit
(40) Rosemary in his shiny new car, a gift from his doting parents. Victor would finish college soon, and his

future appeared bright—if he ever got out of bed, that is.

Something Victor had said last night over dinner
(45) had disturbed her. Now what was it? Oh yes; he had been talking about one of his college courses—a "gut," he had called it. When she had asked him to explain the term, Victor had said it was a course that you took simply because it was easy to pass. Rosemary, who had
(50) not even had a high school education, found the term repellent. If she had been allowed to continue her studies, she would never have taken a "gut" . . . The memory flooded back then, still painful as an open wound all these years later. It was the first day of high
(55) school. She had graduated from grammar school the previous year, but her father had forbidden her to go on to high school that fall, saying she was needed on the farm. After much tearful pleading, she had gotten him to promise that next year, she could start high school.
(60) She had endured a whole year of chores instead of books, with animals and rough farmhands for company instead of people her own age. Now, at last, the glorious day was at hand. She had put on her best dress (she owned two), her heart racing in anticipation.
(65) But her father was waiting for her as she came downstairs.

"Where do you think you're going?" he asked.

"To high school, Papa."

"No you're not. Take that thing off and get back to
(70) work."

"But Papa, you promised!"

"Do as I say!" he thundered.

There was no arguing with Papa when he spoke that way. Tearfully, she had trudged upstairs to change
(75) clothes. Rosemary still wondered what her life would have been like if her father had not been waiting at the bottom of the stairs that day, or if somehow she had found the strength to defy him . . . .

Suddenly, Victor stirred, without waking, and
(80) mumbled something unintelligible. Jarred from her reverie, Rosemary stared at Victor. She wondered if he were having a nightmare.

1. Rosemary's attitude toward the physical afflictions of old age can best be described as one of

   (A) acceptance
   (B) sadness
   (C) resentment
   (D) anxiety
   (E) optimism

2. Rosemary's walk to the guest room (lines 20–31) reveals that she

   (A) feels nostalgia for her family
   (B) is anxious about Victor
   (C) is determined to conquer her ailments
   (D) has an elastic perception of time
   (E) suffers from severe disorientation

3. In context, "if he ever got out of bed" (line 42) suggests that Rosemary thinks Victor

   (A) lacks a sense of humor
   (B) is ashamed of what he said last night
   (C) is promising but undisciplined
   (D) works himself to exhaustion
   (E) has failed to plan for the future

4. The reason Rosemary finds Victor's use of the term *gut* (line 46) repellent is because it

   (A) has unpleasant digestive associations
   (B) is typical of Victor's disregard for traditional values
   (C) signifies a disrespect for education
   (D) reminds Rosemary of her grammar school classes
   (E) implies that Rosemary is lacking in education

5. Lines 60–62 indicate that, for Rosemary, the year after she graduated from grammar school was

   (A) marred by illness and hardship
   (B) filled with travel and adventure
   (C) a year of reading and study
   (D) spent isolated from her peers
   (E) difficult because of her father's temper

   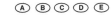

6. Rosemary's memory of the day she finally prepared to start high school indicates that she had

   (A) anticipated her father's command to stay home
   (B) hesitated over her choice of clothes
   (C) done especially well in grammar school
   (D) already decided to pursue a career
   (E) strongly desired to continue her education

7. The passage as a whole is most concerned with

   (A) Rosemary's affectionate concern for Victor
   (B) Rosemary's struggle to suppress painful memories
   (C) the abusive treatment Rosemary suffered at the hands of her father
   (D) the interplay in Rosemary's mind between present and past
   (E) whether Rosemary will wake Victor up

SCORECARD	
Number of Questions Right:	
Number of Questions Wrong:	
Number of Questions Omitted:	
Number of Correct Guesses:	
Number of Wrong Guesses:	
Time Used:	

ANSWERS AND EXPLANATIONS

Practice Passage 7: Rosemary

Next up is a fiction passage about Rosemary, an elderly woman, who recalls parts of her childhood as she waits for her grandson Victor to wake up. There's nothing too difficult here. The most interesting thing about this passage is the way it swings back and forth between the present and the past, by way of Rosemary's wandering mind. Notice the contrast between Victor's cavalier attitude towards his schooling and Rosemary's painful memories of being denied an education—that's sure to generate some questions. Let's take a look at them now.

1. A

The last four sentences of paragraph one discuss Rosemary's attitude towards old age. Thankful that she could write at all, she decided that growing old was like turning to stone: "You couldn't take anything for granted." The attitude that best sums this up is (A) **acceptance.**

She doesn't talk about things she can't do or misses, so (B) **sadness** is incorrect. Since she's not complaining or worrying, (C) and (D) are wrong, too. And though Rosemary is not unhappy, (E) **optimism** is too positive. There's no sense that she believes her life is going to improve.

2. D

A Little Picture question. When we read the lines around the lines cited, we see that the trip, though short, "seemed to take a long while," and that Rosemary "often experienced an expanded sense of time." (D) restates this perfectly, since **elastic** means to be able to expand and contract.

(A) is wrong because at this point in the passage, she's just thinking about her life on the farm, not her **family.** Though Rosemary may be anxious about **Victor,** he is not mentioned in the lines cited in the stem, so (B) is also wrong. (C) tries to catch you because it picks up on the gist of the last question, but in lines 20–32, she is not thinking about her physical problems. Finally, (E) is much too strong, even though it's related to (D).

Rosemary's mind is flooded with memories of her childhood, but she's not **severely disoriented.**

3. C

Rosemary refers to Victor as a "lazy bones" who's been given every advantage by his "doting parents . . . his future appeared bright—*if he ever got out of bed,* that is." (C) sums up that idea well.

HINT: *When you see the phrase in context in a question stem, always find the "keyed" part of the passage and start reading a few lines earlier.*

There's nothing in the passage about Victor's **sense of humor,** so (A) is unsupported. (B) is out of context and remember, this is a context question. Victor's remark isn't discussed until paragraph three. (D) is almost the exact opposite of what the cited lines say about Rosemary's feelings towards Victor. (E) sounds right, but it makes an assumption that's not supported in the passage. Rosemary says his "future appeared bright." Victor may be lazy, but the only things we know about his future are positive.

4. C

The line reference points you to the start of paragraph three. Notice the definition of the term *gut*—"a course you took simply because it was easy to pass." Rosemary thinks the word is "repellent," a very strong word, and believes that "if she had been allowed to continue her studies, she would never had taken a 'gut.'" Obviously, Rosemary has different feelings about education than did Victor. Given her **respect for education,** you can infer that she is reacting to what she feels is Victor's lack of respect. (C) is the right choice.

No one is talking about anyone's stomach here, so (A) is just silly. (B) feels close, but since the passage is concerned only with education and not things like family, religious beliefs, and society, it's too vague to be correct. (D) suggests that Rosemary didn't enjoy her own schooling, which we know is false. It's true that the word upsets her because it makes her think about her experiences, but the experiences were good ones. She's not repelled by thinking about them. Finally, while Rosemary may not have a broad education, Victor was only referring to his own classes. (E) is definitely wrong.

5. D

Again, go straight to the lines cited in the question stem, here one sentence at the end of the third paragraph. "She had endured a whole year of chores instead of books, with animals and rough farmhands for company instead of people her own age." Comparing the answer choices to this clear statement, we see that (D) is the right selection. Her **peers** are "people her own age."

Working on the farm may have been hard, but **illness** is never mentioned, so (A) is out. In fact, Rosemary is referred to as "a sturdy little girl." Since she was on the farm the whole time, she could not have been **traveling** and having **adventures,** as (B) claims. The phrase says that she spent the year with "chores instead of books," so (C) directly contradicts the stem. (E) may be tempting, because it's true that her **father** had a **temper.** This isn't mentioned, however, as a reason the year is so difficult, so (E) is wrong.

HINT: *If you have a choice between an answer that paraphrases something in the cited context and an answer that may be true but has no direct reference in the text, go with the paraphrase.*

6. E

Even though the stem doesn't direct you to a specific point of reference, this is a relatively easy question. The question refers to Rosemary on that "glorious" day when she was going to high school, which is found near the end of paragraph three. She gets up, puts on her "best dress, her heart racing in anticipation." All together, these facts point to (E) as the right choice.

Though you may have **anticipated** that Rosemary's father would stop her from going to school, there's no evidence that Rosemary did, so (A) is wrong. Remember that Rosemary had only two dresses, which makes it unlikely that she **hesitated** in **her choice,** as (B) says. Again, as with (A) you may be tempted to make an assumption with (C) that's not supported. The passage makes it clear that Rosemary enjoyed **grammar school,** but nowhere does it says she did **especially well.** Same with (D): One can guess that she wanted a **career,** but nothing is said about it in the passage.

7. D

A Big Picture question. What is the primary concern of the passage?

Though Victor is important in this passage, his real role is to awaken thoughts in Rosemary about her **past.** Most of the passage is about Rosemary and her life. When you look at the answer choices, (D) is really the only one that addresses this in a wide enough way.

(A) is too narrow. It deals only with Victor and doesn't take into account all the memories Rosemary has. (B) feels close, but we never get the sense that she's trying to **suppress** the **unhappy memories.** (C) is a distortion; we're told that Rosemary was forbidden from attending school, but there's no suggestion she was victimized by her **father.** (E) is too trivial. This is a small and incorrect answer to a Big Picture question.

HINT: *Take a few seconds (no more) to predict an answer. Then find a choice that best matches your prediction.*

Suggested Time: 13 Minutes

Directions: Answer the questions below based on the information in the accompanying passages.

Practice Passage 8: Miles Davis Pair

This pair of passages presents contrasting views of the music of jazz trumpeter Miles Davis, who died in 1993. The author of Passage 1 argues that Davis's artistry reached its peak in the 1950s. The author of Passage 2 claims that Davis remained an important creative force in jazz to the end of his life.

Passage 1

The recent death of trumpeter Miles Davis brought an end to one of the most celebrated careers in the history of jazz. Few musicians have ever enjoyed
Line such popularity for so long. Much has been made of
(5) Davis's influence on the historical development of jazz, his ability to "show the way" to other musicians. Yet it must be said that Miles reached the artistic high point of his career in the 1950s.

Davis came to New York City from the Midwest in
(10) the mid-1940s while still a teenager. Studying at the Juilliard School of Music by day, he haunted the city's jazz clubs by night, receiving another education entirely. Bebop, the hot, frantic new sound in jazz, was being played by such musical revolutionaries as
(15) Charlie Parker, Dizzy Gillespie, and Thelonious Monk, and Davis was sometimes invited up on the bandstand to play with them. Though obviously talented, Davis had to struggle to keep up with these musicians, and he worked tirelessly to perfect his
(20) technique.

Even at this early stage, Davis's sound and style on trumpet set him apart. Rather than filling the air with a headlong rush of musical notes, as other bebop musicians did, Davis played sparingly. He seemed
(25) more interested in the silences between the notes than in the notes themselves. This less-is-more approach became the basis of "Cool" jazz, the counter-revolution Davis led which dominated West Coast jazz in the 1950s. The Miles Davis quintet set the standard
(30) for all other jazz combos of the era, and produced a series of recordings culminating in the classic *Kind of Blue.*

Although *Kind of Blue* represents the high-water mark of Davis's career, his artistic decline was not
(35) immediately apparent. In the early 1960s, playing with a different set of musicians, he produced some

excellent albums. But the end was near. His last pure jazz album is named, fittingly enough, *In a Silent Way.* After issuing this recording in 1969, Davis turned his
(40) back on traditional jazz, disappointingly opting for an electronic "fusion" sound that blurred the lines between jazz and rock. Yes, he continued to enjoy a lucrative recording career and public adulation. But for all those who learned to love jazz by listening to the
(45) plaintive sounds of the Miles Davis of the 1950s, it was as if he had already fallen silent.

Passage 2

Miles Davis was a protean* figure in jazz; like some musical Picasso, he mastered and then shed a series of styles throughout the course of his career.
(50) This is rare in any artist, but almost unheard of in the world of jazz, where a musician's style is usually formed extremely early, and then refined and repeated for the remainder of his or her life. Although Davis could have earned millions by continuing to play the
(55) music that had first made him famous in the 1950s, he refused to repeat himself. He consistently sought to expand his musical horizons, working with young, emerging musicians, restlessly searching for new sounds.

(60) After cutting his teeth on the bebop jazz of the 1940s, Davis developed a "cooler" style and made his name in the 1950s with a five-man combo. The so-called "purists" have often claimed that this period represents the zenith of Davis's achievement. But this
(65) argument reveals more about the narrow tastes of certain critics than it does about the supposed limitations of Miles Davis. The groups Davis led in the 1960s featured a new generation of superb musicians such as Wayne Shorter and Herbie Hancock, and
(70) produced music that explored new and complex rhythmic textures.

Yet critics continued to complain. And when Davis released *Bitches Brew* in 1970, the jazz "purists" were horrified: His band was using electronic
(75) instruments, and its music borrowed heavily from rock rhythms and the psychedelic sound of "acid" rock. Typically, Davis ignored the storm of protest, secure in his artistic vision. Throughout the early 1970s, he continued to attract the best new players to his side.
(80) They benefited from his vast experience and mastery, and he from their youthful energy and fresh approach to the music.

After a six-year retirement brought on by illness, Davis re-emerged in 1981. Ever willing to court
(85) controversy, he wore outrageous clothes, grew his hair long, and even did a television commercial. But

musically, Davis was as exciting as ever. Once again, he sought out some of the finest young musicians, and played to great acclaim. A restless innovator to the end (90) of his life, Miles Davis deserves his place as the dominant figure in jazz in the second half of the 20th century.

*protean: able to assume different shapes or roles

1. In paragraph 1, the phrase *show the way* most nearly means

   (A) lead a band
   (B) bring publicity to
   (C) teach novice musicians
   (D) affect the creative development of
   (E) compose music of high quality

   Ⓐ Ⓑ Ⓒ Ⓓ Ⓔ

2. The author suggests that "Cool" jazz was a "counter-revolution" (lines 26–29) because it

   (A) reflected Davis's unique sound on trumpet
   (B) improved the quality of jazz on the West Coast
   (C) marked Davis's emergence as the premier trumpeter of his generation
   (D) represented a stylistic alternative to bebop jazz
   (E) grew out of Davis's disagreements with Parker, Gillespie, and Monk

   Ⓐ Ⓑ Ⓒ Ⓓ Ⓔ

3. In lines 35–37, when discussing the Davis group of the early 1960s, the author of Passage 1 suggests that

   (A) critics persuaded Davis that he should reject the "Cool" sound of the 1950s
   (B) Davis's individual style of play became even more spare and economical
   (C) Davis continued to produce music of high quality even though past his prime
   (D) musicians and audiences alike began treating Davis with increased respect
   (E) Davis gave up electronic instruments and returned to playing traditional jazz

   Ⓐ Ⓑ Ⓒ Ⓓ Ⓔ

4. The author of Passage 1 suggests that the music Miles Davis played after *In a Silent Way*

   (A) ignored current musical trends
   (B) alienated most of his listeners
   (C) revived bebop jazz
   (D) disappointed influential music critics
   (E) remained highly profitable

   Ⓐ Ⓑ Ⓒ Ⓓ Ⓔ

5. By saying that "it was as if he had already fallen silent" (lines 45–46), the author of Passage 1 suggests that

   (A) it would have been preferable if Davis had not played at all, rather than play "fusion" jazz
   (B) by 1970, Davis no longer had the ability to play in the plaintive style that had made him famous
   (C) people who loved traditional jazz stopped buying recordings after the use of electronic instruments became popular
   (D) Davis lost most of his popular following when he began to blur the lines between jazz and rock music
   (E) younger listeners learned about jazz in a completely different way than those who had first heard it in the 1950s

   Ⓐ Ⓑ Ⓒ Ⓓ Ⓔ

6. The author of Passage 2 suggests that, unlike Miles Davis, most jazz musicians

   (A) find it difficult to earn a living playing music
   (B) know very little about the tradition of jazz
   (C) solidify their playing style early in life
   (D) refuse to work with musicians younger than themselves
   (E) prefer to play a "hot" style of jazz

   Ⓐ Ⓑ Ⓒ Ⓓ Ⓔ

7. The phrase *cutting his teeth* (line 60) most nearly means

   (A) getting excited about
   (B) acquiring skill
   (C) becoming injured by
   (D) memorizing fully
   (E) criticizing sharply

   Ⓐ Ⓑ Ⓒ Ⓓ Ⓔ

8. The references in Passage 2 to "purists" (line 63) and "supposed limitations" (lines 66–67) serve to

   (A) emphasize the shortcomings of Miles Davis as a bebop player
   (B) show what Davis might have accomplished had he continued to play "cool" jazz
   (C) give an assessment of Davis's reaction to his critics
   (D) criticize those who would say negative things about Miles Davis
   (E) prove that Davis entered a period of artistic decline in the 1960s

   Ⓐ Ⓑ Ⓒ Ⓓ Ⓔ

9. According to the author of Passage 2, the relationship between Davis and the musicians he played with in the early 1970s can best be summarized as which of the following?

   (A) It was similar to that of teacher and pupil.
   (B) It was filled with dissension and conflict.
   (C) It was the focus of critical acclaim.
   (D) It lacked the "chemistry" of Davis's earlier groups.
   (E) It was mutually beneficial.

   Ⓐ Ⓑ Ⓒ Ⓓ Ⓔ

10. The author of Passage 1 would most likely react to the characterization of Miles Davis as a "restless innovator" (line 89) by arguing that

    (A) Davis was no longer the dominant figure in jazz after 1950
    (B) only a critic can properly judge the extent of a musician's artistic achievement
    (C) Davis should have concentrated less on innovation and more on perfecting his technique
    (D) the artistic quality of any musical innovation depends largely on the caliber of the musicians involved
    (E) Davis should have realized that change for change's sake is not always a positive thing

    Ⓐ Ⓑ Ⓒ Ⓓ Ⓔ

11. Both passages are primarily concerned with

    (A) describing the evolution of jazz from the 1940s onward
    (B) explaining why Miles Davis continually played with new groups of musicians
    (C) showing how the music of Miles Davis was heavily influenced by bebop jazz
    (D) evaluating the career and achievements of Miles Davis
    (E) indicating the high point of Miles Davis's career

    Ⓐ Ⓑ Ⓒ Ⓓ Ⓔ

SCORECARD

Number of Questions Right:	
Number of Questions Wrong:	
Number of Questions Omitted:	
Number of Correct Guesses:	
Number of Wrong Guesses:	
Time Used:	

ANSWERS AND EXPLANATIONS

Practice Passage 8: Miles Davis Pair

In this pair of passages about jazz trumpet player Miles Davis, each author has a different take on Davis's career. Passage 1 says Davis played his best music in the 1950s and then went off in the wrong direction—eventually switching to electronic instruments and borrowing from rock music. Passage 2 celebrates the very thing Passage 1 criticizes: Davis's ability to change styles over the course of his career. You don't need to be a musical expert to do well here. The paragraphs of each passage are organized chronologically, which makes it doubly easy to go back and relocate material pertinent to the questions.

1. D

Look at the entire third sentence in which the keyed phrase occurs: "Much has been made of Davis's influence on the historical development of jazz, his ability to 'show the way' to other musicians." "Show the way" is equivalent in meaning to "influenc[ing] the historical development of jazz." So (D) is best: Davis was able to **affect the creative development** of other musicians, even his peers, which is one reason he was so influential.

(A) **leading a band,** (B) **bringing publicity to** jazz, and even (E) **composing** excellent **music** can all be done without necessarily being historically influential. Likewise, (C) **teaching novice** jazz players influences *their* development, but not necessarily the historical development of jazz.

2. D

Paragraph three of Passage 1 says Davis played differently from other bebop players. Earlier, paragraph two describes bebop jazz as "the hot, frantic new sound" being played by "revolutionaries." So the "Cool" sound Davis developed was "counter-revolutionary" because stylistically it differed dramatically from bebop. Correct choice (D) restates this idea.

(A) and (B) touch on other details mentioned in paragraph three, but neither creates the direct opposition of "revolution" and "counter-revolution." (C) distorts the final sentence of paragraph three, which says that Davis's quintet "set the standard" for all other jazz combos of the era. The author of Passage 1 never calls Davis the **premier trumpeter of his generation.** Finally, (E) is plausible but unsupported by the text. We don't know whether Davis **disagreed** with beboppers **Parker, Gillespie, and Monk** or simply followed his own instincts.

3. C

This inference question is keyed to the top of the last paragraph of Passage 1. The author says that, after the "high-water mark" of *Kind of Blue*, Davis's "artistic decline was not immediately apparent"; that in the early 1960s he played with another group and "produced some excellent albums." So (C) is correct: In the 1960s Davis still made **high-quality music, although** he was **past his prime.**

Critics are not mentioned in Passage 1, so choice (A) is a poor guess. Nor does the author say Davis's playing became (B) **more economical.** (D) distorts the assertion, near the end of Passage 1, that Davis "continued to enjoy . . . public adulation." This suggests that his popularity remained high, not that it **increased.** And (E) gets it backwards: Davis gave up traditional jazz and turned to electronic instruments.

4. E

This is a question about Davis's music after 1969. In Passage 1, the second half of the last paragraph says that after *In a Silent Way*, Davis "turned his back on traditional jazz," so you can eliminate choice (C). (A) is wrong because Davis *was* influenced during this time by **current trends**—i.e., by rock music. (B) is wrong because Davis "continued to enjoy . . . public adulation."

(D) is tempting, but we don't know that Passage 1 was written by a critic, and the author never suggests that **influential music critics** were **disappointed.** That leaves (E) as correct. It's based on the reference to Davis continuing to enjoy a "lucrative recording career."

5. A

This is a question about the last sentence of Passage 1. The phrase *fallen silent* intentionally echoes the title of *In a Silent Way,* the album that marked the end of

Davis's traditional jazz playing. The suggestion is that Davis *should have* fallen silent, rather than make music the author disliked. Correct choice (A) restates this.

(B) is wrong because there's no suggestion that Davis was **unable** to play traditional jazz. Rather, he *chose* to play a different style. (C) is completely unwarranted; we know nothing about the record-buying habits of **people who love traditional jazz.** (D) is contradicted by the reference to Davis continuing to enjoy public adulation. And (E) has nothing to do with the issue of Davis falling silent.

6. C

Now you're into Passage 2. The first paragraph says Davis "mastered and then shed a variety of styles" during his career. It goes on to say that this is rare in the jazz world, "where a musician's style is usually formed extremely early, and then refined and repeated for the remainder of his or her life." So choice (C) is correct: Davis is different from most jazz players, who **solidify their playing style early in life.**

(A) is wrong: We're told Davis earned "millions," but the passage never mentions whether most jazz musicians find it hard **to earn a living.** There's no evidence for (B) or (D). And (E) refers only to bebop players, not *most jazz musicians.*

7. B

We talk about babies teething or cutting their first teeth. The figurative use of the phrase conveys the image of a beginner learning and improving, which points to (B) **acquiring skill** as correct. If you aren't familiar with this expression, information in Passage 1 can help you answer correctly. Davis "cut his teeth" on the bebop in the 1940s, at the earliest phase of his career.

(A) has nothing to do with "cutting one's teeth." (C) and (E) try to distract you by playing off the use of the verb *cut,* (C) literally and (E) figuratively. Memorization (D) is related to learning, but doesn't fit the cliché; you don't always need to **memorize** in order to acquire skill.

8. D

The question stem quotes from two successive sentences in paragraph two of Passage 2, and a careful reading of context helps here. Responding to critics who think Davis's 1950s music was the "zenith," or highest point, of his career, the author argues that this "reveals more about the narrow tastes of . . . critics than it does about the supposed limitations of Miles Davis." In other words, the author is attacking Davis's critics; (D) is correct.

(A), (B), and (E) incorrectly focus on Davis's music instead of his detractors, and (C) wrongly puts the author's words in Davis's mouth.

9. E

Always check the context—in this case, the last two sentences of paragraph three. During the early '70s, Davis played with the best young jazz musicians, who "benefited from his vast experience and mastery," as he did from their "youthful energy and fresh approach." In other words, both sides got something good; the relationship **was mutually beneficial,** so (E) is correct.

(A) fails on two counts: First, Davis was playing with the younger musicians as peers, and second, **teacher-pupil** relationships are not necessarily mutually beneficial. The passage suggests neither (B) **conflict** between Davis and the young players, nor a drop-off in (D) **"chemistry."** Finally, in (C), the critics did not praise the work of Davis and the musicians he played with; on the contrary, in 1970 purists complained when his band was using electronic instruments, so (C) is wrong.

10. E

Here you're asked to compare the viewpoints in Passages 1 and 2. An "innovator" introduces something new, or changes the way things are done. While Author 2 praises Davis for restlessly changing musical styles, Author 1 wishes Davis had continued playing traditional jazz. So Author 1 would argue that Davis's "innovations" were a mistake, and this suggests (E): **Davis [failed to] realize that change for the sake of change is not always [good].**

(A) doesn't address whether Davis's innovations were a good thing; in addition, Author 1 thought Davis reached his peak **after 1950.** (B) is a poor guess, since the author of Passage 1 never takes this position. The first half of (C) is accurate, but the second half is untrue: Author 1 thinks Davis's decline stemmed from the kind of music he chose to play, *not* from **imperfect technique.** Nor does Author 1 suggest that Davis's mistake was playing with inferior musicians, as (D) suggests.

11. D

This Big Picture question asks about the main point of *both* passages. The wording suggests they share the same primary purpose. Though each author has a different opinion of Davis, both **evaluate** his music and trace the arc of his **career,** so (D) is correct.

(A) is too broad; it doesn't even mention Davis. (B) reflects Passage 2, but not Passage 1, which argues that Davis should have stayed with his '50s music. (C) relates only to a minor point in each passage—how Davis got started in jazz. And (E) accurately describes Passage 1, but not Passage 2, which argues that Davis's career was a succession of **high points.**

SAT
Vocabulary

How to Use the SAT Word and Root Lists

The Kaplan SAT Word List is a minidictionary of SAT-level vocabulary words. These are the right words to study, with brief definitions based on the meanings likely to be tested. The SAT Root List breaks these words into their component parts. Use the Kaplan Word List and Root List in three ways to help build your vocabulary:

1. Anytime you come across a word or root in this workbook that you don't know, look it up on the appropriate list. Think about the word or root for a moment. Try to come up with a way to remember it. Put a check mark next to anything you look up so that you can come back to review. Here are some ways to help lodge new words or roots in your head:

   • Create and use flashcards

   • Make a vocabulary notebook

   • Make a vocabulary tape

   • Use rhymes, mental pictures, or other mnemonics (memory aids)

2. Use these Lists to study from, concentrating on the things you check off. It takes repetition and review to memorize new words. Cover up the definitions, and quiz yourself every now and then to make sure you still remember what you've studied.

3. Read through the Lists whenever you have some time. Relax. Browse around. The more familiar you get with the look and feel of SAT-level vocabulary, the more comfortable you'll be on Test Day.

You don't need to use any particular method to build your vocabulary. Use whatever works for you. All of the Verbal question types will become easier for you as your word mastery grows.

SAT Word List

A

☐ ABANDON (n.)—total lack of inhibition

With her strict parents out of the way, Kelly danced all night with *abandon*.

☐ ABASE—to humble; disgrace

After his immature behavior, John was *abased* in my eyes.

☐ ABATE—decrease, reduce

As the hurricane's force *abated*, the winds dropped and the sea became calm.

☐ ABDICATE—to give up a position, right, or power

With the angry mob clamoring outside the palace, the king *abdicated* his throne and fled.

☐ ABERRATION—something different from the usual

Due to the bizarre *aberrations* in the author's behavior, her publicist decided that the less the public saw of her, the better.

☐ ABET—to aid; act as accomplice

While Derwin robbed the bank, Marvin *abetted* his friend by pulling up the getaway car.

☐ ABEYANCE—temporary suppression or suspension

Michelle held her excitement in *abeyance* while the college review board considered her application.

☐ ABHOR—to loathe, detest

After she repeatedly failed to learn the Pythagorean theorem, Susan began to *abhor* geometry.

☐ ABJECT—miserable, pitiful

When we found the *abject* creature lying on the ground, we took it inside and tended to its broken leg.

☐ ABJURE—to reject, abandon formally

Claiming he had changed, the president *abjured* his old beliefs during his speech.

☐ ABLUTION—act of cleansing

Taking off her makeup was the last step in Minnie's evening *ablutions*.

☐ ABNEGATE—to deny; renounce

The monks had dedicated themselves to a humble and self-*abnegating* lifestyle, refusing all comforts.

☐ ABOLITIONIST—one who opposes the practice of slavery

Harriet Beecher Stowe, a known *abolitionist*, portrayed the evils of slavery in her novel *Uncle Tom's Cabin*.

☐ ABORTIVE—interrupted while incomplete

Her attempt at reaching the other side of the lake was *abortive*—her sailboat capsized halfway across.

☐ ABRIDGE—to condense, shorten

The teacher assigned an *abridged* version of *Tristram Shandy* to her class, as the original was very long.

❑ ABROGATE—to put an end to, abolish by authority

The immigration authorities agreed to *abrogate* their original decision to deport Juan after evidence was submitted that he was in fact a political refugee, as he had claimed.

❑ ABSCOND—to depart secretly

After being fired, the disgruntled ex-employee *absconded* with six company computers in the middle of the night.

❑ ABSOLVE—to forgive, free from blame

The queen *absolved* the general from blame for the disastrous military campaign, much to his relief.

❑ ABSTAIN—to choose not to do something

During Lent, practicing Catholics *abstain* from eating meat.

❑ ABSTRACT (adj.)—theoretical; complex, difficult

The theory was too *abstract* for the students to comprehend.

❑ ABSTRUSE—difficult to comprehend

The philosopher's elucidation was so clear that he turned an *abstruse* subject into one his audience could grasp.

❑ ACCEDE—to express approval; agree to

When the mayor proposed lower taxes, the people readily *acceded*.

❑ ACCESSIBLE—attainable, available; approachable

Preeti was surprised that the famous professor was so *accessible*, inviting students to visit him at all hours.

❑ ACCESSORY—attachment, ornament; accomplice, partner

You can use this safety pin for practical purposes or just as an *accessory*.

❑ ACCOLADE—praise, distinction

The winner of the spelling bee beamed as *accolades* were heaped upon her from all sides.

❑ ACCOST—to approach and speak to someone

Furious, Maria *accosted* the man who had trampled her flower bed and demanded that he apologize.

❑ ACCRETION—growth in size or increase in amount

The committee's strong fund-raising efforts resulted in an *accretion* in available scholarship money.

❑ ACCRUE—to accumulate, grow by additions

Before he knew it, Cliff had *accrued* an overwhelmingly large debt.

❑ ACERBIC—bitter, sharp in taste or temper

Gina's *acerbic* wit and sarcasm were feared around the office.

❑ ACME—highest point; summit

The dictator was assassinated just as he reached the *acme* of his power.

❑ ACQUIESCE—to agree; comply quietly

The princess *acquiesced* to demands that she marry a nobleman, but she was not happy about it.

❑ ACQUITTAL—release from blame

The public was astonished at the jury's *acquittal* of the serial killer—how could they let a man like that go?

❑ ACRID—harsh, bitter

The *acrid* smell of vinegar drove the children out of the kitchen.

❑ ACRIMONY—bitterness, animosity

The *acrimony* the newly divorced couple showed towards each other made everyone feel uncomfortable.

❑ ACUITY—sharpness

Although Dr. Patel is in her mid-80's, her mental *acuity* is still impressive.

❑ ACUMEN—sharpness of insight

The portfolio manager's financial *acumen* helped him to select high-yield stocks for his clients.

❑ ACUTE—sharp, pointed, severe

There is an *acute* shortage of food in the city, and people will starve if food is not brought in soon.

❑ ADAGE—old saying or proverb

"A penny saved is a penny earned" is a popular *adage*.

❑ ADAMANT—uncompromising, unyielding

The lawyer was *adamant* in his tireless defense of the death penalty.

❑ ADAPT—to accommodate; adjust

Although it may be difficult at first, we all have to *adapt* to the new computer system.

ADHERE—to cling or follow without deviation

He was a strict Catholic who *adhered* to all the teachings of the Church.

ADJACENT—next to

The photocopier is down the hall, *adjacent* to the water cooler.

ADJUNCT—something added, attached, or joined

An *adjunct* professor is one not given the same full-time status as other faculty members.

ADMONISH—to caution or reprimand

My mother began to *admonish* me about my poor grades.

ADROIT—skillful, accomplished, highly competent

The *adroit* athlete completed even the most difficult obstacle course with ease.

ADULATION—high praise

After Ana's piano recital, the audience lavished her with *adulation*.

ADULTERATE—to corrupt or make impure

The restaurateur made his ketchup last longer by *adulterating* it with water.

ADUMBRATE—to sketch, outline in a shadowy way

There was only time to *adumbrate* an escape plan before the cyclone hit.

ADVANTAGEOUS—favorable, useful

Derek found his Spanish-speaking skills to be *advantageous* in his travels in Mexico.

ADVERSARIAL—antagonistic, competitive

The brothers' *adversarial* relationship made it impossible for them to support each other in times of need.

ADVERSE—unfavorable, unlucky; harmful

They cancelled the baseball game due to *adverse* weather conditions.

AERIAL—having to do with the air

From the plane, we took several *aerial* pictures of the mountain tops.

AERIE—nook or nest built high in the air

The eagle's *aerie*, filled with eggs, was perched high in the trees.

AERODYNAMIC—relating to objects moving through the air

We made the paper airplane more *aerodynamic* by folding the wings at an angle.

AESTHETIC—pertaining to beauty or art

The museum curator, with her fine *aesthetic* sense, created an exhibit that was a joy to behold.

AFFABLE—friendly, easy to approach

The *affable* postman was on good terms with everyone on his route.

AFFECTED (adj.)—pretentious, phony

The *affected* hairdresser spouted French phrases continually, even though she had never been to France.

AFFINITY—fondness, liking; similarity

George felt an instant *affinity* for his new neighbor when he realized that he, too, was a Broncos fan.

AFFLUENT—rich, abundant

An *affluent* woman, Enid was able to give large sums of money to charity.

AFFRONT (n.)—personal offense, insult

Clyde took the waiter's insulting remark as an *affront* to his whole family.

AGENDA—plan, schedule

The board put the urgent issue at the top of the *agenda* for their next meeting.

AGGRANDIZE—to make larger or greater in power

All the millionaire really wanted was to *aggrandize* his personal wealth as much as possible.

AGGREGATE (n.)—collective mass or sum; total

An *aggregate* of panic-stricken customers mobbed the bank, demanding their life savings.

AGGRIEVE—to afflict, distress

Elizabeth, the chambermaid, felt *aggrieved* at the harsh treatment she received from her mistress.

AGILE—well coordinated, nimble

The *agile* monkey leapt onto the table and snatched the boy's banana away in the blink of an eye.

AGITATION—commotion, excitement; uneasiness

The patient's *agitation* was obvious; she was terrified at the thought of undergoing the operation.

AGNOSTIC—one who doubts that God exists

When she could find no evidence to affirm the existence of God, she proclaimed herself an *agnostic*.

AGRARIAN—relating to farming or rural matters

She took a course in *agrarian* accounting in order to help her family run the farm after college.

ALACRITY—cheerful willingness, eagerness; speed

The eager dog fetched with *alacrity* the stick that had been tossed for him.

ALCHEMY—medieval chemical philosophy aimed at trying to change metal into gold

Scientists of old struggled to master the secrets of *alchemy*, but could never change metal to gold.

ALGORITHM—mechanical problem-solving procedure

Sara's new computer used *algorithms* to solve equations.

ALIAS—assumed name

The criminal who goes by the *alias* "Big Bad Bobby" was just arrested.

ALIENATED—distanced, estranged

Anthony made an effort to make the new student feel less *alienated* by inviting her out with the group.

ALIGNED—precisely adjusted; committed to one side

Jackie always made sure her pens were perfectly *aligned* in her drawer.

ALLAY—to lessen, ease, or soothe

The nurse tried to *allay* the couple's fears that their son's health had deteriorated.

ALLEGORY—symbolic representation

The novelist used the stormy ocean as an *allegory* for her life's struggles.

ALLEVIATE—to relieve, improve partially

This medicine will help to *alleviate* the pain.

ALLITERATION—repetition of the beginning sounds of words

The poet was fond of using *alliteration* in her work, as in her poem "Preening Pigeons Perch Prettily."

ALLOCATION—allowance, portion, share

The treasurer will be in charge of the *allocation* of funds during the campaign.

ALLURE (v.)—to entice by charm; attract

The video arcade owner *allured* teenage customers by installing the coolest, most desirable new games.

ALLUSION—indirect reference

He was sometimes referred to as "the Slugger," an *allusion* to his ability to hit the baseball very hard.

ALLUSIVENESS—quality of making many indirect references

Joyce found Michael's *allusiveness* increasingly irritating—sometimes she wished he'd just get to the point.

ALOOF—detached, indifferent

The newcomer remained *aloof* from all our activities and therefore made no new friends.

ALTERCATION—noisy dispute

When the drunken cowboy knocked someone's beer bottle off the table, a serious *altercation* ensued.

ALTRUISM—unselfish concern for others' welfare

The woman's *altruism* revealed itself in the way she gave out money to all who seemed needy.

AMALGAMATE—to mix, combine

Giant Industries *amalgamated* with Mega Products to form Giant-Mega Products Incorporated.

AMBIDEXTROUS—able to use both hands equally well

The *ambidextrous* man was able to chop vegetables with both hands simultaneously, making him one of the fastest short-order cooks in the business.

AMBIGUOUS—uncertain; subject to multiple interpretations

The directions he gave were so *ambiguous* that we disagreed on which way to turn.

AMBIVALENCE—attitude of uncertainty; conflicting emotions

Jane was filled with *ambivalence*—on the one hand, switching jobs would get her away from her tyrannical boss, but on the other hand, she'd lose her high salary and corner office.

AMELIORATE—to make better, improve

Conditions in the hospital were *ameliorated* by the hiring of dozens of expertly trained nurses.

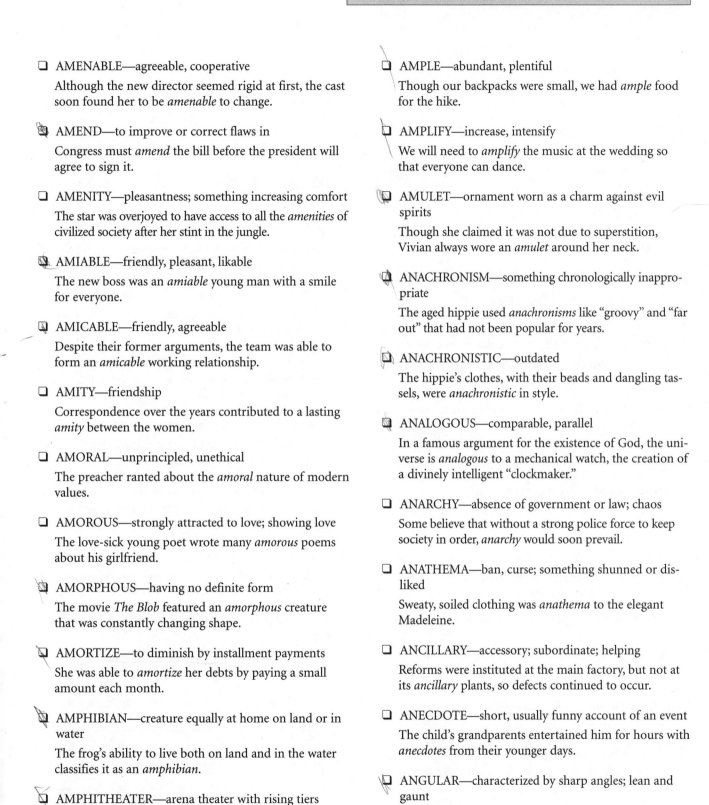

❑ AMENABLE—agreeable, cooperative

Although the new director seemed rigid at first, the cast soon found her to be *amenable* to change.

❑ AMEND—to improve or correct flaws in

Congress must *amend* the bill before the president will agree to sign it.

❑ AMENITY—pleasantness; something increasing comfort

The star was overjoyed to have access to all the *amenities* of civilized society after her stint in the jungle.

❑ AMIABLE—friendly, pleasant, likable

The new boss was an *amiable* young man with a smile for everyone.

❑ AMICABLE—friendly, agreeable

Despite their former arguments, the team was able to form an *amicable* working relationship.

❑ AMITY—friendship

Correspondence over the years contributed to a lasting *amity* between the women.

❑ AMORAL—unprincipled, unethical

The preacher ranted about the *amoral* nature of modern values.

❑ AMOROUS—strongly attracted to love; showing love

The love-sick young poet wrote many *amorous* poems about his girlfriend.

❑ AMORPHOUS—having no definite form

The movie *The Blob* featured an *amorphous* creature that was constantly changing shape.

❑ AMORTIZE—to diminish by installment payments

She was able to *amortize* her debts by paying a small amount each month.

❑ AMPHIBIAN—creature equally at home on land or in water

The frog's ability to live both on land and in the water classifies it as an *amphibian*.

❑ AMPHITHEATER—arena theater with rising tiers around a central open space

The *amphitheater* in the park is the perfect place for a summer concert.

❑ AMPLE—abundant, plentiful

Though our backpacks were small, we had *ample* food for the hike.

❑ AMPLIFY—increase, intensify

We will need to *amplify* the music at the wedding so that everyone can dance.

❑ AMULET—ornament worn as a charm against evil spirits

Though she claimed it was not due to superstition, Vivian always wore an *amulet* around her neck.

❑ ANACHRONISM—something chronologically inappropriate

The aged hippie used *anachronisms* like "groovy" and "far out" that had not been popular for years.

❑ ANACHRONISTIC—outdated

The hippie's clothes, with their beads and dangling tassels, were *anachronistic* in style.

❑ ANALOGOUS—comparable, parallel

In a famous argument for the existence of God, the universe is *analogous* to a mechanical watch, the creation of a divinely intelligent "clockmaker."

❑ ANARCHY—absence of government or law; chaos

Some believe that without a strong police force to keep society in order, *anarchy* would soon prevail.

❑ ANATHEMA—ban, curse; something shunned or disliked

Sweaty, soiled clothing was *anathema* to the elegant Madeleine.

❑ ANCILLARY—accessory; subordinate; helping

Reforms were instituted at the main factory, but not at its *ancillary* plants, so defects continued to occur.

❑ ANECDOTE—short, usually funny account of an event

The child's grandparents entertained him for hours with *anecdotes* from their younger days.

❑ ANGULAR—characterized by sharp angles; lean and gaunt

Her *angular* frame contrasted sharply with that of her overweight sister.

❑ ANIMATION—enthusiasm, excitement

Ben's face filled with *animation* as he described his wonderful, exciting trip to Venice.

ANIMOSITY—hatred, hostility

The deep-rooted *animosity* between them made it difficult for the cousins to work together.

ANNUL—to cancel, nullify, declare void, or make legally invalid

The couple asked the court to *annul* their marriage, as they had made a mistake in wedding each other.

ANODYNE—something that calms or soothes pain

The skittish patient asked the dentist for an *anodyne* to dull the pain.

ANOINT—to apply oil to, especially as a sacred rite

The ceremony required the woman to *anoint* her child's head with oil.

ANOMALY—irregularity or deviation from the norm

Albino animals may display too great an *anomaly* in their coloring to attract normally colored mates.

ANONYMITY—condition of having no name or an unknown name

After abandoning her movie career at a relatively youthful age, Garbo retreated into relative *anonymity*.

ANTAGONIST—foe, opponent, adversary

The child and the cat became bitter *antagonists* after the child pulled the cat's tail.

ANTECEDENT (adj.)—coming before in place or time

Though the war appeared to be over, the *antecedent* events made the soldiers wary of retreating.

ANTEDILUVIAN—prehistoric, ancient beyond measure

The *antediluvian* fossils were displayed in the museum.

ANTEPENULTIMATE—third from last

In the word "ultimate," the spoken stress is on the *antepenultimate* syllable, "ul."

ANTERIOR—preceding, previous, before, prior (to)

Following tradition, the couple's wedding was *anterior* to the honeymoon.

ANTHOLOGY—collection of literary works

Whenever the student needed a quotation, she consulted her *anthology*.

ANTHROPOMORPHIC—attributing human qualities to nonhumans

Milo's *anthropomorphic* behavior towards his computer was evident when he called it "Fred."

ANTIPATHY—dislike, hostility; extreme opposition or aversion

The *antipathy* between the French and the English regularly erupted into open warfare.

ANTIQUATED—outdated, obsolete

The old man's typewriter was completely *antiquated*, especially when compared to his son's computer.

ANTIQUITY—ancient times; the quality of being old

It was obviously a castle of great *antiquity*, unchanged since before the Middle Ages.

ANTITHESIS—exact opposite or direct contrast

The ill-mannered boy was often described as the *antithesis* of his sweet sister.

APATHETIC—indifferent, unconcerned

The author seemed *apathetic*, going along with all the editor's proposed changes without an argument.

APATHY—lack of feeling or emotion

The *apathy* of voters is so great that less than half the people who are eligible to vote bother to do so.

APHASIA—inability to speak or use words

Stroke victims often suffer from *aphasia*, making it difficult for them to communicate with others.

APHELION—point in a planet's orbit that is farthest from the sun

When the Earth is at its *aphelion*, it has reached its greatest distance from the sun.

APHORISM—old saying or short, pithy statement

The country doctor was given to *aphorisms* such as "Still waters run deep."

APOCRYPHAL—not genuine; fictional

Sharon suspected that the stories she was hearing about alligators in the sewer were *apocryphal*.

APOSTATE—one who renounces a religious faith

The king declared himself an *apostate* before flouting the Church's doctrines to divorce his wife.

❑ APOSTROPHE—an address to the reader or someone not present

The author often used *apostrophe* to present a viewpoint directly to the reader.

❑ APOTHEOSIS—glorification; glorified ideal

In her heyday, many people considered Jackie Kennedy to be the *apotheosis* of stylishness.

❑ APPEASE—to satisfy, placate, calm, pacify

We all sang lullabies to try to *appease* the bawling infant.

❑ APPROBATION—praise; official approval

Billy was sure he had gained the *approbation* of his teacher when he received a glowing report card.

❑ APPROPRIATE (v.)—to take possession of

Lucia came up with the great idea to *appropriate* the abandoned building for storage.

❑ AQUATIC—belonging or living in water

The heaviest *aquatic* creature, the whale, dwarfs heavy land animals, as its weight is supported by water.

❑ ARABLE—suitable for cultivation

The overpopulated country desperately needed more *arable* land to grow food for its starving people.

❑ ARBITRARY—depending solely on individual will; inconsistent

Nancy won a prize, but not Fred, making the judges' decisions seem completely *arbitrary*.

❑ ARBITRATE—mediate, negotiate

Since the couple could not come to agreement, a judge was forced to *arbitrate* their divorce proceedings.

❑ ARBOREAL—relating to trees; living in trees

The squirrel is an *arboreal* mammal, spending much of its time running up and down trees.

❑ ARBORETUM—place where trees are displayed and studied

The botanist spent many hours in the *arboretum* doing research.

❑ ARCANE—secret, obscure, known only to a few

The *arcane* rituals of the sect were passed down through many generations.

❑ ARCHAIC—antiquated, from an earlier time; outdated

Her *archaic* Commodore computer could not run the latest software.

❑ ARCHIPELAGO—large group of islands

Boat taxis are the only form of transportation between villages in the Stockholm *archipelago*.

❑ ARDENT—passionate, enthusiastic, fervent

After a 25-game losing streak, even the Mets' most *ardent* fans realized the team wouldn't finish first.

❑ ARDOR—great emotion or passion

Bishop's *ardor* for landscape was evident when he passionately described the beauty of the Hudson Valley.

❑ ARDUOUS—extremely difficult, laborious

Amy thought she would pass out after completing the *arduous* climb up the mountain.

❑ ARID—extremely dry or deathly boring

The *arid* farmland produced no crops.

❑ ARRAIGN—to call to court to answer an indictment

The conman was *arraigned* yesterday, but failed to show up in court.

❑ ARROGATE—to demand, claim arrogantly

Lynn watched in astonishment as her boss *arrogated* all the credit for Lynn's brilliant work on the project.

❑ ARSENAL—ammunition storehouse

The soldiers rushed to the *arsenal* to fetch more cannonballs.

❑ ARTICULATE (adj.)—well spoken, expressing oneself clearly

She is such an *articulate* defender of labor that unions are among her strongest supporters.

❑ ARTIFACT—historical relic, item made by human craft

The archaeologist discovered hundreds of interesting *artifacts* in the ruins of the mansion.

❑ ARTISAN—craftsperson; expert

Artisans were among the most valued citizens of the kingdom for their skills in tool-making.

❑ ASCEND—to rise or climb

As Mr. Boggs *ascended* the stairs, he panted heavily.

❑ ASCENDANCY—state of rising, ascending; power or control

The devious politician's *ascendancy* to the top ranks of government seemed inevitable.

❑ ASCERTAIN—to determine, discover, make certain of

Try as he might, the archaeologist couldn't *ascertain* the correct age of the Piltdown man's skeleton.

❑ ASCETIC—self-denying, abstinent, austere

The monk lived an *ascetic* life deep in the wilderness, denying himself all forms of luxury.

❑ ASCRIBE—to attribute to, assign

Aunt Fran was shocked when she heard about the negative qualities her family *ascribed* to her.

❑ ASHEN—resembling ashes; deathly pale

The *ashen* look on Jesse's face made it clear he had already heard the bad news.

❑ ASKEW—crooked, tilted

I was so late for work that I rushed out of the house with my hair uncombed and my hat *askew*.

❑ ASPERSION—false rumor, damaging report, slander

It is unfair to cast *aspersions* on someone behind his or her back.

❑ ASPIRE—to have great hopes; to aim at a goal

Although Sid started out in the mailroom, he *aspired* to owning the company someday.

❑ ASSAIL—to attack, assault

The foreign army *assailed* the fort for days, but did not manage to take it.

❑ ASSENT—to express agreement

I want to make money, but I would never *assent* to doing anything illegal.

❑ ASSERT—to affirm, attest

Some people look favorably on politicians who are willing to *assert* their views boldly.

❑ ASSIDUOUS—diligent, persistent, hard-working

The chauffeur scrubbed the limousine *assiduously*, hoping to make a good impression on his employer.

❑ ASSIGNATION—appointment for lovers' meeting; assignment

Romeo and Juliet made an *assignation* to meet at her balcony.

❑ ASSIMILATION—act of blending in, becoming similar

Language classes were offered to aid in the *assimilation* of the immigrants with the native citizens.

❑ ASSONANCE—resemblance in sound, especially in vowel sounds; partial rhyme

The professor pointed out how *assonance* among the words contributed to the flow of the poem.

❑ ASSUAGE—to make less severe, ease, relieve

Like many people, Philip Larkin used alcohol to *assuage* his sense of meaninglessness and despair.

❑ ASTRINGENT—harsh, severe, stern

The principal's punishments seemed overly *astringent*, but the students did not dare to complain.

❑ ASTUTE—having good judgment

The novelist Judy Blume is an *astute* judge of human nature; her characters ring true.

❑ ASUNDER (adv.)—into different parts

Though the boat was strong, the violent storm tore it *asunder*.

❑ ASYMMETRICAL—not corresponding in size, shape, position, etcetera

The hairstylist was shocked to find that the two sides of his customer's hair were *asymmetrical*.

❑ ATONE—to make amends for a wrong

Many people go to church to *atone* for their wrongdoings and seek forgiveness.

❑ ATROCIOUS—monstrous, shockingly bad, wicked

The British officer committed the *atrocious* act of slaughtering a large group of peaceful Indian villagers.

❑ ATROPHY—to waste away, wither from disuse

When Mimi stopped exercising, her muscles began to *atrophy*.

❑ ATTAIN—to accomplish, gain

It is clear that Clem's hard work will help him *attain* that raise he's been hoping for.

❑ ATTENUATE—to make thin or slender; weaken

The Bill of Rights *attenuated* the traditional power of government to change laws at will.

❑ ATTEST—to testify, stand as proof of, bear witness

Once her husband had *attested* to the fact that Mrs. Martin was with him on the night of the murder, the jury had no choice but to acquit her of the crime.

❑ AUDACIOUS—bold, daring, fearless

"And you, your majesty, may kiss my bum!" replied the *audacious* peasant.

❑ AUDIBLE—capable of being heard

The shy boy's voice was barely *audible* as he answered the teacher's questions.

❑ AUDIT—formal examination of financial records

The grocer cursed the IRS's decision to *audit* him, as he couldn't pay all the back taxes they demanded.

❑ AUDITORY—having to do with hearing

Sometimes, people's *auditory* canals become blocked by large quantities of wax.

❑ AUGMENT—to expand, extend

Ben *augmented* his salary with overtime hours as much as possible.

❑ AUGURY—prophecy, prediction of events

Troy hoped the rainbow was an *augury* of good things to come.

❑ AUGUST—dignified, awe inspiring, venerable

The *august* view of the summit of the Grand Teton filled the climbers with awe.

❑ AUSPICIOUS—having favorable prospects, promising

Tamika thought that having lunch with the boss was an *auspicious* start to her new job.

❑ AUSTERE—stern, strict, unadorned

The lack of decoration makes Zen temples seem *austere* to the untrained eye.

❑ AUTHORITARIAN—extremely strict, bossy

The *authoritarian* manager alienated his employees with his bossy manner.

❑ AUTOCRAT—dictator

Mussolini has been described as an *autocrat* who did not tolerate opposition.

❑ AUTONOMOUS—separate, independent

There is a movement underway to make Scotland an independent country, *autonomous* from England.

❑ AUXILIARY—supplementary, reserve

Gasping for air, the astronaut was forced to open his *auxiliary* canister of oxygen.

❑ AVARICE—greed

Rebecca's *avarice* motivated her to stuff the $100 bill in her pocket instead of returning it to the man who had dropped it.

❑ AVENGE—to retaliate, take revenge for an injury or crime

"You'll regret humiliating me! Someday, I will *avenge* this insult!" shouted the furious count.

❑ AVER—to declare to be true, affirm

The witness *averred* that the man had in fact been holding a gun.

❑ AVERSION—intense dislike

Laura took an instant *aversion* to Mike because of his obnoxious personality.

❑ AVERT—to turn (something) away; prevent, hinder

The queasy medical school student had to *avert* her eyes when the operation began.

❑ AVIARY—large enclosure housing birds

The tourists brought their cameras to the city's famous *aviary*, hoping to capture its exotic birds on film.

❑ AVOW—to state openly or declare

The groom *avowed* his love for his bride to the rabbi.

❑ AWRY—crooked, askew, amiss

Something must have gone *awry* in the computer system, because some of my files are missing.

❑ AXIOM—premise, postulate, self-evident truth

Halle lived her life based on the *axioms* her grandmother had passed on to her.

Beawk

B

BALEFUL—harmful, with evil intentions

The sullen teenager gave his nagging mother a *baleful* look.

BALK—to refuse, shirk; prevent

The horse *balked* at jumping over the high fence and instead threw his rider off.

BALLAD—folk song, narrative poem

We heard the singer perform many romantic *ballads* at the country inn.

BALM—soothing, healing influence

"Let me give you some lip *balm* for your chapped lips," said Donna.

BAN—to forbid, outlaw

After getting drunk one night and smashing dozens of bottles, Joe was *banned* from the bar for life.

BANAL—trite, overly common

He used *banal* phrases like "Have a nice day" or "Another day, another dollar."

BANE—something causing death, destruction, or ruin

Speeches were the *bane* of Jenny's existence; she hated having to stand up in front of a crowd.

BANTER—playful conversation

The eligible young man's cheerful *banter* was misinterpreted as flirtation by the woman who adored him.

BASTION—fortification, stronghold

The club was well known as a *bastion* of conservative values in the liberal city.

BAY (v.)—to bark, especially in a deep, prolonged way

The dog *bayed* all night, much to the annoyance of the neighbors.

BECALM—to make calm or still; keep motionless by lack of wind

Most of the sailors fell prey to scurvy as the *becalmed* ship made little or no progress for weeks on end.

BECLOUD—to confuse; darken with clouds

The ink of the squid *beclouded* the water.

BEGUILE—to deceive, mislead; charm

Beguiled by the songs of the Sirens, Odysseus wanted to abandon all his men and forget his family.

BEHEMOTH—huge creature

Titanic's budget became such a *behemoth* that observers predicted that the film would never make a profit.

BELABOR—to insist repeatedly or harp on

I understand completely; you do not need to *belabor* the point.

BELATED—late

George handed Jerry a *belated* birthday gift with a sheepish grin.

BELEAGUER—to harass, plague

Mickey's *beleaguered* parents finally gave in to his request for a Nintendo.

BELFRY—bell tower, room in which a bell is hung

The town was shocked when a bag of money was found stashed in the old *belfry* of the library.

BELIE—to misrepresent; expose as false

The first lady's carefree appearance *belied* rumors that she was on the verge of divorcing her husband.

BELITTLE—to represent as unimportant, make light of

Carla's parents scolded her for constantly *belittling* her younger sister's views.

BELLICOSE—warlike, aggressive

Immediately after defeating one of his enemies, the *bellicose* chieftain declared war on another.

BELLIGERENT—hostile, tending to fight

The bartender realized that it would be fruitless to try to subdue the *belligerent* drunk by himself.

BELLOW—to roar, shout

The poor acoustics of the lecture hall required the professor to *bellow* as loud as she could.

BEMUSE—to confuse, stupefy; plunge deep into thought

The computer technician, continually *bemused* by the complex problems he had to deal with each day, decided to quit and find an easier job.

*Banal, platitud
adj se.*

❑ BENCHMARK—standard of measure

The average scores of the previous year's students are used as a *benchmark* against which new applicants are measured.

❑ BENEFACTOR—someone giving aid or money

A mysterious *benefactor* paid off all Robin's bills, making it possible for her to send her children to college.

❑ BENEFICENT—kindly, charitable; doing good deeds; producing good effects

Despite his tough reputation, Kirk was a *beneficent* man, donating millions of dollars to worthy charities.

❑ BENIGHTED—unenlightened

Ben scoffed at the crowd, as he believed it consisted entirely of *benighted* individuals.

❑ BENIGN—kindly, gentle, or harmless

Suraj was relieved to discover that his tumor was *benign* and he did not have cancer after all.

❑ BEQUEATH—to give or leave through a will; to hand down

Grandpa *bequeathed* the house to his daughter and the car to his son.

❑ BERATE—to scold harshly

Andy was embarrassed when his mother *berated* him in public for smashing the family car.

❑ BESEECH—to beg, plead, implore

She *beseeched* him to give her a second chance, but he refused.

❑ BESTIAL—beastly, animal-like

The *bestial* nature of the growl in the dark made the campers shake with fright.

❑ BESTOW—to give as a gift

The students *bestowed* gifts upon the teacher, attempting to procure better grades.

❑ BETOKEN—to indicate, signify, give evidence of

She turned her back to us, *betokening* her hostility.

❑ BEVY—group

As predicted, a *bevy* of teenagers surrounded the rock star's limousine.

❑ BIAS—prejudice, slant

Racial *bias* in employment is illegal in the United States.

❑ BIBLIOGRAPHY—list of books

Please include a *bibliography* at the end of your paper so I can identify your sources.

❑ BIBLIOPHILE—book lover

The librarian was a real *bibliophile*; she knew every author we mentioned.

❑ BILATERAL—two-sided

The battle finally came to a halt when the two sides signed a *bilateral* treaty.

❑ BILK—to cheat, defraud

Though the lawyer seemed honest, the woman feared he would try to *bilk* her out of her money.

❑ BILLET—board and lodging for troops

The old cabins served as the soldiers' *billets* for two months.

❑ BIPED—two-footed animal   *smthntts sly*

Human beings are *bipeds*, whereas horses are quadrupeds.

❑ BISECT—to cut into two (usually equal) parts

We were so hungry that we *bisected* the cake and each ate half.

❑ BLANCH—to pale; take the color out of

The murderess *blanched* when the man she thought she had killed walked into the room.

❑ BLANDISH—to coax with flattery

We *blandished* the bouncer with compliments until he finally let us into the club.

❑ BLASPHEMOUS—cursing, profane, irreverent

The protesters found the politician's offhanded biblical references *blasphemous* and inappropriate.

❑ BLATANT—glaring, obvious, showy

That movie was a *blatant* ripoff of *Star Wars*; they didn't even change the name of the villain!

❑ BLIGHT (v.)—to afflict, destroy

The farmers feared that the previous night's frost had *blighted* the potato crops entirely.

❑ BLITHE—joyful, cheerful, or without appropriate thought

She *blithely* assumed that no one would care if she took the only printer in the office home with her.

❑ BLUDGEON—to hit as with a short, heavy club

Mrs. Smyth became worried when her son confessed to *bludgeoning* the family car with a baseball bat.

❑ BOISTEROUS—rowdy, loud, unrestrained

The *boisterous* football fans ran riot in the streets until the police restrained them.

❑ BOMBASTIC—using high-sounding but meaningless language

Mussolini's speeches were mostly *bombastic*; his boasting and outrageous claims had no basis in fact.

❑ BONANZA—extremely large amount; something profitable

Judi was overjoyed at the unexpected *bonanza* of winning the lottery.

❑ BONHOMIE—good-natured geniality; atmosphere of good cheer

The general *bonhomie* that characterized the party made it a joy to attend.

❑ BOON—blessing, something to be thankful for

Dirk realized that his new coworker's computer skills would be a real *boon* to the company.

❑ BOOR—crude person, one lacking manners or taste

"That utter *boor* ruined my recital with his constant guffawing!" wailed the pianist.

❑ BOTANIST—scientist who studies plants

The *botanist* spent endless hours studying the orchids that fascinated her.

❑ BOUNTIFUL—plentiful

Food is *bountiful* in the United States, yet some people are still hungry.

❑ BOURGEOIS—middle-class

The *bourgeois* family was horrified when the lower-class family moved in next door.

❑ BOVINE—cowlike; relating to cows

An illness commonly known as "mad cow disease" devastated Britain's *bovine* population not long ago.

❑ BRAZEN—bold, shameless, impudent; of or like brass

"That *brazen* slut had better stay away from my husband!" fumed Mrs. Hayward.

❑ BREACH—act of breaking, violation

The record company sued the singer for *breach* of contract when he recorded for another company without permission.

❑ BRIGAND—bandit, outlaw

Brigands held up the bank and made off with the contents of the safe.

❑ BROACH (v.)—to mention or suggest for the first time

Polly was nervous about *broaching* the subject of a raise to her boss.

❑ BRUSQUE—rough and abrupt in manner

The bank teller's *brusque* treatment of his customers soon evoked several complaints.

❑ BUFFET (v.)—to toss about

The swing, *buffeted* by the wind, smashed into the tree and broke.

❑ BUFFOON—clown or fool

The boy was known as the school *buffoon*, so he wasn't taken seriously as a candidate for class president.

❑ BULWARK—defense wall; anything serving as defense

The villagers used logs to construct a *bulwark* against the invading army.

❑ BURGEON—to sprout or flourish

We will need major subway expansion to accommodate the *burgeoning* population of the city.

❑ BURLY—brawny, husky

Freddy was a bit intimidated by the tall, *burly* man standing by the bar.

❑ BURNISH—to polish, make smooth and bright

Mr. Frumpkin loved to stand in the sun and *burnish* his luxury car until it gleamed.

❑ BURSAR—treasurer

For billing concerns, please contact the *bursar* via telephone or e-mail.

❑ BUSTLE—commotion, energetic activity

The *bustle* of the crowd made Andrea remember how much she hated Christmas shopping.

❑ BUTT—person or thing that is object of ridicule

Chip's unusual haircut made him the *butt* of jokes at the high school prom.

❑ BUTTRESS (v.)—to reinforce or support

The construction workers attempted to *buttress* the ceiling with pillars.

❑ BYWAY—back road

During rush hour, it is wise to use the *byway* and avoid the traffic.

C

❑ CACOPHONY—jarring, unpleasant noise

The junior high orchestra created an almost unbearable *cacophony* as they tried to tune their instruments.

❑ CADENCE—rhythmic flow of poetry; marching beat

Pierre spoke with a lovely *cadence*, charming all those who heard him.

❑ CAJOLE—to flatter, coax, persuade

The spoiled girl could *cajole* her father into buying her anything.

❑ CALAMITOUS—disastrous, catastrophic

Everyone hoped this year's event would be less *calamitous* than last year's fiasco.

❑ CALLOUS—thick-skinned, insensitive

Mrs. Meriwether *callously* ignored the pathetic whining of the injured puppy.

❑ CALLOW—immature, lacking sophistication

The young and *callow* fans hung on every word the talk show host said.

❑ CALUMNY—false and malicious accusation, misrepresentation, slander

The unscrupulous politician used *calumny* to bring down his opponent in the senatorial race.

❑ CANDOR—honesty of expression

The *candor* of his confession impressed his parents, and they gave him a light punishment as a result.

❑ CANNY—smart; founded on common sense

The executive's *canny* business sense saved the company from bankruptcy.

❑ CANONIZE—to declare a person a saint; raise to highest honors

Discrimination may be the reason certain authors have not been *canonized* by the literary establishment.

❑ CANVASS—to examine thoroughly; conduct a poll

After *canvassing* people for months, the market researchers finally tabulated the results.

❑ CAPACIOUS—large, roomy; extensive

We wondered how many hundreds of stores occupied the *capacious* mall.

❑ CAPITULATE—to submit completely, surrender

After atom bombs devastated Hiroshima and Nagasaki, the Japanese had little choice but to *capitulate*.

❑ CAPRICIOUS—impulsive, whimsical, without much thought

Queen Elizabeth I was quite *capricious*; her courtiers could never be sure who would catch her fancy.

❑ CARDIOLOGIST—physician specializing in diseases of the heart

Although a famous *cardiologist* performed the operation, Kevin's heart transplant was unsuccessful.

❑ CARICATURE—exaggerated portrait, cartoon

The star was extremely upset by the unflattering *caricature* of him that appeared in the magazine.

❑ CARNAL—of the flesh

Although nothing of a truly intimate, *carnal* nature had occurred between the senator and his intern, he was forced to resign when the scandal broke out.

❑ CARNIVOROUS—meat-eating

Dogs, as *carnivorous* animals, generally do not do well on purely vegetarian diets.

❑ CARP (v.)—to find fault, complain constantly

If the new employee hadn't *carped* all the time, she might not have been fired.

❑ CARTOGRAPHY—science or art of making maps

Shawn's interest in *cartography* may stem from the extensive traveling he did as a child.

❑ CAST (n.)—copy, replica

The proud parents made a *cast* of their infant's first pair of shoes.

❑ CAST (v.)—to fling, to throw

Embarrassed, the fisherman *cast* his empty line back into the water.

❑ CASTIGATE—to punish, chastise, criticize severely

Authorities in Singapore harshly *castigate* perpetrators of what would be considered minor crimes in the United States.

❑ CATALYST—something causing change without being changed

The imposition of harsh taxes was the *catalyst* that finally brought on the revolution.

❑ CATEGORICAL—absolute, without exception

Annette *categorically* denied any involvement in the crime that led to her husband's arrest.

❑ CATHARSIS—purification, cleansing

Plays can be more satisfying if they end in some sort of emotional *catharsis* for the characters involved.

❑ CATHOLIC—universal; broad and comprehensive

Hot tea with honey is a *catholic* remedy for a sore throat.

❑ CAUCUS—smaller group within an organization; a meeting of such a group

The president met with the delegated *caucus* to discuss the national crisis.

❑ CAULK—to make watertight

As a precaution, the sailors *caulked* the ship's windows with fiberglass.

❑ CAUSALITY—cause-and-effect relationship

There was definite *causality* between the dog's shedding fur and the humid weather.

❑ CAUSTIC—biting, sarcastic; able to burn

Dorothy Parker gained her reputation for *caustic* wit from her cutting, yet clever, insults.

❑ CAVALIER—carefree, happy; with lordly disdain

The nobleman's *cavalier* attitude to the suffering of the peasants working for him made them hate him.

❑ CAVORT—to frolic, frisk

The puppies looked adorable as they *cavorted* in the grass.

❑ CEDE—to surrender possession of something

Argentina *ceded* the Falkland Islands to Britain after a brief war in which it was soundly defeated.

❑ CELEBRITY—fame, widespread acclaim

Some stars find that the price of *celebrity* is too high when they are stalked by crazed fans.

❑ CENSORIOUS—severely critical

Saddam, unconcerned by the *censorious* attitude of the U.N., continued his nuclear weapons testing.

❑ CENTRIPETAL—directed or moving towards the center

It is *centripetal* force that keeps trains from derailing as they round curves.

❑ CERTITUDE—assurance, freedom from doubt

According to Oliver Wendell Holmes, *certitude* is not the test of certainty.

❑ CESSATION—temporary or complete halt

The *cessation* of hostilities ensured that soldiers were able to spend the holidays with their families.

❑ CESSION—act of surrendering something

After the *cession* of his crown to his younger brother, the former king felt extremely depressed.

❑ CHAGRIN—shame, embarrassment, humiliation

No doubt, the president felt a good deal of *chagrin* after vomiting on his neighbor at the state banquet.

❑ CHALICE—goblet, cup

The knight drank from the jewel-encrusted *chalice* with great enjoyment.

❑ CHAMPION (v.)—to defend or support

Ursula continued to *champion* the rights of the prisoner, even after it was proven beyond a doubt that he was guilty.

❑ CHAOTIC—extremely disorderly

His office was so *chaotic* that he couldn't find the proposal he was supposed to present.

❑ CHARLATAN—quack, fake

"That *charlatan* of a doctor prescribed the wrong medicine for me!" complained the patient.

❑ CHARY—watchful, cautious, extremely shy

Mindful of the fate of the Titanic, the captain was *chary* of navigating the iceberg-filled sea.

❑ CHASTISE—to punish, discipline, scold

The little girl was *chastised* for breaking the priceless vase.

❑ CHERUBIC—sweet, innocent, resembling a cherub angel

Her *cherubic* appearance made people think her personality was also sweet, when the opposite was true.

❑ CHICANERY—trickery, fraud, deception

Dishonest used car salesmen often use *chicanery* to sell their beat-up old cars.

❑ CHIDE—to scold, express disapproval

Florence *chided* her poodle for eating the birthday cake she had baked for her friend.

❑ CHIMERICAL—fanciful, imaginary, visionary, impossible

The inventor's plans seemed *chimerical* to the conservative businessman from whom he was asking for financial support.

❑ CHOLERIC—easily angered, short-tempered

The *choleric* principal raged at the students who had come late to school.

❑ CHOICE (adj.)—specially selected, preferred

Wendell took the *choicest* cut of beef for himself, annoying the others at the dinner.

❑ CHORTLE—to chuckle

The jolly old man *chortled* as he watched the amusing sitcom.

❑ CHROMATIC—relating to color

Because he was color blind, his *chromatic* senses were different from those of other people.

❑ CHRONICLER—one who keeps records of historical events

The court *chronicler* wrote a description of the battle, so that future generations could read about the king's heroic exploits.

❑ CIRCUITOUS—roundabout

The cab driver took a *circuitous* route to the airport, making me miss my plane.

❑ CIRCUMFERENCE—boundary or distance around a circle or sphere

The space shuttle set a course around the *circumference* of the Earth.

❑ CIRCUMLOCUTION—roundabout, lengthy way of saying something

He avoided discussing the real issues with endless *circumlocutions*.

❑ CIRCUMNAVIGATE—to sail completely around

The explorer discovered many new lands in his attempt to *circumnavigate* the globe.

❑ CIRCUMSCRIBE—to encircle; set limits on, confine

Diego Buenaventura's country estate is *circumscribed* by rolling hills.

❑ CIRCUMSPECT—cautious, wary

His failures have made Jack far more *circumspect* in his exploits than he used to be.

❑ CIRCUMVENT—to go around; avoid

Laura *circumvented* the hospital's visiting schedule, slipping into her boyfriend's room long after visiting hours were over.

❑ CISTERN—tank for rainwater

When their water supply was cut off, the Rileys had to rely on the rainwater captured by their *cistern*.

❑ CITADEL—fortress or stronghold

The nobleman retreated to his mountain *citadel* to protect himself from a counterattack.

❑ CIVIL—polite; relating to citizens

Police officers are instructed to be *civil* to the general public, although cases of police brutality do occur.

❑ CIVILITY—courtesy, politeness

The subway ticket seller treated his customers with the utmost *civility*, which they appreciated.

❑ CLAIRVOYANT (adj.)—having ESP, psychic

The *clairvoyant* fortuneteller claimed to have communicated with the ghost of Abraham Lincoln.

❑ CLAMOR (v.)—to make a noisy outcry

The chicks *clamored* for worms from their mother's beak.

❑ CLAMOR (n.)—noisy outcry

The *clamor* of children playing outside made it impossible for me to study.

❑ CLANDESTINE—secretive, concealed for a darker purpose

The intern paid many *clandestine* visits to the president's office in the dead of night.

❑ CLARITY—clearness; clear understanding

Henrietta explained the plan to Greg with the utmost *clarity*, but he still failed to understand.

❑ CLAUSTROPHOBIA—fear of small, confined places

Isaac's *claustrophobia* made it impossible for him to join his friends in exploring the cave.

❑ CLEAVE—to split or separate or to stick, cling, adhere

Brent *cleaved* the log in two in one mighty blow.

❑ CLEMENCY—merciful leniency

Kyle begged for *clemency*, explaining that he had been under the influence of hallucinogens when he robbed the bank.

❑ CLOISTER (v.)—to confine, seclude

The Montagues *cloistered* their wayward daughter in a convent, hoping to keep her out of trouble.

❑ COAGULATE—to clot or change from a liquid to a solid

Hemophiliacs can bleed to death because their blood is incapable of *coagulating*.

❑ COALESCE—to grow together or cause to unite as one

The different factions of the organization *coalesced* to form one united front against their opponents.

❑ CODDLE—to baby, treat indulgently

The strict grandmother frowned disapprovingly as her daughter *coddled* the spoiled, whining infant.

❑ COERCE—to compel by force or intimidation

The thief *coerced* the cashier into handing over all the money in her cash register.

❑ COFFER—strongbox, large chest for money

The taxman chuckled gleefully as he stuffed huge quantities of money into his *coffer*.

❑ COGENT—logically forceful, compelling, convincing

Swayed by the *cogent* argument of the defense, the jury had no choice but to acquit the defendant.

❑ COGNATE—related, similar, akin

The young man was *cognate* to several royal families, making him a hot prospect on the marriage market.

❑ COGNITION—mental process by which knowledge is acquired

If scientists completely understood the processes of *cognition*, the ways in which people learn could be mapped out and education could be revolutionized.

❑ COGNOMEN—family name; any name, especially a nickname

The gambler went by the *cognomen* "Lucky Luke."

❑ COHABIT—to live together

The couple *cohabited* for years before finally deciding to get married.

❑ COHERENT—intelligible, lucid, understandable

Cathy was so tired that her speech was barely *coherent*.

❑ COLLATERAL—accompanying

"Let's try to stick to the main issue here and not get into all the *collateral* questions," urged the CEO.

❑ COLLOQUIAL—characteristic of informal speech

The book was written in a *colloquial* style so that the information in it would be more user-friendly.

❑ COLLOQUY—dialogue or conversation, conference

The congressmen held a *colloquy* to determine how to proceed with the environmental legislation.

❑ COLLUSION—collaboration, complicity, conspiracy

It came to light that the police chief and the mafia were in *collusion* in running the numbers racket.

❑ COMELINESS—physical grace and beauty

Ann's *comeliness* made her perfect for the role of Sleeping Beauty.

❑ COMMEND—to compliment, praise

The teacher *commended* Yumi on her brilliant performance on the exam.

❑ COMMENSURATE—proportional

Steve was given a salary *commensurate* with his experience.

❑ COMMISSION—fee payable to an agent; authorization

The realtor earned a hefty *commission* on every property he sold.

❑ COMMODIOUS—roomy, spacious

Raqiyah was able to stretch out fully in the *commodious* bathtub.

❑ COMMONPLACE—ordinary, found every day

Computers are *commonplace* in modern offices.

❑ COMMUNICABLE—transmittable

Nurses must wear surgical masks as a precaution when treating people with *communicable* diseases.

❑ COMMUTE—to change a penalty to a less severe one

His death sentence was *commuted* when it was discovered that he was in fact innocent of the crime.

❑ COMPATRIOT—fellow countryman

Halfway across the world from home, Jeff felt most comfortable in the company of his *compatriots*.

❑ COMPELLING (adj.)—having a powerful and irresistible effect

The defense lawyer's *compelling* arguments made the jurors sympathize with the cold-blooded killer.

❑ COMPENSATE—to repay or reimburse

The moving company *compensated* me for the furniture it broke while moving my stuff to the new house.

❑ COMPLACENT—self-satisfied, smug

Philip smiled *complacently* as he was showered with compliments for his handling of the Buckman deal.

❑ COMPLEMENT—to complete, perfect

Gina's pink sweater *complemented* her red hair perfectly.

❑ COMPLIANT—submissive and yielding

Lowell used to fight with his stubborn ex-wife, but his new girlfriend has a more *compliant* personality.

❑ COMPLICITY—knowing partnership in wrongdoing

The two boys exchanged a look of sly *complicity* when their father shouted "Who broke the window?"

❑ COMPOUND (adj.)—complex; composed of several parts

A *compound* word is one containing components that are words in themselves.

❑ COMPOUND (v.)—to combine, augment

After spitting out his food, he *compounded* the insult to the hostess by giving his plate to the dog to finish.

❑ COMPRESS—to reduce, squeeze

The campers *compressed* the six-man tent into a tiny package.

❑ COMPULSIVE—obsessive, fanatic

A *compulsive* liar, Reggie told his boss that he had once climbed Mount Everest with a yak on his back.

❑ COMPUNCTION—feeling of uneasiness caused by guilt or regret

It is often said that psychopaths have no consciences, suffering little *compunction* for the pain they cause.

❑ CONCAVE—curving inward

The *concave* shape of the inside of a bowl makes it ideal for holding food.

❑ CONCEDE—to yield, admit

Ralph *conceded* that he should have checked that he had enough gas before driving into the wilderness.

❑ CONCEPTUALIZE—to envision, imagine

It was difficult for me to *conceptualize* how Bert's crackpot scheme could possibly work.

❑ CONCERTO—musical composition for orchestra and one or more soloists

The orchestra performed the *concerto* every night for weeks.

❑ CONCILIATORY—overcoming distrust or hostility

Fred made the *conciliatory* gesture of buying Abby flowers after their big fight.

❑ CONCORD—agreement

The manager and her employees were in *concord* over the necessity of improving the product.

❑ CONCUR—to agree

When Jamal proposed that the staff devote more time to quality control, everyone *concurred*, and the change was made.

❑ CONDONE—to pardon or forgive; overlook, justify, or excuse a fault

"We cannot *condone* your behavior," said Raj's parents after he missed his curfew. "You're grounded."

❑ CONDUIT—tube, pipe, or similar passage

The *conduit* carried excess rainwater down to the ocean, preventing flooding.

❑ CONFECTION—something sweet to eat

The children begged for a taste of the delicious *confection*.

❑ CONFISCATE—to appropriate, seize

The FBI agents *confiscated* the heroin shipment and arrested the drug dealers.

❑ CONFLAGRATION—big, destructive fire

After the *conflagration* had finally died down, the city center was nothing but a mass of blackened embers.

❑ CONFLUENCE—meeting place; meeting of two streams

The town of Harper's Ferry, Virginia, was built at the *confluence* of two rivers.

❑ CONFOUND—to baffle, perplex

Vince, *confounded* by the difficult algebra problems, threw his math book at the wall in frustration.

❑ CONGEAL—to become thick or solid, as a liquid freezing

The melted butter *congealed* on the floor, forming a sticky mass.

❑ CONGENIAL—similar in tastes and habits

Couples with *congenial* personalities stay together longer than couples who are polar opposites.

❑ CONGENITAL—existing since birth

The infant's *congenital* deformity was corrected through surgery.

❑ CONGLOMERATE—collected group of varied things

The Acme *conglomerate* manufactured everything from diapers to trucks.

❑ CONGRESS—formal meeting or assembly

The *congress* debated the thorny issues long into the night, but could not reach a compromise.

❑ CONGRUITY—correspondence, harmony, agreement

There was an obvious *congruity* between Mark's pleasant personality and his kind actions towards others.

❑ CONJECTURE—speculation, prediction

The actor refused to comment, forcing gossip columnists to make *conjectures* on his love life.

❑ CONJUGAL—pertaining to marriage

Larry terminated all *conjugal* relations with his wife after he discovered that she was having an affair.

❑ CONJURE—to evoke a spirit, cast a spell

The cotton candy *conjured* up the image of the fairgrounds he used to visit as a child in Arthur's mind.

❑ CONNIVE—to conspire, scheme

The customs officials were not above *conniving* with criminals in smuggling drugs into the country.

❑ CONSANGUINEOUS—of the same origin; related by blood

The geologist discovered that the rocks of the two sides of the canyon were *consanguineous*, indicating that at one point in time they had been joined together.

❑ CONSCIENTIOUS—governed by conscience; careful and thorough

Harrison wrote *conscientiously* in his diary, never missing a day if he could help it.

❑ CONSECRATE—to declare sacred; dedicate to a goal

The priest *consecrated* the clothing of the saint, and it was placed in the church to be worshipped.

❑ CONSENSUS—unanimity, agreement of opinion or attitude

The jurors finally reached a *consensus* and declared the defendant guilty as charged.

❑ CONSIGN—to commit, entrust

Gertrude *consigned* her cat to the care of her neighbor while she vacationed in Costa Rica.

❑ CONSOLATION—something providing comfort or solace for a loss or hardship

The millions she inherited were little *consolation* to the grief-stricken widow.

❑ CONSOLIDATE—to combine, incorporate

The author *consolidated* various articles she had previously published into one book.

❑ CONSONANT (adj.)—consistent with, in agreement with

The pitiful raise Ingrid received was *consonant* with the low opinion her manager had of her performance.

❑ CONSTITUENT—component, part; citizen, voter

A machine will not function properly if one of its *constituents* is defective.

❑ CONSTRAINED—forced, compelled; confined, restrained

Oscar, *constrained* by the limitations his editor imposed upon him, had to cut 2,000 pages from his book.

❑ CONSTRAINT—something that forces or compels; something that restrains or confines

The madman was put in a strait jacket, but this *constraint* was insufficient to prevent him from injuring five orderlies.

❑ CONSTRUE—to explain or interpret

"I wasn't sure how to *construe* that last remark he made," said Delia, "but I suspect it was an insult."

❑ CONSUMMATE (adj.)—accomplished, complete, perfect

The skater delivered a *consummate* performance, perfect in every aspect.

❑ CONSUMMATE (v.)—to complete, fulfill

Since the marriage was never *consummated*, the couple was able to legally annul it.

❑ CONTEND—to battle, clash; compete

No boxer, past or present, would have been able to *contend* with Muhammad Ali in his prime.

❑ CONTENTIOUS—quarrelsome, disagreeable, belligerent

The *contentious* gentleman in the bar angrily ridiculed whatever anyone said.

❑ CONTINENCE—self-control, self-restraint

Lucy exhibited impressive *continence* in steering clear of fattening foods, and she lost 50 pounds.

❑ CONTRAVENE—to contradict, deny, act contrary to

The watchman *contravened* his official instructions by leaving his post for an hour.

❑ CONTRITE—deeply sorrowful and repentant for a wrong

After three residents were mugged in the lobby while the watchman was away from his post, he felt very *contrite*.

❑ CONTUSION—bruise

The boxer had ugly *contusions* all over his face after the fight.

❑ CONUNDRUM—riddle, puzzle or problem with no solution

The old man puzzled over the *conundrum* for hours, but eventually gave up in disgust.

❑ CONVALESCENCE—gradual recovery after an illness

During her *convalescence* from the malaria attack, Tatiana read dozens of novels.

❑ CONVENE—to meet, come together, assemble

The members of the board *convene* at least once a week.

❑ CONVENTIONAL—typical, customary, commonplace

Conventional wisdom today says that a good job requires a college education.

❑ CONVEX—curved outward

The *convex* shape of his pot belly contrasted sharply with his wife's tautly concave stomach.

❑ CONVIVIAL—sociable; fond of eating, drinking, and people

The restaurant's *convivial* atmosphere contrasted starkly with the gloom of Maureen's empty apartment.

❑ CONVOKE—to call together, summon

The president *convoked* a group of experts to advise him on how to deal with the crisis.

❑ CONVOLUTED—twisted, complicated, involved

Although many people bought *A Brief History of Time*, few could follow its *convoluted* ideas and theories.

❑ COPIOUS—abundant, plentiful

The hostess had prepared *copious* amounts of food for the banquet.

❑ COQUETTE—woman who flirts

The *coquette* flirted shamelessly with all the married men in the room.

❑ CORPOREAL—having to do with the body; tangible, material

Makiko realized that the supposed ghost was *corporeal* in nature when it bumped into a chair.

❑ CORPULENCE—obesity, fatness, bulkiness

Egbert's *corpulence* increased as he spent several hours each day eating and drinking.

❑ CORRELATION—association, mutual relation of two or more things

All too often, there is little *correlation* between the amount of money someone makes and her intelligence.

❑ CORROBORATE—to confirm, verify

Fingerprints *corroborated* the witness's testimony that he saw the defendant in the victim's apartment.

❑ CORRUGATE—to mold in a shape with parallel grooves and ridges

The *corrugated* tin roofs of the shanty town glinted in the haze.

❑ COSMETIC (adj.)—relating to beauty; affecting the surface of something

Cosmetic surgery such as a nose job is generally not covered by insurance.

❑ COSMOGRAPHY—science that deals with the nature of the universe

The scientist's bizarre claims about the universe were not accepted by leading experts in *cosmography*.

❑ COSMOPOLITAN—sophisticated, free from local prejudices

Diplomats are usually more *cosmopolitan* than farmers who have never left the towns they were born in.

❑ COSSET—to pamper, treat with great care

Mimi *cosseted* her toy poodle, feeding it gourmet meals and buying it a silk pillow to sleep on.

❑ COTERIE—small group of persons with a similar purpose

Judith invited a *coterie* of fellow stamp enthusiasts to a stamp-trading party.

❑ COUNTENANCE (n.)—facial expression; look of approval or support

Jeremy was afraid of the new Music Appreciation instructor because she had such an evil *countenance*.

❑ COUNTENANCE (v.)—to favor, support

When the girls started a pillow fight, the baby-sitter warned them, "I will not *countenance* such behavior."

❑ COUNTERMAND—to annul, cancel, make a contrary order

Protestants were relieved when the king *countermanded* his decree that they should be burned at the stake as heretics.

❑ COUNTERVAIL—to counteract, to exert force against

The guerrillas *countervailed* the army offensive by hiding in the jungle and picking off the soldiers one by one.

❑ COVEN—group of witches

The *coven* of witches cackled evilly as they brewed a potion that would turn the prince into a frog.

❑ COVERT—hidden; secret

Spies typically engage in *covert* operations.

❑ COVET—to desire strongly something possessed by another

Harold *coveted* his neighbor's new Mercedes Benz, but he did not have enough money to buy his own.

❑ CRASS—crude, unrefined

Miss Manners watched in horror as her *crass* date belched loudly and snapped his fingers at the waiter.

❑ CRAVEN—cowardly

The *craven* lion cringed in the corner of his cage, terrified of the mouse.

❑ CREDENCE—acceptance of something as true or real

Mr. Biggles couldn't give any *credence* to the charge that his darling son had cheated on his SAT test.

❑ CREDIBLE—plausible, believable

With such a *credible* witness testifying against his client, the lawyer's chances of winning the case were small.

❑ CREDULOUS—gullible, trusting

Although some 4-year-olds believe in the Easter Bunny, only the most *credulous* 9-year-olds do.

❑ CREED—statement of belief or principle

It was a basic tenet of the old man's *creed* that killing was indefensible.

❑ CRESCENDO—gradual increase in volume of sound

The *crescendo* of tension became unbearable as Evel Knievel prepared to jump his motorcycle over the school buses.

CRITERION—standard for judging, rule for testing

Only recently has intelligence become an important *criterion* in the judging of beauty pageants.

CRYPTIC—puzzling

Sherlock Holmes was baffled by the *cryptic* message left on his doorstep.

CUISINE—characteristic style of cooking

French *cuisine* is delicious, yet fattening.

CULMINATION—climax, final stage

Fireworks marked the *culmination* of the festivities.

CULPABLE—guilty, responsible for wrong

The CEO is *culpable* for the bankruptcy of the company; he was, after all, in charge of it.

CULPRIT—guilty person

The police caught the *culprit* eating a doughnut he had stolen in the street outside the burglarized deli.

CUMULATIVE—resulting from gradual increase

"The *cumulative* effect of all this downsizing will be that one day, there won't be enough staff to do the work around here!" exclaimed the exasperated manager.

CUPIDITY—greed

The poverty-stricken man stared at the shining jewels with *cupidity* in his gleaming eyes.

CURATOR—caretaker and overseer of an exhibition, especially in a museum

The *curator* resigned when he could no longer bear begging for donations to keep his museum open.

CURMUDGEON—cranky person

The old man was a notorious *curmudgeon* who snapped at anyone who disturbed him for any reason.

CURSORY—hastily done, superficial

The copy editor gave the article a *cursory* once-over, missing dozens of errors.

CURT—abrupt, blunt

The grouchy shop assistant was curt with one of her customers, and she was reprimanded by her manager.

CURTAIL—to shorten

I had to *curtail* my vacation in the Bahamas after I ran out of money.

CUTLERY—cutting instruments; tableware

The restaurant was notorious for not washing its *cutlery* properly.

CYGNET—young swan

Cygnets may look like ugly, clumsy ducklings, but they grow up to be graceful swans.

CYNIC—person who distrusts the motives of others

Have we become a nation of *cynics* who have lost faith in our own system of government?

D

DAINTY—delicate, sweet

The slim, *dainty* girl made a perfect ballerina.

DAUNT—to discourage, intimidate

She was *daunted* by the enormity of the task before her.

DEARTH—lack, scarcity, insufficiency

The *dearth* of supplies in our city made it difficult to hold out for long against the attack of the aliens.

DEBASE—to degrade or lower in quality or stature

The president's deceitful actions *debased* the stature of his office.

DEBAUCH—to corrupt, seduce from virtue or duty; indulge

After the unscrupulous count *debauched* the innocent girl, she was shunned by her fellow villagers.

DEBILITATE—to weaken, enfeeble

Debilitated by the flu, the postman was barely able to finish his rounds.

DEBUNK—to discredit, disprove

It was the teacher's mission in life to *debunk* the myth that girls are bad at math.

DEBUTANTE—young woman making debut in high society

The *debutante* spent hours dressing for her very first ball, hoping to catch the eye of an eligible bachelor.

DECAPITATE—to behead

In late 18th-century France, the guillotine was used to *decapitate* the enemies of the revolution.

❑ DECATHLON—athletic contest with ten events

Only the most versatile athletes can do well on an event like the *decathlon*.

❑ DECIDUOUS—losing leaves in the fall; short-lived, temporary

Deciduous trees are bare in winter, which is why coniferous trees such as evergreens are used as Christmas trees.

❑ DECLIVITY—downward slope

Because the village was situated on the *declivity* of a hill, it never flooded.

❑ DECOROUS—proper, tasteful, socially correct

The countess trained her daughters in the finer points of *decorous* behavior, hoping they would make a good impression when she presented them at Court.

❑ DECORUM—proper behavior, etiquette

The duke complained that the vulgar peasants lacked the *decorum* appropriate for a visit to the palace.

❑ DECRY—to belittle, openly condemn

Governments all over the world *decried* the dictator's vicious massacre of the helpless peasants.

❑ DEFACE—to mar the appearance of, vandalize

After the wall was torn down, statues of Communist leaders were *defaced* all over the former Eastern bloc.

❑ DEFAMATORY—slanderous, injurious to the reputation

The tabloid was sued for making *defamatory* statements about the celebrity.

❑ DEFENDANT—person required to answer a legal action or suit

The *defendant* sat impassively as witness after witness described the dreadful crimes she had committed.

❑ DEFERENTIAL—respectful and polite in a submissive way

The respectful young law clerk treated the Supreme Court justice very *deferentially*.

❑ DEFILE—to dirty, spoil; to disgrace, dishonor

The natives became enraged after the insensitive explorer spat in their temple, *defiling* it.

❑ DEFINITIVE—clear-cut, explicit or decisive

The brilliant 1949 production has been hailed as the *definitive* version of *A Doll's House*.

❑ DEFLATION—decrease, depreciation

The *deflation* of the currency resulted in financial disaster for many ordinary Russians.

❑ DEFORM—to disfigure, distort

Betty shrieked at the sight of the *deformed* features of the circus freak.

❑ DEFT—skillful, dexterous

It was a pleasure to watch the *deft* carpenter as he repaired the furniture.

❑ DEFUNCT—no longer existing, dead, extinct

That factory, which used to produce bowler hats, has been *defunct* for many years.

❑ DELECTABLE—appetizing, delicious

"That cake was simply *delectable*!" cooed Mrs. Vanderbilt, congratulating the chef.

❑ DELEGATE (v.)—to give powers to another

After learning to *delegate* more work to his assistants, the manager reduced his stress level significantly.

❑ DELETERIOUS—harmful, destructive, detrimental

If we put these defective clocks on the market, it could be quite *deleterious* to our reputation.

❑ DELINEATION—depiction, representation

Mrs. Baxter was very satisfied with the artist's *delineation* of her new mansion.

❑ DELTA—tidal deposit at the mouth of a river

The *delta* of the Nile river is a very impressive sight from the air.

❑ DELUGE (n.)—flood

The president's veto of the housing bill brought a *deluge* of angry calls from people all over America.

❑ DELUGE (v.)—to submerge, overwhelm

The popular actor was *deluged* with fan mail.

❑ DEMAGOGUE—leader, rabble-rouser, usually using appeals to emotion or prejudice

Hitler began his political career as a *demagogue*, giving fiery speeches in the beer halls of Munich.

❑ DEMARCATION—borderline; act of defining or marking a boundary or distinction

The Berlin Wall formed a clear *demarcation* between East and West Berlin.

❑ DEMEAN—to degrade, humiliate, humble

The editor felt that it would *demean* the newspaper to publish letters containing obscenities.

❑ DEMOGRAPHICS—data relating to study of human population

Demographics seem to indicate that the population of the world will double within the foreseeable future.

❑ DEMOTE—to reduce to a lower grade or rank

The army will *demote* any soldier who disobeys orders.

❑ DEMOTION—lowering in rank or grade

Disgruntled by his *demotion*, the accountant planned to search for a new job.

❑ DEMUR—to express doubts or objections

When scientific authorities claimed that all the planets revolved around the Earth, Galileo, with his superior understanding of the situation, was forced to *demur*.

❑ DEMYSTIFY—to remove mystery from, clarify

The process by which traits are inherited was *demystified* by the discovery of the gene.

❑ DENIGRATE—to slur or blacken someone's reputation

The people still loved the president, despite his enemies' attempts to *denigrate* his character.

❑ DENOUNCE—to accuse, blame

After Stella *denounced* her coworkers for stealing pencils from the office, she was promoted.

❑ DENUDE—to make bare, uncover, undress

The mountain was completely *denuded* by uncontrolled logging.

❑ DENUNCIATION—public condemnation

The church staged a public *denunciation* of Galileo for his controversial beliefs.

❑ DEPICT—to describe, represent

Official royal portraits generally *depict* their subjects in a flattering light.

❑ DEPLETE—to use up, exhaust

The ozone layer is gradually being *depleted* by pollution.

❑ DEPLORE—to express or feel disapproval of; regret strongly

"I simply *deplore* your table manners," she told him, as he stuck his head into the bowl to lick up the last of the oatmeal.

❑ DEPLOY—to spread out strategically over an area

The general *deployed* his troops all over the region, overwhelming the enemy through sheer numbers.

❑ DEPOSE—to remove from a high position, as from a throne

After being *deposed* from his throne, the king spent the rest of his life in exile.

❑ DEPRAVITY—sinfulness, moral corruption

The *depravity* of the actor's Hollywood lifestyle shocked his traditional parents.

❑ DEPRECATE—to belittle, disparage

Ernest *deprecated* his own contribution, instead praising the efforts of his coworkers.

❑ DEPRECIATE—to lose value gradually

The Barrettas sold their house, fearful that its value would *depreciate* due to the nuclear reactor being built around the corner.

❑ DERIDE—to mock, ridicule, make fun of

The awkward child was often *derided* by his "cooler" peers.

❑ DERIVATIVE—copied or adapted; not original

The TV show was so obviously *derivative* of *Seinfeld* that viewers who prize originality were not interested in watching it.

❑ DERIVE—to originate; take from a certain source

Maple syrup is *derived* from the sap of maple trees.

❑ DEROGATE—to belittle, disparage

The sarcastic old man never stopped *derogating* the efforts of his daughter, even after she won the Nobel Prize.

❑ DESECRATE—to abuse something sacred

The archaeologist tried to explain to the explorer that he had *desecrated* the temple by spitting in it, but to no avail.

❑ DESICCATE—to dry completely, dehydrate

After a few weeks of lying on the desert's baking sands, the cow's carcass became completely *desiccated*.

❑ DESIST—to stop doing something

The old man was ordered to *desist* from breeding rats in his apartment by the manager.

❑ DESPONDENT—feeling discouraged and dejected

Mr. Baker was lonely and *despondent* after his wife's death.

❑ DESPOT—tyrannical ruler

The *despot* executed half the nobles in his court on a whim.

❑ DESTITUTE—very poor, poverty-stricken

After the stock market crash, Jeanette was *destitute*, forced to beg on the streets in order to survive.

❑ DESULTORY—at random, rambling, unmethodical

Diane had a *desultory* academic record; she had changed majors 12 times in 3 years.

❑ DETER—to discourage; prevent from happening

Some sociologists claim that the death penalty does not really *deter* criminals from committing crimes.

❑ DETERMINATE—having defined limits; conclusive

The sweeper violated the *determinate* rules of his caste by shaking hands with the Brahmin priest.

❑ DETRIMENTAL—causing harm or injury

It is generally acknowledged that cigarette smoking can be *detrimental* to your health.

❑ DEVIATE—to stray, wander

As long as you don't *deviate* from the trail, you should be fine out there in the wilderness.

❑ DEVIATION—departure, exception, anomaly

The supervisor would not tolerate any *deviation* from his established way of doing things.

❑ DEVOID—totally lacking

Roger is utterly *devoid* of tact; did you hear him tell that off-color joke at the funeral?

❑ DEVOUT—deeply religious

Priests and nuns are known to be *devout* people.

❑ DEXTEROUS—skilled physically or mentally

The gymnast who won the contest was far more *dexterous* than the other competitors.

❑ DIABOLICAL—fiendish; wicked

Sherlock Holmes's archenemy is the *diabolical* Professor Moriarty.

❑ DIALECT—regional style of speaking

Jay has lost his original southern *dialect* completely; he sounds like he was born in New York City.

❑ DIAPHANOUS—allowing light to show through; delicate

Ginny's *diaphanous* gown failed to disguise the fact that she was wearing ripped panty hose.

❑ DIATRIBE—bitter verbal attack

During the CEO's lengthy *diatribe*, the board members managed to remain calm and self-controlled.

❑ DICHOTOMY—division into two parts

Westerns often feature a simple *dichotomy* between good guys and bad guys.

❑ DICTUM—authoritative statement; popular saying

Chris tried to live his life in accordance with the *dictum* "Two wrongs don't make a right."

❑ DIDACTIC—excessively instructive

The father was overly *didactic* with his children, turning every activity into a lesson.

❑ DIFFERENTIATE—to distinguish between two items

Ned hoped that his fiancée would not be able to *differentiate* between a real diamond ring and the ring he had bought her.

❑ DIFFIDENCE—shyness, lack of confidence

Steve's *diffidence* during the job interview stemmed from his nervous nature and lack of experience.

❑ DIFFRACT—to cause to separate into parts, especially light

The crystal *diffracted* the ray of sunlight, separating it into beams of all the colors of the spectrum.

❑ DIFFUSE—widely spread out

The smoke was *diffuse*, spreading instead of concentrating in the room in which the fire had started.

❑ DIGRESS—to turn aside; to stray from the main point

The professor *digressed* repeatedly from the subject of the lecture, boring his students.

❑ DILAPIDATED—in disrepair, run down, neglected

It was amazing that the *dilapidated* jalopy could still be driven.

❑ DILATE—to enlarge, swell, extend

When you enter a darkened room, the pupils of your eyes *dilate* to let in more light.

❑ DILATORY—slow, tending to delay

The congressman used *dilatory* measures to delay the passage of the bill.

❑ DILUVIAL—relating to a flood

Mandy came home after the flood to find her basement filled with *diluvial* deposits.

❑ DIMINUTIVE—small

Napoleon made up for his *diminutive* stature with his aggressive personality, terrifying his courtiers.

❑ DIPLOMACY—discretion, tact

Ambassadors need to be skilled in the art of *diplomacy* in order to deal with erratic foreign governments.

❑ DIRGE—funeral hymn

The deceased's relatives wept as the mournful *dirge* was played on the funeral home's organ.

❑ DISAFFECTED—discontented and disloyal

The *disaffected* employee spent most of his time at work surfing the Web for job opportunities and sending out résumés.

❑ DISARRAY—clutter, disorder

Johnny's room fell into *disarray* after his mother decided to stop cleaning it up for him.

❑ DISBAND—to break up

The rock group decided to *disband* after their record sold fewer than 100 copies.

❑ DISBAR—to expel from legal profession

The lawyer was *disbarred* after he was accused of bribing a juror.

❑ DISBURSE—to pay out

The government *disbursed* millions of dollars to reform elementary schools.

❑ DISCERN—to perceive something obscure

It is easy to *discern* the difference between real butter and butter-flavored topping.

❑ DISCLAIM—to deny, disavow

Francine's statement was so silly that she later *disclaimed* it, pretending she had never made it.

❑ DISCLOSE—to confess, divulge

The CIA agent *disclosed* that he had been selling top secret information to the enemy for years.

❑ DISCONCERTING—bewildering, perplexing, slightly disturbing

Brad found his mother-in-law's hostile manner so *disconcerting* that he acted like a fool in her presence.

❑ DISCORDANT—harsh-sounding, badly out of tune

The harpsichord sounded completely *discordant* after not having been played for 50 years.

❑ DISCREDIT—to dishonor or disgrace

The war hero was *discredited* after it was revealed that he had fled in terror from the scene of the battle.

❑ DISCREDITED—disbelieved, discounted; disgraced, dishonored

The *discredited* evangelist struggled to win back his flock, begging their forgiveness for his sins.

❑ DISCREPANCY—difference between

The obvious *discrepancy* between the appearance of the man and the photo in his passport led officials to believe that the passport was a fake.

❑ DISCRETIONARY—subject to one's own judgment

Ambassadors have some *discretionary* powers, though they must bow to the authority of the secretary of state.

❑ DISCURSIVE—wandering from topic to topic

The professor, known for his *discursive* speaking style, covered everything from armadillos to zebras in his zoology lecture.

❑ DISDAIN—to regard with scorn and contempt

The gorgeous contestant *disdained* her competitors, certain that she would win the Miss America crown.

❑ DISDAINFUL—contemptuous, scornful

The interior designer's face took on a *disdainful* expression as he inspected the tacky, vulgar apartment.

❑ DISENGAGED—disconnected, disassociated

Disengaged from the proceedings, the aged senator didn't notice when the fire drill went off.

❑ DISGORGE—to vomit, discharge violently

The drunken man *disgorged* huge quantities of beer, then passed out.

❑ DISHEVELED—untidy, disarranged, unkempt

After his car broke down and he had to walk to work through the rain, Pete showed up at work *disheveled*.

❑ DISINCLINED—averse, unwilling, lacking desire

Harry was *disinclined* to put a lot of effort into his homework, since the teacher never checked it.

❑ DISPARAGE—to belittle, speak disrespectfully about

Gregorio loved to *disparage* his brother's dancing skills, pointing out every mistake he made on the floor.

❑ DISPARATE—dissimilar, different in kind

Although the twins appear to be identical physically, their personalities are *disparate*.

❑ DISPARITY—contrast, dissimilarity

There was a marked *disparity* between his high opinion of himself and the low opinion others had of him.

❑ DISPASSIONATE—free from emotion; impartial, unbiased

Judges should be as *dispassionate* as possible when adjudicating a court case.

❑ DISPEL—to drive out or scatter

Arnie's heroic rescue of the family from the flames *dispelled* any doubts that he could be a good fireman.

❑ DISPENSE—to distribute, administer

Pharmacists will only *dispense* medicine to customers with doctors' prescriptions.

❑ DISPENSE WITH—to suspend the operation of, do without

"I think we can *dispense with* the formalities, now that we know each other so well," said Mr. Rollins.

❑ DISPERSE—to break up, scatter

The workers *dispersed* after receiving their paychecks, many of them heading for the local bar.

❑ DISPIRIT—to dishearten, make dejected

"Henry's been looking *dispirited* since the failure of his business. I'm worried about him," sighed his wife.

❑ DISREPUTE—disgrace, dishonor

The law firm fell into *disrepute* after it was revealed that one of its lawyers was guilty of jury tampering.

❑ DISSEMBLE—to pretend, disguise one's motives

The villain could *dissemble* to the police no longer—he finally had to confess to the forgery.

❑ DISSEMINATE—to spread far and wide

The wire service *disseminates* information so rapidly that events get reported shortly after they happen.

❑ DISSENSION—difference of opinion

The government was forced to abandon the extensive reforms it had planned, due to continued *dissension* within its party ranks about the form these reforms should take.

❑ DISSIPATE—to scatter; to pursue pleasure to excess

The fog gradually *dissipated*, revealing all the ships docked in the harbor.

❑ DISSOCIATE—to separate; remove from an association

Yun-fat *dissociated* himself from the project when he realized how badly it would turn out.

❑ DISSONANT—harsh and unpleasant sounding

The screeching of the opera singer was completely *dissonant* to the ears of her audience.

❑ DISSUADE—to persuade someone to alter original intentions

I tried to *dissuade* him from climbing Everest without an oxygen tank, but he refused to listen.

❑ DISTEND—to swell, inflate, bloat

Her stomach was *distended* after she gorged on the six-course meal.

❑ DISTRAUGHT—very worried and distressed

The *distraught* mother searched desperately for her missing children.

❑ DISTRUST (n.)—disbelief and suspicion

An atmosphere of *distrust* pervaded the office after a rash of burglaries; no one knew who the culprit was.

❑ DITHER—to move or act confusedly or without clear purpose

Ellen *dithered* around her apartment, uncertain how to tackle the family crisis.

❑ DIURNAL—daily

Diurnal creatures tend to become inactive during the night.

❑ DIVINE (v.)—to foretell or know by inspiration

The fortune-teller *divined* from the pattern of the tea leaves that her customer would marry five times.

❑ DIVISIVE—creating disunity or conflict

The leader used *divisive* tactics to pit his enemies against each other.

❑ DOCILE—tame, willing to be taught

Wolves are not as *docile* as dogs, which is why they are not recommended as house pets.

❑ DOCTRINAIRE—rigidly devoted to theories

The professor was *doctrinaire* in his devotion to the theories of Ayn Rand.

❑ DOGMATIC—rigidly fixed in opinion, opinionated

The dictator was *dogmatic*—he, and only he, was right.

❑ DOLEFUL—sad, mournful

Looking into the *doleful* eyes of the lonely pony, the girl decided to take him home with her.

❑ DOLT—idiot, dimwit, foolish person

"You *dolt*," she yelled, spitting out her coffee, "you put salt in the sugar bowl!"

❑ DOMINEER—to rule over something in a tyrannical way

The powerful butcher *domineered* over his timid wife and children.

❑ DONOR—benefactor, contributor

Blood *donors* should be tested for diseases before their blood is used in transfusions.

❑ DORMANT—at rest, inactive, in suspended animation

The volcano seemed *dormant*, but a devastating eruption was brewing deep in the earth beneath it.

❑ DOTARD—senile old person

The *dotard*, unable to care for himself any longer, was sent to a nursing home.

❑ DOTING—excessively fond, loving to excess

Tony's *doting* father let him get away with all sorts of bad behavior.

❑ DOUR—sullen and gloomy; stern and severe

The *dour* hotel concierge demanded payment for the room in advance.

❑ DOWRY—money or property given by a bride to her husband

Because her parents could offer a large *dowry*, Sonal had her pick of husbands.

❑ DRAFT (v.)—to plan, outline; to recruit, conscript

The boys were *drafted* into the army on their 18th birthday.

❑ DRIVEL—stupid talk; slobber

"I don't want to hear any more of that *drivel*," the impatient wife shouted at her whining husband.

❑ DROLL—amusing in a wry, subtle way

Although the play couldn't be described as hilarious, it was certainly *droll*.

❑ DROSS—waste produced during metal smelting; garbage

The steel mill tried to come up with ways to dispose of *dross* in an environmentally friendly manner.

❑ DULCET—pleasant sounding, soothing to the ear

The *dulcet* tone of her voice lulled me to sleep.

❑ DUPE (v.)—to deceive, trick

Bugs Bunny was able to *dupe* Elmer Fudd by dressing up as a lady rabbit.

❑ DUPE (n.)—fool, pawn

But one day, Elmer Fudd decided that he would be Bugs Bunny's *dupe* no longer; he ripped the lady rabbit's clothes off, only to discover that she was in fact a lady rabbit after all.

❑ DUPLICITY—deception, dishonesty, double-dealing

Diplomatic relations between the two superpowers were outwardly friendly, yet characterized by *duplicity*.

❑ DURABILITY—strength, sturdiness

The all-terrain pickup truck was built for *durability*.

❑ DURATION—period of time that something lasts

Doreen was seasick in her cabin for the entire *duration* of the voyage.

❑ DURESS—threat of force or intimidation; imprisonment

Under *duress*, the political dissident revealed the names of others in his organization to the secret police.

❑ DYSPEPTIC—suffering from indigestion; gloomy and irritable

The *dyspeptic* young man cast a gloom over the party the minute he walked in.

E

❑ EBB—to fade away, recede

Melissa enjoyed watching the *ebb* and flow of the tide from her beachside balcony.

❑ EBULLIENT—exhilarated, full of enthusiasm and high spirits

The *ebullient* child exhausted the baby-sitter, who lacked the energy to keep up with her.

❑ ECLECTIC—selecting from various sources

Budapest's architecture is an *eclectic* mix of eastern and western styles.

❑ ECSTATIC—joyful

Mortimer's parents were *ecstatic* when they learned of his 1600 SAT score.

❑ EDDY—air or wind current

When water gets pulled down a drain, it forms a small *eddy*.

❑ EDICT—law, command, official public order

Pedestrians often disobey the *edict* that they should not jaywalk.

❑ EDIFICE—building

The towering *edifice* dominated the city skyline.

❑ EDIFY—to instruct morally and spiritually

The guru was paid to *edify* the actress in the ways of Buddhism.

❑ EDITORIALIZE—to express an opinion on an issue

Most of the papers in the country *editorialized* on the subject of the president's impeachment.

❑ EFFACE—to erase or make illegible

Benjamin attempted to *efface* all traces of his troubled past by assuming a completely new identity.

❑ EFFERVESCENT—bubbly, lively

Tina's *effervescent* personality made her perfect for the job of game show host.

❑ EFFICACIOUS—effective, efficient

Penicillin was one of the most *efficacious* drugs on the market when it was first introduced; the drug completely eliminated almost all bacterial infections for which it was administered.

❑ EFFIGY—stuffed doll; likeness of a person

The anti-American militants burned Uncle Sam in *effigy* during their demonstration.

❑ EFFLUVIA—outpouring of gases or vapors

Poisonous *effluvia* from the factory contaminated the surrounding countryside.

❑ EFFRONTERY—impudent boldness; audacity

The receptionist had the *effrontery* to laugh out loud when the CEO tripped over a computer wire and fell flat on his face.

❑ EFFULGENT—brilliantly shining

The *effulgent* angel hovering in the dark evening sky dazzled the sharecroppers.

❑ EFFUSIVE—expressing emotion without restraint

The teacher praised Brian *effusively* for his brilliant essay.

❑ EGOCENTRIC—acting as if things are centered around oneself

Craig was so *egocentric* that he didn't even notice that his comments were hurting Pat's feelings.

❑ EGREGIOUS—conspicuously bad

The English text book contained several *egregious* errors; for example, "grammar" was misspelled as "gramer" throughout.

❑ EGRESS—exit

Airplanes should have points of convenient *egress* so that passengers can escape in the event of a crash.

ELATION—exhilaration, joy

The actress was filled with *elation* when she heard that she had been awarded the Emmy.

ELEGY—mournful poem, usually about the dead

Although Thomas Gray's *Elegy Written in a Country Churchyard* is about death and loss, it urges its readers to endure this life, and to trust in spirituality.

ELICIT—to draw out, provoke

The tough policeman was not able to *elicit* the confession he wanted from the murder suspect.

ELOQUENCE—fluent and effective speech

The Gettysburg Address is moving because of its lofty sentiments as well as its *eloquence*.

ELUCIDATE—to explain, clarify

The teacher *elucidated* the reasons why she had failed the student to his upset parents.

EMACIATED—skinny, scrawny, gaunt, especially from hunger

The *emaciated* stray dog begged for scraps from the picnickers.

EMANCIPATE—to set free, liberate

After the slaves were *emancipated*, many of them moved to eastern cities in search of new opportunities.

EMBELLISH—to ornament; make attractive with decoration or details; add details to a statement

Sanjev's story is too short: it needs to be *embellished* with more details about life among the penguins.

EMBEZZLE—to steal money in violation of a trust

The accountant *embezzled* millions of dollars from the company before management discovered what he was up to.

EMBROIL—to involve in; cause to fall into disorder

Lawyers became *embroiled* in the dispute when it became obvious that no compromise could be reached without them.

EMEND—to correct a text

The catalog was *emended* so that correct prices were given for the products on sale.

EMINENT—celebrated, distinguished; outstanding, towering

They were amazed that such an *eminent* scholar could have made such an obvious error.

EMOLLIENT—having soothing qualities, especially for skin

After using the *emollient* lotion for a couple of weeks, Donna's skin changed from scaly to smooth.

EMOTIVE—appealing to or expressing emotion

The film had a strong *emotive* appeal, reducing the audience to tears.

EMPATHY—identification with another's feelings

Having taught English herself, Julie felt a strong *empathy* for the troubled English teacher in the film.

EMULATE—to copy, imitate

The graduate student sought to *emulate* the professor he admired in every way.

ENCIPHER—to translate a message into code

The spy *enciphered* the top-secret document before sending it to headquarters via radio transmitter.

ENCORE—additional performance, often demanded by audience

The soprano performed three *encores*, much to the delight of the enthusiastic audience.

ENCUMBER—to hinder, burden, restrict motion

Encumbered by her huge backpack, Luisa could not run fast enough to catch the bus.

ENDEMIC—belonging to a particular area, inherent

The health department determined that the outbreak was *endemic* to the small village, so they quarantined the inhabitants before the virus could spread.

ENDURANCE—ability to withstand hardships

To prepare for the marathon, Becky built up her *endurance* by running ten miles every day.

ENERVATE—to weaken, sap strength from

The guerrillas hoped that a series of surprise attacks would *enervate* the regular army.

ENGENDER—to produce, cause, bring about

His fear of clowns was *engendered* when he witnessed the death of his father at the hands of a clown.

❑ ENIGMATIC—puzzling, inexplicable

Because he spoke in riddles and dressed in robes, his peers considered the artist's behavior *enigmatic*.

❑ ENJOIN—to urge, order, command; forbid or prohibit, as by judicial order

The stalker was *enjoined* from coming within 100 yards of the woman with whom he was obsessed.

❑ ENMITY—hostility, antagonism, ill-will

After McDonald was killed by McDuff, the *enmity* between their families continued for hundreds of years.

❑ ENNUI—boredom, lack of interest and energy

Joe tried to alleviate the *ennui* he felt while doing his tedious job by flirting with all his coworkers.

❑ ENORMITY—state of being gigantic or terrible

The manager underestimated the *enormity* of the problem and did not act quickly to solve it, which resulted in disaster.

❑ ENSCONCE—to settle comfortably into a place

Wayne sold the big, old family house and *ensconced* his aged mother in a cozy little cottage.

❑ ENSHROUD—to cover, enclose with a dark cover

The Chinese *enshroud* themselves in white cloths at funerals, since white is the color of mourning.

❑ ENTAIL—to involve as a necessary result, necessitate

The reforms you are suggesting would *entail* massive changes in the way we do things around here.

❑ ENTHRALL—to captivate, enchant, enslave

The children were *enthralled* by the spectacular circus show.

❑ ENTITY—something with its own existence or form

Attempts have been made to preserve Hong Kong as a territorial *entity*, separate from China.

❑ ENTOMOLOGIST—scientist who studies insects

Entomologists protested when several animated movies were released in which ants were given the wrong number of legs.

❑ ENTREAT—to plead, beg

I *entreated* him to just tell me what the problem was instead of bottling it up inside, but he refused.

❑ ENUMERATE—to count, list, itemize

Moses returned from the mountain with tablets on which the commandments were *enumerated*.

❑ ENUNCIATE—to pronounce clearly

Airport announcers must learn to *enunciate* clearly so that international passengers can understand them.

❑ EPHEMERAL—momentary, transient, fleeting

The lives of mayflies seem *ephemeral* to us, since the flies' average life span is a matter of hours.

❑ EPICURE—person with refined taste in food and wine

Restaurant critics should be *epicures*, as people rely on their judgments in choosing where to eat.

❑ EPIGRAM—short, witty saying or poem

The poet was renowned for his skill in making up amusing *epigrams*.

❑ EPIGRAPH—quotation at the beginning of a literary work

The *epigraph* of the book didn't seem to have a connection to the content that followed it.

❑ EPILOGUE—concluding section of a literary work

In the *epilogue* of the novel, the author described the ultimate fate of its characters.

❑ EPITOME—representative of an entire group; summary

The host was the *epitome* of graciousness, making all of his guests feel perfectly comfortable.

❑ EPOCHAL—very significant or influential; defining an epoch or time period

Martin Luther King's "I Have a Dream" speech was *epochal* for the Civil Rights era.

❑ EQUANIMITY—calmness, composure

Kelly took the news that she had been fired with outward *equanimity*, though she was crying inside.

❑ EQUESTRIAN—one who rides on horseback

The *equestrian* visited a horse show to select a new mare for her personal use.

❑ EQUINE—relating to horses

Many donkeys have *equine* characteristics, although they are not horses.

❑ EQUIVOCAL—ambiguous, open to more than one interpretation

Poems are inherently *equivocal*, and there is no point in trying to assign a definitive meaning to them.

❑ EQUIVOCATE—to use vague or ambiguous language intentionally

When faced with criticism of his policies, the politician *equivocated* and left all parties thinking he agreed with them.

❑ ERADICATE—to erase or wipe out

It is unlikely that poverty will ever be completely *eradicated* in this country, though the general standard of living has significantly improved in recent decades.

❑ ERRANT—straying, mistaken, roving

The *errant* elephant was eventually caught and sent back to the zoo.

❑ ERUDITE—learned, scholarly

The annual meeting of professors brought together the most *erudite*, respected individuals in the field.

❑ ESCHEW—to abstain from, avoid

Models generally *eschew* rich desserts because such desserts are fattening.

❑ ESOTERIC—understood by only a learned few

Only a handful of experts are knowledgeable about the *esoteric* world of particle physics.

❑ ESPOUSE—to support or advocate; to marry

Due to his religious beliefs, the preacher could not *espouse* the practice of abortion.

❑ ESTRANGE—to alienate, keep at a distance

Estranged from his family for many years, Alan had not heard that his both his parents had died.

❑ ETHEREAL—not earthly, spiritual, delicate

Her delicate, *ethereal* beauty made her a popular model for Pre-Raphaelite artists.

❑ ETHOS—beliefs or character of a group

In accordance with the *ethos* of his people, the teenage boy underwent a series of initiation rituals to become a man.

❑ ETYMOLOGY—origin and history of a word; study of words

The professor devoted himself to an ambitious study of the *etymology* of all words beginning with "E."

❑ EULOGY—high praise, often in a public speech

His best friend gave the *eulogy*, outlining his many achievements and talents.

❑ EUPHEMISM—use of an inoffensive word or phrase in place of a more distasteful one

The funeral director preferred to use the *euphemism* "passed away" instead of the word "dead."

❑ EUPHONY—pleasant, harmonious sound

To their loving parents, the children's orchestra performance sounded like *euphony*, although an outside observer probably would have called it a cacophony of hideous sounds.

❑ EUPHORIA—feeling of well-being or happiness

Euphoria overwhelmed her when she discovered that she had scored a perfect 1600 on her SAT.

❑ EURYTHMICS—art of harmonious bodily movement

Ballerinas must be skilled in the art of *eurythmics*.

❑ EUTHANASIA—mercy killing; intentional, easy, and painless death

The widow claimed that she had committed *euthanasia*, not murder, when she gave her terminally ill husband an overdose.

❑ EVADE—to avoid, dodge

He *evaded* answering my question by pretending not to hear me and changing the subject.

❑ EVANESCENT—momentary, transitory, short-lived

It is lucky that eclipses are *evanescent*, or the world would never see sunlight.

❑ EVICT—to put out or force out

Mrs. Rose was *evicted* from the apartment when she failed to pay rent for three months in a row.

❑ EVINCE—to show clearly, display, signify

The new secretary *evinced* impressive typing and filing skills.

❑ EVOKE—to inspire memories; to produce a reaction

The sight of the old elm tree *evoked* memories of the treehouse she had built as a little girl.

❑ EXACERBATE—to aggravate, intensify the bad qualities of

It is unwise to take aspirin to relieve heartburn; instead of providing relief, the drug will only *exacerbate* the problem.

❑ EXASPERATION—irritation

The catcher couldn't hide his *exasperation* when the pitcher refused to listen to his advice, throwing a series of pitches that resulted in home runs for the opposing team.

❑ EXCERPT (n.)—selection from a book or play

If you want to reprint an *excerpt* from that play, you'll have to get permission from the author.

❑ EXCOMMUNICATE—to bar from membership in the church

The king was *excommunicated* from the Church when he decided to divorce his wife and remarry.

❑ EXCRUCIATING—agonizing, intensely painful

Although it's a minor injury, stubbing your toe can be *excruciatingly* painful.

❑ EXCULPATE—to clear of blame or fault, vindicate

The adversarial legal system is intended to convict those who are guilty and to *exculpate* those who are innocent.

❑ EXECRABLE—utterly detestable, abhorrent

The stew tasted utterly *execrable* after the cook accidentally dumped a pound of salt into it.

❑ EXHILARATION—state of being energetic or filled with happiness

Fred was filled with *exhilaration* after he learned that he had won the lottery.

❑ EXHORT—to urge or incite by strong appeals

Rob's friends *exhorted* him to beware of ice on the roads when he insisted on driving home in the middle of a snowstorm.

❑ EXHUME—to remove from a grave; uncover a secret

The murder victim's corpse was *exhumed*, but no new evidence was discovered and it was reburied the following day.

❑ EXIGENT—urgent; excessively demanding

The patient was losing blood so rapidly that it was *exigent* to stop the source of the bleeding.

❑ EXONERATE—to clear of blame, absolve

The fugitive was *exonerated* when another criminal confessed to committing the crime.

❑ EXORBITANT—extravagant, greater than reasonable

After the harvest was destroyed by freezing temperatures, shops charged *exorbitant* prices for oranges.

❑ EXORCISE—to expel evil spirits

The priest struggled to *exorcise* the spirit of the Devil from the body of the little girl.

❑ EXOTIC—foreign; romantic, excitingly strange

The atmosphere of the restaurant was *exotic*, but the food was ordinary.

❑ EXPANSIVE—sweeping, comprehensive; tending to expand

"Soon, all this will be mine!" declared the evil emperor, indicating the city below him with an *expansive* sweep of his arm.

❑ EXPATRIATE (n.)—one who lives outside one's native land

He spent much of his adult life as an *expatriate*, only returning to his own country for his retirement.

❑ EXPATRIATE (v.)—to drive someone from his/her native land

Imelda Marcos was *expatriated* from the Phillipines after her husband was deposed.

❑ EXPEDIENT (adj.)—convenient, efficient, practical

It was considered more *expedient* to send the fruit directly to the retailer instead of through a middleman.

❑ EXPIATE—to atone for, make amends for

The nun *expiated* her sins by scrubbing the floor of the convent on her hands and knees.

❑ EXPIRE—to come to an end; die; breathe out

Since her driver's license was about to *expire*, she had to go and exchange it for a new one.

❑ EXPLICABLE—capable of being explained

"I'm sure that all these bizarre events are completely *explicable*," said Nancy, trying to reassure her family that the terrifying sounds coming from the haunted house were nothing to worry about.

❑ EXPLICIT—clearly defined, specific; forthright in expression

The owners of the house left a list of *explicit* instructions detailing their house-sitters' duties.

❑ EXPLODE—to debunk, disprove; blow up, burst

The "free love" common in the '60s *exploded* conventional theories of marriage and courtship.

❑ EXPONENT—one who champions or advocates

The vice president was an enthusiastic *exponent* of computer technology.

❑ EXPOUND—to elaborate; to expand or increase

The teacher *expounded* on the theory of relativity for hours, boring his students.

❑ EXPUNGE—to erase, eliminate completely

The censor wanted to *expunge* all the parts of Joyce's *Ulysses* he thought were obscene.

❑ EXPURGATE—to censor

Government propagandists *expurgated* all negative references to the dictator from the film.

❑ EXTEMPORANEOUS—unrehearsed, on the spur of the moment

Jan gave an *extemporaneous* performance of a Monty Python skit at her surprise birthday party.

❑ EXTENUATE—to lessen the seriousness, strength, or effect of

The fact that the man whom Ronnie shot was trying to strangle him at the time was considered an *extenuating* circumstance, and the judge gave him a fairly light sentence.

❑ EXTINCTION—end of a living thing or species

The dodo was hunted to *extinction* by man many years ago.

❑ EXTOL—to praise

The salesman *extolled* the virtues of the used car he was trying to convince the customer to buy.

❑ EXTORT—to obtain something by threats

The president's ex-lover *extorted* a cushy job from him, threatening to reveal their affair if he did not do as she wished.

❑ EXTRANEOUS—irrelevant, unrelated, unnecessary

When none of the committee members acknowledged that she had even spoken, June realized that her presence at the meeting was completely *extraneous*.

❑ EXTREMITY—outermost or farthest point

The *extremities* of the body, such as toes, are vulnerable to frostbite in extreme cold weather.

❑ EXTRICATE—to free from, disentangle

The fly was unable to *extricate* itself from the flypaper.

❑ EXTRINSIC—not inherent or essential, coming from without

"While it's a cute idea, I'd say that the espresso machine accessory is *extrinsic* to our basic concept of a good, functional car," said the Ford executive.

❑ EXUBERANT—lively, happy, and full of good spirits

The *exuberant* puppy jumped up and licked the face of its master, happy to see him home again.

❑ EXUDE—to give off, ooze

The job candidate *exuded* an aura of self-confidence, impressing his interviewers.

❑ EXULT—to rejoice

The investor *exulted* as the price of the stocks he had bought skyrocketed

F

❑ FABRICATE—to make or devise; construct

A prefab house is one that is *fabricated* before it is transported to a plot of land.

❑ FABRICATED—constructed, invented; faked, falsified

The reporter was disgraced when it was uncovered that the stories he'd published were largely *fabricated*.

❑ FACADE—face, front; mask, superficial appearance

The drug dealers conducted business from a small bodega in order to maintain a *facade* of respectability.

❑ FACILE—very easy

She was alarmingly *facile* when it came to telling lies; they seemed to roll off her tongue.

❑ FACILITATE—to aid, assist

The organizers tried to *facilitate* the social interaction of the delegates by giving everyone name tags.

❑ FACILITY—aptitude, ease in doing something

Bob had a *facility* for trigonometry problems, although he could not do algebra at all.

❑ FALLACIOUS—wrong, unsound, illogical

We now know that the statement "the Earth is flat" is *fallacious*.

❑ FALLOW—uncultivated, unused

This field should lie *fallow* for a year so that the soil does not become completely depleted.

❑ FANATICISM—extreme devotion to a cause

The stormtroopers' *fanaticism* in their devotion to the Emperor was so great that they would readily have sacrificed their lives for him.

❑ FARCICAL—absurd, ludicrous

"The idea that I would burn down my own house is completely *farcical*," sneered the arson suspect.

❑ FASTIDIOUS—careful with details

Brett was normally so *fastidious* that Rachel was astonished to find his desk littered with clutter.

❑ FATHOM (v.)—to measure the depth of, gauge

The marine scientists used their sophisticated equipment to attempt to *fathom* the depth of the underwater canyon.

❑ FATUOUS—stupid; foolishly self-satisfied

Ted's *fatuous* comments always embarrassed his keen-witted wife at parties.

❑ FAULT—break in a rock formation; mistake or error

The San Andreas *fault* runs under several major urban areas in California, making earthquakes a frequent occurrence.

❑ FAWN (v.)—to flatter excessively, seek the favor of

The understudy *fawned* over the director in hopes of being cast in the part on a permanent basis.

❑ FAZE—to bother, upset, or disconcert

Strangely, the news that his car had been stolen did not *faze* Nathan, although his wife was hysterical.

❑ FEASIBLE—possible, capable of being done

It was decided that the idea of giving away free fur coats was not *feasible*, and it was abandoned.

❑ FECKLESS—ineffective, careless, irresponsible

Anja took on the responsibility of caring for her aged mother, realizing that her *feckless* sister was not up to the task.

❑ FECUND—fertile, fruitful, productive

The *fecund* housewife gave birth to a total of twenty children.

❑ FEDERATION—union of organizations; union of several states, each of which retains local power

The states formed a *federation* in order to put together a united army to resist the attacking foreign power.

❑ FEIGN—to pretend, give a false impression; to invent falsely

Although Sean *feigned* indifference, he was very much interested in the contents of the envelope.

❑ FEISTY—excitable, easily drawn into quarrels

The *feisty* old lady alienated her neighbors with her habit of picking fights with anyone who crossed her.

❑ FELICITOUS—suitable, appropriate; well-spoken

The father of bride made a *felicitous* speech at the wedding, contributing to the success of the event.

❑ FELL (v.)—to chop, cut down

The muscular logger *felled* the tree in one powerful blow.

❑ FERVID—passionate, intense, zealous

The fans of Maria Callas were particularly *fervid*, doing anything to catch a glimpse of the great singer.

❑ FETID—foul-smelling, putrid

The *fetid* stench from the outhouse caused Laura to wrinkle her nose in disgust.

❑ FETTER—to bind, chain, confine

The chain gang, *fettered* together in a long line, trudged slowly through the mud.

❑ FIASCO—disaster, utter failure

After the soloist turned up drunk, it was hardly surprising that the concert proved to be an utter *fiasco*.

❑ **FICTIVE**—fictional, imaginary

The boy had a *fictive* friend who kept him company during the long hours he had to spend alone.

❑ **FIDELITY**—loyalty

A traitor is someone whose *fidelity* is questioned.

❑ **FILCH**—to steal

The pickpocket managed to *filch* ten wallets in the rush hour crowd.

❑ **FILIBUSTER**—use of obstructive tactics in a legislative assembly to prevent adoption of a measure

Democrats *filibustered* for hours, desperately trying to prevent the adoption of the Republican measure.

❑ **FINICKY**—fussy, difficult to please

The *finicky* child rejected every dish on the menu, to the exasperation of his parents.

❑ **FISSION**—process of splitting into two parts

The discovery of the process of nuclear *fission* enabled scientists to construct the atom bomb.

❑ **FITFUL**—intermittent, irregular

The water came through the tap in *fitful* spurts at first, then began to pour in a steady flow.

❑ **FLACCID**—limp, flabby, weak

The woman jiggled her *flaccid* arms in disgust, resolving to begin lifting weights as soon as possible.

❑ **FLAGRANT**—outrageous, shameless

His *flagrant* disregard for the rules has resulted in his dismissal from the job.

❑ **FLAMBOYANT**—flashy, garish; exciting, dazzling

Reginald's *flamboyant* clothing made him stick out like a sore thumb at his conservative office.

❑ **FLAMMABLE**—combustible, being easily burned

It is not a good idea to keep highly *flammable* objects close to open fires.

❑ **FLAUNT**—to show off

Rhonda *flaunted* her engagement ring all over the office.

❑ **FLEDGLING**—young bird just learning to fly; beginner, novice

The *fledgling* eagle clung to the edge of the cliff, afraid to take its first plunge into the open air.

❑ **FLORA**—plants

The local *flora* of the Kenyan savannah includes the baobab tree.

❑ **FLORID**—gaudy, extremely ornate; ruddy, flushed

The palace had been decorated in an excessively *florid* style; every surface had been carved and gilded.

❑ **FLOUNDER**—to falter, waver; to muddle, struggle

The previously glib defendant began to *flounder* when the prosecutor found a hole in his story.

❑ **FLOUT**—to treat contemptuously, scorn

The motorist *flouted* the traffic cop's instructions, cutting several cars off to barrel across the intersection.

❑ **FLUCTUATE**—to alternate, waver

Certain stock prices *fluctuate* so much that it is risky to invest in them.

❑ **FODDER**—raw material; feed for animals

The gossip columnist chatted with as many celebrities as possible, seeking *fodder* for her articles.

❑ **FOIBLE**—minor weakness or character flaw

Her habit of licking out the centers of Oreo cookies is a *foible*, not a serious character flaw.

❑ **FOIL (v.)**—to defeat, frustrate

James Bond *foiled* the villain's evil plot to take over the world.

❑ **FOLIATE**—to grow, sprout leaves

The plant looked dead, so Victor was astonished when it began to *foliate*.

❑ **FOMENT**—to arouse or incite

The protesters tried to *foment* feeling against the war through their speeches and demonstrations.

❑ **FORBEARANCE**—patience, restraint, leniency

In light of the fact that he was new on the job, Collette decided to exercise *forbearance* with her assistant's numerous errors.

❑ **FORECLOSE**—to rule out; to seize debtor's property for lack of payments

The bank *foreclosed* on the Okie family farm, forcing them to drive to California to look for work.

❑ FORD (v.)—to cross a body of water at a shallow place

Because of the recent torrential rains, the cowboys were unable to *ford* the swollen river.

❑ FOREBODING—dark sense of evil to come

Carrie felt an acute sense of *foreboding* when she thought about the upcoming high school prom.

❑ FORENSIC—relating to legal proceedings; relating to debates

The law school offered an excellent program in *forensics*.

❑ FORESTALL—to prevent, delay; anticipate

The landlord *forestalled* Bob's attempt to avoid paying the rent by waiting for him outside his door.

❑ FORETHOUGHT—anticipation, foresight

If you had given a little *forethought* to your presentation, I'm sure it would have turned out better.

❑ FORGO—to go without, refrain from

In an effort to lose weight, Lisa decided to *forgo* dessert for the next month or so.

❑ FORLORN—dreary, deserted; unhappy; hopeless, despairing

Ying felt *forlorn* at the prospect of moving out of the house in which she had been born.

❑ FORMULATE—to conceive, devise; to draft, plan; to express, state

The marketers *formulated* an advertising strategy to launch the new product on the market.

❑ FORSAKE—to abandon, withdraw from

It is common for criminals on Death Row to feel that everyone they know has *forsaken* them.

❑ FORSWEAR—to repudiate, renounce, disclaim, reject

I was forced to *forswear* french fries after the doctor told me that my cholesterol was too high.

❑ FORTE—strong point, something a person does well

Since math was Dan's *forte*, his friends always asked him to calculate the bill whenever they went out to dinner together.

❑ FORTUITOUS—happening by luck, fortunate

Rochelle got her start in the music industry when a powerful agent happened, *fortuitously*, to attend one of her gigs.

❑ FOSTER—to nourish, cultivate, promote

The record agent *fostered* the development of his clients by sending them to singing lessons.

❑ FOUNDATION—groundwork, support; institution established by donation to aid a certain cause

The claim that the sun revolves around the Earth has no *foundation*; scientific evidence disproves it.

❑ FOUNDER (v.)—to fall helplessly; sink

After colliding with the jagged rock, the ship *foundered*, forcing the crew to abandon it.

❑ FRACAS—noisy dispute

When the bandits discovered that the gambler was cheating them at cards, a violent *fracas* ensued.

❑ FRACTIOUS—unruly, rebellious

The general had a hard time maintaining discipline among his *fractious* troops.

❑ FRAGMENTATION—division, separation into parts, disorganization

After the *fragmentation* of the former India into India, Pakistan, and Bangladesh, ethnic violence erupted.

❑ FRANK—honest and straightforward

"Let me be *frank*: there's no way I would ever hire you," said the recruiter to the job applicant.

❑ FRAUD—deception, hoax

The salesman was arrested for *fraud* after selling 500 acres of mosquito-infested swamp, which he claimed was choice beachside property, to the senior citizens.

❑ FRAUDULENT—deceitful, dishonest, unethical

The factory engaged in *fraudulent* practices, producing radios with no internal components.

❑ FRAUGHT—full of, accompanied by

The sea voyage was *fraught* with peril; the crew had to contend with storms, sharks, and scurvy on board.

❑ FRENETIC—wildly frantic, frenzied, hectic

The *frenetic* manager worked insane hours, trying desperately to finish the important project on time.

❑ FRENZIED—feverishly fast, hectic, and confused

The family made a *frenzied* dash through the airport, arriving at their gate just before their plane took off.

❑ FRIVOLOUS—petty, trivial; flippant, silly

The biggest problem in the world for the *frivolous* debutante was that her ribbon was the wrong color.

❑ FROND—leaf

The fern *fronds* made a beautiful pattern against the window.

❑ FULSOME—sickeningly excessive; repulsive

Diana felt nauseous at the sight of the rich, *fulsome* dishes weighing down the table at the banquet.

❑ FUNEREAL—mournful, appropriate to a funeral

Depressed by the party's *funereal* atmosphere, Suzanne decided to leave early.

❑ FURTIVE—secret, stealthy

Glenn *furtively* peered out of the corner of his eye at the stunningly beautiful model.

❑ FUSION—process of merging things into one

Cement is a *fusion* formed from a combination of shale and limestone.

G

❑ GALL (n.)—bitterness; careless nerve

I cannot believe she had the *gall* to show up late her first day of work.

❑ GALL (v.)—to exasperate and irritate

My uncle constantly *galls* my aunt by putting his feet up on the coffee table.

❑ GAMBOL—to dance or skip around playfully

The parents gathered to watch the children *gambol* about the yard.

❑ GAMELY—courageously

Though Xena lacked sufficient weapons, she *gamely* faced her opponent.

❑ GARGANTUAN—giant, tremendous

Cleaning a teenager's room can often be a *gargantuan* task.

❑ GARNER—to gather and store

The director managed to *garner* financial backing from several different sources for his next project.

❑ GARRULOUS—very talkative

The *garrulous* parakeet distracted its owner with its continuous talking.

❑ GAUNT—thin and bony

The actress's *gaunt* frame led the press to speculate that she was anorexic.

❑ GAVEL—mallet used for commanding attention

The judge pounded the desk with his *gavel* to silence the crowd.

❑ GENRE—type, class, category

My sister loves mysteries, but I can't stand that *genre* of books.

❑ GERMINATE—to begin to grow (as with a seed or idea)

Three weeks after planting, the seeds will *germinate*.

❑ GESTATION—growth process from conception to birth

The longer the *gestation* period of an organism is, the more developed the baby is at birth.

❑ GIBE—to make heckling, taunting remarks

Tina *gibed* at her brothers mercilessly as they clumsily attempted to pitch the tent.

❑ GIRTH—distance around something

The young boy marvelled at the *girth* of his pregnant cat's stomach.

❑ GLIB—fluent in an insincere manner; offhand, casual

The slimy politician managed to continue gaining supporters because he was a *glib* speaker.

❑ GLOBAL—involving the entire world; relating to a whole

People all over the world are finally realizing that pollution is a *global* problem.

❑ GLOWER—to glare, stare angrily and intensely

The cranky waitress *glowered* at the indecisive customer.

❑ GLUTTONY—eating and drinking to excess

It took days for the guests to recover their appetites after the *gluttony* that had taken place at the party.

❑ GNARL—to make knotted, deform

The old oak was extremely *gnarled* after withstanding the force of powerful winds for centuries.

GNOSTIC—having to do with knowledge

The *gnostics* were distrusted by the Church because of their preference for knowledge over faith.

GOAD—to prod or urge

Denise *goaded* her sister Leigh into running the marathon with her.

GRADATION—process occurring by regular degrees or stages; variation in color

The paint store offers so many different *gradations* of red that it's impossible to choose among them.

GRANDILOQUENCE—pompous talk, fancy but meaningless language

The pompous headmistress was notorious for her *grandiloquence* as well as for her ostentatious clothes.

GRANDIOSE—magnificent and imposing; exaggerated and pretentious

The house had a *grandiose* facade that disguised its humble and simple interior.

GRANULAR—having a grainy texture

The chemist poured the *granular* substance into the test tube.

GRASP (v.)—to perceive and understand; to hold securely

Peggy could not *grasp* the concept that Dwight had dumped her, and she continued to call him every day.

GRATIS—free, costing nothing

The college students swarmed around the *gratis* buffet in the lobby.

GRATUITOUS—free, voluntary; unnecessary and unjustified

Matt's snubbing of his old friend seemed *gratuitous*, as there had been no bad blood between the two of them previously.

GRATUITY—something given voluntarily, tip

At many restaurants, an 18 percent *gratuity* is added to the bill when the dining party is large enough.

GREGARIOUS—outgoing, sociable

She was so *gregarious* that when she found herself alone she felt quite sad.

GRIEVOUS—causing grief or sorrow; serious and distressing

Maude and Bertha sobbed loudly throughout the *grievous* event.

GRIMACE—facial expression showing pain or disgust

The count *grimaced* when his wife, drunk as usual, spilled a carafe of wine on the king.

GRIMY—dirty, filthy

Beth was displeased when her date, Spike, showed up in a *grimy* t-shirt and torn jeans.

GROSS (adj.)—obscene; blatant, flagrant

Spike's comment that he liked the "casual" look was a *gross* understatement.

GROSS (n.)—total before deductions

The company's *gross* earnings exceeded their predictions.

GROVEL—to humble oneself in a demeaning way

The dog *groveled* at his owner's feet, hoping for a few table scraps.

GUILE—trickery, deception

Greg used considerable *guile* to acquire his rent-controlled apartment, even claiming to be a Vietnam Vet.

GULLIBLE—easily deceived

The *gullible* landlord believed Rich's story that he was only going away for a few days, despite the moving boxes that littered the apartment.

GUSTATORY—relating to sense of taste

Murdock claimed that he loved cooking because he enjoyed the *gustatory* pleasures in life.

H

HABITAT—dwelling place

A rabbit's *habitat* should be a large, dry area with plenty of food, water, and hay available.

HACKNEYED—worn out by overuse

We always mock my father for his *hackneyed* expressions and dated hairstyle.

❑ HALLOWED—holy; treated as sacred

The Constitution is a *hallowed* document in the United States.

❑ HAMLET—small village

Did you know her husband grew up in a *hamlet* in Sweden? No wonder he can't adjust to New York City.

❑ HAPLESS—unfortunate, having bad luck

I wish someone would give that poor, *hapless* soul some food and shelter.

❑ HARBINGER—precursor, sign of something to come

The groundhog's appearance on February 2 is a *harbinger* of spring.

❑ HARDY—robust, vigorous

Heidi was a strong, *hardy* girl who beat up her older brothers on a daily basis.

❑ HARROWING—extremely distressing, terrifying

We stayed up all night listening to Dave and Will talk about their *harrowing* adventures on the sea.

❑ HASTEN—to hurry, to speed up

Juanita *hastened* to the post office to send off her presents in time for Christmas.

❑ HAUGHTY—arrogant and condescending

The teacher resented Sally's *haughty* attitude and gave her a D for the semester.

❑ HEADSTRONG—reckless; insisting on one's own way

Sally was *headstrong* and brought her teacher up before the school board for unfair grading.

❑ HEATHEN—pagan; uncivilized and irreligious

The missionaries considered it their duty to convert as many of the *heathen* natives as possible.

❑ HECTIC—hasty, hurried, confused

Breakfast at their house was always a *hectic* affair, with ten children running around and screaming.

❑ HEDONISM—pursuit of pleasure as a goal

Michelle lay on the couch eating cookies all day, claiming *hedonism* was her philosophy of life.

❑ HEGEMONY—leadership, domination, usually by a country

When Germany claimed *hegemony* over Russia, Stalin was outraged.

❑ HEIGHTEN—to raise

In the past decade, doctors have worked to *heighten* women's awareness of breast cancer.

❑ HEINOUS—shocking, wicked, terrible

Nobody could believe the *heinous* crime the baby-sitter had committed.

❑ HEMICYCLE—semicircular form or structure

The architect sketched the building in the shape of a *hemicycle*.

❑ HEMORRHAGE (n.)—heavy bleeding

The wounded soldiers worried they would have *hemorrhages* as they awaited the doctor's return.

❑ HEMORRHAGE (v.)—to bleed heavily

The girl applied a bandage to her wound to keep from *hemorrhaging* and losing too much blood.

❑ HERETICAL—opposed to an established religious orthodoxy

After the onset of the Inquisition, the *heretical* priest was forced to flee the country to escape the Church's punishment.

❑ HERMETIC—tightly sealed

The *hermetic* seal of the jar proved impossible to break.

❑ HETERODOX—unorthodox, not widely accepted

After the preacher had delivered his *heterodox* sermon, the congregation was speechless.

❑ HETEROGENEOUS—composed of unlike parts, different, diverse

The United Nations is by nature a *heterogenous* body.

❑ HEW—to cut with an ax

Vlad *hewed* down the trees in order to build himself a cabin.

❑ HIATUS—break, interruption, vacation

Julia Roberts returned to acting after a lengthy *hiatus*.

❑ HIDEBOUND—excessively rigid; dry and stiff

The *hidebound* old patriarch would not tolerate any opposition to his orders.

❑ HINDSIGHT—perception of events after they happen

In *hindsight*, Hank realized that drinking the entire bottle of vodka himself was probably not a wise idea.

❑ HINTERLAND—wilderness

The anthropologists noticed that the people had moved out of the cities and into the *hinterland*.

❑ HOARY—very old; whitish or gray from age

The old man's *hoary* beard contrasted starkly to the new stubble of his teenage grandson.

❑ HOLISTIC—emphasizing importance of the whole and interdependence of its parts

Angie is studying internal medicine and believes in a *holistic* approach to healing.

❑ HOLOCAUST—widespread destruction, usually by fire

The city was desolate, utterly destroyed by a *holocaust*.

❑ HOMAGE—public honor and respect

Upon arriving at the village, the warriors paid *homage* to its chief.

❑ HOMOGENEOUS—composed of identical parts

Finland was a very *homogenous* country until immigrants began to settle there several decades ago.

❑ HOMONYM—word identical in pronunciation and spelling but different in meaning

"Right" as in the direction and "right" meaning "correct" are *homonyms*.

❑ HONE—to sharpen

You might want to *hone* your writing skills before filling out college applications.

❑ HONOR—to praise, glorify, pay tribute to

The ceremony *honored* the community leaders who had risked their lives to defend everyone's civil rights.

❑ HUMANE—merciful, kindly

A *humane* man, the camp commander made sure to treat all the prisoners of war fairly.

❑ HUSBAND (v.)—to farm; manage carefully and thriftily

The farmer's wife *husbanded* the money she had made from her strawberry preserves all year.

❑ HUTCH—pen or coop for animals; shack, shanty

The rabbits bred so rapidly that soon their *hutch* could not contain them all.

❑ HYDRATE—to add water to

You'll need to *hydrate* these powdered eggs in order to make an omelet from them.

❑ HYGIENIC—clean, sanitary

A century or two ago, it was realized that surgery should be performed under *hygienic* conditions.

❑ HYMN—religious song, usually of praise or thanks

The churchgoers sang a number of *hymns* together in the course of the service.

❑ HYPERBOLE—purposeful exaggeration for effect

When the mayor claimed his town was one of the seven wonders of the world, outsiders classified his statement as *hyperbole*.

❑ HYPERVENTILATE—to breathe abnormally fast

During her anxiety attack, Joan *hyperventilated* and sweated profusely.

❑ HYPOCHONDRIA—unfounded belief that one is often ill

Dr. Pradesh groaned when he saw Mr. Crupp on his appointment list yet again; the man was a classic victim of *hypochondria*.

❑ HYPOCRITE—person claiming beliefs or virtues he or she doesn't really possess

The prudish evangelist was accused of being a *hypocrite* when he was discovered with a prostitute.

❑ HYPOTHERMIA—abnormally low body temperature

The Arctic explorer, suffering from *hypothermia*, was wrapped in thick blankets by his companions.

❑ HYPOTHESIS—assumption subject to proof

It's an interesting *hypothesis*, but I'll need proof before I'll believe that Pluto is made of cheese.

❑ HYPOTHETICAL—theoretical, speculative

The official claimed that his radical proposal to close half the hospitals in the city was only *hypothetical*.

I

❑ ICONOCLAST—one who attacks traditional beliefs

His lack of regard for traditional beliefs soon established him as an *iconoclast*.

❑ IDEALISM—pursuit of noble goals

"I admire his *idealism*, but how does Bola think he can support ten orphans?" complained his sister.

❑ IDIOSYNCRASY—peculiarity of temperament, eccentricity

His numerous *idiosyncrasies* included a fondness for wearing bright green shoes with mauve socks.

❑ IGNOBLE—dishonorable, not noble in character

The *ignoble* grocer took pleasure in selling his customers flour that was laced with dust.

❑ IGNOMINIOUS—disgraceful and dishonorable

He was humiliated by his *ignominious* dismissal.

❑ ILK—type or kind

"I try not to associate with men of his *ilk*," sniffed the respectable old lady.

❑ ILLICIT—illegal, improper

The mafia is heavily involved in *illicit* activities such as prostitution and drugs.

❑ ILLIMITABLE—limitless

The universe is considered *illimitable*, or in any case so large that humans cannot fathom its end.

❑ ILLUSORY—unreal, deceptive

The desert explorer was devastated to discover that the lake he had seen in the distance was in fact *illusory*.

❑ ILLUSTRIOUS—famous, renowned

The *illustrious* composer produced masterpiece after masterpiece, entrancing her fans.

❑ IMBUE—to infuse; dye, wet, moisten

Marcia struggled to *imbue* her children with decent values, a difficult task in this day and age.

❑ IMMACULATE—spotless; free from error

After I cleaned my apartment for hours, it was finally *immaculate*.

❑ IMMATERIAL—extraneous, inconsequential, nonessential; not consisting of matter

"Where you get the money is *immaterial* to me; just pay up!" grumbled the loanshark.

❑ IMMENSE—enormous, huge

In the main hall of the museum, the *immense* dinosaur skeleton towered over the children.

❑ IMMERSE—to bathe, dip; to engross, preoccupy

The Japanese snow monkey *immersed* itself in the hot spring.

❑ IMMOBILE—not moveable; still

Although Gerald's legs have been *immobile* since the accident, he gets around pretty well with his crutches.

❑ IMMUNE—exempt; protected from harm or disease; unresponsive to

After you get chicken pox once, you are *immune* to the disease.

❑ IMMUNOLOGICAL—relating to immune system

Her *immunological* system was severely damaged by the onset of AIDS, making her vulnerable to illness.

❑ IMMUTABLE—unchangeable, invariable

Poverty was an *immutable* fact of life for the unfortunate Wood family; every moneymaking scheme they tried failed.

❑ IMPAIR—to damage, injure

After embroidering in poor light for decades, Doris's vision became *impaired*.

❑ IMPASSE—blocked path, dilemma with no solution

The rock slide produced an *impasse* so that we could proceed no further on the road.

❑ IMPASSIONED—with passion

The protesters made an *impassioned* plea for the life of the condemned man.

❑ IMPASSIVE—showing no emotion

The queen looked on *impassively* as the traitor argued desperately that his life should be spared.

❑ IMPEACH—to charge with misdeeds in public office; accuse

The senators debated whether or not the president should be *impeached* for his crimes.

❑ IMPECCABLE—flawless, without fault

The dress rehearsal was *impeccable*; nothing needed to be changed before the actual performance.

❑ IMPECUNIOUS—poor, having no money

After the stock market crashed, many former millionaires found themselves *impecunious*.

❑ IMPEDIMENT—barrier, obstacle; speech disorder

Ludmila's speech *impediment* made it difficult to understand what she was saying.

❑ IMPERATIVE—essential; mandatory

It's *imperative* that you follow the instructions of the crew in the event of a crash, or chaos will result.

❑ IMPERIOUS—arrogantly self-assured, domineering, overbearing

The *imperious* princess demanded that her servants do back flips every time they came into her presence.

❑ IMPERTINENT—rude

The *impertinent* boy stuck his tongue out at the policeman.

❑ IMPERTURBABLE—not capable of being disturbed

Due to her experience with distraught children, the counselor seemed *imperturbable*, even when faced with tantrums.

❑ IMPERVIOUS—impossible to penetrate; incapable of being affected

A good raincoat should be *impervious* to moisture.

❑ IMPETUOUS—quick to act without thinking

The *impetuous* day trader rushed to sell his stocks at the first hint of trouble, and lost $300,000.

❑ IMPIOUS—not devout in religion

The nun cut herself off from her *impious* family after she entered the convent.

❑ IMPLACABLE—inflexible, incapable of being pleased

His rage at the betrayal was so great that he remained *implacable* for weeks.

❑ IMPLANT (v.)—to set securely or deeply; to instill

The reform school sought to *implant* the virtues of law-abiding citizens in the minds of its juvenile delinquent charges.

❑ IMPLAUSIBLE—improbable, inconceivable

A skeptical man by nature, Max found his neighbor's claim that he'd seen a UFO highly *implausible*.

❑ IMPLICATE—to involve in a crime, incriminate

In an effort to save himself, the criminal *implicated* his friends in the murder.

❑ IMPLICIT—implied, not directly expressed

Implicit in Jake's request that Sheila return his keys was his desire to terminate their relationship.

❑ IMPORTUNE—to ask repeatedly, beg

The assistant *importuned* her boss with constant requests for a raise and promotion.

❑ IMPOSE—to inflict, force upon

The patriarch *imposed* his will upon his daughter, refusing to allow her to marry the butler.

❑ IMPOSING—dignified, grand

The *imposing* facade of the mansion intimidated the governess who had come to work there.

❑ IMPOTENT—powerless, ineffective, lacking strength

Mr. Cliff was *impotent* to prevent his daughter's spiralling plunge into drug addiction.

❑ IMPOUND—to seize and confine

The car was *impounded* when the Hendersons could not keep up with the payments for it.

❑ IMPOVERISH—to make poor or bankrupt

Though he had more money than he could count, Bruce did nothing to help his *impoverished* relatives.

❑ IMPRECATION—curse

Spouting violent *imprecations*, Hank searched for the man who had totally destroyed his truck.

❑ IMPREGNABLE—totally safe from attack, able to resist defeat

The fortress was *impregnable*—until, that is, the defenders allowed the Trojan Horse to enter its gates.

❑ IMPRESSIONABLE—easily influenced or affected

After attending the Spice Girls concert, the *impressionable* girl began to dress like Sporty Spice every day.

❑ IMPROMPTU—spontaneous, without rehearsal

During the interview, the Beatles suddenly decided to give an *impromptu* performance of "Love Me Do."

❑ IMPROVIDENT—without planning or foresight, negligent

The *improvident* woman spent all the money she received in her court settlement within two weeks.

❑ IMPUDENT—arrogant, audacious

The teacher raged inwardly at the *impudent* comments of his student, but kept outwardly calm.

❑ IMPUGN—to call into question, attack verbally

"How dare you *impugn* my honorable motives?" protested the lawyer on being accused of ambulance chasing.

❑ IMPULSE—sudden tendency, inclination

On *impulse,* Sarah bought a leather jacket for her boyfriend, although she couldn't really afford it.

❑ IMPULSIVE—spontaneous, unpredictable

Last Christmas she was on her way to London, but at the last minute she *impulsively* canceled the trip and went to Hawaii instead.

❑ INADVERTENTLY—unintentionally

As he was backing out of the driveway, Diego *inadvertently* ran over a rose bush.

❑ INANE—foolish, silly, lacking significance

The talk show host desperately tried to make the star's *inane* comments seem more interesting.

❑ INAUGURATE—to begin or start officially; to induct into office

The president was *inaugurated* in a lavish ceremony attended by thousands.

❑ INCANDESCENT—shining brightly

The moon had an *incandescent* glow on that romantic night we met.

❑ INCARCERATE—to put in jail; to confine

The thief was *incarcerated* for two years, but he got out on parole after six months.

❑ INCARCERATION—imprisonment

In order to avoid *incarceration,* the swindler struck a plea bargain with the district attorney's office.

❑ INCARNADINE—blood-red in color

At first glance, Theo's *incarnadine* shirt made people think he was bleeding profusely.

❑ INCARNATE—having bodily form

The serial killer was so sadistic that many people thought he might be the devil *incarnate.*

❑ INCENDIARY—combustible, flammable, burning easily

Gasoline is so *incendiary* that cigarette smoking is forbidden at gas stations.

❑ INCENSE (v.)—to infuriate, enrage

The general became thoroughly *incensed* when his subordinates failed to follow his orders.

❑ INCEPTION—beginning

Even from its *inception,* those who were involved in the plan knew that it probably wouldn't succeed.

❑ INCESSANT—continuous, never ceasing

Otis's wife complained *incessantly* about the way he sat watching TV all day instead of looking for a job.

❑ INCHOATE—imperfectly formed or formulated

As her thoughts on the subject were still in *inchoate* form, Amy could not explain what she meant.

❑ INCIPIENT—beginning to exist or appear; in an initial stage

At that point, her cancer was only *incipient* and she could still work full time.

❑ INCISIVE—perceptive, penetrating

The psychologist's *incisive* analysis of her patient's childhood helped him to understand his own behavior.

❑ INCLINATION—tendency towards

Her natural *inclination* was to refuse Max's invitation to dinner, but since he was her boss she felt obligated to accept it.

❑ INCLUSIVE—comprehensive, all-encompassing

It took 30 years, but the publisher managed to produce the most *inclusive* encyclopedia on the market.

❑ INCOGNITO—in disguise, concealing one's identity

Fearful of damaging her reputation, the politician gambled in Atlantic City *incognito.*

❑ INCONCEIVABLE—impossible, unthinkable

It was *inconceivable* to the dictator that his subjects could hate him, although they obviously did.

❑ INCONSEQUENTIAL—unimportant, trivial

The king dismissed the concerns of his horrified advisers as *inconsequential,* and decided to go ahead with his marriage to the beautiful young woman despite rumors that she was criminally insane.

❑ INCONTROVERTIBLE—unquestionable, beyond dispute

The fact that Harvard would be too expensive for Lisa without scholarship money was *incontrovertible.*

❑ INCORRIGIBLE—incapable of being corrected

The puppy was *incorrigible*; however many times he was told not to chew on his master's shoes, he persisted in doing it.

❑ INCREDULOUS—skeptical, doubtful

I was *incredulous* as I listened to Ishmael's wild fishing story about "the one that got away."

❑ INCULCATE—to teach, impress in the mind

Most parents blithely *inculcate* their children with their religious beliefs instead of allowing their children to select their own faith.

❑ INCULPATE—to blame, charge with a crime

His suspicious behavior after the crime tended to *inculpate* him.

❑ INCUMBENT—holding a specified office, often political

Incumbents often have an advantage over unknown parties in political races.

❑ INCURSION—sudden invasion

The army was unable to resist the *incursion* of the rebel forces into their territory.

❑ INDEFATIGABLE—never tired

Theresa seemed *indefatigable*, barely sweating after a 10-mile run.

❑ INDEFENSIBLE—inexcusable, unforgivable

"Your rudeness tonight was *indefensible*; I never want to see you again!" Amelia shouted at her boyfriend.

❑ INDELIBLE—permanent, not erasable

Rita was enraged when her infant daughter drew pictures on the wall in *indelible* ink.

❑ INDICATIVE—showing or pointing out, suggestive of

The looting of the shop was *indicative* of the general lawlessness that was taking possession of the city.

❑ INDICT—to accuse formally, charge with a crime

The mafioso was *indicted* for tax evasion because the FBI could not prove any of his other crimes.

❑ INDIGENOUS—native, occurring naturally in an area

Palm trees are *indigenous* to Florida, unlike penguins.

❑ INDIGENT—very poor

Because the suspect was *indigent*, the state paid for his legal representation.

❑ INDIGNANT—angry, incensed, offended

The innocent passerby was *indignant* when the police treated him as a suspect in the crime.

❑ INDOLENT—habitually lazy, idle

Her *indolent* ways got her fired from many jobs.

❑ INDOMITABLE—fearless, unconquerable

Samson was *indomitable* in battle until the treacherous Delilah cut off his hair, taking away his strength.

❑ INDUBITABLE—unquestionable

His *indubitable* cooking skills made it all the more astonishing when the Thanksgiving dinner he prepared tasted awful.

❑ INDUCE—to persuade; bring about

Tom attempted to *induce* his girlfriend to go skydiving with him, but she refused.

❑ INDUCT—to place ceremoniously in office

The pitcher was proud to be *inducted* into the Baseball Hall of Fame.

❑ INDULGE—to give in to a craving or desire

Jenny *indulged* herself with a weekend at a luxurious spa.

❑ INDUSTRY—business or trade; diligence, energy

The car *industry* was completely transformed by the rise of the large Japanese automakers.

❑ INEBRIATED—drunk, intoxicated

Obviously *inebriated*, the best man slurred his words during his speech at the wedding.

❑ INEPT—clumsy, awkward

He was so *inept* in the garden that he dug up roses and fertilized weeds.

❑ INERT—unable to move, tending to inactivity

In the heat of the desert afternoon, lizards lie *inert*.

❑ INESTIMABLE—too great to be estimated

"The value of this acquisition to our company is *inestimable*," bragged the CEO.

❑ INEVITABLE—certain, unavoidable

With all the obstacles in their path, it was perhaps *inevitable* that their affair should end unhappily.

❑ INEXORABLE—inflexible, unyielding

The *inexorable* force of the twister swept away their house.

❑ INEXTRICABLE—incapable of being disentangled

The gum caught in the sheepdog's fur was *inextricable*, and his owner had to shave him to remove it.

❑ INFALLIBLE—incapable of making a mistake

I considered my mother to be *infallible* until she got fired from her job when I was 10.

❑ INFAMY—reputation for bad deeds

The corrupt mayor's *infamy* was legendary in the city.

❑ INFANTILE—childish, immature

The young man's *infantile* behavior in the presence of his mother annoyed his fiancée intensely.

❑ INFATUATED—strongly or foolishly attached to, inspired with foolish passion, overly in love

After seeing her picture in a fashion magazine, Lester became completely *infatuated* with the beautiful model.

❑ INFER—to conclude, deduce

I think we can *infer* from the results of this study that the quality of old-age homes needs to be improved.

❑ INFILTRATE—to pass secretly into enemy territory

The spy *infiltrated* the CIA, gaining access to highly classified information.

❑ INFINITESIMAL—extremely tiny

Infinitesimal specks of dust marred the camera lens, blotching the pictures that were taken through it.

❑ INFIRMITY—disease, ailment

Plagued by a variety of *infirmities*, the old man rarely left his bed during his final years.

❑ INFRINGE—to encroach, trespass; to transgress, violate

Koca-Cola was sued by Coca-Cola for *infringing* on its copyright.

❑ INFURIATE—to anger, provoke, outrage

Malcolm knew that his irresponsible behavior would *infuriate* his mother.

❑ INFURIATING—provoking anger or outrage

The girl had an *infuriating* habit of rudely insulting her elders.

❑ INGENIOUS—original, clever, inventive

Luther found an *ingenious* way to solve the complex math problem.

❑ INGENUOUS—straightforward, open; naive and unsophisticated

She was so *ingenuous* that her friends feared that her innocence would be exploited when she visited the big city.

❑ INGRATE—ungrateful person

When none of her relatives thanked her for the fruit cakes she had sent them, Doris condemned them all as *ingrates.*

❑ INGRATIATE—to bring oneself purposely into another's good graces

Walter *ingratiated* himself with his new coworkers by bringing them doughnuts every morning.

❑ INGRESS—entrance

Ed hoped that the mailroom job would provide him with an *ingress* into the company.

❑ INHIBIT—to hold back, prevent, restrain

Paulette was too *inhibited* to tell Rod that she resented him borrowing money and never paying her back.

❑ INIMICAL—hostile, unfriendly

Even though a cease-fire had been in place for months, the two sides were still *inimical* to each other.

❑ INIQUITY—sin, evil act

"I promise to close every den of *iniquity* in this town!" thundered the conservative new mayor.

❑ INITIATE—to begin, introduce; to enlist, induct

Jewish boys have a Bar Mitzvah when they are *initiated* into manhood.

❑ INJECT—to force into; to introduce into conversation

The doctor *injected* the boy with a large dose of penicillin to cure his illness.

❑ INJUNCTION—command, order

The Catholic religion has an *injunction* against the use of birth control.

❑ INKLING—hint; vague idea

Niles had had no *inkling* that he was about to be promoted, and was shocked when his manager gave him the news.

❑ INNATE—natural, inborn

Her *innate* levelheadedness will help her to withstand the enormous pressure she's under.

❑ INNATENESS—state of being natural or inborn

The *innateness* of intelligence is a topic that is under debate in today's society.

❑ INNOCUOUS—harmless; inoffensive

Some snakes are poisonous, but most species are *innocuous* and pose no danger to humans.

❑ INNOVATE—to invent, modernize, revolutionize

Coco Chanel *innovated* a popular new suit design, transforming the fashion industry.

❑ INNUENDO—indirect and subtle criticism, insinuation

Through hints and *innuendo*, the yellow journalist managed to ruin the star's reputation while ensuring that he could not be sued for slander.

❑ INNUMERABLE—too many to be counted

There are *innumerable* stars in the universe.

❑ INOFFENSIVE—harmless, innocent

Margie found Mike's off-color jokes relatively *inoffensive*, but Liz was outraged by them.

❑ INOPERABLE—not operable; incurable by surgery

Fred's brain cancer was *inoperable*, but drugs kept it under control.

❑ INQUEST—investigation; court or legal proceeding

At the *inquest*, it was determined that Ruby's death was an accident.

❑ INSATIABLE—never satisfied

Myrtle's *insatiable* appetite made it difficult for her to lose weight.

❑ INSCRUTABLE—impossible to understand fully

The judge's face was *inscrutable* as he read the jurors' verdict, giving no clue as to what it would be.

❑ INSENTIENT—unfeeling, unconscious

I was completely *insentient* during the operation due to the anesthetic I was given.

❑ INSIDIOUS—sly, treacherous, devious

Iago's *insidious* comments about Desdemona fuelled Othello's feelings of jealousy regarding his wife.

❑ INSINUATE—to suggest, say indirectly, imply

Brenda *insinuated* that Deirdre's brother had stolen her watch without accusing him outright.

❑ INSIPID—bland, lacking flavor; lacking excitement

The critic claimed that the soup was *insipid*, lacking any type of spice.

❑ INSOLENT—insulting and arrogant

"How dare you, *insolent* wretch!" roared the king when the peasant laughed at the sight of him stumbling into the mud.

❑ INSOLUBLE—not able to be solved or explained

When a mathematician finds the solution to a problem that others have declared *insoluble*, he is hailed as a genius.

❑ INSOLVENT—bankrupt, unable to pay one's debts

The company became *insolvent* after overinvesting in many failed projects and had to go out of business.

❑ INSTIGATE—to incite, urge, agitate

The man who had *instigated* the rebellion escaped, although all his followers were arrested.

❑ INSUBSTANTIAL—modest, insignificant

The losses we risk are *insubstantial* compared with the massive profits we stand to gain.

❑ INSULAR—isolated, detached

The inhabitants of the *insular* little village were shocked when Mrs. Malone set up a belly-dancing school in her home.

❑ INSUPERABLE—insurmountable, unconquerable

The difficulties we face may seem *insuperable*, but I'm confident that we will achieve all we set out to do.

❑ INSURGENT (adj.)—rebellious, insubordinate

The *insurgent* crew staged a mutiny and threw the captain overboard.

❑ INSURRECTION—rebellion

After the Emperor's troops crushed the *insurrection*, its leaders fled the country.

❑ INTEGRAL—central, indispensable

Paper is an *integral* part of a book.

❑ INTEGRITY—decency, honesty; wholeness

The candidate's *integrity* made him a refreshing contrast to his sleazy political opponents.

❑ INTEMPERATE—not moderate

The *intemperate* climate in the Sahara Desert makes it hard for plants that need lots of water to survive.

❑ INTER—to bury

After giving the masses one last chance to file past his remains and pay their respects, the authorities *interred* the leader's body.

❑ INTERDICT—to forbid, prohibit

The matron *interdicted* male visits to the girls' dorm rooms after midnight.

❑ INTERJECT—to interpose, insert

"We have a money-back guarantee!" shouted the salesman. "But only if you have a valid receipt!" *interjected* his assistant.

❑ INTERLOCUTOR—someone taking part in a dialogue

The tapes revealed that the drug dealer had planned a criminal act with an unidentified *interlocutor*.

❑ INTERLOPER—trespasser; meddler in others' affairs

The wolf pack rejected the lone pup as an *interloper*.

❑ INTERMINABLE—endless

By the time the *interminable* play ended, the last train home had already left.

❑ INTERMITTENT—starting and stopping

The flow of traffic was *intermittent* on the highway, but the commuters were thankful that it hadn't stopped completely.

❑ INTERNECINE—deadly to both sides

The disadvantage of *internecine* chemical weapons is that they are devastating to both sides in a conflict.

❑ INTERPOLATE—to insert; change by adding new words or material

The editor *interpolated* a few new sentences into the manuscript, and the new edition was ready to print.

❑ INTERPOSE—to insert; to intervene

The policeman *interposed* himself between the two men who were about to start fighting.

❑ INTERREGNUM—interval between reigns

During the *interregnum*, no one knew who was in charge and all hell broke loose in the country.

❑ INTERROGATE—to question formally

The secret police *interrogated* the suspected rebel for days, demanding the names of his co-conspirators.

❑ INTERSECT—to divide by passing through or across

The rambling country path was *intersected* by a busy freeway.

❑ INTERSPERSE—to distribute among, mix with

Mushrooms were *interspersed* among the bushes and clumps of moss in the shady forest.

❑ INTIMATION—clue, suggestion

Abby chose to ignore Babu's *intimation* that her essay was not as good as it could have been.

❑ INTRACTABLE—not easily managed

The problem of reforming hardened criminals has proved to be an *intractable* one.

❑ INTRAMURAL—within an institution, such as a school

Betty played on the *intramural* badminton team, although she was not good enough for the varsity team.

❑ INTRANSIGENT—uncompromising, refusing to be reconciled

The professor was *intransigent* on the deadline, insisting that everyone turn the assignment in on Friday.

❑ INTREPID—fearless

The *intrepid* hiker completed his ascent to the peak, despite the freezing winds that cut through his body.

❑ INTRINSIC—inherent, internal

The *intrinsic* value of this diamond is already considerable, and its elegant setting makes it truly priceless.

❑ INTROSPECTIVE—contemplating one's own thoughts and feelings

The *introspective* young man toured the countryside on his own, writing poetry based on his reflections.

❑ INTROVERT—someone given to self-analysis

Janet's a real *introvert*; she rarely pays attention to what the people around her are doing.

❏ INTRUSION—trespass, invasion of another's privacy
Despite the Do Not Disturb sign on their door, the Smiths had to put up with constant *intrusions* from the hotel staff.

❏ INTUITIVE—instinctive, untaught
"My Riya's talent with numbers is completely *intuitive*; I never taught her a thing," bragged her mother.

❏ INUNDATE—to cover with water; overwhelm
The tidal wave *inundated* Atlantis, which was lost beneath the water.

❏ INURE—to harden; accustom; become used to
Eventually, Hassad became *inured* to the sirens that went off every night and could sleep through them.

❏ INVALIDATE—to negate or nullify
Niko's driver's license was *invalidated* after he was caught speeding in a school zone.

❏ INVECTIVE—verbal abuse
A stream of *invective* poured from Mrs. Pratt's mouth as she watched the vandals smash her ceramic frog.

❏ INVESTITURE—ceremony conferring authority
After his *investiture*, the Supreme Court justice was ready to preside at his first case.

❏ INVETERATE—confirmed, long-standing, deeply rooted
An *inveterate* gambler, Lori tried her luck at roulette every chance she got.

❏ INVIDIOUS—envious; obnoxious
It is cruel and *invidious* for parents to play favorites with their children.

❏ INVINCIBLE—invulnerable, unbeatable
At the height of his career, Mike Tyson was considered practically *invincible*.

❏ INVIOLABLE—safe from violation or assault
The relieved refugees felt *inviolable* in the camp under the protection of the U.N. troops.

❏ INVOKE—to call upon, request help
Baxter *invoked* the financial assistance of all his relatives when his business ran into serious trouble.

❏ IOTA—very tiny amount
"If I even got one *iota* of respect from you, I'd be satisfied!" raged the father at his insolent son.

❏ IRASCIBLE—easily angered
Attila the Hun's *irascible* and violent nature made all who dealt with him fear for their lives.

❏ IRIDESCENT—showing many colors
The tourists sighed at the beautiful vision of the *iridescent* tropical butterfly fluttering among the orchids.

❏ IRRESOLVABLE—unable to be resolved; not analyzable
The conflict between Catholics and Protestants in Northern Ireland seemed *irresolvable* until just recently.

❏ IRREVERENT—disrespectful, gently or humorously mocking
Kevin's *irreverent* attitude in Sunday School annoyed the priest, but amused the other children.

❏ IRREVOCABLE—conclusive, irreversible
Once he had pushed the red button, the president's decision to launch a missile was *irrevocable*.

❏ ITINERANT—wandering from place to place, unsettled
The *itinerant* tomcat came by the Johansson homestead every six months or so.

❏ ITINERARY—route of a traveler's journey
The travel agent provided her customer with a detailed *itinerary* of his journey.

J

❏ JADED—tired by excess or overuse; slightly cynical
While the naive girls stared at the spectacle in awe, the *jaded* matrons dozed in their chairs.

❏ JANGLING—clashing, jarring; harshly unpleasant (in sound)
The *jangling* of the bells of all the Santa Clauses outside the store assaulted the shoppers' ears.

❏ JARGON—nonsensical talk; specialized language
You need to master technical *jargon* in order to communicate successfully with engineers.

❏ JAUNDICE—yellowish discoloration of skin
Her *jaundice* was so advanced that her head looked like a big lemon.

☑ JAUNDICED—affected by jaundice; prejudiced or embittered

The cynical man was *jaundiced* by his past unhappy marriages, and refused to fall in love again.

☑ JETTISON—to cast off, throw cargo overboard

The sinking ship *jettisoned* its cargo in a desperate attempt to reduce its weight.

☑ JINGOISM—belligerent support of one's country

The president's *jingoism* made him declare war on other countries at the slightest provocation.

☑ JOCULAR—jovial, playful, humorous

The *jocular* old man entertained his grandchildren with jokes for hours.

☑ JUBILEE—special anniversary

At the queen's Silver *Jubilee*, the entire country celebrated her long reign.

☑ JUDICIOUS—sensible, showing good judgment

The wise and distinguished judge was well known for having a *judicious* temperament.

☑ JUGGERNAUT—huge force destroying everything in its path

The *juggernaut* of Napoleon's army surged ahead until it was halted in its tracks by the brutal winter.

☑ JUNCTURE—point where two things are joined

At this *juncture*, I think it would be a good idea for us to take a coffee break.

☑ JURISPRUDENCE—philosophy of law

An expert in *jurisprudence*, the esteemed lawyer was often consulted by his colleagues.

☑ JUXTAPOSITION—side-by-side placement

The porcelain dog was placed in *juxtaposition* with the straw dog house on the mantelpiece.

K

☑ KEEN (adj.)—having a sharp edge; intellectually sharp, perceptive

With her *keen* intelligence, she figured out the puzzle in seconds flat.

☑ KERNEL—innermost, essential part; seed grain, often in a shell

The parrot cracked the hard shell of the seed in order to get at its delicious *kernel*.

☑ KEYNOTE—note or tone on which a musical key is founded; main idea of a speech, program, etcetera

The university administration asked a prominent historian to deliver the *keynote* speech at the conference.

☑ KINDLE—to set fire to or ignite; excite or inspire

With only damp wood to work with, Tilda had great difficulty in *kindling* the camp fire.

☑ KINETIC—relating to motion; characterized by movement

The *kinetic* sculpture moved back and forth, startling the museum visitors.

☑ KNELL—sound of a funeral bell; omen of death or failure

When the townspeople heard the *knelling* from the church belfry, they knew that their mayor had died.

☑ KUDOS—fame, glory, honor

The actress happily accepted *kudos* from the press for her stunning performance in the indie film.

L

☑ LABYRINTH—maze

When Peichi finally reached the center of the *labyrinth*, she realized that she had no idea how to get back to its entrance.

☑ LACERATION—cut or wound

The chopping knife slipped and slashed Frank's arm, making a deep *laceration*.

☑ LACHRYMOSE—tearful

Heather always became *lachrymose* when it was time to bid her daughter good-bye.

☑ LACKADAISICAL—idle, lazy; apathetic, indifferent

The clerk yawned openly in the customer's face, not bothering to hide his *lackadaisical* attitude.

❑ LACONIC—using few words

She was a *laconic* poet who built her reputation on using words as sparingly as possible.

❑ LAGGARD—dawdler, loafer, lazy person

The manager hesitated to fire Biff, his incompetent *laggard* of an assistant, because Biff was the CEO's son.

☑ LAMENT (v.)—to deplore, grieve

The children continued to *lament* the death of the goldfish weeks after its demise.

❑ LAMPOON—to attack with satire, mock harshly

The mayor hated being *lampooned* by the press for his efforts to make the inhabitants of his city more polite.

❑ LANGUID—lacking energy, indifferent, slow

The cat *languidly* cleaned its fur, ignoring the viciously snarling dog chained a few feet away from it.

☑ LAP (v.)—to drink using the tongue; to wash against

The dog eagerly *lapped* up all the water in its bowl, thirsty after barking non-stop for two hours.

❑ LAPIDARY—relating to precious stones

"This ring is of no *lapidary* value; you could buy it in any cheap department store," sneered the jeweller.

☑ LARCENY—theft of property

The crime of stealing a wallet can be categorized as petty *larceny*.

❑ LARDER—place where food is stored

Dottie was horrified to discover that rats had eaten all the potatoes in her *larder*.

❑ LARGESS—generosity; gift

Because the mafia don had extended considerable *largess* to his neighbors, they supported him.

☑ LARYNX—organ containing vocal cords

The opera singer's *larynx* was damaged in the accident, spelling doom for her career.

❑ LASSITUDE—lethargy, sluggishness

The defeated French army plunged into a state of depressed *lassitude* as they trudged home from Russia.

❑ LATENT—present but hidden; potential

Milton's latent *paranoia* began to emerge as he was put under more and more stress at the office.

❑ LAUDABLE—deserving of praise

Kristin's dedication is *laudable*, but she doesn't have the necessary skills to be a good paralegal.

❑ LAXITY—carelessness

Our newspaper delivery boy's *laxity* is the reason why our paper lands in a puddle more often than not.

❑ LEERY—suspicious

After being swindled once, Ruth became *leery* of strangers trying to sell things to her.

❑ LEGERDEMAIN—trickery

The magician was skilled in the arts of *legerdemain*.

☑ LEGIBLE—readable

Gordon's chickenscratch handwriting was barely *legible*.

❑ LEGISLATE—to decree, mandate, make laws

Some congressmen make every effort to *legislate* in favor of powerful interest groups.

☑ LENIENT—easygoing, permissive

When the pitcher was fined only $50 for punching the batter, fans felt the punishment was too *lenient*.

❑ LETHARGY—indifferent inactivity

The worker sank into a state of *lethargy*, letting dozens of defective toys pass him by on the assembly line.

☑ LEVITATE—to rise in the air or cause to rise

The magician caused his assistant to *levitate* in the air, astonishing the audience.

❑ LEVITY—humor, frivolity, gaiety

At Christmas, an atmosphere of *levity* fills our office as people prepare to have fun with their families.

☑ LEXICON—dictionary, list of words

You may not find the word "supercalifragilisticexpialidocious" in the *lexicon*.

☑ LIBERAL—tolerant, broad-minded; generous, lavish

Kate's *liberal* parents trusted her, and allowed her to manage her own affairs to a large extent.

☑ LIBERATION—freedom, emancipation

After the *liberation* of the slaves, the southern plantation fell into disrepair after its entire workforce left to find paid employment.

❑ LIBERTARIAN—one who believes in unrestricted freedom

The *libertarian* refused to pay taxes to the government, as he didn't recognize its jurisdiction over him.

❑ LIBERTINE—one without moral restraint

The *libertine* took pleasure in gambling and seducing innocent youths.

❑ LICENTIOUS—immoral; unrestrained by society

Religious citizens were outraged by the *licentious* exploits of the community of artists living in the town.

❑ LIEN—right to possess and sell the property of a debtor

The bank took a *lien* on the lender's house to protect themselves in case he defaulted on his loan.

❑ LIMPID—clear, transparent

Shelley could see all the way to the bottom through the pond's *limpid* water.

❑ LINEAGE—ancestry

Manuela could trace her *lineage* back through many generations.

❑ LINGUISTICS—study of language

Her study of *linguistics* helped her to master new languages more easily.

❑ LINIMENT—medicinal liquid used externally to ease pain

Vernon rubbed the soothing *liniment* into his aching joints.

❑ LIONIZE—to treat as a celebrity

After the success of his novel, the author was *lionized* by the press.

❑ LISSOME—easily flexed, limber, agile

The *lissome* yoga instructor twisted herself into shapes that her students could only dream of.

❑ LISTLESS—lacking energy and enthusiasm

Listless and depressed after breaking up with his girlfriend, Nick spent his days moping on the couch.

❑ LITERATE—able to read and write; well-read and educated

The only *literate* man in the village, Abraham was asked to read his neighbors' letters to them.

❑ LITHE—moving and bending with ease; graceful

The dancer's movements were *lithe* and graceful, even when she was not performing.

❑ LITIGATION—lawsuit

Mr. Prather finally won his court case after years of *litigation*.

❑ LIVID—discolored from a bruise; reddened with anger

Irving was *livid* when he discovered that someone had spilled grape juice all over his cashmere coat.

❑ LOATHE—to abhor, despise, hate

Stuart *loathed* the subject so much that he could barely stand to sit through his physics class.

❑ LOCOMOTION—movement from place to place

The *locomotion* of trains became more rapid after steam engines were replaced by electrically powered ones.

❑ LOGO—corporate symbol

Kaplan's company *logo* can be found on all of its products.

❑ LOITER—to stand around idly

The teenagers *loitered* on the corner, waiting for something to happen.

❑ LOQUACIOUS—talkative

She was naturally *loquacious*, which was a problem in situations in which listening was more important than talking.

❑ LOW (v.)—to make a sound like a cow, moo

The *lowing* of the cows woke the milkmaid from her deep slumber.

❑ LUCID—clear and easily understood

Explanations should be written in a *lucid* manner so that people can understand them.

❑ LUDICROUS—laughable, ridiculous

The scientist thought his colleague's claims were *ludicrous*, but kept quiet because he didn't want to offend his old friend.

❑ LUGUBRIOUS—sorrowful, mournful; dismal

Irish wakes are a rousing departure from the *lugubrious* funeral services most people are accustomed to.

❑ LUMBER (v.)—to move slowly and awkwardly

The bear *lumbered* towards the garbage, drooling at the prospect of the Big Mac leftovers he smelled.

❑ LUMINARY—bright object; celebrity; source of inspiration

Logan's father was a *luminary* of the New York theater world, and many sought his advice.

❑ LUMINOUS—bright, brilliant, glowing

The *luminous* moon shone right through the curtains into the bedroom.

❑ LUNAR—relating to the moon

The scientists analyzed the *lunar* rocks collected by the space shuttle crew for traces of water.

❑ LURID—harshly shocking, sensational; glowing

The politician nearly had a heart attack when he saw the *lurid* headlines about his past indiscretions.

❑ LURK—to prowl, sneak

The burglar *lurked* in the bushes until the Jeffersons had left the house, then broke in.

❑ LUSCIOUS—tasty

These *luscious* strawberries are the best I've ever tasted!

❑ LUXURIANCE—elegance, lavishness

The *luxuriance* of the couches made them an obvious choice for the palace sitting room.

❑ LYRICAL—suitable for poetry and song; expressing feeling

Ambrose's *lyrical* talents made him a gifted poet and songwriter.

M

❑ MACHINATION—plot or scheme

Tired of his enemies' endless *machinations* to remove him from the throne, the king had them executed.

❑ MACROBIOTICS—art of prolonging life by special diet of organic nonmeat substances

A devout believer in *macrobiotics*, Rosemary fed her children nothing but fruit and bran.

❑ MACROCOSM—the entire universe; a complex that is a large-scale reproduction of one of its parts

In a welfare society, the state can be considered a *macrocosm* of the family in that it takes care of the elderly and children.

❑ MAELSTROM—whirlpool; turmoil; agitated state of mind

The transportation system of the city had collapsed in the *maelstrom* of war.

❑ MAGNANIMOUS—generous, noble in spirit

Although at first he seemed mean, Uncle Frank turned out to be a very *magnanimous* fellow.

❑ MAGNATE—powerful or influential person

The entertainment *magnate* bought two cable TV stations to add to his collection of magazines and publishing houses.

❑ MAGNITUDE—extent, greatness of size

When she saw the huge leaks in her ceiling, she realized the full *magnitude* of the repairs her house needed.

❑ MALADROIT—clumsy, tactless

"So, when is your baby due?" said the *maladroit* guest to his overweight but not pregnant hostess.

❑ MALADY—illness

Elizabeth visited the doctor many times, but he could not identify her mysterious *malady*.

❑ MALAPROPISM—humorous misuse of a word

When the infant pointed to the puppy and said "Look at the fluffy," his *malapropism* delighted his parents.

❑ MALCONTENT—discontented person, one who holds a grudge

Dinah had always been a *malcontent*, so no one was surprised when she complained about the new carpet in the lobby.

❑ MALEDICTION—curse

The prince-frog looked for a princess to kiss him and put an end to the witch's evil *malediction*.

❑ MALEFACTOR—evil-doer; culprit

Many organizations are still trying to bring Nazi *malefactors* to justice.

- MALEVOLENT—ill-willed; causing evil or harm to others

  The *malevolent* gossiper spread false rumors about people just for the pleasure of upsetting them.

- MALFUNCTION (v.)—to fail to work

  When his computer *malfunctioned* yet again, Derek decided to throw it out and buy a new one.

- MALFUNCTION (n.)—breakdown, failure

  The *malfunction* of the booster rocket meant that the space shuttle could not be launched on schedule.

- MALICE—animosity, spite, hatred

  Kendra felt such *malice* towards the insurance company that she celebrated when it went bankrupt.

- MALINGER—to evade responsibility by pretending to be ill

  A common way to avoid the draft was by *malingering*—pretending to be ill so as to avoid being taken by the Army.

- MALNUTRITION—undernourishment

  The child's distended stomach and spindly limbs was a sure sign that she suffered from *malnutrition*.

- MALODOROUS—foul smelling

  The *malodorous* beggar, who had not bathed in many months, could barely stand his own smell.

- MANDATORY—necessary, required

  It is *mandatory* for all subway employees to wear blue uniforms while on the job.

- MANIFEST (adj.)—obvious

  The fact that she had had plastic surgery was *manifest*, since she looked 20 years younger than she had done the week before.

- MANIFOLD—diverse, varied, comprised of many parts

  The *manifold* tourist attractions of London make it a great place to visit.

- MANNERED—artificial or stilted in character

  Igor was so nervous about attending a high society dinner for the first time that his behavior was *mannered* and unnatural.

- MANUAL (adj.)—hand operated; physical

  When the power lines went down, the secretary dug out his old *manual* typewriter to type his letters.

- MAR—to damage, deface; spoil

  Telephone poles *marred* the natural beauty of the countryside.

- MARGINAL—barely sufficient

  Because her skills were *marginal*, Edith was not a valued employee and was paid a very low salary.

- MARITIME—relating to the sea or sailing

  At the *maritime* museum, historic ships and sailing equipment are displayed.

- MARTIAL—warlike, pertaining to the military

  Experts in *martial* arts know how to physically defend themselves if anyone attacks them.

- MARTINET—strict disciplinarian, one who rigidly follows rules

  A complete *martinet*, the official insisted that Pete fill out all the forms again even though he was already familiar with his case.

- MARTYR—person dying for his or her beliefs

  Joan of Arc became a famous *martyr* after she was burned at the stake for her beliefs.

- MASOCHIST—one who enjoys pain or humiliation

  Only a *masochist* would volunteer to take over this nightmarish project.

- MASQUERADE—disguise; action that conceals the truth

  I dressed up as President Nixon for last year's *masquerade* party.

- MATERIALISM—preoccupation with material things

  The couple's *materialism* revealed itself in the way they had to buy the most up-to-date model of every consumer item.

- MATRICULATE—to enroll as a member of a college or university

  When Suda-May *matriculates* at Yale University this coming fall, she'll move to New Haven.

- MATRILINEAL—tracing ancestry through mother's line rather than father's

  In the *matrilineal* society, inheritances were passed on through the mother's line rather than the father's.

MAUDLIN—overly sentimental

The mother's death should have been a touching scene, but the movie's treatment of it was so *maudlin* that, instead of making the audience cry, it made them cringe.

MAWKISH—sickeningly sentimental

The poet hoped to charm his lover with his romantic poem, but its *mawkish* tone sickened her instead.

MEDDLER—person interfering in others' affairs

Mickey is a real *meddler*, always sticking his nose in where it doesn't belong.

MEDIEVAL—relating to the Middle Ages (about A.D. 500–1500)

In *medieval* times, countless Europeans died of diseases because medicine was not very far advanced.

MEGALITH—huge stone used in prehistoric structures

The archaeologist wondered how the prehistoric tribe had managed to move the gigantic *megalith* to the top of the hill.

MEGALOMANIA—mental state with delusions of wealth and power

Suffering from *megalomania*, the mental patient demanded that the hospital staff bow to him.

MELANCHOLY—sadness, depression

The gloomy, rainy weather made James feel *melancholy*.

MELODY—pleasing musical harmony; related musical tunes

The hit pop song had the same basic *melody* as Beethoven's Fifth.

MENAGERIE—various animals kept together for exhibition

The lion would have eaten all the other animals in the circus *menagerie* if given the chance.

MENDACIOUS—dishonest

So many of her stories were *mendacious* that I decided she must be a pathological liar.

MENDICANT—beggar

"Please, sir, can you spare a dime?" begged the *mendicant* as the businessman walked past.

MENTOR—experienced teacher and wise adviser

After being accepted at several colleges, Luisa asked her *mentor* which one she should choose.

MERCENARY (n.)—soldier for hire in foreign countries

Because his own army was so small, the dictator was forced to hire foreign *mercenaries* to protect him.

MERCENARY (adj.)—motivated only by greed

Many celebrated "explorers" were actually *mercenary* plunderers.

MERCURIAL—quick, shrewd, and unpredictable

Her *mercurial* personality made it difficult to guess how she would react to the bad news.

MERETRICIOUS—gaudy, falsely attractive

The casino's *meretricious* decor horrified the cultivated interior designer.

MERIDIAN—circle passing through the two poles of the earth

The explorer attempted to follow the *meridian* from the North Pole to the South Pole, but he failed when his ship ran into a solid sheet of ice and he could go no further.

MERITORIOUS—deserving reward or praise

The student's performance in all subjects was so *meritorious* that I'm sure she'll be awarded a scholarship.

METAMORPHOSIS—change, transformation

The *metamorphosis* of a caterpillar into a butterfly is a fascinating process.

METAPHOR—figure of speech comparing two different things

The *metaphor* "a sea of troubles" suggests a lot of troubles by comparing their number to the vastness of the sea.

METICULOUS—extremely careful, fastidious, painstaking

To find all the clues at the crime scene, the investigators *meticulously* examined every inch of the area.

METRONOME—time-keeping device used in music

Even with the help of a *metronome*, the talentless piano student couldn't keep the rhythm as she played the simple tune.

❑ METTLE—courageousness; endurance

The helicopter pilot showed her *mettle* as she landed in the battlefield to rescue the wounded soldiers.

❑ MICROBE—microorganism

A major medical breakthrough occurred when it was discovered that *microbes* were responsible for the spread of disease.

❑ MICROCOSM—tiny system used as analogy for larger system

The social order of a beehive can serve as a *microcosm* for the social order of human society.

❑ MIGRATORY—wandering from place to place with the seasons

The *migratory* geese flew in from Canada at around the same time every year.

❑ MILITATE—to operate against, work against

Lenin *militated* against the tsar for years before he overthrew him and established the Soviet Union.

❑ MINIMAL—smallest in amount, least possible

Add only a *minimal* amount of rum to the cake, or it will overwhelm the taste of all the other ingredients.

❑ MINUSCULE—very small

Dave needed a magnifying glass to read the *miniscule* print on the lease.

❑ MIRTH—frivolity, gaiety, laughter

Vera's hilarious jokes contributed to the general *mirth* at the dinner party.

❑ MISANTHROPE—person who hates human beings

Scrooge was such a *misanthrope* that even the sight of children singing made him angry.

❑ MISAPPREHEND—to misunderstand, fail to know

The policeman *misapprehended* the situation and arrested Mark, although Peter was guilty of the crime.

❑ MISCONSTRUE—to misunderstand, fail to discover

Because I don't what I've said to be *misconstrued*, I'll distribute transcripts of my speech to all of you.

❑ MISERLINESS—extreme stinginess

Although Scrooge was a rich man, his *miserliness* prevented him from helping others who were in need.

❑ MISGIVING—apprehension, doubt, sense of foreboding

Jews had serious *misgivings* about Hitler's intentions towards them, and they fled Germany in large numbers.

❑ MISHAP—accident; misfortune

In an unfortunate *mishap*, the actress broke her arm and could not perform that night as planned.

❑ MISNOMER—an incorrect name or designation

Some feel that to call a nuclear missile a "peacemaker" is a *misnomer*.

❑ MISSIVE—note or letter

Lydia spent hours composing a romantic *missive* for Leo, which she sent off in the evening mail.

❑ MITIGATE—to soften, or make milder

A judge may *mitigate* a sentence if she decides that a person committed a crime out of need.

❑ MNEMONIC—relating to memory; designed to assist memory

The *mnemonic* "King Phillip Swiftly Came Over For Good Sushi" can help you remember the order of classificatory divisions when you study for a biology test.

❑ MOBILITY—ease of movement

The wheelchair increased Stanley's *mobility*; previously, he had been confined to his bed all day.

❑ MOCK—to deride, ridicule

Charles suspected that Toni was *mocking* him behind his back, but in fact, she respected him greatly.

❑ MODERATE (adj.)—reasonable, not extreme

"Please make sure my dish is *moderately* spiced; I like a little spice, but not too much," the customer instructed the waiter.

❑ MODERATE (v.)—to make less excessive, restrain; regulate

The engineer *moderated* the flow of electricity to the house after its fuses blew repeatedly.

❑ MOLLIFY—to calm or make less severe

Their argument was so intense that it was difficult to believe any compromise would *mollify* them.

❑ MOLLUSK—sea animal with soft body

Mollusks often develop hard shells in order to protect their soft, vulnerable bodies.

❑ MOLT (v.)—to shed hair, skin, or an outer layer periodically

The snake *molted* its skin and left it behind in a crumpled mass.

❑ MONASTIC—extremely plain or secluded, as in a monastery

The philosopher retired to his *monastic* lodgings to contemplate life free from any worldly distraction.

❑ MONOCHROMATIC—having one color

The multicolored butterfly really stood out in the *monochromatic* foliage of the clearing.

❑ MONOGAMY—custom of marriage to one person at a time

Monogamy is the accepted norm in American culture, though some members of certain religions take several wives.

❑ MONOLITH—large block of stone

The looming *monolith* dominated the horizon for miles around.

❑ MONOLOGUE—dramatic speech performed by one actor

Olivier's *monologue* in the film version of *Hamlet* is a well-known example of classical acting.

❑ MONTAGE—composite picture

The artist created a *montage* of photographs, newspaper articles, and everyday objects in her work of art.

❑ MOOT—debatable; purely academic, deprived of practical significance

Charles couldn't decide what to get Alison for her birthday, but after they broke up the issue became *moot*.

❑ MORBID—gruesome; relating to disease; abnormally gloomy

Mrs. Fletcher had a *morbid* fascination with her dead daughter, displaying photos of her everywhere.

❑ MORES—customs or manners

In accordance with the *mores* of ancient Roman society, Nero held an orgy every weekend.

❑ MORIBUND—dying, decaying

Thanks to feminism, many sexist customs are now *moribund* in this society.

❑ MOROSE—gloomy, sullen, or surly

After hearing that he had been rejected by the university of his choice, Lenny was *morose* for weeks.

❑ MORSEL—small bit of food

The timid bird darted forward and quickly grabbed the *morsel* of food from between the girl's fingers.

❑ MOTE—small particle, speck

Monica's eye watered, irritated by the *mote* of dust that had blown into it.

❑ MOTLEY—many colored; composed of diverse parts

The club was made up of a *motley* crew of people from all kinds of different backgrounds.

❑ MOTTLE—to mark with spots

Food stains *mottled* the tablecloth.

❑ MULTIFACETED—having many parts, many sided

The *multifaceted* emerald sparkled in different ways depending on which angle you looked at it from.

❑ MULTIFARIOUS—diverse

Ken opened the hotel room window, letting in the *multifarious* noises of the great city.

❑ MUNDANE—worldly; commonplace

The plot of that thriller was completely *mundane*; as usual, the film ended in a huge explosion.

❑ MUNIFICENT—generous

The *munificent* millionaire donated ten million dollars to the hospital.

❑ MUNITIONS—ammunition

Soon after the *munitions* plant was blown up, the troops ran out of ammunition and surrendered.

❑ MUTABILITY—changeability

We need stable substances for this solution, and the *mutability* of this compound makes it unsuitable for our experiment.

❑ MYOPIC—nearsighted

The *myopic* old man needed a magnifying glass to read the morning paper.

❑ MYRIAD—immense number, multitude

Naomi moved to the city to take advantage of the *myriad* of modeling opportunities available to her there.

N

NADIR—lowest point

As Lou waited in line to audition for the diaper commercial, he realized he had reached the *nadir* of his acting career.

NARRATIVE—account, story

The police took notes as the witness gave a detailed *narrative* of the events that had taken place.

NASCENT—starting to develop, coming into existence

The advertising campaign was still in a *nascent* stage, and nothing had been finalized yet.

NATAL—relating to birth

The pregnant woman and her husband searched for a hospital specializing in *natal* care.

NEBULOUS—vague, cloudy

The candidate's *nebulous* plans to fight crime lacked the concrete detail that skeptical voters demanded.

NECROMANCY—black magic

Maya's mother forbade her to practice *necromancy* or witchcraft of any kind.

NEFARIOUS—vicious, evil

Nefarious deeds are never far from an evil-doer's mind.

NEGLIGENT—careless, inattentive

The court determined that Mr. Glass had been *negligent* in failing to keep his vicious dog chained up.

NEGLIGIBLE—not worth considering

It's obvious from our *negligible* dropout rate that our students love our program.

NEOLOGISM—new word or expression

Many *neologisms* are actually words we borrow from other languages and add to the English vocabulary.

NEONATE—newborn child

The intensive care unit was filled with tiny, vulnerable *neonates* having respiratory problems.

NEOPHYTE—novice, beginner

A relative *neophyte* at bowling, Seth rolled all of his balls into the gutter.

NETHER—located under or below

Paul hunted for his favorite tie in the *nether* regions of the closet.

NETTLE (v.)—to irritate

I don't particularly like having blue hair—I just do it to *nettle* my parents.

NEUTRALITY—disinterest, impartiality

Switzerland is well known for its *neutrality* in times of international conflict.

NEUTRALIZE—to balance, offset

Dr. Schwartz poured acid in the beaker to *neutralize* the basic solution.

NICETY—elegant or delicate feature; minute distinction

Lani went to fancy parties all summer, enjoying the *niceties* of upper-crust society.

NICHE—recess in a wall; best position for something

The thieves tucked the stolen money into a hidden *niche* in the wall.

NIGGARDLY—stingy, ungenerous

Sarah received only *niggardly* praise from her jealous supervisor for her brilliant performance.

NIHILISM—belief that existence and all traditional values are meaningless

Robert's *nihilism* expressed itself in his lack of concern with the norms of decent, moral society.

NOCTURNAL—pertaining to night; active at night

Bats are *nocturnal* creatures, sleeping all day and emerging only at night.

NOISOME—stinking, putrid

A dead mouse trapped in your walls produces a *noisome* odor.

NOMADIC—moving from place to place

The *nomadic* Berber tribe travels from place to place, searching for grasslands for their herds.

NOMENCLATURE—terms used in a particular science or discipline

Although I've been studying medicine for six months, I can't seem to get the hang of the *nomenclature*.

NOMINAL—existing in name only; negligible

A *nominal* but far from devout Catholic, she rarely if ever went to church.

NON SEQUITUR—conclusion not following from apparent evidence

The FBI agent's conclusion that Jimmy had committed the murder was a total *non sequitur* to the evidence he'd presented.

NONDESCRIPT—lacking interesting or distinctive qualities; dull

The celebrity showed up wearing sunglasses and a *nondescript* black outfit.

NOTORIETY—unfavorable fame

Wayne realized from the silence that greeted him as he entered the bar that his *notoriety* preceded him.

NOVICE—apprentice, beginner

Although Jen is only a *novice* at sailing, she shows great potential.

NOVITIATE—state of being a beginner or novice

Women who want to enter a convent must go through a lengthy *novitiate* before they can be accepted as full-fledged nuns.

NOXIOUS—harmful, unwholesome

The workers wore face masks to avoid breathing in the *noxious* chemical fumes.

NUANCE—shade of meaning

The scholars argued for hours over tiny *nuances* in the interpretation of the last line of the poem.

NULLIFY—to make legally invalid; to counteract the effect of

Crystal *nullified* her contract with her publisher when she received a better offer from another company.

NUMISMATICS—coin collecting

Cleo picked up dozens of rare coins at the *numismatics* convention.

NUPTIAL—relating to marriage

Pamela would not consent to marriage until Leland agreed to draw up a pre-*nuptial* agreement.

NUTRITIVE—relating to nutrition or health

Try as he might, George could not convince us of the *nutritive* benefits of seaweed.

O

OBDURATE—stubborn

The president was *obdurate* on the issue, and no amount of persuasion would change his mind.

OBFUSCATE—to confuse, obscure

Benny always *obfuscates* his own arguments by using complicated words that he doesn't understand.

OBLIQUE—indirect, evasive; misleading, devious

Usually open and friendly, Allie has been behaving in a curiously *oblique* manner lately.

OBLITERATE—demolish, wipe out

The city center was completed *obliterated* by the atom bomb.

OBLIVIOUS—unaware, inattentive

Gandhi calmly made his way through the crowd, seemingly *oblivious* to the angry rioters around him.

OBSCURE (adj.)—dim, unclear; not well known

The speaker's style was so confusing that it *obscured* his main point rather than made it clear.

OBSCURITY—a state of being obscure

The mayor hoped that the scandal that had almost torn the community apart would fade into *obscurity*.

OBSEQUIOUS—overly submissive, brownnosing

The *obsequious* new employee complimented her supervisor's tie and agreed with him on every issue.

OBSESSIVE—preoccupying, all-consuming

Jorge is *obsessive* about his work; he never leaves the office before ten at night.

OBSOLETE—no longer in use

Black-and-white television is now almost completely *obsolete*.

OBSTINATE—stubborn

The *obstinate* child could not be made to eat any food that he disliked.

OBSTREPEROUS—troublesome, boisterous, unruly

The *obstreperous* toddler, who was always breaking things, was the terror of his nursery school.

❑ OBTRUSIVE—pushy, too conspicuous

I think that huge portrait of yourself that you hung in the hall is a bit *obtrusive*, don't you?

❑ OBTUSE—insensitive, stupid, dull

Alfred was too *obtuse* to realize that the sum of the angles of a triangle is 180 degrees.

❑ OBVIATE—to make unnecessary; to anticipate and prevent

The river was shallow enough for the riders to wade across, which *obviated* the need for a bridge.

❑ OCCLUDE—to shut, block

A shadow is thrown across the Earth's surface during a solar eclipse, when the light from the sun is *occluded* by the moon.

❑ ODIOUS—hateful, contemptible

While most people consider studying vocabulary an *odious* task, there are a few who find it enjoyable.

❑ OFFICIOUS—too helpful, meddlesome

The *officious* waiter butted into the couple's conversation, advising them on how to take out a mortgage.

❑ OFFSHOOT—branch

The company's main store is closing, but its *offshoots* in other areas are doing surprisingly well.

❑ OMINOUS—menacing, threatening, indicating misfortune

The sky filled with *ominous* dark clouds before the storm.

❑ OMNIPOTENT—having unlimited power

The manager clearly thinks he is *omnipotent*, the way he orders everyone around.

❑ OMNISCIENT—having infinite knowledge, all-seeing

Christians believe that because God is *omniscient*, they cannot hide their sins from Him.

❑ OMNIVOROUS—eating everything; absorbing everything

She is an *omnivorous* reader, covering everything from comic books to Plutarch.

❑ ONEROUS—burdensome

The assignment was so difficult to manage that it proved *onerous* to the team in charge of it.

❑ ONTOLOGY—theory about the nature of existence

There will probably never be a definitive *ontology* that people all over the world accept.

❑ OPALESCENT—iridescent, displaying colors

The infant, fascinated by the *opalescent* stone, stared at it for hours on end.

❑ OPAQUE—impervious to light; difficult to understand

The heavy buildup of dirt and grime on the windows almost made the.m *opaque*.

❑ OPERATIVE (adj.)—functioning, working

We all thought the photocopier was finally *operative*, until it broke down yet again.

❑ OPINE—to express an opinion

The talk show audience member *opined* that the guest under discussion was a pathetic excuse for a human being.

❑ OPPORTUNE—appropriate, fitting

Her investment in plastics, made just before the invention of plastic bags, was *opportune*.

❑ OPPORTUNIST—one who takes advantage of circumstances

Dozens of *opportunists* traveled to the earthquake-stricken region to sell food and water to the victims.

❑ OPPROBRIOUS—disgraceful, contemptuous

Despite his *opprobrious* addiction to gambling, the governor was re-elected once again.

❑ OPULENCE—wealth

Livingston considered his BMW to be a symbol of both *opulence* and style.

❑ ORACLE—person who foresees the future and gives advice

Opal decided to consult an *oracle* when she could not make the decision on her own.

❑ ORATION—lecture, formal speech

The class valedictorian gave an impressive *oration* on graduation day.

❑ ORATOR—lecturer, speaker

The new professor's dull tone of voice and lack of energy make her a particularly poor *orator*.

❑ ORB—spherical body; eye

Polly sighed at the sight of the lantern *orbs* glowing like small moons above the tables in the romantic restaurant garden.

❑ ORCHESTRATE—to arrange music for performance; to coordinate, organize

Though the president took all the credit, it was his wife who had actually *orchestrated* the entire event.

❑ ORDAIN—to make someone a priest or minister; to order

Stephanie sat proudly in the front row to watch her mother be *ordained* as the first female minister in the church's history.

❑ ORNITHOLOGIST—scientist who studies birds

The team of *ornithologists* devoted their research to the study of extinct species such as dodo birds.

❑ OSCILLATE—to move back and forth

The fans, *oscillating* from the ceiling, did little to cool down the humid Florida restaurant.

❑ OSSIFY—to turn to bone; to become rigid

Under certain conditions, cartilage in the body can *ossify* into bone.

❑ OSTENSIBLE—apparent

The *ostensible* reason for his visit was to borrow a book, but secretly he wanted to chat with lovely Wanda.

❑ OSTENTATIOUS—showy

The billionaire's 200-room palace was considered by many to be an overly *ostentatious* display of wealth.

❑ OSTRACISM—exclusion, temporary banishment

Larry knew that *ostracism* would be his fate when, after he made an obnoxious comment, all the other guests at the party turned their backs to him.

❑ OUSTER—expulsion, ejection

After his insane behavior at the meeting, the chairman faced an *ouster* by his fellow board members.

❑ OVERSTATE—to embellish, exaggerate

I do not want to *overstate* this, but I need you to understand the seriousness of the situation.

❑ OVERTURE—musical introduction; proposal, offer

The director received *overtures* from several big studios after his indie film success.

❑ OVERWROUGHT—agitated, overdone

The lawyer's *overwrought* voice on the phone made her clients worry about the outcome of their case.

P

❑ PACIFIC—calm, peaceful

The Pacific ocean was named for its comparatively subdued, *pacific* waves.

❑ PACIFIST—one opposed to war

For one who claimed to be a *pacifist*, Doug was surprisingly fond of weapons of war.

❑ PACIFY—to restore calm, bring peace

Nothing the king offered could *pacify* the angry princess, so he finally locked her in the dungeon.

❑ PALATIAL—like a palace, magnificent

After living in a one-room apartment for five years, Alicia thought the modest one bedroom looked downright *palatial*.

❑ PALAVER—idle talk

The journalist eagerly recorded the *palaver* among the football players in the locker room.

❑ PALEONTOLOGY—study of past geological eras through fossil remains

Janine decided to go into *paleontology* because of her interest in fossils and ancient civilizations.

❑ PALETTE—board for mixing paints; range of colors

The art instructor told the class to put only red, yellow, and blue paint on their *palettes*.

❑ PALISADE—fence made up of stakes

The tall iron *palisade* loomed menacingly over the prison.

❑ PALL (n.)—covering that darkens or obscures; coffin

A *pall* fell over the landscape as the clouds obscured the moon in the night sky.

❑ PALL (v.)—to lose strength or interest

Over time, the model's beauty *palled*, though her haughty attitude remained intact.

❑ PALLIATE—to make less serious, ease

The accused's crime was so vicious that the defense lawyer could not *palliate* it for the jury.

❑ PALLID—lacking color or liveliness

The old drugstore's *pallid* window could not compete with Wal-Mart's extravagant display next door.

❑ PALPABLE—obvious, real, tangible

As soon as Nicola disembarked from the plane in Mexico City, she noticed the *palpable* humidity.

❑ PALPITATION—trembling, shaking

Matthew hoped the *palpitations* of his hands would not betray how nervous he was to see her.

❑ PALTRY—pitifully small or worthless

Bernardo paid the ragged boy the *paltry* sum of ten cents to carry his luggage all the way to the hotel.

❑ PANACEA—cure-all

Some claim that Vitamin C is a *panacea* for all sorts of illnesses, but I have my doubts.

❑ PANACHE—flamboyance, verve

Even when she has to plan them last minute, Leah always manages to pull off parties with *panache*.

❑ PANDEMIC—spread over a whole area or country

Pandemic alarm spread throughout Colombia after the devastating earthquake.

❑ PANEGYRIC—elaborate praise; formal hymn of praise

The director launched into a *panegyric* in praise of the man whose donation had kept his charity going.

❑ PANOPLY—impressive array

Corrina casually sifted through a *panoply* of job offers before finally deciding on one.

❑ PANORAMA—broad view; comprehensive picture

The tourists gazed in awe at the *panorama* of mountains and valleys lying before them.

❑ PARADIGM—ideal example, model

The ribs restaurant owner used McDonald's as a *paradigm* for the expansion of his business.

❑ PARADOX—contradiction, incongruity; dilemma, puzzle

It is a *paradox* that those most in need of medical attention are often those least able to obtain it.

❑ PARADOXICAL—self-contradictory but true

The civics teacher tried to explain to the class that *paradoxically*, rules and regulations helped to ensure freedom.

❑ PARAGON—model of excellence or perfection

She is the *paragon* of what a judge should be: honest, intelligent, hardworking, and just.

❑ PARAMOUNT—supreme, dominant, primary

It is of *paramount* importance that we make it back to camp before the storm hits, or we'll freeze to death.

❑ PARAPHRASE—to reword, usually in simpler terms

In *paraphrasing* the poet, she lost the eloquence of his style and the complexity of his message.

❑ PARASITE—person or animal that lives at another's expense

It is not in the *parasite's* interest to harm its host, because in doing so the parasite will reduce its own chances of survival.

❑ PARCH—to dry or shrivel

The *parched* traveler searched desperately for a water source.

❑ PARE—to trim

The scullery maid's hands were sore after she *pared* hundreds of potatoes for the banquet.

❑ PARIAH—outcast

The *pariah* dog hovered at the outskirts of the camp, begging for scraps.

❑ PARITY—equality

Mrs. Lutskaya tried to maintain *parity* between her children, although each claimed she gave the other preferential treatment.

❑ PARLEY—discussion, usually between enemies

The peace organization tried in vain to schedule a *parley* between Israel and Iraq.

❑ PAROCHIAL—of limited scope or outlook, provincial

It was obvious that Victor's *parochial* mentality would clash with Ivonne's liberal open-mindedness.

❑ PARODY—humorous imitation

Shana's new play is a thinly veiled *parody* of the corruption in the White House.

❑ PAROLE—conditional release of a prisoner

John hoped he would be released from Attica on *parole* for good behavior within three years.

❑ PARRY—to ward off or deflect

Kari *parried* every question the army officer fired at her, much to his frustration.

❑ PARSIMONY—stinginess

Ethel gained a reputation for *parsimony* when she refused to pay for her daughter's college education.

❑ PARTISAN (n.)—strong supporter

After speaking out at every meeting, Evelia became known as a *partisan* of her cause.

❑ PARTISAN (adj.)—biased in favor of

Though we claim to have a non-*partisan* democratic system, it is clear that decisions always boil down to party lines.

❑ PASTICHE—piece of literature or music imitating other works

The playwright's clever *pastiche* of the well-known Bible story had the audience rolling in the aisles.

❑ PATENT (adj.)—obvious, unconcealed

Moe could no longer stand Frank's *patent* brownnosing to the boss, and confronted him about it directly.

❑ PATENT (n.)—official document giving exclusive right to sell an invention

Margaret claims she had the idea for that computer system years ago but never got the *patent* for it.

❑ PATERNITY—fatherhood; descent from father's ancestors

In this week's episode, the soap opera's star refuses to reveal the *paternity* of her child.

❑ PATHOGENIC—causing disease

Bina's research on *pathogenic* microorganisms and their origins should help stop the spread of disease.

❑ PATHOS—pity, compassion

Dr. Irwin's cold lack of *pathos* for his patients got him fired from the hospital.

❑ PATRICIAN—aristocrat

Though he was born a pauper, Claudius hoped eventually to acquire a *patrician* standing in society.

❑ PATRICIDE—murder of one's father

Freud interpreted *patricide* as a manifestation of jealousy of one's father's intimacy with one's mother.

❑ PATRIMONY—inheritance or heritage derived from one's father

After the will was read, Petra asked her brother to donate his share of the *patrimony* to charity.

❑ PATRONIZE—to condescend to, disparage; to buy from

LuAnn *patronized* the students, treating them like idiots, which they deeply resented.

❑ PAUCITY—scarcity, lack

Because of the relative *paucity* of bananas in the country, their price was very high.

❑ PAUPER—very poor person

A common theme in movies is the ascension of a *pauper* up the ranks of society to financial success.

❑ PAVILION—tent or light building used for shelter or exhibitions

The caterers decorated the *pavilion* lavishly with lights, streamers, and balloons.

❑ PECCADILLO—minor sin or offense

Gabriel tends to harp on his brother's *peccadilloes* and never lets him live them down.

❑ PECULATION—theft of money or goods

The news reported the *peculation* of the Monet paintings and described their recovery by the police.

❑ PEDAGOGUE—teacher

Jesus was regarded as an influential *pedagogue* in his society.

❑ PEDANT—uninspired, boring academic

The graduate instructor's tedious commentary on the subject soon gained her a reputation as a *pedant*.

❑ PEDESTRIAN (adj.)—commonplace

Although the restaurant's prices were high, critics considered its food little more than *pedestrian*.

❑ PEDIATRICIAN—doctor specializing in children and their ailments

Although she was first attracted to family medicine, she became a *pediatrician* because she loved working with children.

❑ PEDIMENT—triangular gable on a roof or facade

I notice that the *pediments* on the roof are coming loose; we should get them fixed.

❑ PEER (n.)—contemporary, equal, match

Adults often blame their children's inappropriate actions on pressure from their *peers*.

❑ PEERLESS—unequaled

Hannah's hard work and dedication to this fund-raiser have been *peerless*.

❑ PEJORATIVE—having bad connotations; disparaging

The teacher scolded Mark for his unduly *pejorative* comments about his classmate's presentation.

❑ PELLUCID—transparent; translucent; easily understood

We could not determine whether the clear, *pellucid* liquid in the bottle was water or vodka.

❑ PENANCE—voluntary suffering to repent for a wrong

The aging pirate wanted to do *penance* for his crimes of days gone by.

❑ PENCHANT—inclination

Tiffany's *penchant* for rich, married men made her an object of hatred for their wives.

❑ PENDING (adj.)—not yet decided, awaiting decision

The court has been waiting for the jury to announce the verdict, but the decision is still *pending*.

❑ PENITENT—expressing sorrow for sins or offenses, repentant

The victim's family claimed that the murderer did not feel *penitent* and therefore should not have been released from prison.

❑ PENSIVE—thoughtful

Drew was a *pensive* boy who often spent time alone writing poetry.

❑ PENULTIMATE—next to last

The *penultimate* syllable in the word "later" is stressed.

❑ PENUMBRA—partial shadow

The *penumbras* of the spooky forest frightened Dorothy and her dog, Toto.

❑ PENURY—extreme poverty

The Watsons lived in *penury* after Mr. Watson lost his job at the factory.

❑ PERAMBULATOR—baby carriage

After placing her baby in the *perambulator*, Nan set out for the park.

❑ PERCIPIENT—discerning, able to perceive

The *percipient* detective saw through the suspect's lies and uncovered the truth in the matter.

❑ PERDITION—complete and utter loss; damnation

Faust brought *perdition* upon himself when he made a deal with the Devil in exchange for power.

❑ PEREGRINATE—to wander from place to place

Prehistoric man *peregrinated* from Africa to other parts of the globe.

❑ PERENNIAL—present throughout the years; persistent

Fortunately for me, these flowers are *perennial* and require no maintenance whatsoever.

❑ PERFIDIOUS—faithless, disloyal, untrustworthy

The actress's *perfidious* companion revealed all of her intimate secrets to the gossip columnist.

❑ PERFUNCTORY—done in a routine way; indifferent

The machinelike bank teller processed the transaction and gave the waiting customer a *perfunctory* smile.

❑ PERIHELION—point in orbit nearest to the sun

At *perihelion*, the Earth receives the greatest amount of sunlight.

❑ PERIPATETIC—moving from place to place

Morty claims that his *peripatetic* hot dog stand gives him the opportunity to travel all over the city.

❑ PERJURE—to tell a lie under oath

Benson *perjured* himself to protect his son, claiming that he had spent the evening with him when in fact he had not.

❑ PERMEABLE—penetrable

Karen discovered that her raincoat was *permeable* when she was drenched while wearing it in a rainstorm.

❑ PERNICIOUS—very harmful

The Claytons considered Rocky, a convicted felon, to be a *pernicious* influence on their innocent daughter.

❑ PERPETUAL—endless, lasting

Although objects may appear solid, the electrons that make up matter are actually in *perpetual* motion.

PERSONIFICATION—act of attributing human qualities to objects or abstract qualities

Ellie may take the *personification* of her teddy bear a bit too far—she even shares her dessert with it.

PERSPICACIOUS—shrewd, astute, keen witted

Inspector Poirot used his *perspicacious* mind to solve mysteries.

PERT—lively and bold

The beauty contestant's *pert* personality and attractive appearance made her a natural choice for first prize.

PERTINACIOUS—persistent, stubborn

Despite her parents' opposition, Tina *pertinaciously* insisted on continuing to date her boyfriend.

PERTINENT—applicable, appropriate

The supervisor felt that his employee's complaints were *pertinent* and mentioned them in the meeting.

PERTURBATION—disturbance

Grandpa sleeps so soundly that he wouldn't notice any kind of *perturbation*.

PERUSAL—close examination

When you fly, your carry-on luggage is always subject to the *perusal* of customs officials.

PERVERT (v.)—to cause to change in immoral way; to misuse

Charlene objected when the opposing lawyer seemed to be *perverting* the truth.

PESTILENCE—epidemic, plague

The country went into national crisis when it was plagued by both *pestilence* and floods at the same time.

PETULANCE—rudeness, peevishness

The child's *petulance* annoyed the teacher, who liked her young students to be cheerful and cooperative.

PHALANX—massed group of soldiers, people, or things

Focusing on the importance of the *phalanx* in ancient Greece, the exhibit displayed several shields from the period.

PHILANDERER—pursuer of casual love affairs

The *philanderer*, incapable of being faithful to one woman, had been through several divorces.

PHILANTHROPY—love of humanity; generosity to worthy causes

The Metropolitan Museum of Art owes much of its collection to the *philanthropy* of private collectors who willed their estates to it.

PHILISTINE—narrow-minded person, someone lacking appreciation for art or culture

"These *philistines* are incapable of appreciating true art!" fumed the playwright as he read the terrible reviews of his play.

PHILOLOGY—study of words

Christian's love of *philology* led him to major in linguistics in college.

PHLEGMATIC—calm in temperament; sluggish

The *phlegmatic* old boar snoozed in the grass as the energetic piglets frolicked around him.

PHOBIA—exaggerated, illogical fear

Talia claims her *phobia* of spiders stems from the time she was bitten by one in third grade.

PHOENIX—mythical, immortal bird that lives for 500 years, burns itself to death, and rises from its ashes

Though the family's house had burned down, they knew they would rise from the rubble like the proverbial *phoenix* and rebuild their lives.

PHONETICS—study of speech sounds

The field of *phonetics* had interested Ilya ever since he'd conquered his speech impediment as a teenager.

PHONIC—relating to sound

The CD-ROM had impressive graphics, but it needed *phonic* enhancement as well.

PIETY—devoutness

The nun's *piety* inspired Anne to start going to church again.

PILFER—to steal

Marianne did not *pilfer* the money for herself but rather for her sick brother, who needed medicine.

PILLAGE—to loot, especially during a war

The invading soldiers *pillaged* the town for food and valuables.

PINNACLE—peak, highest point of development

The whole show was excellent, but the *pinnacle* was when the skater did a backwards flip.

PIOUS—dedicated, devout, extremely religious

Saul, a *pious* man, walks to the synagogue on the Sabbath and prays daily.

PIQUE (n.)—fleeting feeling of hurt pride

In a fit of *pique*, the writer tossed his manuscript into the fire after his friend criticized it.

PITHY—profound, substantial; concise, succinct, to the point

Martha's *pithy* comments during the interview must have been impressive, because she got the job.

PITTANCE—meager amount or wage

Zack felt sure he would not be able to buy food for his family with the small *pittance* the government gave him.

PLACATE—to soothe or pacify

The burglar tried to *placate* the snarling doberman by saying, "Nice doggy," and offering it a treat.

PLACID—calm

Looking at Aparna's *placid* expression, no one could tell that she was inwardly seething with rage.

PLAGIARIST—one who steals words or ideas

The notable scientist lost his job when he was exposed as a *plagiarist*; years before, he had copied a paper from a magazine.

PLAINTIFF—injured person in a lawsuit

The lawyer asked the *plaintiff* to rise and show the court his injuries.

PLAIT—to braid

Every morning before school the girl's grandmother *plaited* her long, curly hair.

PLATITUDE—stale, overused expression

Although Jacob has some interesting ideas, he relies too much on *platitudes* in his writing.

PLEBEIAN—crude, vulgar, low-class

The aristocrats would not lower themselves to attend a form of entertainment so *plebeian* as a movie.

PLENITUDE—abundance, plenty

Every Thanksgiving our family gives thanks for our *plenitude* of good fortune.

PLETHORA—excess, overabundance

Assuming that more was better, the defendant offered the judge a *plethora* of excuses.

PLIANT—pliable, yielding

Only those with extremely *pliant* limbs are able to perform complex yoga moves.

PLUCK (v.)—to pull strings on a musical instrument; to remove feathers from a bird

The moment she first *plucked* the strings of the Stradivarius, Nancy knew she had to have it.

PLUCKY—courageous, spunky

The *plucky* young nurse dove bravely into the foxhole, determined to save the life of the wounded soldier.

PLUMMET—to fall, plunge

Marvin screamed as he watched his new Ferrari *plummet* into the depths of the ravine.

PLURALISTIC—including a variety of groups

The United States is a *pluralistic* society, incorporating a wide range of different groups.

PLY (v.)—to use diligently; to engage; to join together

The weaver *plied* the fibers together to make a blanket.

PNEUMATIC—relating to air; worked by compressed air

The rebel launched the dynamite with the help of a *pneumatic* gun.

POACH—to steal game or fish; cook in boiling liquid

He knew it was illegal to *poach* the birds, but he did not have enough money to get a permit.

PODIUM—platform or lectern for orchestra conductors or speakers

The audience could see Tara shaking as she walked up to the *podium*.

POIGNANT—emotionally moving

Maria's speech in honor of her deceased friend was so *poignant* that there was not a dry eye at the funeral.

❑ POLAR—relating to a geographic pole; exhibiting contrast

Though Shawn and Angie are *polar* opposites in many ways, they have been happily married for ten years.

❑ POLARIZE—to tend towards opposite extremes

The leaders feared the conflict would *polarize* the group into two separate camps.

❑ POLEMIC—controversy, argument; verbal attack

The candidate's *polemic* against his opponent was vicious and small-minded rather than well reasoned and convincing.

❑ POLITIC—discreet, tactful

Her prudent and *politic* management of the crisis led her to be elected president the following year.

❑ POLYGLOT—speaker of many languages

Ling's extensive travels have helped her to become a true *polyglot*.

❑ PONDEROUS—weighty, heavy, large

We steeled ourselves before attempting to lift the *ponderous* bureau.

❑ PONTIFICATE—to speak in a pretentious manner

She *pontificated* about the virtues of being rich until we all left the room in disgust.

❑ PORE (v.)—to study closely or meditatively

I've *pored* over this text for over an hour, and I still can't understand it.

❑ POROUS—full of holes, permeable to liquids

Unfortunately, the tent was more *porous* than we thought and the rain soaked us to the bone.

❑ PORTENT—omen

Kylie quaked in fear as she watched a black cat cross her path, a *portent* of bad luck in the future.

❑ PORTLY—stout, dignified

The *portly* man wearily put on the Santa suit and set out for the mall.

❑ POSIT—to put in position; to suggest an idea

She *posited* the hideous vase on the mantelpiece in clear view of the guests who had given it to her.

❑ POSTERIOR—bottom, rear

The veterinarian injected the antibiotics into the *posterior* of the animal.

❑ POSTERITY—future generations; all of a person's descendants

Nadine saved all of her soccer trophies for *posterity*.

❑ POTABLE—drinkable

Though the water was *potable*, it tasted terrible.

❑ POTENTATE—monarch or ruler with great power

Alexander was a much kinder person before he assumed the role of *potentate* and it went to his head.

❑ PRAGMATIC—practical; moved by facts rather than abstract ideals

While daydreaming gamblers think they can get rich by frequenting casinos, *pragmatic* gamblers realize that the odds are heavily stacked against them.

❑ PRATTLE (n.)—meaningless, foolish talk

Her husband's mindless *prattle* drove Hilary insane; sometimes, she wished he would just shut up.

❑ PRECARIOUS—uncertain

The mountain goat almost lost its *precarious* footing on the cliff face.

❑ PRECEPT—principle; law

The Supreme Court justices do their best to abide by the *precepts* of the Constitution.

❑ PRECIPICE—edge, steep overhang

The hikers stood at the *precipice*, staring down over the steep cliff.

❑ PRECIPITATE (adj.)—sudden and unexpected

Since the couple wed after knowing each other only a month, many expected their *precipitate* marriage to end in divorce.

❑ PRECIPITATE (v.)—to throw down from a height; to cause to happen

It's fairly certain that Lloyd's incessant smoking *precipitated* his early death from cancer.

❑ PRECIPITOUS—hasty, quickly, with too little caution

At the sight of the approaching helicopters, Private Johnson *precipitously* shot a flare into the air, not realizing that he was attracting the attention of enemy aircraft.

I am more pragmatic

❑ PRÉCIS—concise summary of facts

The police chief reviewed the *précis* for any missing details.

❑ PRECISION—state of being precise

Molly entered the data into the computer with remarkable *precision* and speed.

❑ PRECLUDE—to rule out

The seriousness of the damage to the car *precluded* any attempt to repair it; it had to be scrapped.

❑ PRECOCIOUS—unusually advanced at an early age

The fact that Beatrice got married at age eighteen did not come as much of a shock, as she had always been *precocious*.

❑ PRECURSOR—forerunner, predecessor

It is amazing to compare today's sleek, advanced computers with their bulky, slow *precursors*.

❑ PREDATOR—one that preys on others, destroyer, plunderer

The lioness is a skilled *predator*, stalking her prey silently until it is close enough to go for the kill.

❑ PREDICAMENT—difficult situation

Because he had spent all of his pay, Bancha found himself in a miserable *predicament* when his rent bill arrived.

❑ PREDICATE (v.)—to found or base on

The new company is *predicated* on the central role of the Internet in modern international commerce.

❑ PREDICTIVE—relating to prediction, indicative of the future

The investors hung on every word of Bill Gates' *predictive* statements.

❑ PREDILECTION—preference, liking

The old woman's *predilection* for candy was evident from the chocolate bar wrappers strewn all over her apartment.

❑ PREDISPOSITION—tendency, inclination

I have a *predisposition* to be suspicious of used car salesmen, even though some of them may be honest.

❑ PREEMINENT—celebrated, distinguished

After he was awarded the Nobel Prize, Dr. Desai was recognized as a *preeminent* scholar in his field.

❑ PREFACE (n.)—introduction to a book; introductory remarks to a speech

Yumiko was thrilled that the famous Oprah Winfrey would be writing the *preface* to her book.

❑ PREMEDITATE—to consider, plan beforehand

The district attorney had to prove that the murder was *premeditated* in order to convince the jury to opt for the death penalty.

❑ PREMONITION—forewarning; presentiment

Mrs. Famuyiwa had a *premonition* that if her son were to marry this woman, he would suffer a terrible fate.

❑ PREPONDERANCE—majority in number; dominance

The *preponderance* of millionaires in his district meant that the Communist candidate stood no chance of being elected.

❑ PREPOSSESSING—attractive, engaging, appealing

The young man's *prepossessing* appearance and manner made him the most eligible bachelor at the party.

❑ PREPOSTEROUS—absurd, illogical

Hamish's *preposterous* plan to save the environment by burning all the cities to the ground made him an object of ridicule.

❑ PRESAGE—to foretell, indicate in advance

The demolition of the Berlin Wall *presaged* the fall of the Soviet Union.

❑ PRESCIENT—having foresight

Jonah's decision to sell the apartment turned out to be a *prescient* one, as its value soon dropped by half.

❑ PRESCRIBE—to set down a rule; to recommend a treatment

The doctor *prescribed* valium to the nervous patient, not realizing how addictive the drug was.

❑ PRESENTIMENT—premonition, sense of foreboding

I had a *presentiment* of doom when I saw the manager heading towards us with an angry look on his face.

❑ PRESTIDIGITATION—sleight of hand

Through some *prestidigitation*, the magician performed a seemingly impossible card trick.

❑ PRESUMPTUOUS—rude, improperly bold

"I don't want to be *presumptuous*, but why on earth did you choose red wallpaper?" said Ceci to her hosts.

❑ PRETEXT—excuse, pretended reason

Under the *pretext* that he needed a cup of coffee, Ted stood close to the managers, trying to overhear their conversation.

❑ PREVALENT—widespread

The teacher struggled to counteract the *prevalent* belief in the school that girls could give boys cooties.

❑ PREVARICATE—to lie, evade the truth

Rather than admit that he had overslept again, the employee *prevaricated*, claiming that traffic had made him late.

❑ PRIMEVAL—ancient, primitive

The archaeologist claimed that the skeleton he had uncovered was of *primeval* origin, though in actuality it was the remains of a monkey who had died at the zoo a few weeks previously.

❑ PRIMORDIAL—original, existing from the beginning

The first organisms were formed eons ago from *primordial* ooze.

❑ PRISTINE—untouched, uncorrupted

Since measures had been taken to prevent looting, the archeological site was still *pristine* when researchers arrived.

❑ PRIVATION—lack of usual necessities or comforts

The convict endured total *privation* while locked up in solitary confinement for a month.

❑ PROBITY—honesty, high-mindedness

The conscientious witness responded with the utmost *probity* to all the questions posed to her.

❑ PROCLIVITY—tendency, inclination

His *proclivity* for speeding got him into trouble with the highway patrol on many occasions.

❑ PROCRASTINATOR—one who continually and unjustifiably postpones

Don't be a *procrastinator*; do your homework now!

❑ PROCURE—to obtain

I was able to *procure* tickets to the premiere of the new *Star Wars* movie.

❑ PRODIGAL (adj.)—wasteful, extravagant, lavish

The *prodigal* son quickly wasted all of his inheritance on a lavish lifestyle devoted to pleasure.

❑ PRODIGIOUS—vast, enormous, extraordinary

The musician's *prodigious* talent made her famous all over the world.

❑ PROFANE—impure; contrary to religion; sacrilegious

His *profane* comments caused him to be banished from the temple for life.

❑ PROFICIENT—expert, skilled in a certain subject

The mechanic was *proficient* at repairing cars, but his horrible temper made it difficult for him to keep jobs for long.

❑ PROFLIGATE—corrupt, degenerate

Some historians claim that it was the Romans' decadent, *profligate* behavior that led to the decline of the Roman Empire.

❑ PROFUSE—lavish, extravagant

Although Janet was angry at Bart for forgetting her birthday, his *profuse* apologies made her forgive him.

❑ PROGENITOR—originator, forefather, ancestor in a direct line

The *progenitor* of the telephone is Alexander Graham Bell.

❑ PROGENY—offspring, children

The old photograph showed Greatgrandma Wells surrounded by her husband and all their *progeny*.

❑ PROGNOSIS—prediction of disease outcome; any prediction

Although his illness is serious, the new drugs on the market have made his *prognosis* relatively good.

❑ PROGRESSIVE—favoring progress or change; moving forward, going step-by-step

The *progressive* party pushed for reforms, while the conservatives tried to maintain the status quo.

❑ PROLIFERATE—propagate, reproduce; enlarge, expand

He only had two guinea pigs initially, but they *proliferated* to such an extent that he soon had dozens.

❑ PROLIFIC—productive, fertile

Stephen King, a *prolific* writer, seems to come out with a new book every six months.

❑ PROLOGUE—introductory section of a literary work or play

In the novel's *prologue*, the narrator of the story is introduced.

❑ PROMONTORY—piece of land or rock higher than its surroundings

The view of the valley from the *promontory* was an impressive sight.

❑ PROMULGATE—to make known publicly

The publicist *promulgated* the news of the celebrity's splendid wedding to the press.

❑ PROPENSITY—inclination, tendency

She has a *propensity* to lash out at others when under stress, so we leave her alone as much as possible.

❑ PROPINQUITY—nearness

The house's close *propinquity* to the foul-smelling pig farm made it impossible to sell.

❑ PROPITIATE—to win over, appease

The management *propitiated* the irate union by agreeing to raise wages for its members.

❑ PROPITIOUS—favorable, advantageous

"I realize that I should have brought this up at a more *propitious* moment, but I don't love you," said the bride to the groom in the middle of their marriage vows.

❑ PROPONENT—advocate, defender, supporter

A devoted *proponent* of animal rights, Rose rescued stray dogs and cats at every opportunity.

❑ PROSAIC—relating to prose; dull, commonplace

Simon's *prosaic* style bored his writing teacher to tears, and she dreaded having to mark his essays.

❑ PROSCRIBE—to condemn; to forbid, outlaw

Treason was *proscribed* in the country's constitution.

❑ PROSE—ordinary language used in everyday speech

The author's ideas were matched by his exquisite *prose* style, which was almost as refined as poetry.

❑ PROSECUTOR—person who initiates a legal action or suit

The *prosecutor*'s aggressive questioning left the defendant flustered, which weakened the defense's case.

❑ PROSELYTIZE—to convert to a particular belief or religion

The Jehovah's Witnesses went from door to door in the neighborhood, *proselytizing* enthusiastically.

❑ PROSTRATE—lying face downward, lying flat on ground

After taking a tumble down the stairs, Millie was found *prostrate* on the floor of the basement.

❑ PROTAGONIST—main character in a play or story, hero

In dramatic tragedy, the *protagonist* often brings about his own downfall.

❑ PROTEAN—readily assuming different forms or characters

The *protean* Scarlet Pimpernel could play a wide variety of different characters convincingly.

❑ PROTESTATION—declaration

Although the music students voiced their *protestation*, the school's music program was canceled.

❑ PROTOCOL—ceremony and manners observed by diplomats

Diplomats must strive to observe the correct *protocol* in their dealings with foreign heads of state.

❑ PROTRACT—to prolong, draw out, extend

Since every member of the committee had to have his or her say, the meeting was a *protracted* affair.

❑ PROTRUSION—something that sticks out

The carpenter noticed a *protrusion* in the piece of wood and sanded it down until it disappeared.

❑ PROVINCIAL—rustic, unsophisticated, limited in scope

Anita, a sophisticated city girl, sneered at the *provincial* attitudes of her country cousins.

❑ PROVOCATION—cause, incitement to act or respond

Poisonous snakes seldom attack without *provocation*; it is usually those who harass the snakes in some way who are bitten.

❑ PROWESS—bravery, skill

She credited her athletic *prowess* to daily practice and intense concentration.

❑ PROXIMITY—nearness

Tim was careful to put the glass out of reach, since the toddler loved to yank down objects in her *proximity*.

❑ PROXY—power to act as a substitute for another

The senile woman's niece produced a document that identified her as her aunt's *proxy* for all legal matters.

❑ PRUDE—one who is excessively proper or modest

The performance was admired by all except the *prude* in the front row, who fainted during the first sex scene.

❑ PRUDENT—careful, cautious

Considering the small size of our army, it would not be *prudent* for us to attack right now.

❑ PRURIENT—lustful, exhibiting lewd desires

The drunken sailor gave the buxom young waitress a *prurient* look.

❑ PRY—to intrude into; force open

I hesitated to ask Fern what had made her cry, since I didn't want to *pry* into her personal life.

❑ PSEUDONYM—pen name; fictitious or borrowed name

The exposé was so thoroughly damning to all parties involved that the author was forced to publish it under a *pseudonym*.

❑ PSYCHIC (adj.)—perceptive of nonmaterial, spiritual forces

Many unsuspecting fools have been robbed of their savings by people claiming to have *psychic* abilities.

❑ PUERILE—childish, immature, silly

Olivia's boyfriend's *puerile* antics are really annoying; sometimes he acts like a five-year-old!

❑ PUDGY—chubby, overweight

The *pudgy* dachshund was put on a diet when its owners realized that its large stomach was practically scraping the ground.

❑ PUGILISM—boxing

Pugilism has been praised a positive outlet for the aggressive impulses of deprived youths; on the down side, many boxers ultimately suffer brain damage from repeated blows to the head.

❑ PUGNACIOUS—quarrelsome, eager and ready to fight

The serene eighty-year-old used to be a *pugnacious* troublemaker in her youth, but she's softer now.

❑ PULCHRITUDE—beauty

The mortals gazed in admiration at Venus, stunned by her incredible *pulchritude*.

❑ PULVERIZE—to pound, crush, or grind into powder; destroy

The polar bear's awesome strength was such that a single blow from its paw would *pulverize* a human.

❑ PUMMEL—to pound, beat

The parents feared that the gorilla would *pummel* their precious baby, but instead, it brought him to safety.

❑ PUNCTILIOUS—careful in observing rules of behavior or ceremony

The *punctilious* butler made sure that all the proper conventions were observed for the important diplomatic dinner.

❑ PUNGENT—strong or sharp in smell or taste

The smoke from the burning tires was extremely *pungent*.

❑ PUNITIVE—having to do with punishment

The teacher banished Jack from the classroom as a *punitive* measure, but the boy was actually overjoyed to be missing class.

❑ PURGATION—catharsis, purification

Some religions require that converts undergo ritual *purgation* before accepting them as full-fledged members of the faith.

❑ PURGE—to cleanse or free from impurities

After *purging* his body of toxins, Roger felt healthy and refreshed.

❑ PURITANICAL—adhering to a rigid moral code

Fred was so *puritanical* that he refused to let his daughters talk to boys, let alone date them.

❑ PURPORT—to profess, suppose, claim

Brad *purported* to be an opera lover, but he fell asleep at every performance he attended.

Q

QUACK—faker; one who falsely claims to have medical skill

Licenses are given to doctors so that patients can be assured that their M.D.'s are qualified professionals rather than *quacks*.

QUADRILATERAL—four-sided polygon

The fortress was shaped as a *quadrilateral*, with watch towers in each of its four corners.

QUADRUPED—animal having four feet

After I threw my back out, the only way I could manage to move around was to clamber about on all fours like a *quadruped*.

QUAGMIRE—marsh; difficult situation

Kevin realized that he needed help to get himself out of this *quagmire*.

QUALIFY—to provide with needed skills; modify, limit

Stacey needed to shave a full minute off her record in order to *qualify* for the Olympic finals.

QUANDARY—dilemma, difficulty

Bill found himself in quite a *quandary* when he realized that he had promised to give the job to two different applicants.

QUARANTINE—isolation period, originally 40 days, to prevent spread of disease

When cholera hit the village, it was *quarantined* to prevent the disease spreading any further.

QUATERNARY—consisting of or relating to four units or members

The Rio Trio was hard pressed to come up with a new name when a fourth member turned their group into a *quaternary*.

QUELL—to crush or subdue

The dictator dispatched troops to *quell* the rebellion.

QUERULOUS—inclined to complain, irritable

Curtis's complaint letter received prompt attention after the company labeled him a *querulous* potential troublemaker.

QUERY (n.)—question

When the congressman refused to answer her *query*, the journalist repeated it in a louder voice.

QUIBBLE—to argue about insignificant and irrelevant details

Ignoring the widening crack in the dam, the engineers *quibbled* over whose turn it was to make coffee.

QUICKEN (v.)—to hasten, arouse, excite

The car had been well constructed, but continuous exposure to sea air *quickened* its deterioration, and it had to be replaced.

QUIESCENCE—inactivity, stillness

Bears typically fall into a state of *quiescence* when they hibernate during the winter months.

QUINTESSENCE—most typical example; concentrated essence

As far as I'm concerned, Julio Iglesias is the *quintessence* of Spanish manliness.

QUIVER—to shake slightly, tremble, vibrate

The *quivering* mobile unfastened from its weak nail and came crashing down.

QUIXOTIC—overly idealistic, impractical

The practical Danuta was skeptical of her roommate's *quixotic* plans to build a rollercoaster in their yard.

QUOTIDIAN—occurring daily; commonplace

The sight of people singing on the street is so *quotidian* in New York that passersby rarely react to it.

R

RACONTEUR—witty, skillful storyteller

The *raconteur* kept all the passengers entertained with his stories during the six-hour flight.

RADICAL—fundamental; drastic

Bored with her appearance, Lucinda decided to make a *radical* change and dyed her hair bright purple.

RAIL (v.)—to scold with bitter or abusive language

When the teacher assigned twice as much homework as usual, his students *railed* against such an impossible work load.

❑ RALLY (v.)—to assemble; recover, recuperate

Martina's neighbors *rallied* to her side after the fire destroyed her home, collecting donations for her.

❑ RAMBLE—to roam, wander; to babble, digress

Central Park was designed to invite both open-air lounging and random *rambling* down various paths.

❑ RAMIFICATION—an implication, outgrowth, or consequence

Deb was too young to comprehend the *ramifications* of her actions at the time she committed the crime.

❑ RAMSHACKLE—likely to collapse

The homeless man lived in a *ramshackle* lean-to that had long been abandoned by its previous owners.

❑ RANCID—spoiled, rotten

Oleta's body was discovered after neighbors complained about *rancid* odors emanating from her apartment.

❑ RANCOR—bitter hatred

Herbert was so filled with *rancor* that he could think of nothing but taking revenge on those who had humiliated him.

❑ RANT—to harangue, rave, forcefully scold

The teenager barely listened as her father *ranted* on and on about her disrespectful behavior.

❑ RAPPORT—relationship of trust and respect

Initially, they disliked one another, but working together eventually forged a *rapport* between the two men.

❑ RAPT—deeply absorbed

Surprisingly, the normally wild infant sat *rapt* during the classical music performance.

❑ RAREFY—to make thinner, purer, or more refined

The atmosphere *rarefies* as altitude increases, so the air at the top of high mountains is too thin to breathe.

❑ RASH (adj.)—careless, hasty, reckless

Lewis *rashly* jumped to the conclusion that the employee was completely incompetent after she made a small error.

❑ RATIFY—to approve formally, confirm

The Senate *ratified* the treaty after only a brief debate, much to the delight of its supporters.

❑ RATIOCINATION—methodical, logical reasoning

Reading Plato's work teaches a young person the *ratiocination* necessary to evaluate experiences.

❑ RATION (n.)—portion, share

After wolfing down her own *ration*, the soldier helped herself to the new recruit's meager portion.

❑ RATION (v.)—to supply; to restrict consumption of

The hikers had to *ration* their food so that it would last until they reached the safety of the camp.

❑ RATIONAL—logical, reasonable

Desiree offered no *rational* reasons for quitting school and taking her show on the road, which infuriated her parents.

❑ RAUCOUS—harsh sounding; boisterous

The grade school cafeteria was a *raucous* place at lunch time.

❑ RAVAGE—to destroy, devastate

Floods periodically *ravaged* the small town, but life was so pleasant there that residents refused to relocate.

❑ RAVENOUS—extremely hungry

The refugee had not had a bite of food for days and was *ravenous*.

❑ RAVINE—deep, narrow gorge

Police officers scoured the crime scene for days before finding the murder weapon buried in a *ravine*.

❑ RAZE—to tear down, demolish

The house had been *razed*: where it once stood there was nothing but splinters and bricks.

❑ REACTIONARY—marked by extreme conservatism, especially in politics

The former bra-burning hippie had turned into quite a *reactionary*, and the press dwelled on her about-face, attempting to expose her as a hypocrite.

❑ REBUFF (n.)—blunt rejection

The princess coldly *rebuffed* her suitor's marriage proposal, turning her back on him and walking away.

❑ REBUKE—to reprimand, scold

Sergeants often *rebuke* newly enlisted soldiers to teach them discipline.

❑ REBUT—to refute by evidence or argument

The moderator was careful to allow sufficient time for callers to *rebut* claims made by her guest speakers.

❑ RECALCITRANT—resisting authority or control

The *recalcitrant* mule refused to go down the treacherous path, however hard its master pulled at its reins.

❑ RECANT—to retract a statement, opinion, etcetera

The statement was so damning that the politician had no hopes of recovering his credibility, even though he tried to *recant* the words.

❑ RECAPITULATE—to review by a brief summary

After the long-winded president had finished his speech, his assistant *recapitulated* the points he had made for the press.

❑ RECEPTIVE—open to others' ideas; congenial

The leading software company was *receptive* to new ideas and fearless about making changes to incorporate new technology.

❑ RECLUSIVE—shut off from the world

Anthony's *reclusive* tendencies led him to leave the city and move into a lonely cabin in Montana.

❑ RECONDITE—relating to obscure learning; known to only a few

The ideas expressed in the ancient philosophical treatise were so *recondite* that only a few scholars could appreciate them.

❑ RECOUNT—to describe facts or events

Suspiciously, the witness changed her story when asked to *recount* the events leading up to the crime.

❑ RECRUIT (v.)—to draft, enlist; to seek to enroll

Companies often send representatives to college campuses to *recruit* bright young employees.

❑ RECTIFY—to correct

Most people would *rectify* errors they had made if they were given the opportunity.

❑ RECTITUDE—moral uprightness

Young women used to be shipped off to finishing schools to teach them proper manners and *rectitude*.

❑ RECURRENCE—repetition

The frequent *recurrence* of cancer even after it is seemingly cured makes it a particularly terrible disease.

❑ REDRESS—relief from wrong or injury

Seeking *redress* for the injuries she had received in the accident, Doreen sued the driver of the truck that had hit her.

❑ REDUNDANCY—unnecessary repetition

Let's delete a few paragraphs to cut down on the *redundancy* in this section of the book.

❑ REFECTORY—room where meals are served

The students rushed down to the *refectory* for their evening meal.

❑ REFLECTION—image, likeness; opinion, thought, impression

The vain young man admired his own *reflection* in the mirror for hours on end.

❑ REFORM—to change, correct

The new mayor struggled to *reform* the corrupt government, as she had promised the voters she would.

❑ REFRACT—to deflect sound or light

The crystal *refracted* the rays of sunlight so that they made a beautiful pattern on the wall.

❑ REFUGE—escape, shelter

The couple took *refuge* from the storm underneath the awning.

❑ REFURBISH—to renovate

This old house is charming, but it's kind of shabby and definitely needs to be *refurbished*.

❑ REFUTE—to contradict, discredit

The president managed to *refute* the charges against him by proving that his accuser had been bribed to lie by his enemies.

❑ REGIMEN—government rule; systematic plan

His marathon training *regimen* dictated that he had to run ten miles every morning.

❑ REGRESS—to move backward; revert to an earlier form or state

Elderly people who suffer from senility often *regress* to the early years of their childhood.

❑ REHABILITATE—to restore to good health or condition; re-establish a person's good reputation

The star checked herself into a clinic in order to *rehabilitate* herself from her drug addiction.

❑ REITERATE—to say or do again, repeat

The teacher was forced to *reiterate* the instructions because the class hadn't been listening the first time.

❑ REJOINDER—response

Patrick tried desperately to think of a clever *rejoinder* to Marcy's joke, but he couldn't.

❑ REJUVENATE—to make young again; renew

Martina looked and felt completely *rejuvenated* after her plastic surgery was completed.

❑ RELEGATE—to assign to a class, especially an inferior one

Because of his poor standardized test scores, Abe was *relegated* to a lower grade level than his peers.

❑ RELINQUISH—to renounce or surrender something

The toddler was forced to *relinquish* the toy when the girl who owned it asked for it back.

❑ RELISH (v.)—to enjoy greatly

Cameron *relished* the tasty sandwich, but he didn't like the pickle that came with it.

❑ REMEDIABLE—capable of being corrected

In the belief that the juvenile delinquent was *remediable* and not a hardened criminal, the judge put him on probation.

❑ REMEDY (v.)—to cure, correct

We can *remedy* this disastrous situation by putting our emergency backup plan into effect right now.

❑ REMINISCENCE—remembrance of past events

The old timer's *reminiscence* of his childhood was of a time when there were no cars.

❑ REMISSION—lessening, relaxation

Johnetta was relieved to discover that her cancer had gone into *remission*.

❑ REMIT—to send (usually money) as payment

Every month, the Pakistani sailors had to *remit* part of their salaries to people at home to whom they owed money.

❑ REMOTE—distant, isolated

The island was so *remote* that Chan's cell phone wouldn't operate on it.

❑ REMUNERATION—pay or reward for work, trouble, etcetera

You can't expect people to do this kind of boring work without some form of *remuneration*.

❑ RENASCENT—reborn, coming into being again

After decades of unemployment, industry in the city is *renascent* and jobs are becoming available.

❑ RENEGADE—traitor, person abandoning a cause

The *renegades* plotted in secret to overthrow the government.

❑ RENEGE—to go back on one's word

Hitler *reneged* on his promise that he would never attack the Soviet Union when his troops invaded the country during World War II.

❑ RENOUNCE—to give up or reject a right, title, person, etcetera

Edward *renounced* his right to the British throne in order to marry the divorcée, Mrs. Simpson.

❑ RENOWN—fame, widespread acclaim

Having spent her whole childhood banging on things, Jane grew up to be a drummer of great *renown*.

❑ REPAST—meal or mealtime

Ravi prepared a delicious *repast* of chicken tikka and naan.

❑ REPEAL—to revoke or formally withdraw (often a law)

The U.S. government *repealed* Prohibition when they realized that the law was not functioning as it had been intended.

❑ REPEL—to rebuff, repulse; disgust, offend

So far, the castle defenders have managed to *repel* the attackers, but they will not be able to hold out much longer.

❑ REPENT—to regret a past action

"If you don't *repent* your sins, you will rot in hell!" shouted the evangelical preacher.

❑ REPENTANT—apologetic, guilty, remorseful

After stealing from the church collection box, Ralph was *repentant* and confessed his sin to the priest.

❑ REPLETE—abundantly supplied

The gigantic supermarket was *replete* with consumer products of every kind.

❑ REPLICATE—to duplicate, repeat

If we're going to *replicate* last year's profit margins, we're going to have to work really, really hard.

❑ REPOSE—relaxation, leisure

After the stress you've endured at work recently, I hope you'll find some *repose* in this quiet village.

❑ REPRESS—to restrain or hold in

Sheila *repressed* the urge to tell the obnoxious man to shut up, as he was one of her best customers.

❑ REPRESSION—act of restraining or holding in

Many psychologists feel that too much *repression* is not a good thing; certain feelings need to be expressed.

❑ REPREHENSIBLE—blameworthy, disreputable

Lowell was thrown out of the bar because of his *reprehensible* behavior towards the other patrons.

❑ REPRISE—repetition, especially of a piece of music

The soloist ended her aria with a *reprise* of its beautiful refrain.

❑ REPROACH—to find fault with; blame

Renee *reproached* her boyfriend for forgetting to buy her a Christmas present.

❑ REPROBATE—morally unprincipled person

If you ignore your society's accepted moral code, you will be considered a *reprobate*.

❑ REPROVE—to criticize or correct

Mrs. Hernandez *reproved* her daughter for her poor grades and ordered her to work harder in school.

❑ REPUDIATE—to reject as having no authority

The old woman's claim that she was Russian royalty was *repudiated* when DNA tests showed she was not related to them.

❑ REPULSE—repel, fend off; sicken, disgust

He thinks women can't resist him, when in actuality many of them are *repulsed* by his arrogance.

❑ REQUIEM—hymns or religious service for the dead

The musician composed a moving *requiem* in honor of the recently deceased and beloved leader.

❑ REQUITE—to return or repay

Thanks for offering to lend me $500,000, but I know I'll never be able to *requite* your generosity.

❑ RESCIND—to repeal, cancel

The car company *rescinded* the offer of an advertising contract it had made to the celebrity after he was accused of murder.

❑ RESIDUE—remainder, leftover, remnant

The fire burned everything, leaving only a *residue* of ash and charred debris.

❑ RESILIENT—able to recover quickly after illness or bad luck; able to bounce back to shape

Luckily, Ramon was a *resilient* person, and was able to pick up the pieces and move on with his life after losing his business.

❑ RESOLUTE—determined; with a clear purpose

Louise was *resolute*; she would get into medical school no matter what.

❑ RESOLVE (n.)—determination, firmness of purpose

I admire your *resolve*, but is it really a good idea to go through with the marathon in this bad weather?

❑ RESOLVE (v.)—to conclude, determine

The conflict was finally *resolved* when Wanda dropped the criminal charges against her ex-boyfriend.

❑ RESONATE—to echo

The cries of the bald eagle *resonated* throughout the canyon.

❑ RESPIRE—to breathe

Humans need oxygen in order to *respire*.

❑ RESPITE—interval of relief

The brief *respite* was over; once again, Bo's phone was ringing off the hook with customer complaints.

❑ RESPLENDENT—splendid, brilliant

The bride looked *resplendent* in her long train and sparkling tiara.

❑ RESTITUTION—act of compensating for loss or damage

The concentration camp survivors demanded *restitution* from the German government for their suffering.

❑ RESTIVE—impatient, uneasy, restless

The passengers became *restive* after having to wait in line for hours, and began to shout complaints at the airline staff.

RESTORATIVE—having the power to renew or revitalize

Inge told all her friends about the miraculous *restorative* powers of the herbal tea.

RESTRAINED—controlled, repressed, restricted

The formerly wild girl became *restrained* and serious after a month in the strict boarding school.

RESUSCITATE—to revive, bring back to life

The doctor managed to *resuscitate* the heart attack victim one minute after he had stopped breathing.

RETAIN—to hold, keep possession of

Britain had to give up most of its colonies, but it *retained* control over Hong Kong until very recently.

RETARD (v.)—to slow, hold back

The Chinese tradition of footbinding involved *retarding* the growth of women's feet through binding them in heavy bandages.

RETICENT—not speaking freely; reserved

Physically small and *reticent*, Joan Didion often went unnoticed by those upon whom she was reporting.

RETINUE—group of attendants with an important person

The nobleman had to make room in his mansion not only for the princess, but also for her entire *retinue*.

RETIRING—shy, modest, reserved

A shy and *retiring* man, Chuck was horrified at the idea of having to speak in public.

RETORT (n.)—cutting response

It was only after Lance had left the room that Vera came up with the perfect *retort* to his insulting remark.

RETRACT—to draw in or take back

After Lance had *retracted* his insulting remark, Vera decided to forgive him.

RETRENCH—to regroup, reorganize

After their humiliating defeat, the troops *retrenched* back at the base to decide what to do next.

RETRIEVE—to bring, fetch; reclaim

The eager labrador *retrieved* the Frisbee from the lake.

RETROACTIVE—applying to an earlier time

Employee raises will be *retroactive* to the beginning of this year, although they only recently were awarded.

RETROGRADE—having a backward motion or direction

The *retrograde* motion of the comet puzzled the astronomists, who had expected it to move forwards.

RETROSPECTIVE—review of the past

The cinema held a *retrospective* of the director Kurosawa's greatest works.

REVELRY—boisterous festivity

An atmosphere of *revelry* filled the school after its basketball team's surprising victory.

REVERE—to worship, regard with awe

All the nuns in the convent *revered* their wise Mother Superior.

REVERT—to backslide, regress

Just when Liz thought he was finally becoming more mature, Kyle *reverted* to his usual childish ways.

REVILE—to criticize with harsh language, verbally abuse

Resentful of the traumas she had inflicted upon him, George *reviled* his mother at every opportunity.

REVITALIZE—to renew; give new energy to

The new CEO's upbeat, supportive managerial style *revitalized* the previously demoralized staff.

REVOKE—to annul, cancel, call back

Jonas's green card was *revoked* when it was proven that he had illegally worked outside the country.

REVULSION—strong feeling of repugnance or dislike

Rebecca was filled with *revulsion* at the stench that the rotten melon slices in her fridge gave off.

RHAPSODY—emotional literary or musical work

The rock group Queen played on a long musical tradition with their hit song "Bohemian Rhapsody."

RHETORIC—persuasive use of language

Lincoln's talent for *rhetoric* was evident in his beautifully expressed Gettysburg Address.

RHYTHM—regular pattern or variation of sounds and stresses

Darren, who had no sense of *rhythm*, was a terrible dancer.

❑ RIBALD—humorous in a vulgar way

The court jester's *ribald* brand of humor delighted the rather uncouth king.

❑ RIDDLE (v.)—to make many holes in; permeate

The helicopter was *riddled* with bullet holes after its flight into the combat zone.

❑ RIFE—widespread, prevalent; abundant

The essay was so *rife* with grammatical errors that it had to be rewritten.

❑ RISQUÉ—bordering on being inappropriate or indecent

Some of the more conservative audience members found the *risqué* variety act offensive.

❑ ROBUST—strong and healthy; hardy

Many of those around her fell ill, but the *robust* Sharon remained healthy throughout the flu epidemic.

❑ ROCOCO—very highly ornamented

The *rococo* palace was a little too fancy for the minimalist architect's taste.

❑ ROOT (v.)—to dig with a snout (like a pig)

The trained pig *rooted* happily in the mud for truffles and even managed to swallow a few before his master grabbed them.

❑ ROSTRUM—stage for public speaking

The college lecture hall was occasionally used as a *rostrum* for political speeches.

❑ ROTUND—round in shape; fat

The *rotund* matron spent her days baking cookies and then eating a good share of them herself.

❑ RUE—to regret

I *rue* the day I agreed to take care of that evil little cat.

❑ RUMINATE—to contemplate, reflect upon

The scholars spent days at the retreat, *ruminating* upon the complexities of the geopolitical situation.

❑ RUSTIC—rural

The *rustic* cabin was an ideal setting for a vacation in the country.

S

❑ SACCHARINE—excessively sweet or sentimental

Geoffrey's *saccharine* love poems nauseated Lucy, and she wished he'd stop sending them to her.

❑ SACROSANCT—extremely sacred; beyond criticism

Many people considered Mother Teresa to be *sacrosanct* and would not tolerate any criticism of her.

❑ SAGACIOUS—shrewd

Owls have a reputation for being *sagacious*, perhaps because of their big eyes which resemble glasses.

❑ SALIENT—prominent or conspicuous

His most *salient* characteristic is his tendency to dominate every conversation in which he takes part.

❑ SALLOW—sickly yellow in color

Due to the long hours she spent working in the sweatshop, Bertha's skin looked *sallow* and unhealthy.

❑ SALUBRIOUS—healthful

Rundown and sickly, Rita hoped that the fresh mountain air would have a *salubrious* effect on her health.

❑ SALUTATION—greeting

Many people keep in touch by exchanging Christmas *salutations* once a year.

❑ SANCTION (n.)—permission, support; law; penalty

"The court cannot *sanction* this type of criminal behavior, and it must stop," declared the stern judge.

❑ SANCTUARY—haven, retreat

Seeking *sanctuary* from the bloodthirsty crowd that wanted to burn her at the stake, the accused witch banged on the gate of the convent.

❑ SANGUINE—ruddy; cheerfully optimistic

A *sanguine* person thinks the glass is half full, while a depressed person thinks it's half empty.

❑ SARDONIC—cynical, scornfully mocking

Denise was offended by the *sardonic* way in which her date made fun of her ideas and opinions.

❑ SATIATE—to satisfy

His desire for power was so great that nothing less than complete control of the country could *satiate* it.

❑ SAUNTER—to amble; walk in a leisurely manner

The plainclothes policeman *sauntered* casually down the street, hoping he would not attract attention.

❑ SAVANT—learned person

The *savant* was happy to give advice to those who were not as intellectually gifted as she was.

❑ SAVORY—agreeable in taste or smell

The banquet guests consumed the *savory* treats with pleasure.

❑ SCABBARD—sheath for sword or dagger

The knight drew his sword from its *scabbard* and prepared to attack the villain.

❑ SCALE (v.)—to climb to the top of

The army recruits *scaled* the wall as fast as they could and raced to the end of the obstacle course.

❑ SCATHING—harshly critical; painfully hot

After the *scathing* criticism her book of poems received, Alicia swore off poetry writing for good.

❑ SCENARIO—plot outline; possible situation

I think this triangle drama between you, your husband, and the hairdresser would make an interesting *scenario* for a play.

❑ SCINTILLA—trace amount

This poison is so powerful that no more of a *scintilla* of it is needed to kill a horse.

❑ SCINTILLATE—to sparkle, flash

The society hostess was famous for her great wit and *scintillating* conversation.

❑ SCOFF—to deride, ridicule

The toddler *scoffed* at the notion that cows could jump over the moon; he was too smart to believe that.

❑ SCORE (n.)—notation for a musical composition

The *score* of the film was wonderful, but the musicians who performed it were not very skilful.

❑ SCORE (v.)—to make a notch or scratch

The prisoner *scored* a mark in the door for every day he passed in captivity.

❑ SCRIVENER—professional copyist

The illiterate peasant dictated her letter to a local *scrivener*.

❑ SCRUPULOUS—restrained; honest; careful and precise

David could not have stolen Carmen's money; he's too *scrupulous* to do such a thing.

❑ SCRUTINY—careful observation

The prehistoric fossils were given careful *scrutiny* by a team of scientists.

❑ SCURRILOUS—vulgar, low, indecent

The decadent aristocrat took part in *scurrilous* activities every night, unbeknownst to his family.

❑ SECANT—straight line intersecting a curve at two points

The mathematician used the *secant* to calculate the area of the curved shape.

❑ SECEDE—to withdraw formally from an organization

When the U.N. recognized the independence of Platvia's former colony, the country angrily *seceded* from the organization.

❑ SECLUDED—isolated and remote

The hermit lived in a *secluded* cottage, far from the other villagers.

❑ SECTARIAN—narrow-minded; relating to a group or sect

Since the fall of Communism in the former Yugoslavia, its various ethnic groups have plunged into *sectarian* violence.

❑ SECULAR—not specifically pertaining to religion

Although his favorite book was the Bible, the archbishop also read *secular* works such as mysteries.

❑ SEDENTARY—inactive, stationary; sluggish

Americans, who often work in *sedentary* office jobs, are becoming more overweight and out of shape.

❑ SEDITION—behavior promoting rebellion

Li was arrested for *sedition* after he gave a fiery speech condemning the government in the main square.

❑ SEISMOLOGY—science of earthquakes

Architects in San Francisco need to be familiar with *seismology* to design earthquake-proof structures.

❑ SEMINAL—relating to the beginning or seeds of something

The professor's theory is regarded as *seminal* in the discipline, in that many other theories build upon it.

❑ SENESCENT—aging, growing old

Fearful of becoming *senescent*, Jobim worked out several times a week and ate only health foods.

❑ SENSUAL—satisfying or gratifying the senses; suggesting sexuality

Although the movie was admittedly rather *sensual*, I don't think it deserved an X rating.

❑ SENTENTIOUS—having a moralizing tone

The pastor took on a *sententious* tone when he lectured the teenage couple on their loose morals.

❑ SENTIENT—aware, conscious, able to perceive

The anaesthetic didn't work and I was still *sentient* when the surgeon made her cut, so the operation was agony for me.

❑ SEQUEL—anything that follows

I hear they're making another *sequel* to the *Friday the 13th* movies.

❑ SEQUESTER—to remove or set apart; put into seclusion

The witness in the mafia case was *sequestered* for his own protection when it was determined that his life might be in danger.

❑ SERAPHIC—angelic, pure, sublime

Selena's sweet, *seraphic* appearance belied her nasty, bitter personality.

❑ SERENDIPITY—habit of making fortunate discoveries by chance

Rosemary's *serendipity* revealed itself in many ways, such as in her habit of finding money on the street.

❑ SERENITY—calm, peacefulness

Lisette's meditation helps her to achieve true *serenity*.

❑ SERPENTINE—serpentlike; twisting, winding

The princess fled down the seemingly endless *serpentine* staircase of the castle keep.

❑ SERRATED—saw-toothed, notched

A saw will not cut through wood if you do not use its *serrated* edge.

❑ SERVILE—submissive, obedient

As the wealthy widow screamed in rage at him, the *servile* butler apologized profusely for his mistake.

❑ SHARD—piece of broken glass or pottery

Barbara picked up the *shards* of the broken vase and attempted to glue them back together.

❑ SHEEPISH—timid, meek, or bashful

The dog sat near the mangled remains of its owner's fur coat with a guilty, *sheepish* look on its face.

❑ SHIRK—to avoid a task due to laziness or fear

The garbageman *shirked* his responsibilities by picking up the trash on only half of the streets he was supposed to cover.

❑ SIGNIFY—denote, indicate; symbolize

These ancient arrowheads I found *signify* that a Native American tribe once hunted in these woods.

❑ SIMIAN—apelike; relating to apes

Early man was more *simian* in appearance than modern man, as he was more closely related to apes.

❑ SIMPER—to smirk, smile foolishly

The spoiled girl *simpered* as her mother praised her extravagantly to the guests at the party.

❑ SINECURE—well-paying job or office that requires little or no work

The corrupt mayor made sure to set up all his relatives in lucrative *sinecures* in government offices.

❑ SINGE—to burn slightly, scorch

Martha *singed* the hairs on her arm while cooking food over the gas flame.

❑ SINUOUS—winding; intricate, complex

Thick, *sinuous* vines wound around the trunk of the tree.

❑ SKEPTICAL—doubtful, questioning

Although her parents still tried to make her believe that Santa Claus existed, the girl was *skeptical*.

❑ SKULK—to move in a stealthy or cautious manner; sneak

The private detective *skulked* behind a tree, waiting for the lovers to emerge from the motel room.

❑ SLIGHT—to treat as unimportant; insult

Pete *slighted* his old friend Matt by not inviting him to his annual Superbowl party.

❑ SLIPSHOD—careless, hasty

Because he was so stressed out, Kirk did a rather *slip-shod* job on his last project.

❑ SLOTH—sluggishness, laziness

The formerly dynamic CEO sank into *sloth* upon retiring, staying in bed until 3 in the afternoon.

❑ SLOUGH—to discard or shed

The rattlesnake *sloughed* off its old skin and slithered away, shiny and new looking.

❑ SLOVENLY—untidy, messy

The cook's clothes were so stained and *slovenly* that no restaurant would hire him.

❑ SLUGGARD—lazy, inactive person

Helga's *sluggard* of a husband watches TV on the couch all day instead of looking for a job.

❑ SMELT (v.)—to melt metal in order to refine it

We could make jewelry out of this silver ore, but it would look more elegant if we *smelted* it first.

❑ SNIPPET—tiny part, tidbit

From the brief *snippet* of conversation she overheard, Ida realized that her job was in danger.

❑ SOBRIETY—seriousness

Wendell's witty comments alleviated the *sobriety* of the budget conference.

❑ SOBRIQUET—nickname

One of Ronald Reagan's *sobriquets* was "The Gipper."

❑ SODDEN—thoroughly soaked; saturated

My shoes were thoroughly *sodden* after trekking through the damp Irish bog.

❑ SOJOURN—visit, stay

After graduating from college, Iliani embarked on an extended *sojourn* in China.

❑ SOLACE—comfort in distress; consolation

Upset as she was by her poodle's death, Florence took *solace* in the fact that he had died happy.

❑ SOLARIUM—room or glassed-in area exposed to the sun

After a few hours too many in the *solarium*, Annette's skin took on an orangish shade.

❑ SOLECISM—grammatical mistake

The applicant's letter was filled with embarrassing *solecisms*, such as "I works here at 20 years."

❑ SOLICITOUS—concerned, attentive; eager

The *solicitous* waiter stood at the star's elbow throughout the meal, ready to serve her.

❑ SOLIDARITY—unity based on common aims or interests

The company's owner felt a certain *solidarity* with the striking workers because of his own humble origins.

❑ SOLILOQUY—literary or dramatic speech by one character, not addressed to others

Rachel's *soliloquy* gave the audience more insight into her thoughts than the other characters in the play had.

❑ SOLIPSISM—belief that oneself is the only reality

Arthur's *solipsism* meant that he treated other people as if they didn't exist, which tended to annoy them.

❑ SOLSTICE—shortest and longest day of the year

In Sweden, the summer *solstice* is celebrated with parties that last all night.

❑ SOLUBLE—capable of being solved or dissolved

Sugar is *soluble* in cold water, but it dissolves more easily in hot water.

❑ SOMBER—dark and gloomy; melancholy, dismal

Everyone at the funeral was wearing dark, *somber* clothes except for the little girl in the flowered dress.

❑ SOMNAMBULIST—sleepwalker

The *somnambulist* climbed out of bed, walked to the kitchen, made himself a sandwich, and suddenly woke up.

❑ SOMNOLENT—drowsy, sleepy; inducing sleep

Carter became *somnolent* after taking a couple of sleeping pills.

❑ SONIC—relating to sound

The *sonic* capabilities of the speakers were impressive, and Gerry couldn't wait to listen to his favorite CD on them.

❑ SONOROUS—producing a full, rich sound

The *sonorous* blaring of the foghorn woke Lily up at 4:30 in the morning.

☑ SOPHIST—person good at arguing deviously

The philosopher was known as a masterful *sophist*; people respected his abilities, but did not trust him.

❑ SOPHISTRY—deceptive reasoning or argumentation

The politician used *sophistry* to cloud the issue whenever he was asked a tough question in a debate.

☑ SOPHOMORIC—immature and overconfident

The *sophomoric* young man was sure he would have no problems in writing the book, although there was no way he could accomplish the task.

❑ SOPORIFIC—sleepy or tending to cause sleep

The movie proved to be so *soporific* that soon loud snores were heard throughout the theater.

❑ SORDID—filthy; contemptible and corrupt

The details of the president's affair were so *sordid* that many people were too disgusted to read them.

❑ SOVEREIGN—having supreme power

The king did not take kindly to those who refused to recognize his *sovereign* power.

❑ SPARTAN—austere, severe, grave; simple, bare

The athlete's room was *spartan*, containing nothing but a bed and a pair of dumbbells.

❑ SPAWN—to generate, produce

The frog *spawned* hundreds of tadpoles.

❑ SPECULATION—contemplation; act of taking business risks for financial gain

If you want to ensure that you have a nest egg to retire on, you should not engage in too much wild financial *speculation*.

❑ SPECULATIVE—involving assumption; uncertain; theoretical

The theories I'm presenting are purely *speculative*, and they shouldn't be acted upon until more research has been done to test them out.

❑ SPONTANEOUS—on the spur of the moment, impulsive

Jean made the *spontaneous* decision to go to the movies instead of visiting her in-laws as she had planned.

❑ SPORADIC—infrequent, irregular

Since he followed the diet *sporadically*, lapsing into his old bad eating habits, Mick did not lose weight.

❑ SPORTIVE—frolicsome, playful

The lion roared in pain as the *sportive* lion cub bit his tail playfully.

❑ SPRIGHTLY—lively, animated, energetic

He was quite *sprightly* and active for a 98-year-old.

❑ SPUR (v.)—to prod

The rider *spurred* the horse on to leap over the tall hedge.

☑ SPURIOUS—lacking authenticity; counterfeit, false

Quoting from a *spurious* bible, the cult leader declared that all property should be signed over to him.

❑ SPURN—to reject or refuse contemptuously; scorn

When Harvey proposed to Harriet, she *spurned* him: she'd always considered him an idiot.

❑ SQUALID—filthy; morally repulsive

The *squalid* living conditions in the tenement building outraged the new tenants.

❑ SQUANDER—to waste

While I've been saving for a piano, my friend Sean has been *squandering* all his earnings on lottery tickets.

❑ STACCATO—marked by abrupt, clear-cut sounds

The *staccato* sounds of the coded radio transmissions filled the ship's cabin.

❑ STAGNANT—immobile, stale

That *stagnant* pond is a perfect breeding ground for mosquitoes; we should drain it.

❑ STAID—self-restrained to the point of dullness

The lively young girl felt bored in the company of her *staid*, conservative date.

☑ STALK (v.)—to hunt, pursue

The rock star put a restraining order on the insane woman who had *stalked* him for many years.

❑ STAND (n.)—group of trees

The Iroquois warriors hid in a *stand* of trees, waiting to ambush the approaching British soldiers.

❑ STARK—bare, empty, vacant

Nancy bought posters to liven up her *stark* new apartment, although she couldn't afford furniture.

❑ STASIS—motionless state; standstill

The rusty, ivy-covered World War II tank had obviously been in *stasis* for at least fifty years.

❑ STIFLE—to smother or suffocate; suppress

Much as she longed to express her anger at the dictator, Maria *stifled* her protests for fear of being arrested.

❑ STIGMA—mark of disgrace or inferiority

In *The Scarlet Letter*, Hester Prynne was required to wear the letter "A" on her clothes as a public *stigma* for her adultery.

❑ STILTED—stiff, unnatural

The nervous father of the bride gave a rather *stilted* speech at the wedding banquet.

❑ STINT (n.)—period of time spent doing something

After his *stint* in the Peace Corps, Tim decided to get a Ph.D. in international relations.

❑ STINT (v.)—to be sparing or frugal

Just don't *stint* on the mayonnaise in my ham sandwich, because I don't like my sandwiches to be too dry.

❑ STIPEND—allowance; fixed amount of money paid regularly

Unable to survive on her small *stipend* from the university, Joyce was forced to take out loans.

❑ STOCKADE—enclosed area forming defensive wall

As the enemy approached, the soldiers took their defensive positions behind the *stockade*.

❑ STOIC—indifferent to or unaffected by emotions

While most of the mourners wept, the dead woman's husband kept up a *stoic*, unemotional facade.

❑ STOLID—having or showing little emotion

The prisoner appeared *stolid* and unaffected by the judge's harsh sentence.

❑ STRATAGEM—trick designed to deceive an enemy

The Trojan Horse must be one of the most successful military *stratagems* used throughout history.

❑ STRATIFY—to arrange into layers

Many Indians use the concept of caste to *stratify* society into levels ranging from the "Untouchables" to the Brahmins.

❑ STRICTURE—something that restrains; negative criticism

The teenagers ignored all the parental *strictures* placed upon them and partied wildly every night.

❑ STRIDENT—loud, harsh, unpleasantly noisy

The customer's *strident* manner annoyed the shop assistant, but she managed to keep her temper.

❑ STRINGENT—imposing severe, rigorous standards

Many people found it difficult to live up to the *stringent* moral standards imposed by the Puritans.

❑ STULTIFY—to impair or reduce to uselessness

The company's leadership was *stultified* by its practice of promoting the owner's dimwitted children to powerful positions.

❑ STUNTED—having arrested growth or development

The bonsai tree's growth is intentionally *stunted* by the Japanese gardeners who cultivate it.

❑ STUPEFY—to dull the senses of; stun, astonish

The stag, *stupefied* by the bright glare of the headlights, stood right in the middle of the highway.

❑ STYLIZE—to fashion, formalize

Nellie *stylized* her wardrobe to match Princess Diana's, and everyone said they could have been sisters.

❑ STYMIE—to block or thwart

The police effort to capture the bank robber was *stymied* when he escaped through a rear window.

❑ SUAVE—smoothly gracious or polite; blandly ingratiating

Nina was a *suave* young woman who knew exactly how to act in any situation.

❑ SUBDUED—suppressed, stifled

The actor was momentarily *subdued* after the director bawled him out, but soon he was his usual confident self again.

❑ SUBJECTION—dependence, obedience, submission

The coach demanded total *subjection* from the athletes on his team.

❑ SUBJUGATE—to conquer, subdue; enslave

The Romans made a practice of *subjugating* all the peoples they conquered, often enslaving them.

❑ SUBLIME—awe-inspiring; of high spiritual or moral value

The music was so *sublime* that it transformed the rude surroundings into a special place.

❑ SUBLIMINAL—subconscious; imperceptible

Subliminal messages flash by so quickly on the TV screen that viewers are not consciously aware that they have seen them.

❑ SUBMISSIVE—tending to be meek and submit

The *submissive* wolf cringed at the feet of the alpha male, leader of the pack.

❑ SUBPOENA—notice ordering someone to appear in court

The lawyer *subpoenaed* the hostile witness, and she had to come to court and testify against her will.

❑ SUBSEQUENT—following in time or order

Elizabeth heard people discussing what a good president she would make, and *subsequently*, she couldn't stop thinking about how wonderful it would be to be president.

❑ SUBTERFUGE—trick or tactic used to avoid something

Spies who are not skilled in the art of *subterfuge* are generally exposed before too long.

❑ SUBTERRANEAN—hidden, secret; underground

Subterranean passages were dug for the subway after it was decided that there was no longer enough room for the tracks above ground in the crowded city.

❑ SUBTLE—hard to detect or describe; perceptive

The pickpocket was so *subtle* that his victims did not even realize they had been robbed until hours later.

❑ SUBVERT—to undermine or corrupt

The traitor intended to *subvert* loyal citizens of the crown with the revolutionary propaganda he distributed.

❑ SUCCINCT—terse, brief, concise

She was sought after by many talk shows, as her remarks were always *succinct* and to the point.

❑ SUCCULENT—juicy; full of vitality or freshness

The famished businessman dug into the *succulent* porterhouse steak with relish.

❑ SUFFERABLE—bearable

The only thing that made his prison term *sufferable* was his beloved pet mouse, Rodolfo.

❑ SUFFRAGIST—one who advocates extended voting rights

Suffragists eventually won voting rights for women, blacks, and other previously powerless groups.

❑ SULLEN—brooding, gloomy

The *sullen* child sat in the corner by herself, refusing to play with her classmates.

❑ SULLY—to soil, stain, tarnish, taint

Reginald was upset to discover that the child's sticky red lollipop had *sullied* his new cashmere overcoat.

❑ SUMPTUOUS—lavish, splendid

The banquet was a *sumptuous* affair, including a seven-course meal and quarts of champagne.

❑ SUPERANNUATED—too old, obsolete, outdated

The manual typewriter has become *superannuated*, although a few loyal diehards still swear by it.

❑ SUPERCILIOUS—arrogant, haughty, overbearing, condescending

She was a shallow and scornful society woman with a *supercilious* manner.

❑ SUPERFICIAL—hasty; shallow and phony

The politician was friendly, but in a *superficial*, unconvincing kind of way.

❑ SUPERFLUOUS—extra, more than necessary

The extra essays Jake included in his application were *superfluous*, as only one essay was required.

❑ SUPERSEDE—to take the place of; replace

Word 2000 will gradually *supersede* older versions of Word on office computers around the world.

❑ SUPERVISE—to direct or oversee the work of others

Among her other duties, a manager must *supervise* the work of her subordinates.

❑ SUPPLANT—replace, substitute

After his miserable performance, the raw young CEO was *supplanted* by a more experienced candidate.

❑ SUPPLE—flexible, pliant

The *supple* stalks of bamboo swayed back and forth in the wind.

❑ SUPPLICANT—one who asks humbly and earnestly

Alf is normally a cocky fellow, but he transformed himself into a *supplicant* when he begged the banker for a loan.

❑ SURFEIT—excessive amount

Because of the *surfeit* of pigs, pork prices have never been lower.

❑ SURLY—rude and bad-tempered

When asked to clean the windshield, the *surly* gas station attendant tossed a dirty rag at the customer and walked away.

❑ SURMISE—to make an educated guess

From his torn pants and bloody nose, I *surmised* that he had been in a fight.

❑ SURMOUNT—to conquer, overcome

The deaf and blind woman *surmounted* great obstacles to become a well-known trial lawyer.

❑ SURPASS—to do better than, be superior to

Ursula is a pretty girl, but her gorgeous sister *surpasses* her in beauty.

❑ SURPLUS—excess

The supermarket donated its *surplus* fruit to a local homeless shelter.

❑ SURREPTITIOUS—characterized by secrecy

The queen knew nothing of the *surreptitious* plots being hatched against her at court.

❑ SURVEY (v.)—to examine in a comprehensive way

Pampers *surveyed* families in the area to determine what they were looking for in a diaper.

❑ SUSCEPTIBLE—vulnerable, unprotected

Because of her weakened state, Valerie was *susceptible* to infection.

❑ SUSPEND—to defer, interrupt; dangle, hang

Construction of the building was *suspended* when an ancient Native American burial ground was discovered at the site.

❑ SUSTAIN—support, uphold; endure, undergo

If we can *sustain* our efforts a little longer, I'm sure our plan will succeed in the end.

❑ SWARTHY—having a dark complexion

The pale British tourist stood out like a sore thumb among the *swarthy* native Egyptians.

❑ SYBARITE—person devoted to pleasure and luxury

A confirmed *sybarite*, the young nobleman fainted at the thought of having to leave his lush palace and live in a tiny cottage.

❑ SYCOPHANT—self-serving flatterer, yes-man

Dreading criticism, the actor surrounded himself with admirers and *sycophants*.

❑ SYLLABUS—outline of a course

Ko looked at the course *syllabus* to figure out how much work he would be expected to do each week.

❑ SYMBIOSIS—cooperation, mutual helpfulness

The rhino and the tick-eating bird live in *symbiosis*; the rhino gives the bird food in the form of ticks, and the bird rids the rhino of parasites.

❑ SYMPOSIUM—meeting with short presentations on related topics

The university's English department held a *symposium* on sexual imagery in the works of D. H. Lawrence.

❑ SYNCOPATION—temporary irregularity in musical rhythm

Christine couldn't tell if the *syncopation* in the song was intentional or the result of a scratch in the CD she was playing.

❑ SYNOPSIS—plot summary

Oren wrote a one-page *synopsis* of a 55-page book.

❑ SYNTHESIS—blend, combination

The methods used in the experiment were a *synthesis* of techniques taken from biology and medicine.

❑ SYNTHETIC—artificial, imitation

The sushi in the window looked so delicious that you could hardly tell it was made out of *synthetic* materials.

T

TABLEAU—vivid description, striking incident or scene

The tourists admired the famous painter's lifelike *tableau* of the Last Supper.

TACIT—silently understood or implied

Although not a word had been said, everyone in the room knew that a *tacit* agreement had been made about which course of action to take.

TACITURN—uncommunicative, not inclined to speak much

The clerk's *taciturn* nature earned him the nickname "Silent Sammy."

TACTILE—relating to the sense of touch

She was a very *tactile* person, constantly touching the objects around her.

TAINT—to spoil or infect; to stain honor

"I will not allow you to *taint* my reputation!" stormed the politician when the blackmailer threatened to expose his corruption.

TAINTED—stained, tarnished; corrupted, poisoned

The lake water was *tainted* with chemicals from the factory, making it impossible to swim in or drink it.

TALON—claw of an animal, especially a bird of prey

A vulture holds its prey in its *talons* while it dismembers it with its beak.

TANG—sharp flavor or odor

After being smoked together with the herring, the bacon had a distinctly fishy *tang*.

TANGENTIAL—digressing, diverting

Your argument is interesting, but it's *tangential* to the matter at hand, so I suggest we get back to the point.

TANGIBLE—able to be sensed, perceptible, measurable

The storming of the castle didn't bring the soldiers *tangible* rewards, but it brought them great honor.

TANTAMOUNT—equivalent in value or significance; amounting to

Her refusal to defend herself against the accusation was *tantamount* to a confession in the eyes of the police officers.

TARNISHED—corroded, discolored; discredited, disgraced

The antique silver plate was so *tarnished* that Nestor had to polish it for hours before using it.

TAWDRY—gaudy, cheap, showy

The performer changed into her *tawdry*, spangled costume and stepped out onto the stage to do her show.

TAXONOMY—science of classification

Certain strange species do not seem to fit into the systems of classification used in traditional *taxonomy*.

TECHNOCRAT—strong believer in technology; technical expert

The *technocrat* could barely hide his disbelief and contempt as the CEO struggled to open a Word file on his computer.

TEMPERANCE—restraint, self-control, moderation

The strict, religious community frowned on newcomers who did not behave with *temperance*.

TEMPERED—moderated, restrained

The atmosphere at the dinner was *tempered* and calm, which made the loud young guest stand out.

TEMPESTUOUS—stormy, raging, furious

Yentl tried to venture out into the *tempestuous* storm to buy food, but she was forced to return home.

TENABLE—defensible, reasonable

Greg burned down his own house so that his ex-wife could not live in it, a scarcely *tenable* action in light of the fact that this also left his children homeless.

TENACIOUS—stubborn, holding firm

For years, against all odds, women *tenaciously* fought for the right to vote.

TENET—belief, doctrine

One of the *tenets* of the Muslim religion is that it is not acceptable to eat pork.

TENSILE—capable of withstanding physical stress

Architects construct buildings using only *tensile* materials in areas which are prone to earthquakes.

TENUOUS—weak, insubstantial

Francine's already *tenuous* connection to her cousins was broken when they moved away and didn't give her their new address.

❑ TEPID—lukewarm; showing little enthusiasm

Roxanne refused to take a bath in the *tepid* water, fearing that she would catch a cold.

❑ TERMINAL (adj.)—concluding, final; fatal

The boy's parents were devastated to learn that his illness was *terminal*.

❑ TERMINAL (n.)—depot, station

The railway *terminal* was filled with commuters during rush hour.

❑ TERRESTRIAL—earthly; down-to-earth, commonplace

Many "extraterrestrial" objects turn out to be *terrestrial* in origin, as when flying saucers turn out to be normal airplanes.

❑ TERSE—concise, brief, free of extra words

Her *terse* style of writing was widely praised for coming directly to the point.

❑ TESTAMENT—statement of belief; will

Guy's children couldn't believe that he had left everything to his chihuahua in his last will and *testament*.

❑ TESTIMONIAL—statement testifying to a truth; something given in tribute to a person's achievement

The defense lawyers presented many *testimonials* to the good character of the defendant during the trial.

❑ TETHER—to bind, tie

The cheetah chewed through its *tether* and ran away.

❑ THEOCRACY—government by priests representing a god

Under the leadership of Ayatollah Khomeini, who claimed to represent Allah, Iran could be characterized as a *theocracy*.

❑ THEOLOGY—study of God and religion

Priests must study *theology* at a seminary for several years before they can be ordained.

❑ THEORETICAL—abstract

The economics professor's advice was too *theoretical* for the company to put to any practical use.

❑ THERAPEUTIC—medicinal

Trent found the hot springs to be very *therapeutic* for his aches and pains, so he bathed in them often.

❑ THESAURUS—book of synonyms and antonyms

A *thesaurus* can be a very useful tool when you can't think of the right word to use in a certain context.

❑ THESIS—theory or hypothesis; dissertation or long, written composition

Henry worked for six years on his Ph.D. *thesis* on the mating habits of African horned toads.

❑ THWART—to block or prevent from happening; frustrate

Thwarted in its attempt to get at the food inside the box, the chimp threw it to the ground in frustration.

❑ TIDINGS—news

"I bring *tidings* of great joy!" shouted the messenger to the assembled court.

❑ TIMOROUS—timid, shy, full of apprehension

A *timorous* woman, Lois relied on her children to act for her whenever aggressive behavior was called for.

❑ TINGE (v.)—to color slightly

Photographs become *tinged* with yellow as they age.

❑ TINGE (n.)—slight amount

Although she no longer loved him, Linda felt a *tinge* of jealousy when she heard that her ex-husband planned to remarry.

❑ TIRADE—long, violent speech; verbal assault

Observers were shocked at the manager's *tirade* over such a minor mistake.

❑ TITAN—person of colossal stature or achievement

Despite his odd personal habits, it can't be denied that Howard Hughes was a *titan* of industry.

❑ TOADY—flatterer, hanger-on, yes-man

The king was surrounded by *toadies* who rushed to agree with whatever outrageous thing he said.

❑ TOLERANCE—capacity to respect different values; capacity to endure or resist something

Dictators are characterized by their lack of *tolerance* for anyone who opposes them in any way.

❑ TOME—book, usually large and academic

The teacher was forced to refer to various *tomes* to find the answer to the advanced student's question.

TONAL—relating to pitch or sound

Although it has interesting lyrics, the song's *tonal* problems make it unpleasant to listen to.

TOPOGRAPHY—art of making maps or charts

A master in the art of *topography*, Leavenworth was hired to create maps of the coast of South America.

TORPID—lethargic; unable to move; dormant

After surgery, the patient was *torpid* until the anesthesia wore off.

TORRID—burning hot; passionate

The *torrid* weather dried out the rice paddies and ruined the entire crop.

TORSION—act of twisting and turning

The cat executed a variety of desperate *torsions* in its attempt to escape the grip of its owner, who planned to give it a bath.

TORTUOUS—having many twists and turns; highly complex

To reach the remote inn, the travelers had to negotiate a winding, *tortuous* path up the steep mountain.

TOTTERING—barely standing

The *tottering* old man still managed to make his way to the corner shop every day to buy his favorite candy bar.

TOXIN—poison

It's essential to keep all *toxins* away from children and animals, as they might eat them unwittingly.

TRACTABLE—obedient, yielding

Though it was exhausted, the *tractable* workhorse obediently dragged the carriage through the mud.

TRANSCEND—to rise above, go beyond

Yoga helps me to *transcend* the petty frustrations of everyday life and to achieve true spirituality.

TRANSCENDENT—rising above, going beyond

For Wendy, the weekend with the Hari Krishnas was a truly *transcendent* experience, and she lost no time in joining their ranks.

TRANSCRIPTION—copy, reproduction; record

The *transcription* of the incriminating conversation was entered into evidence in the court case.

TRANSGRESS—to trespass, violate a law

After *transgressing* against every parking law in the city, Marvin had accumulated over 300 tickets.

TRANSIENT (adj.)—temporary, short-lived, fleeting

The actress's moment in the spotlight proved to be *transient* when her play folded due to poor reviews.

TRANSITORY—short-lived, existing only briefly

The reporter lived a *transitory* life, staying in one place only long enough to cover the current story.

TRANSLUCENT—partially transparent

The man was visible through the *translucent* shower curtain.

TRANSMUTE—to change in appearance or shape

In a series of stages, the caterpillar *transmuted* into a beautiful butterfly.

TRANSPIRE—to happen, occur; become known

It later *transpired* that a faulty gear shift had been responsible for the horrible accident.

TRAVESTY—parody, exaggerated imitation, caricature

When the pickpocket was sentenced to life in prison, many observers called it a *travesty* of justice.

TREMULOUS—trembling, quivering; fearful, timid

The *tremulous* stray cat hardly dared to approach the bowl of milk the boy offered it.

TRENCHANT—acute, sharp, incisive; forceful, effective

Dan's *trenchant* observations in class made him the professor's favorite student.

TREPIDATION—fear and anxiety

Mike approached the door of the principal's office with *trepidation*.

TRIFLING—of slight worth, trivial, insignificant

That little glitch in the computer program is a *trifling* error; in general, it works really well.

TRITE—shallow, superficial

Lindsay's graduation speech was the same *trite* nonsense we've heard hundreds of times in the past.

TROUNCE—to beat severely, defeat

The inexperienced young boxer was *trounced* in a matter of minutes by the seasoned champ.

❑ TROUPE—group of actors

This acting *troupe* is famous for its staging of Shakespeare's romantic comedies.

❑ TRUNCATE—to cut off, shorten by cutting

The mayor *truncated* his standard lengthy speech when he realized that the audience was not in the mood to listen to it.

❑ TRYING—difficult to deal with

Miraculously, she managed to finish the project under the most *trying* of circumstances.

❑ TRYST—agreement between lovers to meet; rendezvous

The knight arranged a secret *tryst* with the nobleman's wife deep in the forest.

❑ TUMULT—state of confusion; agitation

The *tumult* of the demonstrators drowned out the police chief's speech.

❑ TUNDRA—treeless plain found in arctic or subarctic regions

The Siberians set off across the freezing *tundra*, hoping to reach their homes before nightfall.

❑ TURBULENCE—commotion, disorder

The plane shook violently as it passed through the pocket of *turbulence*.

❑ TURGID—swollen, bloated

In the process of osmosis, water passes through the walls of *turgid* cells, ensuring that they never contain too much water.

❑ TURPITUDE—inherent vileness, foulness, depravity

The priest's affair with the teenage parishioner was considered an act of utter *turpitude*.

❑ TYRO—beginner, novice

An obvious *tyro* at salsa, Millicent received no invitations to dance.

U

❑ UBIQUITOUS—being everywhere simultaneously

Burger King franchises are *ubiquitous* in the United States, and are common in foreign countries as well.

❑ UMBRAGE—offense, resentment

The businessman took *umbrage* at the security guard's accusation that he had shoplifted a packet of gum.

❑ UNADULTERATED—absolutely pure

Only bottled waters that are *unadulterated* with chemicals can call themselves "pure."

❑ UNANIMITY—state of total agreement or unity

The *unanimity* of the council on this issue was surprising; I never thought they'd be able to agree on it.

❑ UNAPPEALING—unattractive, unpleasant

The fish dish looked so *unappealing* that Laszlo could not bring himself to taste it.

❑ UNAVAILING—hopeless, useless

Her efforts to drag her couch out of the flooding house were *unavailing*—it was simply too heavy for her.

❑ UNCONSCIONABLE—unscrupulous; shockingly unfair or unjust

The president's betrayal of the loyal employees who had worked to get him elected him was *unconscionable*.

❑ UNCTUOUS—greasy, oily; smug and falsely earnest

The *unctuous* salesman showered the rich customers with exaggerated compliments.

❑ UNDERMINE—to sabotage, thwart

Rumors of his infidelities *undermined* the star's marriage, and it eventually ended in divorce.

❑ UNDOCUMENTED—not certified, unsubstantiated

The journalist's controversial claims turned out to be completely *undocumented*, ruining his reputation.

❑ UNDULATING—moving in waves

The tourists hiked up and down the *undulating* hills of the lush countryside.

❑ UNEQUIVOCAL—absolute, certain

The jury's verdict was *unequivocal*: the sadistic murderer would be locked up for life.

❑ UNFROCK—to strip of priestly duties

The priest was *unfrocked* after it was discovered that he had broken many of his holy vows.

❑ UNHERALDED—unannounced, unexpected, not publicized

The gallant knight's arrival was *unheralded*, so the princess was surprised to discover him in the castle.

❑ UNIDIMENSIONAL—having one size or dimension, flat

The chocolate bars came off the factory conveyor belt in *unidimensional* little packages.

❑ UNIFORM (adj.)—consistent and unchanging; identical

We need to come up with a *uniform* look for our customer-service employees so that they can easily be identified as such.

❑ UNIMPEACHABLE—beyond question

His actions seem suspicious, but he's so honest that I know his motives must be *unimpeachable*.

❑ UNINITIATED—not familiar with an area of study

Uninitiated in the routines of tax assessment, the new employee had to consult his manual constantly.

❑ UNKEMPT—uncombed, messy in appearance

Sam's long hair seemed *unkempt* to his grandmother, and she told him he looked like a bum.

❑ UNOBTRUSIVE—modest, unassuming

"Servants should be *unobtrusive*, carrying out their duties quietly and efficiently," opined the countess.

❑ UNSCRUPULOUS—dishonest

The *unscrupulous* cafe owner watered down his soft drinks so that he could make a bigger profit on them.

❑ UNSOLICITED—unrequested

It is rare that *unsolicited* manuscripts are published; publishers are usually only interested in manuscripts they have requested through agents.

❑ UNWARRANTED—groundless, unjustified

The harshness of the criticism the film received was *unwarranted*, since it was really not all that bad.

❑ UNWITTING—unconscious; unintentional

Not looking where he was going, John charged into the subway car, *unwittingly* knocking down a blind man.

❑ UNYIELDING—firm, resolute

Despite her son's desperate pleas, Mrs. Young was *unyielding*: under no circumstances could he stay out after midnight.

❑ UPBRAID—to scold sharply

The teacher *upbraided* the student for scrawling graffiti all over the walls of the school.

❑ UPROARIOUS—loud and forceful

The *uproarious* soccer fans made a huge racket as they filed out of the stadium after the match.

❑ URBANE—courteous, refined, suave

The *urbane* teenager sneered at the mannerisms of his country-bumpkin cousin.

❑ USURP—to seize by force

The vice-principal was power-hungry, and threatened to *usurp* the principal's power.

❑ USURY—practice of lending money at exorbitant rates

The moneylender was convicted of *usury* for charging 50 percent interest on all his loans.

❑ UTILITARIAN—efficient, functional, useful

The suitcase was undeniably *utilitarian*, with its convenient compartments of different sizes, but it was also ugly.

❑ UTOPIA—perfect place

Wilson's idea of *utopia* was a beautiful, sunny beach on a tropical island.

V

❑ VACILLATE—to waver, show indecision

The customer held up the line as he *vacillated* between ordering chocolate chip or rocky road ice cream.

❑ VACUOUS—empty, void; lacking intelligence, purposeless

The congresswoman's *vacuous* speech angered the voters, who were tired of hearing empty platitudes.

❑ VAGRANT—poor person with no home

Unable to afford a room for the night, the *vagrant* huddled in a sheltered doorway.

❑ VALIDATE—to authorize, certify, confirm

The Disney employee *validated* my guest pass so that I was able to enter Disney World for free.

❑ VANQUISH—to conquer, defeat

Napoleon was *vanquished* by the English at the Battle of Waterloo.

❑ VAPID—tasteless, dull

Todd found his blind date *vapid* and boring, and couldn't wait to get away from her.

❑ VARIABLE—changeable, inconstant

The weather has been so *variable* lately that I never know whether to put on a coat or shorts in the morning.

❑ VARIEGATED—varied; marked with different colors

The *variegated* foliage of the jungle allows it to support thousands of different animal species.

❑ VAUNTED—boasted about, bragged about

The much-*vaunted* new computer program turned out to have so many bugs that it had to be recalled.

❑ VEHEMENTLY—strongly, urgently

Susanne *vehemently* denied the accusation that she had cheated on the test.

❑ VENDETTA—prolonged feud marked by bitter hostility

The *vendetta* between the Montagues and the Capulets resulted in the death of Romeo and Juliet.

❑ VENERABLE—respected because of age

All of the villagers sought the *venerable* old woman's advice whenever they had a problem.

❑ VENERATION—adoration, honor, respect

In traditional Confucian society, the young treat their elders with *veneration*, deferring to the elders' wisdom.

❑ VENT (v.)—to express, say out loud

Bob *vented* his frustrations at his malfunctioning computer by throwing coffee at it, which only served to make the problem worse.

❑ VERACIOUS—truthful, accurate

Uncertain of whether her son's excuse for coming home late was *veracious*, Sue decided to check his story.

❑ VERACITY—accuracy, truth

She had a reputation for *veracity*, so everyone believed her version of the story.

❑ VERBATIM—word for word

A court stenographer's job is to take down testimony in a court case *verbatim*, making no changes whatsoever in what is said.

❑ VERBOSE—wordy

The professor's answer was so *verbose* that his student forgot what the original question had been.

❑ VERDANT—green with vegetation; inexperienced

He wandered deep into the *verdant* woods in search of mushrooms and other edible flora.

❑ VERDURE—fresh, rich vegetation

The settlers admired the *verdure* that covered the land they had bought, knowing it meant that this land was fertile.

❑ VERIFIED—proven true

Before you publish that information, I'll have to make sure that it's been *verified*.

❑ VERISIMILITUDE—quality of appearing true or real

The TV show's *verisimilitude* led viewers to believe that the characters it portrayed were real.

❑ VERITY—truthfulness; belief viewed as true and enduring

The *verity* of the situation was that Roy couldn't bear to step down and let his sons take over the company.

❑ VERMIN—small creatures offensive to humans

Laura called the exterminator to fumigate her *vermin*-infested apartment.

❑ VERNACULAR—everyday language used by ordinary people; specialized language of a profession

Preeti could not understand the local *vernacular* of the southern U.S. region in which she now resided.

❑ VERNAL—related to spring

Bea basked in the balmy *vernal* breezes, happy that winter was at last coming to an end.

❑ VERSATILE—adaptable, all-purpose

This *versatile* little gadget can be used to dice vegetables, open cans, and whip cream!

❑ VESTIGE—trace, remnant

Vestiges of the former tenant still remained in the apartment, although he hadn't lived there for years.

VETO (v.)—to reject formally

Fearful that the new law would be used to reduce her powers, the president *vetoed* it.

VEX—to irritate, annoy; confuse, puzzle

The old man, who loved his peace and quiet, was *vexed* by his neighbor's loud music.

VIABLE—workable, able to succeed or grow

I don't think your plan to increase sales by sending free samples to every household in the city is *viable*.

VIADUCT—series of elevated arches used to cross a valley

The ancient roman *viaduct* stretched across the lush green valley.

VICARIOUS—substitute, surrogate; enjoyed through imagined participation in another's experience

Harriet lived *vicariously* through her daughter, listening avidly to her tales of romance and adventure.

VICISSITUDE—change or variation; ups and downs

Investors must be prepared for *vicissitudes* in the market and not panic when stock prices fall occasionally.

VIE—to compete, contend

The two wrestlers *vied* for the title of champion in the final match of the competition.

VIGILANT—attentive, watchful

Air traffic controllers must be *vigilant* in order to ensure that planes do not collide with one another.

VIGNETTE—decorative design; short literary composition

The writer's clever little *vignette* was published in a respected literary magazine.

VILIFY—to slander, defame

The candidate *vilified* his opponent, accusing him of being a wife-beating liar.

VIM—energy, enthusiasm

The sprightly old woman, still full of *vim* and vigor, walked four miles every day.

VINDICATE—to clear of blame; support a claim

Tess felt *vindicated* when her dire predictions about the impending earthquake came true.

VINDICATION—clearance from blame or suspicion

Many years after he was unjustly accused of treason, Dreyfus finally received full *vindication* from the authorities.

VINDICTIVE—spiteful, vengeful, unforgiving

After her husband left her for a young model, the *vindictive* ex-wife plotted to destroy their relationship.

VIRILE—manly, having qualities of an adult male

John Wayne tended to play *virile*, tough roles rather than effeminate, sensitive roles.

VIRTUOSO—someone with masterly skill; expert musician

He is a *virtuoso* conductor and has performed in all the most prestigious concert halls.

VIRULENT—extremely poisonous; malignant; hateful

Alarmed at the *virulent* hate mail she was receiving, the movie star decided to hire a bodyguard.

VISCOUS—thick, syrupy, and sticky

The *viscous* sap trickled slowly down the trunk of the tree.

VITRIOLIC—burning, caustic; sharp, bitter

Given the opportunity to critique his enemy's new book, the spiteful critic wrote an unusually *vitriolic* review of it for the *New York Times*.

VITUPERATE—to abuse verbally

The crabby old man *vituperated* his wife for forgetting to buy his favorite breakfast cereal at the market.

VIVACIOUS—lively, spirited

She was *vivacious* and outgoing, always ready to try something new.

VIVID—bright and intense in color; strongly perceived

The *vivid* colors of the rose garden were visible from miles away.

VOCIFEROUS—loud, vocal, and noisy

The prime minister continued his speech despite the *vociferous* protests of the members of parliament.

VOID (adj.)—not legally enforceable; empty

The will was declared null and *void* after it was discovered that the butler had forged his wealthy employer's signature on it.

❑ VOID (n.)—emptiness, vacuum

The astronauts released their shuttle's ancillary rockets and watched them drift off into the *void*.

❑ VOID (v.)—to cancel, invalidate

Her credit card was *voided* after she failed to pay her bills for months on end.

❑ VOLITION—free choice, free will; act of choosing

Dorio gave up her property of her own *volition*; no one pressured her into anything.

❑ VOLLEY (n.)—flight of missiles, round of gunshots

The troops fired a *volley* at the enemy, but they could not be sure how many of their bullets had found their targets.

❑ VOLUBLE—speaking much and easily, talkative; glib

The *voluble* man and his silent wife proved the old saying that opposites attract.

❑ VOLUMINOUS—large, having great volume

The bride's *voluminous* train trailed several yards behind her as she walked down the aisle.

❑ VORACIOUS—having a great appetite

The *voracious* farming family consumed a huge meal after a long day of heavy labor.

❑ VULNERABLE—defenseless, unprotected; innocent, naive

The child whisked the *vulnerable* little duckling out of the raging whirlpool just in time.

W

❑ WAIVE—to refrain from enforcing a rule; to give up a legal right

Veronique *waived* her right to half of her ex-husband's property, ridding herself of everything that could remind her of him.

❑ WALLOW—to indulge oneself excessively, luxuriate

He *wallowed* in the luxurious waterbed, sighing contentedly.

❑ WAN—sickly pale

The sick child had a *wan* face, in contrast to her rosy-cheeked sister.

❑ WANTON—undisciplined, unrestrained, reckless

Instead of singling out appropriate targets for his anger, the crazed man struck out in a *wanton* manner.

❑ WARRANTY—guarantee of a product's soundness

I can't believe that the *warranty* on this radio ran out two days before it broke! Now I won't be able to get my money back!

❑ WARY—careful, cautious

The dog was *wary* of Bola at first, only gradually letting its guard down and wagging its tail when he came home at night.

❑ WAYWARD—erratic, unrestrained, reckless

The Vanderbolts' *wayward* son squandered his inheritance and got into trouble with the law.

❑ WEATHER (v.)—to endure, undergo

I'm surprised that the old shack is still standing; I never expected it to *weather* that storm last night.

❑ WHET—to sharpen, stimulate

The delicious odors wafting from the kitchen *whet* Jack's appetite, and he couldn't wait to eat.

❑ WHIMSICAL—playful or fanciful idea

The ballet was *whimsical*, delighting the children with its imaginative characters and unpredictable sets.

❑ WILY—clever, deceptive

Yet again, the *wily* coyote managed to elude the ranchers who wanted to capture it.

❑ WINDFALL—sudden, unexpected good fortune

A sudden *windfall* enabled the old woman to buy the big new house she wanted after all.

❑ WINSOME—charming, happily engaging

Dawn gave the customs officers a *winsome* smile, and they let her pass without searching her bags.

❑ WITHDRAWN—unsociable, aloof; shy, timid

Silent and *withdrawn*, Yuri was not exactly the life of the party.

❑ WIZENED—withered, shriveled, wrinkled

The *wizened* old man was told that the plastic surgery necessary to make him look young again would cost more money than he could imagine.

- WRIT—written document, usually in law

  Writs are considered more legally valid than oral statements, as they provide a permanent record of what has been decided.

- WRY—amusing, ironic

  Although his words sounded very serious, Del's *wry* expression clued his observers into the fact that he was only joking.

X

- XENOPHOBIA—fear or hatred of foreigners or strangers

  Countries in which *xenophobia* is prevalent often have more restrictive immigration policies than countries which are more accepting of foreign influences.

Y

- YOKE (v.)—to join together

  As soon as the farmer had *yoked* his oxen together, he began to plow the fields.

Z

- ZEALOT—someone passionately devoted to a cause

  The religious *zealot* had no time for those who failed to share his strongly held beliefs.

- ZENITH—highest point, summit

  The diva considered her triumphant performance as Carmen at the Metropolitan Opera to be the *zenith* of her career.

- ZEPHYR—gentle breeze

  The *zephyr* blowing in from the ocean made the intense heat on the beach bearable for the sunbathers.

- ZOOLOGIST—scientist who studies animals

  The *zoologist* spent much of his career studying the social interaction of a group of chimpanzees.

SAT Root List

A

❑ **A, AN—not, without**

amoral, atrophy, asymmetrical, anarchy, anesthetic, anonymity, anomaly

❑ **AB, A—from, away, apart**

abnormal, abdicate, aberration, abhor, abject, abjure, ablution, abnegate, abortive, abrogate, abscond, absolve, abstemious, abstruse, annul, avert, aversion

❑ **AC, ACR—sharp, sour**

acid, acerbic, exacerbate, acute, acuity, acumen, acrid, acrimony

❑ **AD, A—to, toward**

adhere, adjacent, adjunct, admonish, adroit, adumbrate, advent, abeyance, abet, accede, accretion, acquiesce, affluent, aggrandize, aggregate, alleviate, alliteration, allude, allure, ascribe, aspersion, aspire, assail, assonance, attest

❑ **ALI, ALTR—another**

alias, alienate, inalienable, altruism

❑ **AM, AMI—love**

amorous, amicable, amiable, amity

❑ **AMBI, AMPHI—both**

ambiguous, ambivalent, ambidextrous, amphibious

❑ **AMBL, AMBUL—walk**

amble, ambulatory, perambulator, somnambulist

❑ **ANIM—mind, spirit, breath**

animal, animosity, unanimous, magnanimous

❑ **ANN, ENN—year**

annual, annuity, superannuated, biennial, perennial

❑ **ANTE, ANT—before**

antecedent, antediluvian, antebellum, antepenultimate, anterior, antiquity, antiquated, anticipate

❑ **ANTHROP—human**

anthropology, anthropomorphic, misanthrope, philanthropy

❑ **ANTI, ANT—against, opposite**

antidote, antipathy, antithesis, antacid, antagonist, antonym

❑ **AUD—hear**

audio, audience, audition, auditory, audible

❑ **AUTO—self**

autobiography, autocrat, autonomous

B

❑ BELLI, BELL—war
belligerent, bellicose, antebellum, rebellion

❑ BENE, BEN—good
benevolent, benefactor, beneficent, benign

❑ BI—two
bicycle, bisect, bilateral, bilingual, biped

❑ BIBLIO—book
Bible, bibliography, bibliophile

❑ BIO—life
biography, biology, amphibious, symbiotic, macrobiotics

❑ BURS—money, purse
reimburse, disburse, bursar

C

❑ CAD, CAS, CID—happen, fall
accident, cadence, cascade, deciduous

❑ CAP, CIP—head
captain, decapitate, capitulate, precipitous, precipitate

❑ CARN—flesh
carnal, carnage, carnival, carnivorous, incarnate

❑ CAP, CAPT, CEPT, CIP—take, hold, seize
capable, capacious, recapitulate, captivate, deception, intercept, precept, inception, anticipate, emancipation, incipient, percipient

❑ CED, CESS—yield, go
cease, cessation, incessant, cede, precede, accede, recede, antecedent, intercede, secede, cession

❑ CHROM—color
chrome, chromatic, monochrome

❑ CHRON—time
chronology, chronic, anachronism

❑ CIDE—murder
suicide, homicide, regicide, patricide

❑ CIRCUM—around
circumference, circumlocution, circumnavigate, circumscribe, circumspect, circumvent

❑ CLIN, CLIV—slope
incline, declivity, proclivity

❑ CLUD, CLUS, CLAUS, CLOIS—shut, close
conclude, reclusive, claustrophobia, cloister, preclude, occlude

❑ CO, COM, CON—with, together
coeducation, coagulate, coalesce, coerce, cogent, cognate, collateral, colloquial, colloquy, commensurate, commodious, compassion, compatriot, complacent, compliant, complicity, compunction, concerto, conciliatory, concord, concur, condone, conflagration, congeal, congenial, congenital, conglomerate, conjure, conjugal, conscientious, consecrate, consensus, consonant, constrained, contentious, contrite, contusion, convalescence, convene, convivial, convoke, convoluted, congress

❑ COGN, GNO—know
recognize, cognition, cognizance, incognito, diagnosis, agnostic, prognosis, gnostic, ignorant

❑ CONTRA—against
controversy, incontrovertible, contravene

❑ CORP—body
corpse, corporeal, corpulence

❑ COSMO, COSM—world
cosmopolitan, cosmos, microcosm, macrocosm

❑ CRAC, CRAT—rule, power
democracy, bureaucracy, theocracy, autocrat, aristocrat, technocrat

❑ CRED—trust, believe
incredible, credulous, credence

❑ CRESC, CRET—grow
crescent, crescendo, accretion

❑ CULP—blame, fault
culprit, culpable, inculpate, exculpate

❑ CURR, CURS—run
current, concur, cursory, precursor, incursion

D

❑ **DE—down, out, apart**
depart, debase, debilitate, declivity, decry, deface, defamatory, defunct, delegate, demarcation, demean, demur, deplete, deplore, depravity, deprecate, deride, derivative, desist, detest, devoid

❑ **DEC—ten, tenth**
decade, decimal, decathlon, decimate

❑ **DEMO, DEM—people**
democrat, demographics, demagogue, epidemic, pandemic, endemic

❑ **DI, DIURN—day**
diary, diurnal, quotidian

❑ **DIA—across**
diagonal, diatribe, diaphanous

❑ **DIC, DICT—speak**
diction, interdict, predict, abdicate, indict, verdict

❑ **DIS, DIF, DI—not, apart, away**
disaffected, disband, disbar, disburse, discern, discordant, discredit, discursive, disheveled, disparage, disparate, dispassionate, dispirit, dissemble, disseminate, dissension, dissipate, dissonant, dissuade, distend, differentiate, diffidence, diffuse, digress, divert

❑ **DOC, DOCT—teach**
doctrine, docile, doctrinaire

❑ **DOL—pain**
condolence, doleful, dolorous, indolent

❑ **DUC, DUCT—lead**
seduce, induce, conduct, viaduct, induct

E

❑ **EGO—self**
ego, egoist, egocentric

❑ **EN, EM—in, into**
enter, entice, encumber, endemic, ensconce, enthrall, entreat, embellish, embezzle, embroil, empathy

❑ **ERR—wander**
erratic, aberration, errant

❑ **EU—well, good**
eulogy, euphemism, euphony, euphoria, eurythmics, euthanasia

❑ **EX, E—out, out of**
exit, exacerbate, excerpt, excommunicate, exculpate, execrable, exhume, exonerate, exorbitant, exorcise, expatriate, expedient, expiate, expunge, expurgate, extenuate, extort, extremity, extricate, extrinsic, exult, evoke, evict, evince, elicit, egress, egregious

F

❑ **FAC, FIC, FECT, FY, FEA—make, do**
factory, facility, benefactor, malefactor, fiction, fictive, beneficent, affect, confection, refectory, magnify, unify, rectify, vilify, feasible

❑ **FAL, FALS—deceive**
false, infallible, fallacious

❑ **FERV—boil**
fervent, fervid, effervescent

❑ **FID—faith, trust**
confident, diffidence, perfidious, fidelity

❑ **FLU, FLUX—flow**
fluent, flux, affluent, confluence, effluvia, superfluous

❑ **FORE—before**
forecast, foreboding, forestall

❑ **FRAG, FRAC—break**
fragment, fracture, diffract, fractious, refract

❑ **FUS—pour**
profuse, infusion, effusive, diffuse

G

❑ **GEN—birth, class, kin**
generation, congenital, homogeneous, heterogeneous, ingenious, engender, progenitor, progeny

❑ GRAD, GRESS—step

graduate, gradual, retrograde, centigrade, degrade, gradation, gradient, progress, congress, digress, transgress, ingress, egress

❑ GRAPH, GRAM—writing

biography, bibliography, epigraph, grammar, epigram

❑ GRAT—pleasing

grateful, gratitude, gratis, ingrate, congratulate, gratuitous, gratuity

❑ GRAV, GRIEV—heavy

grave, gravity, aggravate, grieve, aggrieve, grievous

❑ GREG—crowd, flock

segregate, gregarious, egregious, congregate, aggregate

H

❑ HABIT, HIBIT—have, hold

habit, inhibit, cohabit, habitat

❑ HAP—by chance

happen, haphazard, hapless, mishap

❑ HELIO, HELI—sun

heliocentric, helium, heliotrope, aphelion, perihelion

❑ HETERO—other

heterosexual, heterogeneous, heterodox

❑ HOL—whole

holocaust, catholic, holistic

❑ HOMO—same

homosexual, homogenize, homogeneous, homonym

❑ HOMO—man

homo sapiens, homicide, bonhomie

❑ HYDR—water

hydrant, hydrate, dehydration

❑ HYPER—too much, excess

hyperactive, hyperbole, hyperventilate

❑ HYPO—too little, under

hypodermic, hypothermia, hypochondria, hypothesis, hypothetical

I

❑ IN, IG, IL, IM, IR—not

incorrigible, indefatigable, indelible, indubitable, inept, inert, inexorable, insatiable, insentient, insolvent, insomnia, interminable, intractable, incessant, inextricable, infallible, infamy, innumerable, inoperable, insipid, intemperate, intrepid, inviolable, ignorant, ignominious, ignoble, illicit, illimitable, immaculate, immutable, impasse, impeccable, impecunious, impertinent, implacable, impotent, impregnable, improvident, impassioned, impervious, irregular

❑ IN, IL, IM, IR—in, on, into

infusion, ingress, innate, inquest, inscribe, insinuate, inter, illustrate, imbue, immerse, implicate, irrigate, irritate, invade, inaugurate, incandescent, incarcerate, incense, indenture, induct, ingratiate, introvert, incarnate, inception, incisive, infer

❑ INTER—between, among

intercede, intercept, interdiction, interject, interlocutor, interloper, intermediary, intermittent, interpolate, interpose, interregnum, interrogate, intersect, intervene

❑ INTRA, INTR—within

intrastate, intravenous, intramural, intrinsic

❑ IT, ITER—between, among

transit, itinerant, reiterate, transitory

J

❑ JECT, JET—throw

eject, interject, abject, trajectory, jettison

❑ JOUR—day

journal, adjourn, sojourn

❑ JUD—judge

judge, judicious, prejudice, adjudicate

❑ JUNCT, JUG—join

junction, adjunct, injunction, conjugal, subjugate

❑ JUR—swear, law

jury, abjure, adjure, conjure, perjure, jurisprudence

L

❑ LAT—side
lateral, collateral, unilateral, bilateral, quadrilateral

❑ LAV, LAU, LU—wash
lavatory, laundry, ablution, antediluvian

❑ LEG, LEC, LEX—read, speak
legible, lecture, lexicon

❑ LEV—light
elevate, levitate, levity, alleviate

❑ LIBER—free
liberty, liberal, libertarian, libertine

❑ LIG, LECT—choose, gather
eligible, elect, select

❑ LIG, LI, LY—bind
ligament, oblige, religion, liable, liaison, lien, ally

❑ LING, LANG—tongue
lingo, language, linguistics, bilingual

❑ LITER—letter
literate, alliteration, literal

❑ LITH—stone
monolith, lithograph, megalith

❑ LOQU, LOC, LOG—speech, thought
eloquent, loquacious, colloquial, colloquy, soliloquy, circumlocution, interlocutor, monologue, dialogue, eulogy, philology, neologism

❑ LUC, LUM—light
lucid, illuminate, elucidate, pellucid, translucent

❑ LUD, LUS—play
ludicrous, allude, delusion, allusion, illusory

M

❑ MACRO—great
macrocosm, macrobiotics

❑ MAG, MAJ, MAS, MAX—great
magnify, majesty, master, maximum, magnanimous, magnate, magnitude

❑ MAL—bad
malady, maladroit, malevolent, malodorous

❑ MAN—hand
manual, manuscript, emancipate, manifest

❑ MAR—sea
submarine, marine, maritime

❑ MATER, MATR—mother
maternal, matron, matrilineal

❑ MEDI—middle
intermediary, medieval, mediate

❑ MEGA—great
megaphone, megalomania, megaton, megalith

❑ MEM, MEN—remember
memory, memento, memorabilia, reminisce

❑ METER, METR, MENS—measure
meter, thermometer, perimeter, metronome, commensurate

❑ MICRO—small
microscope, microorganism, microcosm, microbe

❑ MIS—wrong, bad, hate
misunderstand, misanthrope, misapprehension, misconstrue, misnomer, mishap

❑ MIT, MISS—send
transmit, emit, missive

❑ MOLL—soft
mollify, emollient, mollusk

❑ MON, MONIT—warn
admonish, monitor, premonition

❑ MONO—one
monologue, monotonous, monogamy, monolith, monochrome

❑ MOR—custom, manner
moral, mores, morose

❑ MOR, MORT—dead

morbid, moribund, mortal, amortize

❑ MORPH—shape

amorphous, anthropomorphic, metamorphosis, morphology

❑ MOV, MOT, MOB, MOM—move

remove, motion, mobile, momentum, momentous

❑ MUT—change

mutate, mutability, immutable, commute

N

❑ NAT, NASC—born

native, nativity, natal, neonate, innate, cognate, nascent, renascent, renaissance

❑ NAU, NAV—ship, sailor

nautical, nauseous, navy, circumnavigate

❑ NEG—not, deny

negative, abnegate, renege

❑ NEO—new

neoclassical, neophyte, neologism, neonate

❑ NIHIL—none, nothing

annihilation, nihilism

❑ NOM, NYM—name

nominate, nomenclature, nominal, cognomen, misnomer, ignominious, antonym, homonym, pseudonym, synonym, anonymity

❑ NOX, NIC, NEC, NOC—harm

obnoxious, noxious, pernicious, internecine, innocuous

❑ NOV—new

novelty, innovation, novitiate

❑ NUMER—number

numeral, numerous, innumerable, enumerate

O

❑ OB—against

obstruct, obdurate, obfuscate, obnoxious, obsequious, obstinate, obstreperous, obtrusive

❑ OMNI—all

omnipresent, omnipotent, omniscient, omnivorous

❑ ONER—burden

onerous, onus, exonerate

❑ OPER—work

operate, cooperate, inoperable

P

❑ PAC—peace

pacify, pacifist, pacific

❑ PALP—feel

palpable, palpitation

❑ PAN—all

panorama, panacea, panegyric, pandemic, panoply

❑ PATER, PATR—father

paternal, paternity, patriot, compatriot, expatriate, patrimony, patricide, patrician

❑ PATH, PASS—feel, suffer

sympathy, antipathy, empathy, apathy, pathos, impassioned

❑ PEC—money

pecuniary, impecunious, peculation

❑ PED, POD—foot

pedestrian, pediment, expedient, biped, quadruped, tripod

❑ PEL, PULS—drive

compel, compelling, expel, propel, compulsion

❑ PEN—almost

peninsula, penultimate, penumbra

❑ PEND, PENS—hang

pendant, pendulous, compendium, suspense, propensity

❑ PER—through, by, for, throughout

perambulator, percipient, perfunctory, permeable, perspicacious, pertinacious, perturbation, perusal, perennial, peregrinate

❑ PER—against, destruction

perfidious, pernicious, perjure

❑ PERI—around

perimeter, periphery, perihelion, peripatetic

❑ PET—seek, go toward

petition, impetus, impetuous, petulant, centripetal

❑ PHIL—love

philosopher, philanderer, philanthropy, bibliophile, philology

❑ PHOB—fear

phobia, claustrophobia, xenophobia

❑ PHON—sound

phonograph, megaphone, euphony, phonetics, phonics

❑ PLAC—calm, please

placate, implacable, placid, complacent

❑ PON, POS—put, place

postpone, proponent, exponent, preposition, posit, interpose, juxtaposition, depose

❑ PORT—carry

portable, deportment, rapport

❑ POT—drink

potion, potable

❑ POT—power

potential, potent, impotent, potentate, omnipotence

❑ PRE—before

precede, precipitate, preclude, precocious, precursor, predilection, predisposition, preponderance, prepossessing, presage, prescient, prejudice, predict, premonition, preposition

❑ PRIM, PRI—first

prime, primary, primal, primeval, primordial, pristine

❑ PRO—ahead, forth

proceed, proclivity, procrastinator, profane, profuse, progenitor, progeny, prognosis, prologue, promontory, propel, proponent, propose, proscribe, protestation, provoke

❑ PROTO—first

prototype, protagonist, protocol

❑ PROX, PROP—near

approximate, propinquity, proximity

❑ PSEUDO—false

pseudoscientific, pseudonym

❑ PYR—fire

pyre, pyrotechnics, pyromania

Q

❑ QUAD, QUAR, QUAT—four

quadrilateral, quadrant, quadruped, quarter, quarantine, quaternary

❑ QUES, QUER, QUIS, QUIR—question

quest, inquest, query, querulous, inquisitive, inquiry

❑ QUIE—quiet

disquiet, acquiesce, quiescent, requiem

❑ QUINT, QUIN—five

quintuplets, quintessence

R

❑ RADI, RAMI—branch

radius, radiate, radiant, eradicate, ramification

❑ RECT, REG—straight, rule

rectangle, rectitude, rectify, regular

❑ REG—king, rule

regal, regent, interregnum

❑ RETRO—backward

retrospective, retroactive, retrograde

❑ RID, RIS—laugh
ridiculous, deride, derision

❑ ROG—ask
interrogate, derogatory, abrogate, arrogate, arrogant

❑ RUD—rough, crude
rude, erudite, rudimentary

❑ RUPT—break
disrupt, interrupt, rupture

S

❑ SACR, SANCT—holy
sacred, sacrilege, consecrate, sanctify, sanction, sacro-sanct

❑ SCRIB, SCRIPT, SCRIV—write
scribe, ascribe, circumscribe, inscribe, proscribe, script, manuscript, scrivener

❑ SE—apart, away
separate, segregate, secede, sedition

❑ SEC, SECT, SEG—cut
sector, dissect, bisect, intersect, segment, secant

❑ SED, SID—sit
sedate, sedentary, supersede, reside, residence, assiduous, insidious

❑ SEM—seed, sow
seminar, seminal, disseminate

❑ SEN—old
senior, senile, senescent

❑ SENT, SENS—feel, think
sentiment, nonsense, assent, sentient, consensus, sensual

❑ SEQU, SECU—follow
sequence, sequel, subsequent, obsequious, obsequy, non sequitur, consecutive

❑ SIM, SEM—similar, same
similar, semblance, dissemble, verisimilitude

❑ SIGN—mark, sign
signal, designation, assignation

❑ SIN—curve
sine curve, sinuous, insinuate

❑ SOL—sun
solar, parasol, solarium, solstice

❑ SOL—alone
solo, solitude, soliloquy, solipsism

❑ SOMN—sleep
insomnia, somnolent, somnambulist

❑ SON—sound
sonic, consonance, dissonance, assonance, sonorous, resonate

❑ SOPH—wisdom
philosopher, sophistry, sophisticated, sophomoric

❑ SPEC, SPIC—see, look
spectator, circumspect, retrospective, perspective, perspicacious

❑ SPER—hope
prosper, prosperous, despair, desperate

❑ SPERS, SPAR—scatter
disperse, sparse, aspersion, disparate

❑ SPIR—breathe
respire, inspire, spiritual, aspire, transpire

❑ STRICT, STRING—bind
strict, stricture, constrict, stringent, astringent

❑ STRUCT, STRU—build
structure, construe, obstruct

❑ SUB—under
subconscious, subjugate, subliminal, subpoena, subsequent, subterranean, subvert

❑ SUMM—highest
summit, summary, consummate

❑ SUPER, SUR—above
supervise, supercilious, supersede, superannuated, superfluous, insurmountable, surfeit

❑ SURGE, SURRECT—rise
surge, resurgent, insurgent, insurrection

❑ SYN, SYM—together

synthesis, sympathy, synonym, syncopation, synopsis, symposium, symbiosis

T

❑ TACIT, TIC—silent

tacit, taciturn, reticent

❑ TACT, TAG, TANG—touch

tact, tactile, contagious, tangent, tangential, tangible

❑ TEN, TIN, TAIN—hold, twist

detention, tenable, tenacious, pertinacious, retinue, retain

❑ TEND, TENS, TENT—stretch

intend, distend, tension, tensile, ostensible, contentious

❑ TERM—end

terminal, terminus, terminate, interminable

❑ TERR—earth, land

terrain, terrestrial, extraterrestrial, subterranean

❑ TEST—witness

testify, attest, testimonial, testament, detest, protestation

❑ THE—god

atheist, theology, apotheosis, theocracy

❑ THERM—heat

thermometer, thermal, thermonuclear, hypothermia

❑ TIM—fear, frightened

timid, intimidate, timorous

❑ TOP—place

topic, topography, utopia

❑ TORT—twist

distort, extort, tortuous

❑ TORP—stiff, numb

torpedo, torpid, torpor

❑ TOX—poison

toxic, toxin, intoxication

❑ TRACT—draw

tractor, intractable, protract

❑ TRANS—across, over, through, beyond

transport, transgress, transient, transitory, translucent, transmutation

❑ TREM, TREP—shake

tremble, tremor, tremulous, trepidation, intrepid

❑ TURB—shake

disturb, turbulent, perturbation

U

❑ UMBR—shadow

umbrella, umbrage, adumbrate, penumbra

❑ UNI, UN—one

unify, unilateral, unanimous

❑ URB—city

urban, suburban, urbane

V

❑ VAC—empty

vacant, evacuate, vacuous

❑ VAL, VAIL—value, strength

valid, valor, ambivalent, convalescence, avail, prevail, countervail

❑ VEN, VENT—come

convene, contravene, intervene, venue, convention, circumvent, advent, adventitious

❑ VER—true

verify, verity, verisimilitude, veracious, aver, verdict

❑ VERB—word

verbal, verbose, verbiage, verbatim

❑ VERT, VERS—turn

avert, convert, pervert, revert, incontrovertible, divert, subvert, versatile, aversion

❑ VICT, VINC—conquer
victory, conviction, evict, evince, invincible

❑ VID, VIS—see
evident, vision, visage, supervise

❑ VIL—base, mean
vile, vilify, revile

❑ VIV, VIT—life
vivid, vital, convivial, vivacious

❑ VOC, VOK, VOW—call, voice
vocal, equivocate, vociferous, convoke, evoke, invoke, avow

❑ VOL—wish
voluntary, malevolent, benevolent, volition

❑ VOLV, VOLUT—turn, roll
revolve, evolve, convoluted

❑ VOR—eat
devour, carnivore, omnivorous, voracious

Practice Tests
and
Explanations

SAT

Practice Test A

Before taking this practice test, find a quiet room where you can work uninterrupted for 90 minutes. Make sure you have a comfortable desk and several No. 2 pencils.

Use the answer sheet on the following page to record your answers. (You can tear it out or photocopy it.)

Once you start this practice test, don't stop until you've finished. Remember—you can review any questions within a section, but you may not go back or forward a section.

Good luck.

SAT Practice Test A
Answer Sheet

Remove (or photocopy) this answer sheet and use it to complete the practice test.
See the answer key following the test when finished.
The "Compute Your Score" section at the back of the book will show you how to find your score.

Start with number 1 for each section. If a section has fewer questions that answer spaces, leave the extra spaces blank.

SECTION 1

1 (A) (B) (C) (D) (E)	11 (A) (B) (C) (D) (E)	21 (A) (B) (C) (D) (E)	31 (A) (B) (C) (D) (E)
2 (A) (B) (C) (D) (E)	12 (A) (B) (C) (D) (E)	22 (A) (B) (C) (D) (E)	32 (A) (B) (C) (D) (E)
3 (A) (B) (C) (D) (E)	13 (A) (B) (C) (D) (E)	23 (A) (B) (C) (D) (E)	33 (A) (B) (C) (D) (E)
4 (A) (B) (C) (D) (E)	14 (A) (B) (C) (D) (E)	24 (A) (B) (C) (D) (E)	34 (A) (B) (C) (D) (E)
5 (A) (B) (C) (D) (E)	15 (A) (B) (C) (D) (E)	25 (A) (B) (C) (D) (E)	35 (A) (B) (C) (D) (E)
6 (A) (B) (C) (D) (E)	16 (A) (B) (C) (D) (E)	26 (A) (B) (C) (D) (E)	36 (A) (B) (C) (D) (E)
7 (A) (B) (C) (D) (E)	17 (A) (B) (C) (D) (E)	27 (A) (B) (C) (D) (E)	37 (A) (B) (C) (D) (E)
8 (A) (B) (C) (D) (E)	18 (A) (B) (C) (D) (E)	28 (A) (B) (C) (D) (E)	38 (A) (B) (C) (D) (E)
9 (A) (B) (C) (D) (E)	19 (A) (B) (C) (D) (E)	29 (A) (B) (C) (D) (E)	39 (A) (B) (C) (D) (E)
10 (A) (B) (C) (D) (E)	20 (A) (B) (C) (D) (E)	30 (A) (B) (C) (D) (E)	40 (A) (B) (C) (D) (E)

right in section 1

wrong in section 1

SECTION 2

1 (A) (B) (C) (D) (E)	11 (A) (B) (C) (D) (E)	21 (A) (B) (C) (D) (E)	31 (A) (B) (C) (D) (E)
2 (A) (B) (C) (D) (E)	12 (A) (B) (C) (D) (E)	22 (A) (B) (C) (D) (E)	32 (A) (B) (C) (D) (E)
3 (A) (B) (C) (D) (E)	13 (A) (B) (C) (D) (E)	23 (A) (B) (C) (D) (E)	33 (A) (B) (C) (D) (E)
4 (A) (B) (C) (D) (E)	14 (A) (B) (C) (D) (E)	24 (A) (B) (C) (D) (E)	34 (A) (B) (C) (D) (E)
5 (A) (B) (C) (D) (E)	15 (A) (B) (C) (D) (E)	25 (A) (B) (C) (D) (E)	35 (A) (B) (C) (D) (E)
6 (A) (B) (C) (D) (E)	16 (A) (B) (C) (D) (E)	26 (A) (B) (C) (D) (E)	36 (A) (B) (C) (D) (E)
7 (A) (B) (C) (D) (E)	17 (A) (B) (C) (D) (E)	27 (A) (B) (C) (D) (E)	37 (A) (B) (C) (D) (E)
8 (A) (B) (C) (D) (E)	18 (A) (B) (C) (D) (E)	28 (A) (B) (C) (D) (E)	38 (A) (B) (C) (D) (E)
9 (A) (B) (C) (D) (E)	19 (A) (B) (C) (D) (E)	29 (A) (B) (C) (D) (E)	39 (A) (B) (C) (D) (E)
10 (A) (B) (C) (D) (E)	20 (A) (B) (C) (D) (E)	30 (A) (B) (C) (D) (E)	40 (A) (B) (C) (D) (E)

right in section 2

wrong in section 2

SECTION 3

1 (A) (B) (C) (D) (E)	11 (A) (B) (C) (D) (E)	21 (A) (B) (C) (D) (E)	31 (A) (B) (C) (D) (E)
2 (A) (B) (C) (D) (E)	12 (A) (B) (C) (D) (E)	22 (A) (B) (C) (D) (E)	32 (A) (B) (C) (D) (E)
3 (A) (B) (C) (D) (E)	13 (A) (B) (C) (D) (E)	23 (A) (B) (C) (D) (E)	33 (A) (B) (C) (D) (E)
4 (A) (B) (C) (D) (E)	14 (A) (B) (C) (D) (E)	24 (A) (B) (C) (D) (E)	34 (A) (B) (C) (D) (E)
5 (A) (B) (C) (D) (E)	15 (A) (B) (C) (D) (E)	25 (A) (B) (C) (D) (E)	35 (A) (B) (C) (D) (E)
6 (A) (B) (C) (D) (E)	16 (A) (B) (C) (D) (E)	26 (A) (B) (C) (D) (E)	36 (A) (B) (C) (D) (E)
7 (A) (B) (C) (D) (E)	17 (A) (B) (C) (D) (E)	27 (A) (B) (C) (D) (E)	37 (A) (B) (C) (D) (E)
8 (A) (B) (C) (D) (E)	18 (A) (B) (C) (D) (E)	28 (A) (B) (C) (D) (E)	38 (A) (B) (C) (D) (E)
9 (A) (B) (C) (D) (E)	19 (A) (B) (C) (D) (E)	29 (A) (B) (C) (D) (E)	39 (A) (B) (C) (D) (E)
10 (A) (B) (C) (D) (E)	20 (A) (B) (C) (D) (E)	30 (A) (B) (C) (D) (E)	40 (A) (B) (C) (D) (E)

right in section 3

wrong in section 3

Time—30 Minutes   For each of the following questions, choose the best answer and darken the
30 Questions   corresponding oval on the answer sheet.*

Select the lettered word or set of words that best
completes the sentence.

Example:

Today's small, portable computers contrast
markedly with the earliest electronic computers,
which were ----.

(A) effective
(B) invented
(C) useful
(D) destructive
(E) enormous

1 Most of those polled stated that they would vote
to reelect their legislators; this response showed
the public was ---- a change in leadership.

(A) partial to
(B) wary of
(C) inured to
(D) confident of
(E) receptive to

2 Mountain lions are very ---- creatures, able to run
at high speed and capable of climbing any tree.

(A) agile
(B) passive
(C) capricious
(D) attentive
(E) dominant

3 Although organic farming is more labor intensive
and thus initially quite ----, it may be less
expensive in the long term than conventional
farming.

(A) nutritious
(B) tasteful
(C) restrained
(D) costly
(E) arduous

4 Diego Rivera was one of the most ---- painters of
the modern Mexican mural movement, ---- a
generation of young artists with his bold, dramatic
forms.

(A) famous . . displacing
(B) convoluted . . attracting
(C) antagonistic . . prompting
(D) influential . . inspiring
(E) observant . . thwarting

5 Although the Druids, an ancient Celtic priestly
class, were ----, they preferred to use ---- teaching
methods to educate the young.

(A) uneducated . . illegible
(B) enduring . . intelligent
(C) earnest . . unexceptional
(D) religious . . haphazard
(E) literate . . oral

6 Emphysema, a chronic lung disease, can occur in
either a localized or ---- form.

(A) a contained
(B) an acute
(C) a restricted
(D) a diffuse
(E) a fatal

7 Famed for her ---- opposition to the consumption
of alcohol, Carrie Nation used a hatchet to
demolish barrooms in turn-of-the-century Kansas.

(A) characteristic
(B) feeble
(C) adamant
(D) perfunctory
(E) docile

8 Even though her friends described Becky as
amiable and frank, she was really a very ---- and ----
woman.

(A) dependable . . unfriendly
(B) rude . . calculating
(C) gregarious . . insignificant
(D) entertaining . . antagonistic
(E) frugal . . mysterious

9 Despite much educated ----, there remains no ----
relationship between sunspot cycles and the
Earth's weather.

(A) argument . . decisive
(B) confusion . . clear
(C) conjecture . . proven
(D) evidence . . tenuous
(E) disagreement . . systematic

*The directions on the actual SAT will vary slightly.

GO ON TO THE NEXT PAGE ➡

Choose the lettered pair of words that is related in the same way as the pair in capital letters.

Example:

FLAKE : SNOW ::
(A) storm : hail
(B) drop : rain
(C) field : wheat
(D) stack : hay
(E) cloud : fog   Ⓐ ● Ⓒ Ⓓ Ⓔ

10 HOOF : HORSE ::

(A) lion : mane
(B) paw : cat
(C) pace : foot
(D) bicycle : rider
(E) dog : prairie

11 EMERALD : GEMSTONE ::

(A) hydrogen : gas
(B) granite : marble
(C) hue : tint
(D) diamond : ring
(E) iron : tool

12 LETTER : POSTSCRIPT ::

(A) manuscript : book
(B) address : envelope
(C) garden : plant
(D) building : addition
(E) landscape : house

13 SHIP : DOCK ::

(A) car : park
(B) wheel : steer
(C) horse : ride
(D) raft : float
(E) truck : drive

14 GROUCH : ILL-HUMOR ::

(A) creditor : bankruptcy
(B) chauffeur : speed
(C) official : arrogance
(D) writer : wit
(E) scholar : studiousness

15 LIMP : FIRMNESS ::

(A) sinful : weakness
(B) deep : thickness
(C) silky : softness
(D) old : dryness
(E) polished : roughness

GO ON TO THE NEXT PAGE ➡

KAPLAN

Answer the questions below based on the information in the accompanying passages.

Questions 16–24 are based on the following passage.

The following passage was written in 1992 by France Bequette, a writer who specializes in environmental issues.

The ozone layer, the fragile layer of gas surrounding our planet between 7 and 30 miles above the Earth's surface, is being rapidly depleted.
Line
(5) Seasonally occurring holes have appeared in it over the Poles and, recently, over densely populated temperate regions of the northern hemisphere. The threat is serious because the ozone layer protects the Earth from the sun's ultraviolet radiation, which is harmful to all living organisms.

(10) Even though the layer is many miles thick, the atmosphere in it is tenuous and the total amount of ozone, compared with other atmospheric gases, is small. Ozone is highly reactive to chlorine, hydrogen, and nitrogen. Of these chlorine is the
(15) most dangerous since it is very stable and long-lived. When chlorine compounds reach the stratosphere, they bond with and destroy ozone molecules, with consequent repercussions for life on Earth.

(20) In 1958, researchers began noticing seasonal variations in the ozone layer above the South Pole. Between June and October the ozone content steadily fell, followed by a sudden increase in November. These fluctuations appeared to result
(25) from the natural effects of wind and temperature. But while the low October levels remained constant until 1979, the total ozone content over the Pole was steadily diminishing. In 1985, public opinion was finally roused by reports of a "hole" in
(30) the layer.

The culprits responsible for the hole were identified as compounds known as chlorofluorocarbons, or CFCs. CFCs are compounds of chlorine and fluorine.
(35) Nonflammable, nontoxic and noncorrosive, they have been widely used in industry since the 1950s, mostly as refrigerants and propellants and in making plastic foam and insulation.

In 1989 CFCs represented a sizeable market
(40) valued at over $1.5 billion and a labor force of 1.6 million. But with CFCs implicated in ozone depletion, the question arose as to whether we were willing to risk an increase in cases of skin cancer, eye ailments, even a lowering of the
(45) human immune defense system—all effects of further loss of the ozone layer. And not only humans would suffer. So would plant life. Phytoplankton, the first link in the ocean food chain and vital to the survival of most marine

(50) species, would not be able to survive near the ocean surface, which is where these organisms grow.

In 1990, 70 countries agreed to stop producing CFCs by the year 2000. In late 1991, however,
(55) scientists noticed a depletion of the ozone layer over the Arctic. In 1992 it was announced that the layer was depleting faster than expected and that it was also declining over the northern hemisphere. Scientists believe that natural events are making
(60) the problem worse. The Pinatubo volcano in the Philippines, which erupted in June 1991, released 12 million tons of damaging volcanic gases into the atmosphere.

Even if the whole world agreed today to stop all
(65) production and use of CFCs, this would not solve the problem. A single chlorine molecule can destroy 10,000–100,000 molecules of ozone. Furthermore, CFCs have a lifespan of 75–400 years and they take ten years to reach the ozone layer. In
(70) other words, what we are experiencing today results from CFCs emitted ten years ago.

Researchers are working hard to find substitute products. Some are too dangerous because they are highly flammable; others may prove to be toxic
(75) and to contribute to the greenhouse effect—to the process of global warming. Nevertheless, even if there is no denying that the atmosphere is in a state of disturbance, nobody can say that the situation will not improve, either in the short or
(80) the long term, especially if we ourselves lend a hand.

16 As it is described in the passage, the major function of the ozone layer is closest to that of

(A) an emergency evacuation plan for a skyscraper
(B) a central information desk at a convention center
(C) a traffic light at a busy intersection
(D) the structural support for a suspension bridge
(E) the filtering system for a city water supply

GO ON TO THE NEXT PAGE ➡

17 The word *tenuous* in line 11 most nearly means

(A) doubtful
(B) tense
(C) clear
(D) thin
(E) hazy

18 The passage implies which of the following about the "seasonal variations in the ozone layer" (lines 20–21) observed by scientists in 1958?

(A) They were caused by industrial substances other than CFCs.
(B) They created alarm among scientists but not the public.
(C) They were least stable in the months between June and November.
(D) They opened the public's eye to the threat of ozone depletion.
(E) They focused attention on the dangers posed by CFCs.

19 In context, the word *constant* in line 27 means

(A) gentle
(B) steady
(C) pestering
(D) unerring
(E) considerable

20 The author mentions market and workforce figures related to CFC production in lines 39–41 in order to point out that

(A) responsibility for the problem of ozone depletion lies primarily with industry
(B) the disadvantages of CFCs are obvious while the benefits are not
(C) the magnitude of profits from CFCs has turned public opinion against the industry's practices
(D) while the economic stakes are large, they are overshadowed by the effects of CFCs
(E) curbing the use of CFCs will lead to a crippling loss of jobs worldwide

21 In paragraph six, the author cites the evidence of changes in the ozone layer over the northern hemisphere to indicate that

(A) the dangers of ozone depletion appear to be intensifying
(B) ozone depletion is posing an immediate threat to many marine species
(C) scientists are unsure about the ultimate effects of ozone loss on plants
(D) CFCs are not the primary cause of ozone depletion in such areas
(E) ozone levels are beginning to stabilize at the poles

22 Scientists apparently believe which of the following about the "volcanic gases" mentioned in lines 60–63?

(A) They contribute more to global warming than to ozone loss.
(B) They pose a greater long-term threat than CFCs.
(C) They are hastening ozone loss at present.
(D) They are of little long-term consequence.
(E) They contain molecules that are less destructive of ozone than CFCs.

23 The author's reference to the long life of chlorine molecules (lines 68–69) is meant to show that

(A) CFCs are adaptable to a variety of industrial uses
(B) there is more than adequate time to develop a long-term strategy against ozone loss
(C) the long-term effects of ozone loss on human health may never be known
(D) it is doubtful that normal levels of ozone can ever be reestablished
(E) the positive effects of actions taken against ozone loss will be gradual

24 In the final paragraph, the author tries to emphasize that

(A) researchers are unlikely to find effective substitutes for CFCs
(B) human action can alleviate the decline of the ozone layer
(C) people must to learn to live with the damaging effects of industrial pollutants
(D) people have more control over ozone depletion than over the greenhouse effect
(E) atmospheric conditions are largely beyond human control

GO ON TO THE NEXT PAGE ➡

KAPLAN

Questions 25–30 are based on the following passage.

In this excerpt from a short story, the narrator describes an afternoon visit to the farm of Mrs. Hight and her daughter, Esther. The narrator is accompanied on her visit by William, a fisherman.

Line
(5)
(10)
(15)
(20)
(25)
(30)
(35)
(40)
(45)

Mrs. Hight, like myself, was tired and thirsty. I brought a drink of water, and remembered some fruit that was left from my lunch. She revived vigorously, and told me the history of her later years since she had been been struck in the prime of her life by a paralyzing stroke, and her husband had died and left her with Esther and a mortgage on their farm. There was only one field of good land, but they owned a large area of pasture and some woodland. Esther had always been laughed at for her belief in sheep-raising when one by one their neighbors were giving up their flocks. When everything had come to the point of despair she had raised some money and bought all the sheep she could, insisting that Maine lambs were as good as any, and that there was a straight path by sea to the Boston market. By tending her flock herself she had managed to succeed; she had paid off the mortgage five years ago, and now what they did not spend was in the bank. "It has been stubborn work, day and night, summer and winter, and now she's beginning to get along in years," said the old mother. "She's tended me along with the sheep, and she's been good right along, but she should have been a teacher."
We heard voices, and William and Esther entered; they did not know that it was so late in the afternoon. William looked almost bold, like a young man rather than an ancient boy. As for Esther, she might have been Joan of Arc returned to her sheep*, touched with age and gray. My heart was moved by the sight of her face, weather-worn and gentle, her thin figure in its close dress, and the strong hand that clasped a shepherd's staff, and I could only hold William in new awe; this silent fisherman who alone knew the heart that beat within her. I am not sure that they acknowledged even to themselves that they had always been lovers. Esther was untouched by the fret and fury of life; she had lived in sunshine and rain among her sheep and been refined instead of coarsened, while her patience with an angry old mother, stung by defeat and mourning her lost activities, had given back a self-possession and habit of sweet temper. I had seen enough of Mrs. Hight to know that nothing a sheep might do could vex a person who was used to the severities of her companionship.

*Joan of Arc (1412–31): a young shepherdess who led the French army against the English during the Hundred Years' War.

25   The main purpose of the passage is to

(A)   suggest some of the essential attributes of a character
(B)   speculate about a romantic link between two people
(C)   show that people's lives are determined by events beyond their control
(D)   identify the major causes of Mrs. Hight's unhappiness
(E)   recount an incident that changed the narrator's life

26   Mrs. Hight's description of Esther's sheep-raising efforts (lines 8–17) reveals her daughter's

(A)   desire to succeed no matter what the cost
(B)   humility and grace in accepting defeat
(C)   considerable regard for her neighbors' opinions
(D)   calm determination in meeting difficulties
(E)   dogged refusal to admit a mistake

27   In lines 37–39, the narrator speculates that Esther and William may be

(A)   resigned to being permanently separated from one another
(B)   apprehensive about each other's true feelings
(C)   impatient to make a formal commitment to one another
(D)   ambivalent in their regard for one another
(E)   unaware of the extent of their attachment

28   The narrator is most impressed with Esther's

(A)   aloofness and reserve
(B)   serenity and devotion
(C)   lively sense of humor
(D)   stubborn pride
(E)   material success

GO ON TO THE NEXT PAGE ➡

29 Lines 39–48 are meant to convey Mrs. Hight's

(A) strength in the face of adversity
(B) inability to carry on a conversation
(C) dissatisfaction with her life
(D) distrust of her neighbors
(E) ingratitude toward her daughter

30 The "person" referred to in line 46 is

(A) the narrator
(B) William
(C) Esther
(D) Mrs. Hight
(E) Mrs. Hight's husband

IF YOU FINISH BEFORE TIME IS CALLED, YOU MAY CHECK YOUR WORK ON THIS SECTION ONLY. DO NOT TURN TO ANY OTHER SECTION IN THE TEST. **STOP**

Time—30 Minutes
35 Questions

For each of the following questions, choose the best answer and darken the corresponding oval on the answer sheet.

Select the lettered word or set of words that best completes the sentence.

Example:

Today's small, portable computers contrast markedly with the earliest electronic computers, which were ----.

(A) effective
(B) invented
(C) useful
(D) destructive
(E) enormous

1 Liz is ---- person who loves to attend parties and is always full of ----.

(A) a saturnine . . melancholy
(B) a querulous . . zest
(C) a convivial . . bonhomie
(D) an eloquent . . vitriol
(E) an affable . . choler

2 Negritude, a literary movement emphasizing the importance and value of African culture and history, was founded in Paris in the 1930s by a group of ---- students from Martinique, Senegal, and other French-speaking colonies.

(A) animated
(B) didactic
(C) expatriate
(D) radical
(E) sophisticated

3 Maria's performance was so ---- that even Mr. Rhodes, her teacher and harshest critic, was forced to ---- her talent.

(A) magnificent . . denigrate
(B) tentative . . concede
(C) superb . . deny
(D) indifferent . . praise
(E) compelling . . laud

4 Though the Greek author Thucydides used psychological insight rather than documented information to ---- speeches to historical figures, he is still considered an impartial and ---- historian.

(A) dictate . . endless
(B) transmit . . illustrious
(C) disseminate . . relevant
(D) attribute . . accurate
(E) promote . . inventive

5 Clint Eastwood made his reputation playing tough, ---- characters, notable for their expressive yet ---- speech.

(A) laconic . . pithy
(B) narcissistic . . obtuse
(C) pragmatic . . enthusiastic
(D) esoteric . . trite
(E) monotonous . . interesting

6 Though George Balanchine's choreography stayed within a classical context, he challenged convention by recombining ballet idioms in ---- ways.

(A) naive
(B) effective
(C) redundant
(D) unexpected
(E) awkward

7 While many Americans enjoy ---- lifestyle, the official number of Americans living in poverty has been ---- for several years.

(A) an opulent . . increasing
(B) a leisurely . . developing
(C) an acerbic . . varying
(D) a provincial . . ignored
(E) a peripheral . . stabilized

8 The participants allowed the debate to degenerate into ---- dispute; the urgency of the topic precluded the cordiality expected at such events.

(A) an inconsequential
(B) a depraved
(C) an acrimonious
(D) a prudent
(E) a reticent

9 He claimed to usher in a new era of literature, but his novels were mostly ----, resembling those of many other contemporary authors.

(A) realistic
(B) emotional
(C) pastoral
(D) theoretical
(E) derivative

10 Nearly all epiphytic ferns are ---- tropical rainforests; while they do not require soil, they cannot survive without constant moisture.

(A) uprooted to
(B) steeped in
(C) appointed to
(D) decorative in
(E) endemic to

GO ON TO THE NEXT PAGE ➡

Choose the lettered pair of words that is related in the same way as the pair in capital letters.

Example:

FLAKE : SNOW ::
- (A) storm : hail
- (B) drop : rain
- (C) field : wheat
- (D) stack : hay
- (E) cloud : fog

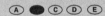

11 MARE : STALLION ::
- (A) fawn : buck
- (B) ewe : ram
- (C) mule : donkey
- (D) alligator : crocodile
- (E) goat : nanny

12 MESS : SOLDIERS ::
- (A) infirmary : patients
- (B) museum : artists
- (C) library : intellectuals
- (D) cafeteria : students
- (E) courtroom : lawyers

13 DAUNTLESS : HERO ::
- (A) ill : hypochondriac
- (B) servile : waiter
- (C) credulous : agnostic
- (D) abstemious : teetotaler
- (E) mendacious : politician

14 QUARANTINE : EPIDEMIC ::
- (A) barricade : building
- (B) cloister : isolation
- (C) boil : bacteria
- (D) eat : famine
- (E) sterilize : infection

15 LION : PRIDE ::
- (A) violinist : quartet
- (B) worker : syndicate
- (C) goose : gaggle
- (D) beaver : dam
- (E) elephant : circus

16 AFFLUENCE : MENDICANT ::
- (A) conformity : maverick
- (B) generosity : altruist
- (C) banality : demagogue
- (D) vanity : sycophant
- (E) innocence : defendant

17 HERBIVORE : PLANT ::
- (A) omnivore : poultry
- (B) historian : history
- (C) choreographer : dance
- (D) carnivore : meat
- (E) vegetarian : calorie

18 TEPID : HEAT ::
- (A) basic : simplicity
- (B) lukewarm : wateriness
- (C) plain : blandness
- (D) regular : familiarity
- (E) mild : spiciness

19 ADMIRE : ADULATION ::
- (A) bore : sadness
- (B) deplete : lending
- (C) hope : adoration
- (D) save : hoarding
- (E) grow : satisfaction

20 MESMERIZING : INTERESTING ::
- (A) incredible : dull
- (B) vile : unpleasant
- (C) wholesome : sour
- (D) nutritious : unwholesome
- (E) unexpected : evil

21 PEERLESS : EQUAL ::
- (A) painless : gain
- (B) unique : consequence
- (C) shapeless : form
- (D) inanimate : object
- (E) inconceivable : idea

22 DESICCATE : MOISTURE ::
- (A) debilitate : strength
- (B) augur : future
- (C) exonerate : verdict
- (D) stem : tide
- (E) exaggerate : confidence

23 ABSTINENT : RESTRAINT ::
- (A) compassionate : sympathy
- (B) eloquent : terseness
- (C) enraged : mistrust
- (D) subservient : deviance
- (E) indifferent : attitude

GO ON TO THE NEXT PAGE ➡

Answer the questions below based on the information in the accompanying passages.

Questions 24–35 are based on the following passage.

The author of the following passage is Juan Carlos Langlois, an Argentine artist whose work has been exhibited in Latin America, North America and Europe.

With the spread of industry, the exodus of people from the countryside, and the resultant transformation of the urban landscape, city-dwellers of the twentieth century have found (5) themselves living in an increasingly colorless environment. Veiled in soot, towns and suburbs have lapsed into grimy taciturnity as an all-pervading drabness has overcome our great, sprawling urban complexes.

(10) From the time of the first industrial revolution, western societies have favored the use of somber, neutral colors in their towns and cities, judging them to be more functional. This anti-color attitude has been accentuated by the desire to (15) imitate the supposed canons of Greek and Roman classicism. As we now know, however, the city-dwellers of antiquity loved color. Our vision of the temples and market-places of old, built solely in white marble, is wrong. On the contrary, judging (20) by the rich and subtle palette found in the art of ancient civilizations, the use of color as a symbolic language seems to have been an important development in human culture. In later times, Romanesque and Gothic architecture also featured (25) great use of color—witness the cathedrals of Siena, Florence, and Venice, with their stained-glass windows, frescoes, mosaics, and precious colored marble.

The facades embellished with traditional (30) paintings still to be seen today in many countries of the world are an indication of the extent to which other peoples continue to nourish their spiritual and imaginative vision through contact with color. This extraordinary ornamental (35) richness can be seen in the cities of Islam, the villages of Greece, the cities, villages and temples of India and Southeast Asia, and the fishing villages of the Caribbean, to name but a few examples. Sensitivity of this kind has found little (40) place in the monotonous environments of our great western cities.

Fortunately, in recent decades the notion of bringing decorative color back into building projects has been gaining some ground. Bold and (45) judicious use of color has an important role to play in the public art of our urban streets, providing a favorable background for a revived form of "urbanity" in its original, positive sense. The whole city becomes more understandable and (50) more convivial as color, the poetry of the street, triumphs over drabness.

Public murals and trompe-l'oeil* facades, which are able to strike a chord in the collective memory by alluding to the important political, (55) religious or artistic events of our cultures, are gradually making a comeback. The first influential muralists of the twentieth century were three great Mexican artists—Diego Rivera, José Clemente Orozco, and David Alfaro Siqueiros. In the 1920s, (60) in search of an art form that would be monumental yet human and popular, they began to paint gigantic frescoes that retraced the major episodes in the history of Mexico. Their initiative brought them many commissions in their own country (65) and, later, in the United States, where they inspired a vast program of publicly financed commissions in the 1930s, designed to provide work for unemployed American artists during the Great Depression. More than 2,500 murals were (70) completed throughout the United States over the next few years under New Deal programs begun by the administration of Franklin D. Roosevelt.

During the 1960s, the creation of murals in public places became the spearhead of an authentic (75) popular art movement. This movement was a community response to the need for expression felt by ethnic and other minority groups to whom access to visual creativity and expression had previously been barred. In 1967, a mural conceived (80) as a "collage" of portraits, photographs and poetic verse was created on a derelict building in the southern suburbs of Chicago by a group of Black American artists led by William Walker. Entitled "Wall of Respect," the work paid tribute to public (85) figures who had fought for civil rights for Black Americans. This group effort by minority artists inspired other similar projects in American cities such as Los Angeles, San Francisco, Baltimore, and New York, and marked a new point of departure (90) for public mural painting in this country.

Improving the quality of life in the city is one of the primary objectives of street art. Color can help to save, rehabilitate or otherwise give new life to neighborhoods and other urban sites doomed to (95) demolition, dereliction or anonymity. The aim is to provide the city-dweller with the opportunity to participate in the rebirth of a more human environment. By its very nature as communal space, the street lends itself to collective creativity (100) which, in turn, leads to an enhanced sense of community pride and well-being.

*Trompe l'oeil (literally, "deception of the eye"): a highly decorative style of mural painting that often depicts architectural or other three-dimensional forms.

GO ON TO THE NEXT PAGE ➡

24 The "transformation of the urban landscape" (line 3) most likely refers to the

(A) diversity of urban ethnic populations
(B) spread and greater density of urban areas
(C) loss of manufacturing jobs in cities
(D) improved visual appearance of cities
(E) loss of parks in modern cities

25 In line 7, the phrase "lapsed into grimy taciturnity" refers to the

(A) growing violence of city life
(B) decay of urban areas
(C) unresponsiveness of politicians to city problems
(D) increasing development of rural areas
(E) passive acceptance by city-dwellers of their surroundings

26 Which of the following best explains why "somber, neutral colors" (lines 11–12) came into wider use in western cities?

(A) They were intended to accentuate other bolder colors.
(B) They were viewed as more modern than the colors of Greece and Rome.
(C) They were considered more beautiful than brighter colors.
(D) They were judged more suitable for an industrial environment.
(E) They recalled the muted colors of Romanesque and Gothic architecture.

27 The author suggests that the admiration of western societies for "the supposed canons of Greek and Roman classicism" (lines 15–16) was

(A) a reaction to the widespread use of functional colors
(B) based on a mistaken belief about the use of color in antiquity
(C) consistent with our love of the colors of Siena, Florence, and Venice
(D) founded on respect for the art of ancient civilizations
(E) inspired by their use of color as a symbolic language

28 In line 17, *vision* most nearly means

(A) image
(B) display
(C) fixation
(D) personal wish
(E) clear-sightedness

29 The cities and villages mentioned in lines 35–38 are noted for their

(A) breathtaking natural scenery
(B) complex histories
(C) uniform architecture
(D) decorative lushness
(E) religious convictions

30 In line 39, the word *sensitivity* most nearly means

(A) sense of community spirit
(B) imaginative use of color
(C) understanding of different cultures
(D) consideration for other people
(E) knowledge of art history

31 *Judicious* in line 45 is best understood as meaning

(A) controversial
(B) objective
(C) determined
(D) informed
(E) judgmental

32 The phrase "strike a chord in the collective memory" (lines 53–54) is used to signify the

(A) adaptability of people living in unfamiliar surroundings
(B) willingness of people to make sacrifices for the good of a community
(C) loyalty shown by people living in small communities
(D) tendency of city-dwellers to lose touch with their cultural roots
(E) ability of art to portray the variety and history of a culture

33 The reference in paragraph 5 to the painters Diego Rivera, José Clemente Orozco, and David Alfaro Siquieros serves to

(A) highlight the poor quality of mural painting in the United States
(B) indicate the wide range of colors and styles to be found in mural painting
(C) shed light on the revival of mural painting in two countries
(D) show the important role that artists have played in Mexican history
(E) emphasize the lack of government funding for public mural painting

GO ON TO THE NEXT PAGE ➡

34 William Walker's "Wall of Respect" project is described as a "new point of departure" (line 89) because

(A) artists who began painting murals went on to success in other art forms

(B) public mural painting had never before been attempted in the United States

(C) other minority groups were inspired to undertake similar community projects

(D) the project popularized a new use for derelict buildings

(E) the artists involved led a revival of the civil rights movement

35 The author most likely considers the street an appropriate location for art because the street

(A) encourages a natural reserve in city-dwellers

(B) carries few traces of past events

(C) is naturally a place of shared activities

(D) forces people to be more alert about their surroundings

(E) features subjects that are interesting to paint

IF YOU FINISH BEFORE TIME IS CALLED, YOU MAY CHECK YOUR WORK ON THIS SECTION ONLY. DO NOT TURN TO ANY OTHER SECTION IN THE TEST.

STOP

Time—15 Minutes
12 Questions

For each of the following questions, choose the best answer and darken the corresponding oval on the answer sheet.

Questions 1–12 are based on the following passages.

The following two passages discuss closely linked periods in European history. In passage 1, the author describes the organization of the guild, an important feature of town life in medieval Europe. The author of passage 2 identifies a fundamental social change that began taking place in Italian towns in the late 1200s.

Passage 1

The membership of guilds in medieval European towns was made up of masters, journeymen, and apprentices. Each guild differed from town to town in
Line its social and political influence, but its primary
(5) economic function was the same everywhere—to protect the merchant and artisan, not just from the competition of foreign merchants, but also from the competition of fellow guild members. Town markets were closed to foreign products, and individual
(10) members were prevented from growing rich at the expense of others.

Each guild adopted strict rules, including fixed hours of work, fixed prices and wages, limits on the numbers of workers in workshops, and regular
(15) workshop inspections. These tightly enforced rules had the effect of dampening personal ambition and initiative. No one was allowed to employ methods of production that were cheaper or more efficient than those used by fellow guild members. In fact,
(20) technical progress and those who favored it were looked on with suspicion.

Each local guild was organized hierarchically. The dominant members were the masters—small merchant proprietors of workshops who owned their
(25) tools, raw materials, products, and all the profits from the sale of those products. Journeymen were wage-earning workers who had completed an apprenticeship. Apprentices were brought into a trade under a master's direction. The number of
(30) masters in each local guild was limited, determined by the needs of the local market and by certain requirements, including citizenship, that were hard to fulfill.

The master functioned as a small, independent
(35) entrepreneur whose primary capital included a house, a workshop, tools, and equipment. The number of workshop employees was restricted, usually to one or two apprentices and journeymen. If a master happened to inherit or marry into a fortune,
(40) it could not be used against other masters, because the guild system left no room for competition. But material inequality among guild merchants was rare. For most of them, the economic structure of the guild meant the same kind of existence and the same

(45) measured resources. While it gave them a secure position, it also prevented them from rising above it. In this sense, the guild system might be described as non-capitalist.

Passage 2

Throughout most of Europe in the late Middle
(50) Ages, human consciousness as we know it today was really only half awake. People thought of themselves as members of a family, organization, or community, but not as individuals. In most countries, the different classes of society lived apart, each with its
(55) own sense of values. Throughout their lives, people tended to remain in the class in which they were born. But in Italy social fluidity appeared early. By the late 1200s, Italy was brimming with the notion of individuality. The Italians of the next two
(60) centuries—the period that we now call the Renaissance—were unafraid of being and appearing different from their neighbors.

Italian towns, primarily because of their control of the Mediterranean trade, were the busiest in
(65) Europe. Town crafts included such sophisticated trades as goldsmithing and stonecarving. Competition between artisans grew so acute that masterpieces began to proliferate, and love of art spread throughout society. A few merchants made
(70) great fortunes, lent their money to foreign princes, and thus became international bankers.

Italy was a place in which the potential for individual achievement—for a privileged few, anyway—seemed unlimited. Since there was no
(75) central Italian government, wealthy merchants were unchecked in their political and social ambitions. They competed for civic power and fame, sponsored public works and cultural institutions, hired armies, and forged alliances. The typical Italian merchant
(80) was fluent in Latin and Greek and read the classic works of Rome and Greece. It was in these circles that private, secular education got its start.

The story of the Medici family of Florence illustrates these changes. Giovanni, an obscure
(85) merchant born in 1360, created the family banking fortune. His son Cosimo became ruler of Florence by scheming against rivals in other Florentine families. Cosimo's grandson and heir, Lorenzo the Magnificent, was an able politician, a famous patron
(90) of the arts and learning, and a reputable scholar and poet. The Medici family's rise to prominence coincided with the decline of the guild and the growth of capitalist individualism in Italy.

GO ON TO THE NEXT PAGE ➡

1 The most important function of the "rules" discussed in lines 12–15 was probably to

(A) guarantee that masters retained strict control over their employees
(B) broaden the political influence of guilds within a town
(C) minimize competition among local artisans and merchants
(D) stimulate the development of more efficient production methods
(E) improve the quality of merchandise in local markets

2 The "requirements" mentioned in line 32 had the effect of

(A) opening local markets to foreign products
(B) controlling the number of those who advanced beyond journeyman status
(C) enlarging the number of those qualified to become town citizens
(D) prohibiting trade with foreign merchants
(E) encouraging economic rivalry among small entrepreneurs

3 In line 45, the word *measured* most nearly means

(A) deliberate
(B) inadequate
(C) rhythmical
(D) cautious
(E) limited

4 The author of Passage 1 describes the guild system as an economic system that was

(A) open and permissive
(B) innovative and energetic
(C) fluid and unpredictable
(D) restrictive and stable
(E) unfair and exploitative

5 In describing human consciousness in most of Europe as being "only half awake" (line 51), the author of Passage 2 seeks to

(A) contrast prevailing social conditions in Europe to those in Italy
(B) criticize a lack of interest in education in medieval European society
(C) imply that some people have always opposed social progress
(D) stress the role of individuality in contemporary society
(E) suggest that a common belief about medieval Europe is wrong

6 The author of Passage 2 uses the term *social fluidity* in line 57 mainly to describe the

(A) dangerous conditions of urban life in Italy
(B) intense competition between families in Italian towns
(C) great disparities of wealth among social classes in Italy
(D) rapid spread of democratic institutions in Italy
(E) unfixed character of social life in Italy

7 The meaning of the word *acute* in line 67 is

(A) chaotic
(B) dangerous
(C) wise
(D) keen
(E) sudden

8 The author discusses the Medici primarily to illustrate which of the following?

(A) The guild system in Italy rewarded individual effort and competitiveness.
(B) There were few restraints on the aspirations of people in Italy.
(C) Political power in Italy was held by a small number of wealthy families.
(D) Family rivalry in Florence was a major social phenomenon.
(E) It was easy for individuals to capture wealth and power in Italy.

9 The author's discussion of the Medici family (lines 83–93) is

(A) nostalgic
(B) disapproving
(C) dispassionate
(D) ironic
(E) defensive

10 Both passages seek to explain the

(A) expanding role of commerce in Italian towns during the Middle Ages
(B) economic structure of the guild system during the Middle Ages
(C) growing importance of individuality in the Middle Ages
(D) circumstances of merchants during the Middle Ages
(E) fast growth of capitalism during the Middle Ages

GO ON TO THE NEXT PAGE ➡

11 What position would the author of Passage 1 most likely take regarding the description of European society in lines 49–53 of Passage 2?

(A) The structure of the medieval guild and its effects support the description.

(B) The description underestimates the extent to which the medieval guild system favored individual initiative.

(C) Trying to describe the complexities of human consciousness is not an appropriate task for historians.

(D) The accuracy of the description cannot be determined without further investigation.

(E) It is unwise to describe European society in such sweeping terms.

12 The merchants discussed in Passage 1 are most different from those discussed in Passage 2 in their

(A) concern for the economic welfare of their towns

(B) interest in exercising their rights as citizens

(C) views regarding the right to own private property

(D) patriotic loyalty to their towns

(E) attitudes regarding personal ambition

IF YOU FINISH BEFORE TIME IS CALLED, YOU MAY CHECK YOUR WORK ON THIS SECTION ONLY. DO NOT TURN TO ANY OTHER SECTION IN THE TEST. **STOP**

ANSWER KEY ON FOLLOWING PAGE ➡

Answer Key

Section 1

1. B
2. A
3. D
4. D
5. E
6. D
7. C
8. B
9. C
10. B
11. A
12. D
13. A
14. E
15. E
16. E
17. D
18. C
19. B
20. D
21. A
22. C
23. E
24. B
25. A
26. D
27. E
28. B
29. C
30. C

Section 2

1. C
2. C
3. E
4. D
5. A
6. D
7. A
8. C
9. E
10. E
11. B
12. D
13. D
14. E
15. C
16. A
17. D
18. E
19. D
20. B
21. C
22. A
23. A
24. B
25. B
26. D
27. B
28. A
29. D
30. B
31. D
32. E
33. C
34. C
35. C

Section 3

1. C
2. B
3. E
4. D
5. A
6. E
7. D
8. B
9. C
10. D
11. A
12. E

Practice Test A Answers and Explanations

SECTION 1

1. B

The clue words here are *reelect* and *change*. If those polled are planning to reelect their legislators, then they are not eager for a change in leadership. The public could not have been (A) **partial to** *a change in leadership,* since they're intending to bring back the same people. And if they were (D) **confident of** or (E) **receptive to** replacing their legislators, they would vote for someone other than the current office holders. (B) and (C) are the only remaining options. If anything, the public is getting used to keeping the same people around, so (C) doesn't fit the blank either. But if *the public was* **wary of** *a change* (that is, cautious or nervous about it), voters might well decide *to reelect their legislators.*

> *inured to: accustomed to something*
> *receptive: open, welcoming*
> *partial to: having a preference or liking for*

2. A

The missing word has to describe an animal that can run at high speed and climb any tree. We could predict that a word like "nimble" would work. (A) **agile** matches our prediction. None of the other choices makes sense—the mountain lion certainly isn't a **passive** creature if it can run at high speed and climb any tree. It makes no sense to call the lion a **capricious** animal. And while the lion may very well be an **attentive** or **dominant** creature, these choices don't make sense in the context of the sentence.

> *capricious: inconsistent*

3. D

The sentence says that *organic farming* is *labor intensive,* that is, it requires a lot of work by human beings (as opposed to machines). It is *thus initially quite ----.* If the sentence ended right after the blank, choice (E) might be the best answer. But the conjunction *although* signals a contrast between the two halves of this sentence. Since the second clause is concerned with how expensive organic farming is compared to conventional farming, the word that fills the blank must have something to do with expense, not labor. **Costly** means "expensive," so (D) is correct.

> *arduous: laborious, involving very hard work*

HINT: *Remember to read the whole sentence. An answer choice that may make sense with one clause of the sentence may not work for the whole sentence.*

4. D

We know that Rivera used *bold, dramatic forms,* so one possible prediction for the first blank would be something like "vivid" or "creative." But none of the answer choices has a first word that matches this prediction. And it's hard to tell what Rivera did to the *generation of young artists.* We won't be able to pick a choice based on one blank.

We'll just have to see which answer choice contains two words that go together *and* make sense when we plug them into the sentence. The other important hint is that the overall tone of the sentence is positive, so whichever pair we choose will probably be positive as well. Choice (D) is the only answer that contains two positive words. When we plug them into the sentence, the two words do reinforce each other: An **influential** artist would be **inspiring** to other painters.

In (A), a famous artist could make it hard for younger artists. But nothing in the sentence indicates that Rivera's fame or his *bold, dramatic forms* **displac**ed other artists. In (B), **convoluted** doesn't really fit with *bold* and *dramatic*. And (C) and (E) both contain highly negative words: **antagonistic** and **thwarting.**

> *convoluted: complex, intricate*
> *antagonistic: hostile, opposing*
> *thwarting: blocking, hindering*

5. E

The backbone of this sentence is a contrast: *Although the Druids . . . were ----, they preferred to use ---- teaching methods to educate the young.* The two words in the correct answer should contrast with each other somehow. The only answer choice that contains two contrasting words is (E). *The Druids . . . were* **literate**— they knew how to read—but they imparted *information* **orally,** that is, by speaking, rather than by writing. The word pairs in (A) and (B) may have a relation in some contexts, but they never contrast each other.

> *literate: able to read and write*
> *oral: using speech*
> *enduring: lasting*
> *haphazard: random*

6. D

The clue words here are *either* and *or*. This offers a choice of two options which do not mean the same thing. If one of the options is a *localized . . . form,* the other has to be *a [nonlocalized] form.* So the correct answer will mean "nonlocalized."

HINT: *If you don't know a vocabulary word, try to remember any similar or related words that you might know.*

Let's say you didn't know the word *localized.* You probably do know the word *local.* It means near you, in

your area, and not all over the place. So *localized* will have something to do with a limited space. The answer has to be "nonlocalized," so (A) and (C) won't work. (D) **diffuse** means "spread out," the opposite of *localized,* so it's correct.

> *localized: restricted to a given area*
> *diffuse: spread out*

7. C

The second part of this sentence states that Carrie Nation demolished barrooms with a hatchet. It's fair to say that this is a "militant," "violent," or "strong" response to alcohol consumption. We can predict that whatever fills the blank will be close to one of those three words.

Right away we can eliminate (B), (D), and (E). None of them describes a strong or violent action. We can eliminate (A) too: **Characteristic** is much too neutral. It's not really saying anything. (C) **adamant** means "inflexible or unyielding." That's what we were looking for. **Adamant** is close to "strong."

> *temperance: abstinence from alcohol*
> *characteristic: typical*
> *adamant: inflexible, unyielding*
> *perfunctory: apathetic, mechanical*
> *docile: obedient, well-behaved*

8. B

The clue words here are *even though.* There must be a strong contrast between the way Becky's friends describe her and the way the author of the sentence sees her. So the words that go in the blanks should be the opposite of *amiable and frank.* We might predict that the correct answer would be something like "disagreeable and secretive." No matter what, both words should certainly be negative. That lets us eliminate (A), (C), and (D) right away, since each of them contains a positive word. And in (E), **frugal** and **mysterious** aren't really negative or positive. Therefore, (B) must be the right answer. A **rude** person is certainly not *amiable;* a **calculating** person isn't *frank,* either.

gregarious: sociable, friendly
frugal: thrifty
calculating: scheming
amiable: pleasing, agreeable
frank: open, honest

9. C

It seems pretty clear that the second blank is going to be filled by something like "definite." On the basis of that prediction alone, choice (D) is wrong.

That still leaves us with four choices in the second words that more or less match the prediction. We need to look at the first blank. The word *despite* is a major clue word. There will be an opposition or contrast between the two parts of the sentence. To contrast with the fact that there is still no definite *relationship between sunspot cycles and the Earth's weather*, the first blank should probably set up a phrase like *educated* "guessing." Though **clear** makes sense in (B), it's out, because *educated* **confusion** doesn't make sense. And (E) won't work, because it wouldn't set up a contrast either. The only remaining choices are (A) and (C). (C) makes the internal logic of the sentence work better. **Conjecture** is pretty close to "guessing" and contrasts very well with **proven.** Also, **proven** is closer to the meaning of "definite" that we had in mind.

tenuous: flimsy, slender
conjecture: speculation, guessing

10. B

A **HORSE**'s foot is called a **HOOF;** a **cat's** foot is called a **paw.**

11. A

An **EMERALD** is a particular type of **GEMSTONE;** **hydrogen** is a particular kind of **gas. Granite** and **marble** are two different types of rock. Both **hue** and **tint** mean "a gradation of color," although **tint** can also mean more specifically "a lighter shade of color."

12. D

A **POSTSCRIPT** (abbreviated as *P. S.*) is, by definition, an afterthought that's added to a **LETTER** after the closing and signature. Similarly, an **addition** is a room or wing that's added to a **building** after the initial construction is finished.

13. A

Here, **steer** has got to be a verb, so you know that all the second position words, including **DOCK,** are verbs. When you **DOCK** a **SHIP,** you stop and leave it someplace temporarily; when you **park** a **car,** you stop and leave it someplace temporarily.

14. E

The defining characteristic of a **GROUCH** is **ILL-HUMOR;** the defining characteristic of a **scholar** is **studiousness. Bankruptcy** is not characteristic of a **creditor;** the **creditor** is the person to whom the debtor owes money.

15. E

By definition, something that's **LIMP** has no **FIRM-NESS;** something that's **polished** has no **roughness.**

The Ozone Passage

Here's a straightforward but somewhat sobering science passage on the topical subject of damage to the ozone layer. Paragraph one summarizes the problem; the layer of ozone, which protects the Earth from the sun's ultraviolet rays, is being depleted. Paragraph two explains the chemical reaction that causes the problem. Paragraph three traces the problem from the first time scientists noticed that something was wrong to the point that the public became aware of it. Paragraph four identifies industry-produced CFCs as the chief culprits in ozone depletion, and paragraph five lists some of the threats the problem poses to life on Earth. Paragraphs six and seven give us the latest news—even though CFCs are being phased out, the long lifespan of CFC molecules means that the effects on the ozone layer can be expected to worsen for the time being. There's a note of optimism at the end of the passage, though—the author advocates continued effort to improve the situation.

16. E

The author describes the *function* of the ozone layer (in lines 6–9). We're told that the ozone layer "protects the Earth from UV radiation," which is "harmful to all living organisms." Choice (E) is the closest analogy here. It captures the idea of something which constantly provides protection against a life-threatening force. The **evacuation plan** mentioned in (A) only helps in **emergencies.** None of the other choices—(B) **information desks,** (C) **traffic lights,** or (D) **suspension bridge supports**—are facilities designed to provide protection against specific threats.

17. D

The author uses *tenuous* to describe the quality of the atmosphere at the ozone layer. Even though the ozone layer is several miles thick, leading us to expect that the atmosphere would be thick too, we're told that the atmosphere is *tenuous.* And so *tenuous* here means (D) **thin,** the opposite of "thick."

(A) **doubtful** is the closest wrong answer because of its negative connotation, but it is not specific enough. (B) **tense** doesn't fit in a discussion of atmosphere. (C) **clear** would contradict the passage by implying that there was no atmosphere at all at this level. Finally, (E) **hazy** is a term that would apply more to the weather than to atmospheric density.

18. C

The "seasonal variations" noticed in 1958 were initially regarded as the "natural effects of wind and temperature" (lines 24–25). According to the passage, it was only much later that the connection between CFCs and ozone depletion became known (lines 31–33). Therefore, we can infer that in 1958, these seasonal variations *were not regarded as a threat,* making (C) correct and (B), (D), and (E) wrong. No other ozone depletants are mentioned (A).

19. B

The key word in line 26 is *while,* because it indicates a contrast. We're told that *while* low October levels stayed *constant,* ozone levels as a whole *diminished,* or fell. *Unlike* the overall figures, in other words, the October levels did not fluctuate—they remained (B) **steady.** (A) **gentle** and (C) **pestering** are unlikely words to use to describe atmospheric measurements. (D) **unerring** suggests that the accuracy of scientists' measurements is the issue. (E) presents a contradiction—the October levels couldn't be both low *and* **considerable** in size.

20. D

The author's point is implied in the first two lines of the paragraph. We're told that CFCs represent a sizeable market. Then we're told that in spite of this, people began to question the risks to human health when CFCs were implicated in ozone depletion. So the author's point in mentioning the CFC market is that the dangers of using CFCs **overshadowed** the **economic** considerations (D).

(A) can't be inferred from the context. The author doesn't explicitly blame industry for the problem. (B) is out because the author makes no mention of **benefits.** (C) gets the issue wrong; it was the health risks, not **industry profits,** that **turned public opinion.** And (E) distorts the author's point of view, since ozone depletion, not **job losses,** is the author's main concern.

21. A

Here the author's giving us a progress report on ozone depletion in the 1990s. We're told that the layer was "depleting faster than expected" in addition to natural events "making the problem worse" (lines 56–60). (A) summarizes this idea that the situation is worsening.

Paragraph six describes the problem as a whole, without relating it to any particular species, even though threats to **marine species** (B) and **plant life** (C) are mentioned elsewhere. (D) goes against the gist of the passage, which basically identifies **CFCs** as the main culprits. Finally, we're told that the ozone layer is depleting over the Arctic, too (E).

22. C

Lines 59–60 say that scientists believe that natural events are "making the problem worse," and the volcanic gases emitted by the Pinatubo volcano are mentioned as one example. (C) is the correct answer.

(A) **global warming** isn't mentioned until paragraph eight. (B) distorts the author's point; **CFCs** are still the biggest **threat**. Since the gases are adding to a **long-term** problem, (D) must be wrong. Finally, (E) can't be inferred here, since the author tells us nothing about how **destructive** the **molecules** in volcanic gases are.

23. E

Even stopping all CFC production today wouldn't solve the problem, we're told, because CFCs can live for up to 400 years. (E) captures the underlying point here; measures against ozone depletion may take years to have an effect.

Choice (A) doesn't fit with the passage at all. (B) is too positive; the author's saying that the problem's going to take years to fix, not that there's plenty of time to deal with it. There's no mention of the implications for **human health** (C) in paragraph seven. (D), finally, is too extreme. The author never states that the problem is insoluble.

24. B

The last paragraph focuses on what scientists are doing about the problem. Even if things are bad, the author says, "nobody can say that the situation will not improve" (lines 78–79) if people lend a hand. (B) captures this positive note.

(A) exaggerates the obstacles to research discussed at the beginning of the paragraph. Choices (C) and (E) just accept ozone depletion as a fact of life, which is not the author's position at all. And finally, ozone depletion and **the greenhouse effect** are never compared in terms of our **control over** them (D).

The Mrs. Hight Passage

This fiction passage is about Mrs. Hight and her daughter Esther, who live together on a farm. Through a conversation with Mrs. Hight, paragraph one gives us some background detail on how Esther saved the family farm by raising sheep singlehandedly. Paragraph two centers on the narrator's admiration for Esther, for her achievement on the farm, and her steadfast loyalty to her mother.

25. A

From line 10 onwards, the story of the passage is really about Esther—her success with sheep farming, and her patience in looking after her mother. The purpose of the passage is to (A) **suggest some of the essential attributes** of her character—determination, good nature, and so on.

Both (B), the **romance** between William and Esther, and (D), **the causes of Mrs. Hight's unhappiness**, are topics only briefly touched on. (C) is not supported by the story at all—Esther's success in sheep raising seems to show that people's lives are very much under **their own control.** And (E) is too extreme—there's no indication that the visit to the farm has **changed the narrator's life** in any major way.

26. D

In *Mrs. Hight's* words, we're told that even though raising the sheep had been "stubborn work," Esther had been "good right along" (lines 20–25). Choice (D) captures Esther's approach here—not only did she overcome **difficulties** with **determination**—she kept **calm** throughout.

(A) is too extreme; Esther didn't put **success** before all other considerations. She wasn't **defeated** (B), and she didn't bow to her **neighbors' opinions** (C). And her success suggests that her efforts were not a **mistake** (E).

27. E

The author speculates that William and Esther had "always been lovers" but had not acknowledged it "even to themselves." In other words, she thinks that William and Esther have a strong attachment that they're not fully aware of. (E) captures this situation.

(B) is wrong because it's their *own* feelings that William and Esther haven't acknowledged, which also makes (C) **a formal commitment** unlikely as yet. (D) **ambivalence** is wrong because there's no suggestion of uncertainty or contradictory feelings. Finally, there's no evidence of a **permanent separation** (A).

28. B

This question touches again on the qualities Esther showed in managing to raise sheep *and* look after her mother at the same time. We're told that she had been "refined instead of coarsened" by her work, and had shown "patience," "self-possession," and "sweet temper" in caring for her mother. (B) **serenity and devotion** fits the bill here.

(B) **aloofness and reserve** sounds like the opposite of "sweet temper." Esther's (C) **sense of humor** is never mentioned, and the author doesn't seem particularly impressed by her (E) **material success.** Finally, (D) **stubborn pride** exaggerates Esther's determination in overcoming adversity, without acknowledging her good points.

29. C

Mrs. Hight, we're told in lines 42–43, was an "angry old mother, stung by defeat and mourning her lost activities." (C) captures the point here—Mrs. Hight is difficult to live with because she's **dissatisfied** with the way her life has run.

(A) **strength in adversity** applies to Esther, but not to her mother. (B) **carrying on a conversation** doesn't seem to be a problem for Mrs. Hight. Mrs. Hight is angry because of her own defeats—not because she (D) **distrusts her neighbors** or (E) **lacks gratitude towards her daughter.**

30. C

The author's focus at the end of the passage is on Esther's relationship with her mother. It's (C) **Esther** who will probably find sheep easier to deal with than the "severity" of Mrs. Hight's company. None of the other characters deals with sheep, or interacts closely with Mrs. Hight.

SECTION 2

1. C

How would you describe someone who likes to *attend parties*? Probably as (C) **convivial,** (E) **affable,** or (a little less likely) (D) **eloquent.** You certainly would not describe her as (A) **saturnine** or (B) **querulous.** Now you've eliminated (A) and (B). Looking at (C), (D), and (E), this person would have to be full of (C) **bonhomie.** She definitely wouldn't be full of (D) **vitriol** or (E) **choler.**

> *convivial: sociable*
> *affable: friendly, approachable*
> *eloquent: well-spoken*
> *saturnine: gloomy*
> *querulous: complaining, irritable*
> *bonhomie: good nature, geniality*
> *vitriol: bitterness*
> *choler: anger*

2. C

The clue here is that Negritude *was founded in Paris* and the students who created it were from *French-speaking colonies.* Thus they must have been (C) **expatriates.** Nothing in the sentence suggests they were (A) **animated,** (D) **radical,** or (E) **sophisticated.**

> *expatriates: people who've left their*
>   *native land*
> *didactic: factual to the point of*
>   *dullness; instructive*

3. E

There are two things to look for in this sentence. The first is the construction *so ---- that.* It tells us that whatever word fills the first blank *forced [Mr. Rhodes] to ---- her talent.* The second is the clue word *even.* If Maria's teacher was her *harshest critic,* and *even* he was forced to say something about *her talent,* chances are that the performance was too good to criticize. Therefore, we can predict that both words will be positive.

Although **praise** appears in choice (D), **indifferent** is not the kind of strongly positive word that would be suitable for the first blank. Similarly, the first word in (B), **tentative,** wouldn't fit the first blank. The first words in (A), (C), and (E) are all strongly positive words, but the second words in (A) and (C) are negative. (E) is the only choice with positive words for both blanks.

> *tentative: hesitant*
> *denigrate: to put down or insult*
> *indifferent: mediocre*
> *compelling: riveting*
> *laud: to honor or praise highly*
> *concede: to admit*

4. D

The clue words *though* and *still* point to a contrast between what Thucydides did and how he is viewed today. We know that *he is still considered an impartial and ---- historian.* Since *impartial* is a good thing for historians to be, the second blank will probably be filled by another positive word. That doesn't help us much, though, since none of the second words in the answer choices is negative. But in (A), it doesn't make much sense to attach **endless** to *historian.* (E) can go, too. How can you **promote** a speech to a historical figure?

With (A) and (E) out of the running, let's go to the first blank. *Thucydides* used speculation or invention *rather than documented* fact, to ---- speeches to historical figures. So Thucydides must have ascribed *to historical figures* words that they never actually spoke. The only choice that gives us that meaning when plugged into the first blank is (D): Thucydides **attributed** *speeches to historical figures* that they may never have made. *Historians* are supposed to be *impartial and* **accurate,** so (D) fills the sentence well all the way around. (B) doesn't work; Thucydides may be *considered* **illustrious,** but there is no evidence in the sentence that he **transmitted** *speeches to historical figures.* Nor does (C) work; the sentence never hints that Thucydides **disseminated** *speeches.*

> *impartial: fair, not taking sides*
> *illustrious: notable*
> *transmit: send*
> *disseminate: distribute*

5. A

The key to completing a sentence is to tie up loose ends without adding any new or unrelated information. The clue word *yet* should help you limit the choices up front. The second word will be something not usually associated with *expressive.* The first word will be one that goes well with *tough.* That lets you eliminate (C) and (E) based on their second blanks.

That leaves (A), (B), and (D) for the first blank. Someone *tough* isn't necessarily be (B) **narcissistic** or (E) **monotonous.** But he could very well be (A) **laconic.** The two words in (A), **laconic** and **pithy,** best fit our predictions.

> *laconic: using as few words as possible, curt*
> *pithy: concise and to the point*
> *narcissistic: self-centered and vain*
> *obtuse: blunt, dull, or stupid*
> *pragmatic: practical*
> *esoteric: relating to knowledge that few people have acquired*

6. D

The problem with the wrong choices here is that they add new information and don't fit the logic of the existing sentence. We're told that Balanchine *stayed within* the format of a particular style of dance, but that he *challenged convention* by doing something new or creative within the established form. (D) **unexpected** ties the whole sentence together—*Balanchine's choreography* was **unexpected** and unconventional, but still stayed within the *context* of *classical* ballet.

HINT: *Remember that your job is to find the one answer that best fits the logic of the sentence.*

naive: innocent, inexperienced
redundant: repetitive

7. A

The first clause says that *Americans enjoy ---- lifestyle.* Since *enjoy* is a very positive verb, the first blank should be filled by a positive adjective. This lets us eliminate (C), (D), and (E).

Now, if the sentence simply read *the official number of Americans has been ---- for several years,* you might generally predict that the blank would be filled by any verb or adjective having to do with quantity, e.g., **increasing,** decreasing, or stable. But the clue word *while* expresses a contrast or opposition between how *Americans* are depicted in the two main clauses. So if the first clause describes the *lifestyle* in positive terms, the second clause must describe it in negative terms. Therefore, we can predict that *the official number of Americans living in poverty has been* rising or **increasing.** In (B), **leisurely,** which means "without haste," doesn't work as well in the first blank; nor does it seem quite right to say that *the official number . . . has been* **developing.** That leaves us with (A) as the right choice.

acerbic: sharp or bitter
provincial: unsophisticated or closed-minded
peripheral: on the periphery or outer boundary, not essential
opulent: wealthy or luxurious
leisurely: without haste

8. C

A *debate* is normally orderly and rational, but this one apparently *degenerate[d] into ---- dispute.* What we have of the sentence before filling in the blank implies that this *debate* became a bitter argument. Therefore, something like "bitter" should go in the blank. (A) won't work; since the sentence talks about *the urgency,* or pressing importance, *of the topic,* the *dispute* would hardly be **inconsequential.** (B) **depraved** seems a bit far-fetched. (D) **prudent** means "careful," which would

go better with rational *debate* than with an uncordial *dispute.* And in (E), a **reticent** dispute means just the opposite of the tumultuous argument we predicted. But (C) **acrimonious** fulfills the prediction exactly.

degenerate: to deteriorate or sink to a lower level
preclude: to prevent
cordiality: affection and kindness
inconsequential: insignificant
depraved: sinful or corrupt
prudent: careful
reticent: silent, reserved
acrimonious: bitter

9. E

This unnamed novelist had delusions of grandeur. *He claimed to usher in a new era of literature,* that is, to be the first to write in a new style or format. But *his novels . . . [resembled] those of many other contemporary authors.* To complete this sentence correctly, you need a choice that reinforces the existing content of the sentence. Whatever fills the blank must support the idea that the author wasn't as innovative as he thought. (E) **derivative** fits the sentence well.

derivative: taken or received from another source
pastoral: relating to the countryside, especially to shepherds or to an idyllic scene

10. E

You don't have to know anything about *epiphytic ferns* to complete this sentence. The heart of a sentence completion is its internal logic, not its scientific topic or specialized technical vocabulary. Look at the parts of the sentence you do understand, and try to figure out how they might fit together with the rest of the sentence. Whatever *epiphytic ferns* are, we know that *they do not require soil* and that *they cannot survive without constant moisture.* What could either of those statements have to do with *tropical rainforests? Tropical rainforests* are extremely humid, so they're probably good places to find plants that need *constant moisture.* Look for an answer that means "found in" or "native to." You should be able to rule out most of the choices, because they don't fit that predicted meaning. But (E) **endemic to** fits; it means "native to" or "found only in."

endemic: native, found only in
steep: to soak or saturate

11. B

A **MARE,** by definition, is a female horse, while a **STALLION** is a male horse. So a **MARE** is the female counterpart of a **STALLION,** just as a **ewe** is the female counterpart of a **ram.** (A) **fawn** means a baby deer, not a female deer. (E) is wrong in part because **goat** can be a male or female. A male goat is a billy goat.

12. D

The **MESS** is the place where **SOLDIERS** eat; the **cafeteria** is the place where **students** eat. None of the other choices is functionally similar to the stem pair. For example, you might find (A) **patients** in an **infirmary,** or (E) **lawyers** in a **courtroom,** but those aren't the places where they eat.

13. D

Bridge: **DAUNTLESS** means "brave," and the quality is thus a characteristic of a **HERO.** Likewise, the quality of being **abstemious** is a characteristic of a **teetotaler.** The other choices present pairs that are not necessarily connected: In (A), a **hypochondriac** is not necessarily **ill;** in (B), a waiter can **serve** you without being **servile.** In (E), a **politician** may or may not be **mendacious.** As for (C), an **agnostic,** one who doubts the existence of God, would certainly not be **credulous.**

teetotaler: one who totally avoids alcohol
abstemious: moderate in eating or drinking
agnostic: one who doubts that God exists
dauntless: brave
hypochondriac: one who always imagines that he or she is ill
servile: submissive
mendacious: dishonest
credulous: trusting

14. E

You **QUARANTINE** someone or something in order to prevent an **EPIDEMIC;** just as you **sterilize** in order to prevent an **infection.** (C) is close but doesn't fit the bridge. In (D), **eat**ing doesn't prevent a **famine** from occurring, although it might prevent you from starving.

15. C

A group of **LIONS** is called a **PRIDE;** a group of **geese** is called a **gaggle.** In (B), a group of **workers** may or may not be a **syndicate,** or union. You might find (A) **violinists** in a **quartet** or (E) **elephants** in a **circus,** but groups of **violinists** are not **quartets** and groups of **elephants** are not **circus**es.

syndicate: union

16. A

A good bridge is: A **MENDICANT** is not characterized by **AFFLUENCE;** a **maverick** is not characterized by **conformity.** (B) is the opposite of the relationship in the stem pair: An **altruist** is interested in others' welfare and would certainly not lack **generosity.** In (D), a **sycophant** appeals to others' **vanity,** but does not necessarily lack **vanity.** In (C), a **demagogue** may or may not possess **banality,** just as in (E), a **defendant** may or may not be **innocent.**

> *affluence: wealth*
> *mendicant: beggar*
> *maverick: nonconformist*
> *sycophant: flatterer*
> *demagogue: rabble rouser*
> *banality: quality of lacking originality*
> *or freshness*

17. D

Bridge: An **HERBIVORE** is, by definition, an animal that eats **PLANT**s.

Since the prefix **OMNI**- means "all" or "everything," an **omnivore** eats both **PLANT**s and animals. But there's no specific or necessary connection between **omnivore** and **poultry**. An **historian** is not someone who eats **history**; nor is a **choreographer** someone who eats **dances**. But a **carnivore** is a **meat**eater. The root **CARN** means **meat**, and **VOR** or **VOUR** (as in *devour*) means "eat." (D) fits the stem bridge: A **carnivore** is an animal that eats **meat.**

> *herbivore: an animal that eats plants*
> *carnivore: an animal that eats meat*

18. E

If you didn't know what **TEPID** meant, your best bet here was to work backwards by defining a bridge for each answer choice. Rule out any answer for which you can't create a strong bridge or whose bridge couldn't possibly fit the stem pair.

Something that's **basic** has **simplicity;** could something **TEPID** have **HEAT?** Possibly . . . .

Lukewarm has nothing to do with **wateriness,** so eliminate (B).

Blandness is the quality of being **plain** in taste. **HEAT** is not the quality of being **TEPID** in flavor, so (C)'s out.

(D) has a rather wishy-washy bridge; **familiarity** *might* stem from a **regular** occurrence of an event or a **regular** association, but the two words don't have to go together.

Finally, something **mild** lacks **spiciness;** could something **TEPID** lack **HEAT?**

As you can see, only the bridges for (A) and (E) sound as though they might fit the stem pair. If you guessed between the two strongest possibilities, you'd have a fifty-fifty chance of picking the right answer. Since **TEPID** means "barely warm," it also means "lacking in **HEAT**." Thus, the words in the stem pair have the same relationship to each other as the words in choice (E).

> *lukewarm: almost cool, only slightly*
> *warm*
> *tepid: barely warm*

19. D

Let's try the same technique here.

The verb **bore** has nothing to do with **sadness,** so (A) is out. **Lending** may or may not **deplete** your resources. (B)'s out. Scratch (C)—**adoration** has nothing to do with **hoping.**

But (D) has a strong bridge: Someone who engages in **hoarding saves** excessively. Could it be that someone who engages in **ADULATION ADMIRES** excessively? That sounds like a reasonable possibility. Since there's no direct connection between **grow** and **satisfaction,** and we've already eliminated the other choices, (D) must be the answer.

> *deplete: to drain, empty, or lessen*
> *adulation: excessive flattery or*
> *admiration*
> *hoarding: accumulating things of value*
> *in a greedy, often secretive, way*

20. B

Although **MESMERIZING** can be used to mean "hypnotizing," it can also mean "extraordinarily **INTERESTING.**" The best option is (B), because something that's **vile** is extraordinarily **unpleasant.**

> *mesmerizing: hypnotizing, or*
> *extraordinarily interesting*

21. C

Bridge: **PEERLESS** means "without **EQUAL**." Despite the time-honored slogan used at gyms everywhere, **painless** doesn't mean "without **gain**," so (A) is wrong. But **shapeless** means "without **form**," so (C) is correct.

> *peerless: without equal inanimate: not*
> *alive*
> *inconceivable: unbelievable or*
> *impossible to imagine*

22. A

In general, the analogies at the end of a set contain more difficult words than the earlier ones. The bridge here is: To **DESICCATE** is to suck all the **MOISTURE** out of something. (A) is right, since to **debilitate** is to take the **strength** from something or someone. You really had to know the definitions of **DESICCATE** and **debilitate** to get this one right. The only small clue was the negative **DE-** prefix that they share in common.

> *dessicate: to take all the moisture out of*
> *something*
> *debilitate: to weaken, sap all the*
> *strength*
> *augur: to predict the future, especially*
> *by interpreting omens or signs*
> *exonerate: to prove innocent of charges*

HINT: *Study the Kaplan Word and Root Lists in this book.*

23. A

The adjective **ABSTINENT** means "showing **RESTRAINT**." Similarly, **compassionate** means "showing **sympathy**."

Although **eloquent** and **terseness** both have to do with speech, there's not much of a connection between them, and **subservient** has nothing to do with

deviance. If you tried to use roots and prefixes to set the meaning of **indifferent,** you would have been misled. Its negative **IN-** prefix would seem to give it a meaning of "the same," or "not different," but its actual meaning is "apathetic or neutral."

> *abstinent: refraining from indulging an*
> *appetite or drinking alcohol*
> *compassionate: showing sympathy*
> *eloquent: expressive and moving*
> *terseness: the quality of using few words*
> *subservient: menial, subordinate,*
> *overly submissive*
> *indifferent: apathetic or neutral*

The Murals Passage

This passage is about the lack of decorative color in our cities. Paragraph one tells us that modern cities have become "increasingly colorless environments." Paragraph two explains why—not only were somber colors believed to be more *functional*, but architects adopted them in order to imitate the traditions of ancient Greece and Rome. Midway through paragraph two, however, we're told that the architects were wrong—that the ancients *had* used a lot of color in their cities. In fact, according to paragraph three, vibrant colors are used almost everywhere outside the monotonous cities of the west. Paragraphs four through six state, however, that color in various forms is coming back; we're told that the work of Mexican mural painters sparked a revival of mural painting in the United States, and the work of William Walker is listed as the first of several mural projects by minority groups undertaken during the 1960s. Paragraph seven concludes the passage by affirming the benefits of street art.

24. B

Resultant is the key word here. We're told that the transformation of the landscape was a result of "the spread of industry" and "the exodus of the people from the countryside." (B)'s the correct answer here. If industry was growing, and people were moving from the country into the towns, we can infer that **urban areas** were **spreading** and growing in **density.**

Ethnic diversity (A) is discussed later in the passage. **Loss of manufacturing jobs** (C) goes against the idea of industry spreading. **Improved visual appearance** (D) goes against the author's critique of "an increasingly colorless environment." **Loss of parks** (E) isn't mentioned at all.

25. B

The author explains the phrase in question in lines 6–9. "Veiled in soot," we're told, towns have "lapsed into grimy taciturnity," as "all-pervading drabness" overcomes our "urban complexes." (B) captures the idea here.

City **violence** (A) isn't an issue in the passage at all. **Politicians** (C) aren't explicitly blamed for the situation and neither are **city-dwellers** (E). It's the state of our cities, not who's responsible, that the author is interested in. Finally, (D)'s out because the author's talking about urban areas, not **rural** ones.

26. D

Two things we're told about "somber, neutral colors" are relevant here. One, they've been widely used since the Industrial Revolution. Two, they were judged to be "more functional." Choice (D) captures these points.

(B)'s wrong because we're also told that somber, neutral colors were favored because people wanted to imitate **Greek and Roman** traditions. There's no basis for (C) in the passage. (A) takes the word *accentuated* (line 14) out of context; the author's point is that somber colors have been used almost exclusively. Finally, we're told that **Romanesque and Gothic architecture** featured "great use of color" (line 25), so (E) is out.

27. B

Western societies' admiration for Greek and Roman classicism was based on **mistaken beliefs.** We're told that somber, neutral colors were used for a long time out of a desire to imitate the Greeks and Romans, but historians now know that they loved color. Therefore (B) is correct.

(A) is wrong because we're told that these beliefs *accentuated* the **widespread** preference for **functional colors.** The cathedrals of **Siena, Florence, and Venice** (C) are described as featuring "great use of color"—so

admiring the ancients for *neutral* colors wouldn't be a consistent attitude. Nor was a **respect for ancient art** (D) the basis of somber color schemes, since we're told that ancient art used a "rich and subtle palette." (E) is wrong for the same reason—using color as a **symbolic language** is using a lot of color, and the admiration for the Greek and Roman canons was based on the idea that they used somber, neutral colors.

28. A

The word *vision* relates to the reverence for Greek and Roman classicism. We're told that our "vision" of marble market places in ancient Rome was all wrong. So *vision* in this context means (A) **image**—our mental picture of what ancient Rome was like.

(B) **display** doesn't make sense. Neither does (D) **personal wish.** (C)'s too extreme; we're not obsessed with the classical colors—we just have a certain idea about them that happens to be wrong. Finally, (E) **clearsightedness** doesn't fit with the author's acknowledgement that the vision is wrong.

29. D

In lines 34–35, we're told that "extraordinary ornamental richness" can be seen in the cities and villages mentioned. The phrase "to name but a few examples" is the giveaway. The cities and villages are listed as *examples of* the (D) **decorative lushness** the author's discussing in the paragraph as a whole.

The author is interested in colorful architecture, not (C) **architecture** that is all the same. (A) **natural scenery** is never discussed in the passage. (B) **complex history** only figures later in paragraph 5 in the discussion of mural painting. Finally, (E) **religious convictions** is a bit of a distortion—we're told that people from these societies derive spiritual nourishment from all the different colors they use.

30. B

The way he introduces the word—"*sensitivity* of this kind"—tells us that the author's referring to a sensitivity that he has just discussed. The topic of the paragraph is the decorative use of color in different cultures—something that has little place in "our great western cities." So the author is talking about *sensitivi-*

ty in the (B) **use of color** in our cities. (A) **sense of community spirit,** (C) **understanding of different cultures,** and (D) **consideration for other people** all suggest possible meanings for sensitivity in other contexts. But the author is talking specifically about the extent to which different societies use decorative color here. Finally, choice (E) is incorrect. We're told that all these people from different cultures are nourished by "contact with color," not that they're all versed in **art history.**

31. D

In lines 44–48, we're told that "bold and *judicious*" use of color makes cities better places to live. *Judicious,* then, is a positive quality. (D) **informed,** meaning "knowledgeable," is the best choice here, since *judicious* means "resulting in good decisions." (A) **controversial** and (E) **judgmental** are both poor choices because both have negative connotations. (B) **objective** conflicts with the word *bold*—could a city planner be both bold and objective about a project? Finally, (C) **determined** simply restates the idea of being bold.

32. E

The author uses the metaphor "striking a chord" here to illustrate how murals work. By "alluding to the important political, religious or artistic events of our cultures," murals make us remember historical events that are significant in our cultures. (E) captures this idea.

It's the function of the mural, not the benefits they present for the community—choices (A), (B), (C)—nor the monotony of cities without murals (D), that the author's referring to here.

33. C

In the lines *surrounding* the quote in question, the author's talking about public murals "making a comeback" (line 56). We're told that the three great Mexican artists were the "first influential muralists of the century" and that "their initiative" subsequently inspired American artists. (C)'s the answer here—the author mentions the Mexican artists to explain why there was a **revival in mural painting** in Mexico and the United States.

(A) is wrong because the author never implies any criticism of American mural painting. (B) is wrong because the history of this revival is the issue in paragraph five. (D)'s a distortion. We're never told that the Mexican artists themselves influenced historical events. Finally, paragraph five does mention the Mexican artists inspiring government funding for murals in the United States (E).

34. C

Turning lines 83–90 around, we're told that Walker's project inspired similar projects in various cities. In other words, it was a "point of departure" since it led to other group projects involving **minorities** (C).

There's no evidence for (A) at all—we're told nothing about specific **artists.** (B) contradicts paragraph five; murals had been commissioned 30 years earlier during the New Deal. (D)'s a bit off the point—the author's more concerned with the revival in murals than with public housing issues. (E) finally, is a distortion; Walker portrayed the **civil rights** pioneers, he didn't **lead** the **movement** himself.

35. C

The question ties quite clearly to the last paragraph's discussion of street art. The author tells us that "by its very nature as communal space" the street "lends itself to collective creativity." So it's the fact that streets are places **shared** by everyone that makes them ideal for this kind of mural painting (C).

(A) **encouraging reserve** goes against the gist of the passage. (B) **carrying few traces of past events** goes against the gist too, since part of the function of murals, according to paragraph five, is to make people aware of their own cultural history. (D) is wrong because the author describes many urban areas as "doomed to demolition, dereliction, or anonymity." If streets already made people aware of **their surroundings,** then presumably murals wouldn't be necessary. (E) is tempting, but the author doesn't mention using the street scenes themselves as **subjects** for painting.

SECTION 3

The Medieval-Guilds Pair

Unlike many others, these paired passages on medieval European society don't present two different perspectives on a single topic. Rather, the second passage here seems to grow out of the first, by depicting the beginning of the transition away from the historical situation described in Passage 1. Author 1 talks about the closed, stable world of the medieval guild, while Author 2 talks about what was going on in Italy in the 13th century, when that world was giving way to the more open, more fluid world of the Renaissance. So Passage 2 is almost like an outgrowth of Passage 1.

1. C

You're asked about the main function of the rules discussed in lines 12–15. In the passage, we read that these rules had the effect of "dampening personal ambition and initiative," which would protect the merchant and artisan from **competition** with other **merchants and artisans.** So (C) answers the question best.

Choice (A) is perhaps the closest wrong choice, but the impression given in the passage is that the rules imposed as much **control** on masters as on the people under those masters. (B) is out, since the **political influence of the guilds** is never discussed at length. (D) and (E), meanwhile, work against the thrust of Passage 1, which is that the guild system discouraged the **development** and innovation.

2. B

We move to the third paragraph of Passage 1. In the last sentence of that paragraph, we read that "the number of masters in each local guild was limited . . . by certain requirements . . . that were hard to fulfill." So the requirements had the effect of limiting the number of masters, or, as correct choice (B) has it, of **controlling the number of those who advanced beyond journeyman status.**

Choices (A) and (E) both contradict the passage, which claims that the guilds kept **foreign products** out of **local markets** (A) and actually discouraged **economic rivalry** (E). (C) is a distortion, since the guild requirements insisted only that one be a **citizen** to

become a master. And in (D), the requirements mentioned in line 32 have to do with becoming a master, not with **trade** restrictions.

3. E

This Vocabulary-in-Context question asks about the adjective *measured* in line 45. It is used to describe the resources of guild merchants. The author has just written about restrictions on the number of workshop employees a merchant could employ, and limits on the amount of their personal wealth they could use against other masters. So their resources were (E) **limited.** (A) **deliberate** and (C) **rhythmical** are other dictionary definitions of *measured,* but neither can be used to describe the word *resources* as it is used in this context. (B) **inadequate** is a close wrong choice, but the passage implies that these resources, while subject to strict limits, were still adequate to get the job done. (D)'s suggestion of **cautious,** meanwhile, is off the mark, since it's not the resources that were cautious.

4. D

This question is asking us to characterize the author's general description of the guild system in economic terms. The author writes at great length of the restrictions the system placed on the guilds. And although these restrictions prevented guild members from "rising above" their position, they did ensure that those positions would be "secure." So choice (D), which incorporates both the **restrictiveness** and the security, or **stability,** looks good as our answer.

(A), (B), and (C) are the opposite of what we want; they seem to describe the post-guild situation that appeared in Italy described in Passage 2—a situation variously described as (A) **open** and (C) **fluid,** and one whose emphasis on competition led to the kind of (B) **innovation** that the guild system tended to stifle. Choice (E), on the other hand, goes too far in the other direction.

5. A

We switch to an examination of Passage 2. The author wants to contrast what was going on in most of Europe with the new developments in Italy. Individuality was replacing group mentality, openness was replacing restrictiveness, and fluidity was replacing social rigidity. So (A) is the best answer.

(B) brings up the red herring of **education,** which isn't discussed until the end of paragraph three. (C) is a distortion, since the author's purpose is to describe the new attitudes in Italy rather than condemn the attitudes in the rest of medieval Europe. (D) is on the right track with its mention of **individuality,** but the author is not interested in **contemporary society.** Finally, (E) fails because the author isn't debunking a **common belief about medieval Europe.**

6. E

The author sets up Italy's new *social fluidity* (line 57) as a contrast to what was going on in the rest of Europe, where social life was rigidly fixed. So it's the **unfixed** quality of **social life in Italy** that the author is describing with the term *social fluidity,* making (E) the best choice.

(A) misses the mark, since the author nowhere indicates that she regards life in Italy at this time as **dangerous.** As for (B), the discussion of rivalries **between Italian families** doesn't come until much later. (C) is a distortion, since the phenomenon described by the author isn't the disparity in **wealth between classes,** but how individuals could jump from one class to another. (D) is closer in spirit, but it tries to fool you by playing to your outside knowledge, since nothing about **democratic institutions** is discussed by Author 2.

7. D

What is described as *acute* in line 67? The competition between artisans, competition that was so sharp, or **keen,** as correct choice (D) says, that it spurred the artisans on to the creation of masterpieces.

As for (A) and (B): Although the competition described definitely could be characterized as energetic, it's not depicted as either out of control or perilous. (C) **wise** could perhaps be seen as a definition of the word *acute* in some contexts, but how can competition itself be described as **wise?** (E) **sudden** has sort of the opposite problem; it could be said to fit the context but there's no way that **sudden** is a synonym for *acute,* which means sharp, penetrating, or extreme.

8. B

Author 2 tells us explicitly in line 84 that the story of the Medici family is meant to illustrate "these changes." She means the changes mentioned in the previous paragraph, that showed how in Italy "the potential for individual achievement . . . seemed unlimited." Therefore (B) is the right choice.

Choice (A) is a distortion, since the Medici family's success is linked to the decline of the **guild system,** which actually hampered the kind of **individual effort** they represent. Although (C) and (D) are true statements, neither is something that the example of the Medicis is meant primarily to illustrate in the passage. (E), meanwhile, is another distortion; no one said that it was **easy** to become successful in Italy at this time, just that it was possible.

9. C

This question asks us to characterize the author's discussion of the Medici family. If you go back and examine that discussion, you'll see that the facts are reported without any kind of emotional slant, so (C) **dispassionate** is the best characterization.

(A) **nostalgic** implies a fondness for old times, but clearly there's nothing affectionate in this description. (B) **disapproving** suggests that the author is passing judgment on the Medicis, but there's no evidence of any such negative evaluation. Finally, choices (D) **ironic** and (E) **defensive** indicate emotions towards the Medici family that are just not supported by the sober delivery of facts in that last paragraph.

10. D

You're asked for a common denominator of the two passages. Passage 1 talks about the guild system and the limits it placed on medieval European merchants. Passage 2 deals with the throwing off of limits for artisans and merchants in Italy in the late Middle Ages. So both passages explain the circumstances of **merchants during the Middle Ages,** choice (D).

All of the wrong choices fail because they don't accurately describe something that's discussed in both passages. Choice (A) can't be the answer, since **Italy** isn't even mentioned in Passage 1. On the other hand, (B) talks about the **structure of the guild system,** which the author of Passage 2 never discusses. (C)'s mention of the **growing importance of individuality** misses the mark, since Passage 1 is about how the guild system discouraged individuality. Similarly, (E)'s mention of capitalism's **fast growth** runs afoul of the thrust of Passage 1.

11. A

We're looking for a likely position taken by Author 1, so we must keep in mind what we know of Author 1. He regards the guild system as closed, restrictive, and stifling of individuality and innovation. So what would he think of the description of most of European society in the first two lines of Passage 2? That's where we hear that human consciousness (in most of Europe) was "half awake," and that people regarded themselves in terms of groups rather than as individuals. Well, this description jibes pretty well with the situation described by Author 1. So choices (A) looks good as the answer.

(B) is way off, since Author 1 tells us how the guild system discouraged **individual initiative.** Meanwhile, there's no evidence that Author 1 has such a restrictive view of the **historian's** job as choice (C) would imply. The wishy-washiness of (D) is also unfounded; we do have evidence that Author 1 would agree with Author 2's **description.** And the general statement in (E) seems unlike our Author 1, who was perfectly willing to make **sweeping** statements about the entire system of medieval guilds.

12. E

The merchants discussed in Passage 1 are very different from the Italian merchants discussed in Passage 2, and this question wants to know in what way they are most different. Well, the merchants in Passage 1 were working within the closed system of the guild, which had numerous restrictions that actually discouraged individual initiative. On the other hand, the merchants in Passage 2 "were unchecked in their political and social ambitions" (lines 75–76). So individual **ambitions** were radically different, making choice (E) the best answer.

Since we don't hear anything about either kind of merchant's attitude towards the **towns** they lived in, we really can't choose either (A) or (D), both of which deal with such attitudes. As for (B), we know nothing about attitudes toward **citizenship** rights. And as for (C), both types of merchant seem to have had **private property,** so it's unclear how their views on the subject would have been vastly different.

Practice Test B

Before taking this practice test, find a quiet room where you can work uninterrupted for 75 minutes. Make sure you have a comfortable desk and several No. 2 pencils.

Use the answer sheet on the following page to record your answers. (You can tear it out or photocopy it.)

Once you start this practice test, don't stop until you've finished. Remember—you can review any questions within a section, but you may not go back or forward a section.

Good luck.

SAT Practice Test B
Answer Sheet

**Remove (or photocopy) this answer sheet and use it to complete the practice test.
See the answer key following the test when finished.
The "Compute Your Score" section at the back of the book will show you how to find your score.**

Start with number 1 for each section. If a section has fewer questions that answer spaces, leave the extra spaces blank.

SECTION 1

1 (A) (B) (C) (D) (E)　11 (A) (B) (C) (D) (E)　21 (A) (B) (C) (D) (E)　31 (A) (B) (C) (D) (E)
2 (A) (B) (C) (D) (E)　12 (A) (B) (C) (D) (E)　22 (A) (B) (C) (D) (E)　32 (A) (B) (C) (D) (E)
3 (A) (B) (C) (D) (E)　13 (A) (B) (C) (D) (E)　23 (A) (B) (C) (D) (E)　33 (A) (B) (C) (D) (E)
4 (A) (B) (C) (D) (E)　14 (A) (B) (C) (D) (E)　24 (A) (B) (C) (D) (E)　34 (A) (B) (C) (D) (E)
5 (A) (B) (C) (D) (E)　15 (A) (B) (C) (D) (E)　25 (A) (B) (C) (D) (E)　35 (A) (B) (C) (D) (E)
6 (A) (B) (C) (D) (E)　16 (A) (B) (C) (D) (E)　26 (A) (B) (C) (D) (E)　36 (A) (B) (C) (D) (E)
7 (A) (B) (C) (D) (E)　17 (A) (B) (C) (D) (E)　27 (A) (B) (C) (D) (E)　37 (A) (B) (C) (D) (E)
8 (A) (B) (C) (D) (E)　18 (A) (B) (C) (D) (E)　28 (A) (B) (C) (D) (E)　38 (A) (B) (C) (D) (E)
9 (A) (B) (C) (D) (E)　19 (A) (B) (C) (D) (E)　29 (A) (B) (C) (D) (E)　39 (A) (B) (C) (D) (E)
10 (A) (B) (C) (D) (E)　20 (A) (B) (C) (D) (E)　30 (A) (B) (C) (D) (E)　40 (A) (B) (C) (D) (E)

right in section 1

wrong in section 1

SECTION 2

1 (A) (B) (C) (D) (E)　11 (A) (B) (C) (D) (E)　21 (A) (B) (C) (D) (E)　31 (A) (B) (C) (D) (E)
2 (A) (B) (C) (D) (E)　12 (A) (B) (C) (D) (E)　22 (A) (B) (C) (D) (E)　32 (A) (B) (C) (D) (E)
3 (A) (B) (C) (D) (E)　13 (A) (B) (C) (D) (E)　23 (A) (B) (C) (D) (E)　33 (A) (B) (C) (D) (E)
4 (A) (B) (C) (D) (E)　14 (A) (B) (C) (D) (E)　24 (A) (B) (C) (D) (E)　34 (A) (B) (C) (D) (E)
5 (A) (B) (C) (D) (E)　15 (A) (B) (C) (D) (E)　25 (A) (B) (C) (D) (E)　35 (A) (B) (C) (D) (E)
6 (A) (B) (C) (D) (E)　16 (A) (B) (C) (D) (E)　26 (A) (B) (C) (D) (E)　36 (A) (B) (C) (D) (E)
7 (A) (B) (C) (D) (E)　17 (A) (B) (C) (D) (E)　27 (A) (B) (C) (D) (E)　37 (A) (B) (C) (D) (E)
8 (A) (B) (C) (D) (E)　18 (A) (B) (C) (D) (E)　28 (A) (B) (C) (D) (E)　38 (A) (B) (C) (D) (E)
9 (A) (B) (C) (D) (E)　19 (A) (B) (C) (D) (E)　29 (A) (B) (C) (D) (E)　39 (A) (B) (C) (D) (E)
10 (A) (B) (C) (D) (E)　20 (A) (B) (C) (D) (E)　30 (A) (B) (C) (D) (E)　40 (A) (B) (C) (D) (E)

right in section 2

wrong in section 2

SECTION 3

1 (A) (B) (C) (D) (E)　11 (A) (B) (C) (D) (E)　21 (A) (B) (C) (D) (E)　31 (A) (B) (C) (D) (E)
2 (A) (B) (C) (D) (E)　12 (A) (B) (C) (D) (E)　22 (A) (B) (C) (D) (E)　32 (A) (B) (C) (D) (E)
3 (A) (B) (C) (D) (E)　13 (A) (B) (C) (D) (E)　23 (A) (B) (C) (D) (E)　33 (A) (B) (C) (D) (E)
4 (A) (B) (C) (D) (E)　14 (A) (B) (C) (D) (E)　24 (A) (B) (C) (D) (E)　34 (A) (B) (C) (D) (E)
5 (A) (B) (C) (D) (E)　15 (A) (B) (C) (D) (E)　25 (A) (B) (C) (D) (E)　35 (A) (B) (C) (D) (E)
6 (A) (B) (C) (D) (E)　16 (A) (B) (C) (D) (E)　26 (A) (B) (C) (D) (E)　36 (A) (B) (C) (D) (E)
7 (A) (B) (C) (D) (E)　17 (A) (B) (C) (D) (E)　27 (A) (B) (C) (D) (E)　37 (A) (B) (C) (D) (E)
8 (A) (B) (C) (D) (E)　18 (A) (B) (C) (D) (E)　28 (A) (B) (C) (D) (E)　38 (A) (B) (C) (D) (E)
9 (A) (B) (C) (D) (E)　19 (A) (B) (C) (D) (E)　29 (A) (B) (C) (D) (E)　39 (A) (B) (C) (D) (E)
10 (A) (B) (C) (D) (E)　20 (A) (B) (C) (D) (E)　30 (A) (B) (C) (D) (E)　40 (A) (B) (C) (D) (E)

right in section 3

wrong in section 3

Time—30 Minutes   For each of the following questions, choose the best answer and darken the
30 Questions   corresponding oval on the answer sheet.*

Select the lettered word or set of words that best completes the sentence.

Example:

Today's small, portable computers contrast markedly with the earliest electronic computers, which were ----.

(A) effective
(B) invented
(C) useful
(D) destructive
(E) enormous

 Ⓐ Ⓑ Ⓒ Ⓓ ⬤

---

1 More insurers are limiting the sale of property insurance in coastal areas and other regions ---- natural disasters.

(A) safe from
(B) according to
(C) despite
(D) which include
(E) prone to

2 Roman legions ---- the mountain ---- of Masada for three years before they were able to seize it.

(A) dissembled . . bastion
(B) assailed . . symbol
(C) besieged . . citadel
(D) surmounted . . dwelling
(E) honed . . stronghold

3 Unlike his calmer, more easygoing colleagues, the senator was ----, ready to quarrel at the slightest provocation.

(A) whimsical
(B) irascible
(C) gregarious
(D) ineffectual
(E) benign

4 Although historians have long thought of Genghis Khan as a ---- potentate, new research has shown he was ---- by many of his subjects.

(A) tyrannical . . abhorred
(B) despotic . . revered
(C) redundant . . venerated
(D) jocular . . esteemed
(E) peremptory . . invoked

5 Jill was ---- by her employees because she often ---- them for not working hard enough.

(A) deified . . goaded
(B) loathed . . berated
(C) disregarded . . eulogized
(D) cherished . . derided
(E) execrated . . lauded

6 Reconstructing the skeletons of extinct species like dinosaurs is ---- process that requires much patience and effort by paleontologists.

(A) a nascent
(B) an aberrant
(C) a disheveled
(D) a worthless
(E) an exacting

7 Nearly ---- by disease and the destruction of their habitat, koalas are now found only in isolated parts of eucalyptus forests.

(A) dispersed
(B) compiled
(C) decimated
(D) infuriated
(E) averted

8 Deep ideological ---- and internal power struggles ---- the government.

(A) disputes . . facilitated
(B) similarities . . protracted
(C) distortions . . accelerated
(D) agreements . . stymied
(E) divisions . . paralyzed

9 Medical experts have viewed high doses of vitamins as a popular remedy whose value is, as yet, ----.

(A) medicinal
(B) prescribed
(C) recommended
(D) unproven
(E) beneficial

---

*The directions on the actual SAT will vary slightly.

GO ON TO THE NEXT PAGE ➡

Choose the lettered pair of words that is related in the same way as the pair in capital letters.

Example:

FLAKE : SNOW ::

(A)   storm : hail
(B)   drop : rain
(C)   field : wheat
(D)   stack : hay
(E)   cloud : fog

Ⓐ ● Ⓒ Ⓓ Ⓔ

10   TROUT : FISH ::

(A)   grain : sand
(B)   human : mammal
(C)   river : stream
(D)   chicken : egg
(E)   frog : toad

11   INHALE : LUNGS ::

(A)   swallow : stomach
(B)   attack : heart
(C)   ache : head
(D)   pump : blood
(E)   travel : foot

12   BRAGGART : BOAST ::

(A)   laggard : tarry
(B)   hypocrite : speak
(C)   extrovert : brood
(D)   mendicant : compromise
(E)   boor : gratify

13   ALLEVIATE : PAIN ::

(A)   soothe : antidote
(B)   depreciate : value
(C)   contract : job
(D)   deviate : standard
(E)   officiate : safety

14   INFURIATE : ANNOY ::

(A)   admire : respect
(B)   indulge : lure
(C)   terrify : frighten
(D)   satiate : deprive
(E)   vex : startle

15   MISERLY : MAGNANIMITY ::

(A)   greedy : mirth
(B)   transient : stupefaction
(C)   admirable : fastidiousness
(D)   innocent : culpability
(E)   offensive : avarice

Alleviate:

GO ON TO THE NEXT PAGE ➡

Answer the questions below based on the information in the accompanying passages.

Questions 16–23 are based on the following passage.

In this excerpt, a Novel Price-winning scientist discusses ways of thinking about extremely long periods of time.

There is one fact about the origin of life which is reasonably certain. Whenever and wherever it happened, it started a very long time ago, so long
Line ago that it is extremely difficult to form any
(5) realistic idea of such vast stretches of time. The shortness of human life necessarily limits the span of direct personal recollection.

Human culture has given us the illusion that our memories go further back than that. Before
(10) writing was invented, the experience of earlier generations, embodied in stories, myths and moral precepts to guide behavior, was passed down verbally or, to a lesser extent, in pictures, carvings, and statues. Writing has made more precise and
(15) more extensive the transmission of such information and, in recent times, photography has sharpened our images of the immediate past. Even so, we have difficulty in contemplating steadily the march of history, from the beginnings of
(20) civilization to the present day, in such a way that we can truly experience the slow passage of time. Our minds are not built to deal comfortably with periods as long as hundreds or thousands of years.

Yet when we come to consider the origin of life,
(25) the time scales we must deal with make the whole span of human history seem but the blink of an eyelid. There is no simple way to adjust one's thinking to such vast stretches of time. The immensity of time passed is beyond our ready
(30) comprehension. One can only construct an impression of it from indirect and incomplete descriptions, just as a blind man laboriously builds up, by touch and sound, a picture of his immediate surroundings.

(35) The customary way to provide a convenient framework for one's thoughts is to compare the age of the universe with the length of a single earthly day. Perhaps a better comparison, along the same lines, would be to equate the age of our earth with
(40) a single week. On such a scale the age of the universe, since the Big Bang, would be about two or three weeks. The oldest macroscopic fossils (those from the start of the Cambrian Period*) would have been alive just one day ago. Modern
(45) man would have appeared in the last ten seconds and agriculture in the last one or two. Odysseus** would have lived only half a second before the present time.

Even this comparison hardly makes the longer

(50) time scale comprehensible to us. Another alternative is to draw a linear map of time, with the different events marked on it. The problem here is to make the line long enough to show our own experience on a reasonable scale, and yet
(55) short enough for convenient reproduction and examination. But perhaps the most vivid method is to compare time to the lines of print themselves. Let us make a 200-page book equal in length to the time from the start of the Cambrian to the present;
(60) that is, about 600 million years. Then each full page will represent roughly 3 million years, each line about ninety thousand years and each letter or small space about fifteen hundred years. The origin of the earth would be about seven books ago and
(65) the origin of the universe (which has been dated only approximately) ten or so books before that. Almost the whole of recorded human history would be covered by the last two or three letters of the book.

(70) If you now turn back the pages of the book, slowly reading *one letter at a time*—remember, each letter is fifteen hundred years—then this may convey to you something of the immense stretches of time we shall have to consider. On this scale the
(75) span of your own life would be less than the width of a comma.

*Cambrian: the earliest period in the Paleozoic era, beginning about 600 million years ago.
**Odysseus: the most famous Greek hero of antiquity; he is the hero of Homer's *The Odyssey*, which describes the aftermath of the Trojan War (ca. 1200 B.C.).

16 The word *span* in line 6 most nearly means

(A) rate of increase
(B) value
(C) bridge
(D) extent
(E) accuracy

GO ON TO THE NEXT PAGE ➡

17 The phrase *to a lesser extent* in line 13 indicates that, before the invention of writing, the wisdom of earlier generations was

  (A) rejected by recent generations when portrayed in pictures, carvings, or statues
  (B) passed down orally, or not at all
  (C) transmitted more effectively by spoken word than by other means
  (D) based on illusory memories that turned fact into fiction
  (E) more strongly grounded in science than in the arts

18 The author most likely describes the impact of writing (lines 14–17) in order to

  (A) illustrate the limitations of the human memory
  (B) provide an example of how cultures transmit information
  (C) indicate how primitive preliterate cultures were
  (D) refute an opinion about the origin of human civilization
  (E) explain the difference between historical facts and myth

19 The word *ready* in line 29 most nearly means

  (A) set
  (B) agreeable
  (C) immediate
  (D) apt
  (E) willing

20 The analogy of the "blind man" (line 32) is presented primarily to show that

  (A) humans are unable to comprehend long periods of time
  (B) myths and legends fail to give an accurate picture of the past
  (C) human history is only a fraction of the time since life began
  (D) humans refuse to learn the lessons of the past
  (E) long periods of time can only be understood indirectly

21 In lines 40–44, the author mentions the Big Bang and the Cambrian Period in order to demonstrate which point?

  (A) The age of the earth is best understood using the time scale of a week.
  (B) Agriculture was a relatively late development in human history.
  (C) No fossil record exists before the Cambrian Period.
  (D) Convenient time scales do not adequately represent the age of the earth.
  (E) The customary framework for thinking about the age of the universe should be discarded permanently.

22 According to lines 52–56, one difficulty of using a linear representation of time is that

  (A) linear representations of time do not meet accepted scientific standards of accuracy
  (B) prehistoric eras overlap each other, making linear representation deceptive
  (C) the more accurate the scale, the more difficult the map is to copy and study
  (D) there are too many events to represent on a single line
  (E) our knowledge of pre-Cambrian time is insufficient to construct an accurate linear map

23 The author of this passage discusses several kinds of time scales primarily in order to illustrate the

  (A) difficulty of assigning precise dates to past events
  (B) variety of choices faced by scientists investigating the origin of life
  (C) evolution of efforts to comprehend the passage of history
  (D) immensity of time since life began on earth
  (E) development of the technology of communication

GO ON TO THE NEXT PAGE ➡

Questions 24–30 are based on the following passage.

The following excerpt is from a speech delivered in 1873 by Susan B. Anthony, a leader in the women's rights movement of the 19th century.

Line
(5)

(10)

Friends and fellow-citizens: I stand before you tonight under indictment for the alleged crime of having voted at the last Presidential election, without having a lawful right to vote. It shall be my work this evening to prove to you that in thus voting, I not only committed no crime, but, instead, simply exercised my citizen's rights, guaranteed to me and all United States citizens by the National Constitution, beyond the power of any State to deny.

The preamble of the Federal Constitution says:

"We, the people of the United States, in order to form a more perfect union, establish justice, insure domestic tranquillity, provide for the common defense, promote the general welfare, and secure the blessings of liberty to ourselves and our posterity, do ordain and establish this Constitution for the United States of America."

(15)

(20)

(25)

It was we, the people; not we, the white male citizens; nor yet we, the male citizens; but we, the whole people, who formed the Union. And we formed it, not to give the blessings of liberty, but to secure them; not to the half of ourselves and the half of our posterity, but to the whole people—women as well as men. And it is a downright mockery to talk to women of their enjoyment of the blessings of liberty while they are denied the use of the only means of securing them provided by this democratic-republican government—the ballot.

(30)

(35)

(40)

(45)

For any State to make sex a qualification that must ever result in the disfranchisement* of one entire half of the people is a violation of the supreme law of the land. By it the blessings of liberty are forever withheld from women and their female posterity. To them this government had no just powers derived from the consent of the governed. To them this government is not a democracy. It is not a republic. It is an odious aristocracy; a hateful oligarchy of sex; this oligarchy of sex, which makes father, brothers, husband, sons, the oligarchs over the mother and sisters, the wife and daughters of every household—which ordains all men sovereigns, all women subjects, carries dissension, discord and rebellion into every home of the nation.

Webster, Worcester and Bouvier all define a citizen to be a person in the United States, entitled to vote and hold office.

(50)

The one question left to be settled now is: Are women persons? And I hardly believe any of our opponents will have the hardihood to say they are

(55)

not. Being persons, then, women are citizens; and no State has a right to make any law, or to enforce any old law, that shall abridge their privileges or immunities. Hence, every discrimination against women in the constitutions and laws of the several States is today null and void, precisely as is every one against Negroes.

*disfranchisement: to deprive of the right to vote.

24 In the first paragraph, Anthony states that her action in voting was

(A) illegal, but morally justified
(B) the result of her keen interest in national politics
(C) legal, if the Constitution is interpreted correctly
(D) an illustration of the need for a women's rights movement
(E) illegal, but worthy of leniency

25 Which best captures the meaning of the word *promote* in line 15?

(A) further
(B) organize
(C) publicize
(D) commend
(E) motivate

26 By saying "we, the people . . . the whole people, who formed the Union" (lines 19–21), Anthony means that

(A) the founders of the nation conspired to deprive women of their rights
(B) some male citizens are still being denied basic rights
(C) the role of women in the founding of the nation is generally ignored
(D) society is endangered when women are deprived of basic rights
(E) all people deserve to enjoy the rights guaranteed by the Constitution

GO ON TO THE NEXT PAGE ➡

27 By "the half of our posterity" (line 23–24), Anthony means

(A) the political legacy passed down from her era
(B) future generations of male United States citizens
(C) those who wish to enjoy the blessings of liberty
(D) current and future opponents of the women's rights movement
(E) future members of the democratic-republican government

28 In the fifth paragraph, lines 30–45, Anthony's argument rests mainly on the strategy of convincing her audience that

(A) any state that denies women the vote undermines its status as a democracy
(B) women deprived of the vote will eventually raise a rebellion
(C) the nation will remain an aristocracy if the status of women does not change
(D) women's rights issues should be debated in every home
(E) even an aristocracy cannot survive without the consent of the governed

29 The word *hardihood* in line 51 could best be replaced by

(A) endurance
(B) vitality
(C) nerve
(D) opportunity
(E) stupidity

30 When Anthony warns that "no State . . . shall abridge their privileges" (line 53–54), she means that

(A) women should be allowed to live a life of privilege
(B) women on trial cannot be forced to give up their immunity
(C) every state should repeal its outdated laws
(D) governments may not deprive citizens of their rights
(E) the rights granted to women must be decided by the people, not the state

IF YOU FINISH BEFORE TIME IS CALLED, YOU MAY CHECK YOUR WORK ON THIS SECTION ONLY. DO NOT TURN TO ANY OTHER SECTION IN THE TEST. **STOP**

Practice Test B—Section 2

Time—30 Minutes
35 Questions

For each of the following questions, choose the best answer and darken the corresponding oval on the answer sheet.

Select the lettered word or set of words that best completes the sentence.

Example:

Today's small, portable computers contrast markedly with the earliest electronic computers, which were ----.

(A) effective
(B) invented
(C) useful
(D) destructive
(E) enormous

1 The rain is so rare and the land is so ---- that few of the men who work there see much ---- in farming.

(A) plentiful . . hope
(B) barren . . difficulty
(C) productive . . profit
(D) infertile . . future
(E) dry . . danger

2 The principal declared that the students were not simply ignoring the rules, but openly ---- them.

(A) accepting
(B) redressing
(C) reviewing
(D) flouting
(E) discussing

3 Some critics believe that the ---- of modern art came with dadaism, while others insist that the movement was a ----.

(A) zenith . . sham
(B) pinnacle . . triumph
(C) decline . . disaster
(D) acceptance . . success
(E) originality . . fiasco

4 She would never have believed that her article was so ---- were it not for the ---- of correspondence which followed its publication.

(A) interesting . . dearth
(B) inflammatory . . lack
(C) controversial . . spate
(D) commonplace . . influx
(E) insignificant . . volume

5 The writings of the philosopher Descartes are ----; many readers have difficulty following his complex, intricately woven arguments.

(A) generic
(B) trenchant
(C) reflective
(D) elongated
(E) abstruse

6 The prisoner was ---- even though he presented evidence clearly proving that he was nowhere near the scene of the crime.

(A) abandoned
(B) indicted
(C) exculpated
(D) exhumed
(E) rescinded

7 Many biologists are critical of the film's ---- premise that dinosaurs might one day return.

(A) scientific
(B) tacit
(C) speculative
(D) unwitting
(E) ambiguous

8 Mozart composed music with exceptional ----; he left no rough drafts because he was able to write out his compositions in ---- form.

(A) audacity . . original
(B) facility . . finished
(C) incompetence . . ideal
(D) prestige . . orchestral
(E) independence . . concise

9 Known for their devotion, dogs were often used as symbols of ---- in Medieval and Renaissance painting.

(A) resistance
(B) benevolence
(C) generosity
(D) fidelity
(E) antagonism

10 It is ---- that a people so capable of treachery and brutality should also exhibit such a tremendous capacity for heroism.

(A) unfortunate
(B) explicable
(C) paradoxical
(D) distressing
(E) appalling

GO ON TO THE NEXT PAGE ➡

Choose the lettered pair of words that is related in the same way as the pair in capital letters.

Example:

FLAKE : SNOW ::

(A) storm : hail
(B) drop : rain
(C) field : wheat
(D) stack : hay
(E) cloud : fog

11 CHARLATAN : SCRUPULOUS ::

(A) confidant : virtuous
(B) laborer : stalwart
(C) officer : mutinous
(D) dullard : irritable
(E) tyrant : just

12 GREED : ACQUIRE ::

(A) fear : disguise
(B) inertia : persuade
(C) gluttony : eat
(D) conformity : agree
(E) ignorance : speak

13 PARRY : BLOW ::

(A) counter : argument
(B) sidestep : offense
(C) defer : ruling
(D) stumble : pitfall
(E) shine : light

14 MALIGN : SLURS ::

(A) satisfy : treaties
(B) persecute : complaints
(C) torment : whispers
(D) court : debates
(E) flatter : compliments

15 LENTIL : LEGUME ::

(A) rice : cereal
(B) nutrition : food
(C) horseshoe : pony
(D) husk : corn
(E) baker : cake

16 INDULGE : APPETITE ::

(A) filter : impurity
(B) infuriate : anger
(C) coddle : emotion
(D) humor : whim
(E) liberate : freedom

17 MELLIFLUOUS : SOUND ::

(A) musical : entertainment
(B) fragrant : smell
(C) pale : color
(D) raucous : discussion
(E) auspicious : occasion

18 GUFFAW : LAUGH ::

(A) sniffle : sneeze
(B) whoop : cough
(C) yell : talk
(D) snore : sleep
(E) chuckle : sigh

19 CELESTIAL : HEAVENS ::

(A) planetary : orbit
(B) scientific : experiment
(C) nautical : ships
(D) solar : heat
(E) viscous : matter

20 ENERVATE : VITALITY ::

(A) consolidate : power
(B) energize : action
(C) daunt : courage
(D) estimate : worth
(E) admit : guilt

21 OLIGARCHY : FEW ::

(A) government : majority
(B) authority : consent
(C) constitution : country
(D) monarchy : one
(E) discrimination : minority

22 UNTRUTHFUL : MENDACIOUSNESS ::

(A) circumspect : caution
(B) timid : behavior
(C) agile : physique
(D) sensitive : patient
(E) trusting : honesty

23 INEXCUSABLE : JUSTIFY ::

(A) isolated : abandon
(B) unassailable : attack
(C) affable : like
(D) famous : admire
(E) splendid : revere

GO ON TO THE NEXT PAGE ➡

Answer the questions below based on the information in the accompanying passages.

Questions 24–35 are based on the following passage.

In the following passage, a nineteenth-century American writer recalls his boyhood in a small town along the Mississippi River.

My father was a justice of the peace, and I supposed he possessed the power of life and death over all men and could hang anybody that offended
Line him. This was distinction enough for me as a
(5) general thing; but the desire to be a steamboatman kept intruding, nevertheless. I first wanted to be a cabin boy, so that I could come out with a white apron on and shake a tablecloth over the side, where all my old comrades could see me. Later I
(10) thought I would rather be the deck hand who stood on the end of the stage plank with a coil of rope in his hand, because he was particularly conspicuous.

But these were only daydreams—too heavenly to be contemplated as real possibilities. By and by
(15) one of the boys went away. He was not heard of for a long time. At last he turned up as an apprentice engineer or "striker" on a steamboat. This thing shook the bottom out of all my Sunday-school teachings. That boy had been notoriously worldly
(20) and I had been just the reverse—yet he was exalted to this eminence, and I was left in obscurity and misery. There was nothing generous about this fellow in his greatness. He would always manage to have a rusty bolt to scrub while his boat was
(25) docked at our town, and he would sit on the inside guard and scrub it, where we could all see him and envy him and loathe him.

He used all sorts of steamboat technicalities in his talk, as if he were so used to them that he
(30) forgot common people could not understand them. He would speak of the "labboard" side of a horse in an easy, natural way that would make you wish he was dead. And he was always talking about "St. Looy" like an old citizen. Two or three of the boys
(35) had long been persons of consideration among us because they had been to St. Louis once and had a vague general knowledge of its wonders, but the day of their glory was over now. They lapsed into a humble silence, and learned to disappear when the
(40) ruthless "cub" engineer approached. This fellow had money, too, and hair oil, and he wore a showy brass watch chain, a leather belt, and used no suspenders. No girl could withstand his charms. He "cut out" every boy in the village. When his
(45) boat blew up at last, it diffused a tranquil contentment among us such as we had not known for months. But when he came home the next week, alive, renowned, and appeared in church all battered up and bandaged, a shining hero, stared at

(50) and wondered over by everybody, it seemed to us that the partiality of Providence for an undeserving reptile had reached a point where it was open to criticism.

This creature's career could produce but one
(55) result, and it speedily followed. Boy after boy managed to get on the river. Four sons of the chief merchant, and two sons of the county judge became pilots, the grandest position of all. But some of us could not get on the river—at least our
(60) parents would not let us.

So by and by I ran away. I said I would never come home again till I was a pilot and could return in glory. But somehow I could not manage it. I went meekly aboard a few of the boats that lay
(65) packed together like sardines at the long St. Louis wharf, and very humbly inquired for the pilots, but got only a cold shoulder and short words from mates and clerks. I had to make the best of this sort of treatment for the time being, but I had
(70) comforting daydreams of a future when I should be a great and honored pilot, with plenty of money, and could kill some of these mates and clerks and pay for them.

24 The author makes the statement that "I supposed he . . . offended him" (lines 1–4) primarily to suggest the

(A) power held by a justice of the peace in a frontier town

(B) naive view that he held of his father's importance

(C) respect in which the townspeople held his father

(D) possibility of miscarriages of justice on the American frontier

(E) harsh environment in which he was brought up

25 As used in line 4, the word *distinction* most nearly means

(A) difference
(B) variation
(C) prestige
(D) desperation
(E) clarity

GO ON TO THE NEXT PAGE ➡

26 The author decides that he would rather become a deck hand than a cabin boy (lines 6–12) because

  (A) the job offers higher wages
  (B) he believes that the work is easier
  (C) he wants to avoid seeing his older friends
  (D) deck hands often go on to become pilots
  (E) the job is more visible to passersby

27 The author most likely mentions his "Sunday-school teachings" in lines 18–19 to emphasize

  (A) the influence of his early education in later life
  (B) his sense of injustice at the engineer's success
  (C) his disillusionment with longstanding religious beliefs
  (D) his determination to become an engineer at all costs
  (E) the unscrupulous nature of the engineer's character

28 The author most likely concludes that the engineer is not "generous" (line 22) because he

  (A) has no respect for religious beliefs
  (B) refuses to share his wages with friends
  (C) flaunts his new position in public
  (D) takes a pride in material possessions
  (E) ignores the disappointment of other people's ambitions

29 The author most probably mentions the use of "steamboat technicalities" (line 28) in order to emphasize the engineer's

  (A) expertise after a few months on the job
  (B) fascination for trivial information
  (C) ignorance on most other subjects
  (D) desire to appear sophisticated
  (E) inability to communicate effectively

30 The word *consideration* in line 35 most nearly means

  (A) generosity
  (B) deliberation
  (C) contemplation
  (D) unselfishness
  (E) reputation

31 According to the passage, the "glory" of having visited St. Louis (lines 36–38) was over because

  (A) the boys' knowledge of St. Louis was much less detailed than the engineer's
  (B) St. Louis had changed so much that the boys' stories were no longer accurate
  (C) the boys realized that traveling to St. Louis was not a mark of sophistication
  (D) the engineer's account revealed that the boys' stories were lies
  (E) travel to St. Louis had become too commonplace to be envied

32 The author describes the engineer's appearance (lines 41–43) primarily in order to

  (A) suggest one reason why many people found the engineer impressive
  (B) convey the way steamboatmen typically dressed
  (C) emphasize the inadequacy of his own wardrobe
  (D) contrast the engineer's behavior with his appearance
  (E) indicate his admiration for fashionable clothes

33 In lines 50–53, the author's response to the engineer's survival is one of

  (A) thankfulness for what he believes is God's providence
  (B) astonishment at the engineer's miraculous escape
  (C) reflection on the occupational hazards of a steamboating career
  (D) outrage at his rival's undeserved good fortune
  (E) sympathy for the extent of the engineer's wounds

34 The major purpose of the passage is to

  (A) sketch the peaceful life of a frontier town
  (B) relate the events that led to a boy's first success in life
  (C) portray the unsophisticated ambitions of a boy
  (D) describe the characteristics of a small-town boaster
  (E) give a humorous portrayal of a boy's conflicts with his parents

GO ON TO THE NEXT PAGE ➡

35 At the end of the passage, the author reflects on

(A) his new ambition to become either a mate or a clerk

(B) the wisdom of seeking a job in which advancement is easier

(C) the prospect of abandoning a hopeless search for fame

(D) the impossibility of returning home and asking his parents' pardon

(E) his determination to keep striving for success in a glorious career

IF YOU FINISH BEFORE TIME IS CALLED, YOU MAY CHECK YOUR WORK ON THIS SECTION ONLY. DO NOT TURN TO ANY OTHER SECTION IN THE TEST.

STOP

KAPLAN 313

Time—15 Minutes   For each of the following questions, choose the best answer and darken the
12 Questions   corresponding oval on the answer sheet.

Questions 1–12 are based on the following passages.

The controversy over the authorship of Shakespeare's plays began in the 18th century and continues to this day. Here, the author of Passage 1 embraces the proposal that Francis Bacon actually wrote the plays, while the author of Passage 2 defends the traditional attribution to Shakespeare himself.

Passage 1

Anyone with more than a superficial knowledge of Shakespeare's plays must necessarily entertain some doubt concerning their true authorship. Can
Line scholars honestly accept the idea that such
(5) masterworks were written by a shadowy actor with limited formal education and a social position that can most charitably be called "humble"? Obviously, the author of the plays must have traveled widely, yet there is no record that Shakespeare ever left his
(10) native England. Even more obviously, the real author had to have intimate knowledge of life within royal courts and palaces, yet Shakespeare was a commoner, with little firsthand experience of the aristocracy. No, common sense tells us that the plays
(15) must have been written by someone with substantial expertise in the law, the sciences, classics, foreign languages, and the fine arts—someone, in other words, like Shakespeare's eminent contemporary, Sir Francis Bacon.

(20) The first person to suggest that Bacon was the actual author of the plays was Reverend James Wilmot. Writing in 1785, Wilmot argued that someone of Shakespeare's educational background could hardly have produced works of such erudition
(25) and insight. But a figure like Bacon, a scientist and polymath* of legendary stature, would certainly have known about, for instance, the circulation of the blood as alluded to in *Coriolanus*. And as an aristocrat, Bacon would have possessed the
(30) familiarity with court life required to produce a *Love's Labour's Lost*.

Delia Bacon (no relation to Sir Francis) was next to make the case for Francis Bacon's authorship. In 1856, in collaboration with Nathaniel Hawthorne,
(35) she insisted that it was ridiculous to look for the creator of Hamlet among "that dirty, doggish group of players, who come into the scene [of the play Hamlet] summoned like a pack of hounds to his service." Ultimately, she concluded that the plays
(40) were actually composed by a committee consisting of Bacon, Edmund Spenser, Walter Raleigh, and several others.

Still, some might wonder why Bacon, if indeed the plays were wholly or partly his work, would not
(45) put his own name on them. But consider the political climate of England in Elizabethan times. Given that it would have been politically and personally damaging for a man of Bacon's position to associate himself with such controversial plays, it is quite
(50) understandable that Bacon would hire a lowly actor to take the credit—and the consequences.

But perhaps the most convincing evidence of all comes from the postscript of a 1624 letter sent to Bacon by Sir Tobie Matthew. "The most prodigious
(55) wit that I ever knew . . . is your lordship's name," Matthew wrote, "though he be known by another." That name, of course, was William Shakespeare.

*polymath: a person of wide and varied learning.

Passage 2

Over the years, there have been an astonishing number of persons put forth as the "true author" of
(60) Shakespeare's plays. Some critics have even gone so far as to claim that only a "committee" could have possessed the abundance of talent and energy necessary to produce Shakespeare's thirty-seven plays. Among the individual figures most seriously
(65) promoted as "the real Shakespeare" is Sir Francis Bacon. Apparently, the fact that Bacon wrote most of his own work in academic Latin does nothing to deter those who would crown him the premier stylist in the English language.

(70) Although the entire controversy reeks of scholarly gamesplaying, the issue underlying it is worth considering: How could an uneducated actor create such exquisite works? But the answer to that is easy. Shakespeare's dramatic gifts had little to do
(75) with encyclopedic knowledge, complex ideas, or a fluency with great systems of thought. Rather, Shakespeare's genius was one of common sense and perceptive intuition—a genius that grows not out of book-learning, but out of a deep understanding of
(80) human nature and a keen grasp of basic emotions, passions, and jealousies.

One of the most common arguments advanced by skeptics is that the degree of familiarity with the law exhibited in a *Hamlet* or a *Merchant of Venice* can
(85) only have been achieved by a lawyer or other man of affairs. The grasp of law evidenced in these plays, however, is not a detailed knowledge of formal law, but a more general understanding of so-called "country law." Shakespeare was a landowner—an
(90) extraordinary achievement in itself for an ill-paid Elizabethan actor—and so would have been

GO ON TO THE NEXT PAGE ➡

knowledgeable about legal matters related to the buying, selling, and renting of real estate. Evidence of such a common understanding of land regulations (95) can be found, for instance, in the gravedigging scene of *Hamlet*.

So no elaborate theories of intrigue and secret identity are necessary to explain the accomplishment of William Shakespeare. Scholars (100) who have made a career of ferreting out "alternative bards" may be reluctant to admit it, but literary genius can flower in any socioeconomic bracket. Shakespeare, in short, was Shakespeare—an observation that one would have thought was (105) obvious to everyone.

1 In line 2, *entertain* most nearly means

- (A) amuse
- (B) harbor
- (C) occupy
- (D) cherish
- (E) engage

2 In Passage 1, the author draws attention to Shakespeare's social standing as a "commoner" (line 13) in order to cast doubt on the Elizabethan actor's

- (A) aptitude for writing poetically
- (B) knowledge of foreign places and habits
- (C) ability to support himself by playwriting
- (D) familiarity with life among persons of high rank
- (E) understanding of the problems of government

3 *Coriolanus* and *Love's Labour's Lost* are mentioned in lines 28–31 as examples of works that

- (A) only Francis Bacon could have written
- (B) exhibit a deep understanding of human nature
- (C) resemble works written by Francis Bacon under his own name
- (D) portray a broad spectrum of Elizabethan society
- (E) reveal expertise more likely held by Bacon than Shakespeare

4 In Passage 1, the quotation from Delia Bacon (lines 36–39) conveys a sense of

- (A) disdain for the disreputable vulgarity of Elizabethan actors
- (B) resentment at the way Shakespeare's characters were portrayed
- (C) regret that conditions for Elizabethan actors were not better
- (D) doubt that Shakespeare could actually have created such unsavory characters
- (E) disappointment at the incompetence of Elizabethan actors

5 The author of Passage 1 maintains that Bacon did not put his own name on the plays attributed to Shakespeare because he

- (A) regarded writing as an unsuitable occupation for an aristocrat
- (B) wished to protect himself from the effects of controversy
- (C) preferred being known as a scientist and politician rather than as a writer
- (D) did not want to associate himself with lowly actors
- (E) sought to avoid the attention that fame brings

6 In the first paragraph of Passage 2, the author calls into question Bacon's likely ability to

- (A) write in a language with which he was unfamiliar
- (B) make the transition between scientific writing and playwriting
- (C) produce the poetic language evident in the plays
- (D) cooperate with other members of a committee
- (E) singlehandedly create thirty-seven plays

7 The word *premier* in line 68 most nearly means

- (A) earliest
- (B) influential
- (C) inaugural
- (D) greatest
- (E) original

8 In line 75, the word *encyclopedic* most nearly means

- (A) technical
- (B) comprehensive
- (C) abridged
- (D) disciplined
- (E) specialized

GO ON TO THE NEXT PAGE ➡

9 The author of Passage 2 cites Shakespeare's status as a landowner in order to

(A) prove that Shakespeare was a success as a playwright

(B) refute the claim that Shakespeare had little knowledge of aristocratic life

(C) prove that Shakespeare didn't depend solely on acting for his living

(D) dispute the notion that Shakespeare was a commoner

(E) account for Shakespeare's apparent knowledge of the law

10 In lines 99–102, the author maintains that literary genius

(A) is not dependent on a writer's external circumstances

(B) must be based on an inborn comprehension of human nature

(C) is enhanced by the suffering that poverty brings

(D) frequently goes unrecognized among those of modest means and position

(E) can be stifled by too much book-learning and academic training

11 The author of Passage 2 would probably respond to the speculation in the fourth paragraph of Passage 1 by pointing out that

(A) Shakespeare's plays would not have seemed particularly controversial to Elizabethan audiences

(B) The extent and range of Bacon's learning has been generally exaggerated

(C) such scenarios are farfetched and unnecessary if one correctly understands Shakespeare's genius

(D) Bacon would not have had the knowledge of the lower classes required to produce the plays

(E) the claim implies that Shakespeare was disreputable when in fact he was a respectable landowner

12 The author of Passage 1 would probably respond to the skepticism expressed in lines 66–69 by making which of the following statements?

(A) The similarities between English and Latin make it plausible that one person could write well in both languages.

(B) Plays written in Latin would not have been likely to attract a wide audience in Elizabethan England.

(C) The premier stylist in the English language is more likely to have been an eminent scholar than an uneducated actor.

(D) Writing the plays in Latin would have shielded Bacon from much of the political damage he wanted to avoid.

(E) The style of the plays is notable mostly for the clarity of thought behind the lines rather than their musicality or beauty.

IF YOU FINISH BEFORE TIME IS CALLED, YOU MAY CHECK YOUR WORK ON THIS SECTION ONLY. DO NOT TURN TO ANY OTHER SECTION IN THE TEST. **STOP**

ANSWER KEY ON FOLLOWING PAGE ➡

Answer Key

Section 1

1. E
2. C
3. B
4. B
5. B
6. E
7. C
8. E
9. D
10. B
11. A
12. A
13. B
14. C
15. D
16. D
17. C
18. B
19. C
20. E
21. A
22. C
23. D
24. C
25. A
26. E
27. B
28. A
29. C
30. D

Section 2

1. D
2. D
3. A
4. C
5. E
6. B
7. C
8. B
9. D
10. C
11. E
12. C
13. A
14. E
15. A
16. D
17. B
18. C
19. C
20. C
21. D
22. A
23. B
24. B
25. C
26. E
27. B
28. C
29. D
30. E
31. A
32. A
33. D
34. C
35. E

Section 3

1. B
2. D
3. E
4. A
5. B
6. C
7. D
8. B
9. E
10. A
11. C
12. C

Practice Test B Answers and Explanations

SECTION 1

1. E

It's easy enough to understand that *insurers* don't like to insure property in places where *natural disasters* are likely to happen. The term **prone to** (E) means "having a tendency to," so it is correct.

2. C

If it took *Roman legions* three years to seize Masada, we can predict that they spent a long time "surrounding or isolating" *the mountain* "fortress or stronghold" *of Masada* before they were finally able to take it. (C) is the best choice. (B) **assailed,** meaning "attacked," would make sense in the first blank, and (E) **stronghold** and (A) **bastion** would fit, too. But (A), (B), and (E)'s first-position words don't make sense when plugged in.

> *besieged: surrounded with armed forces*
> *citadel: fortress*
> *assailed: attacked*
> *bastion: fortified area*
> *dissembled: concealed*
> *honed: sharpened*

3. B

If the senator was *unlike* "his calmer, more easygoing colleagues" and "ready to quarrel at the slightest provocation," it's fair to infer that he was short-tempered or extremely irritable. The best choice is (B)—**irascible.**

> *irascible: easily angered*
> *whimsical: fanciful, erratic, or unpredictable*
> *gregarious: sociable, friendly*
> *ineffectual: futile, unproductive*
> *benign: harmless or gentle*

4. B

You don't have to know that *Genghis Khan* was a violent dictator to get this question right. What's important to know is that the first word of the sentence, *although,* implies that the two blanks have to contain words that contrast with each other. (B) is the best choice—although historians had thought that Genghis Khan was a **despotic** *potentate, new research* shows that *many of his subjects* nevertheless **revered** him. Although (A) **tyrannical** is synonymous with **despotic,** (A)'s second-blank choice, **abhorred,** doesn't provide the predicted contrast. Choice (C) **venerated** doesn't really contrast with **redundant.** And in (E), it doesn't make sense to say that Khan's subjects **invoked** him despite his **peremptory** reputation.

> *despotic: oppressive, dictatorial*
> *potentate: dictator*
> *revered: worshipped, adored*
> *abhorred: hated*
> *venerated: highly respected*
> *redundant: repetitive*
> *jocular: jolly*
> *peremptory: putting an end to debate*
> *invoke: call upon for help*

5. B

The word *because* in the middle of the sentence lets us know that the words in the blanks will be consistent in meaning, which means that they will share the same type of charge. We can predict two positive words, like *Jill was* "appreciated" *by her employees because she often* "forgave" *the fact that they were lazy,* or two negative words like *Jill was* "disliked" *by her employees because she often* "scolded" *them for being lazy.* (B) matches the latter prediction—*Jill was* **loathed** *by her employees because she often* **berated** *them for not working hard enough.* No other choice besides (B) contains two like charges.

> *loathed: hated*
> *berated: scolded*
> *deified: made godlike*
> *lauded: praised or celebrated*
> *derided: made fun of*
> *execrated: condemned, cursed*

6. E

If *reconstructing the skeletons of extinct species like dinosaurs . . . requires much patience and effort by paleontologists,* we can predict that such an activity is a "painstaking or tough, demanding process." (E) **exacting** is our best choice.

> *exacting: requiring lots of attention and extreme accuracy*
> *nascent: introductory or starting*
> *aberrant: abnormal*

7. C

Because of *disease and the destruction of their habitat, koalas are now found only in isolated parts of eucalyptus forests.* The word in the blank must mean something like "killed off" or "destroyed," since things like *disease and habitat destruction* are destructive processes. (C) is our best choice—*nearly* **decimated,** or wiped out, *by disease and habitat destruction, koalas are now found only in isolated parts of eucalyptus forests.* (A) **dispersed,** meaning "scattered," may have been a little tempting, but there's no reason to assume that the koalas were scattered around the forests due to *disease and habitat destruction.*

> *dispersed: scattered*
> *compiled: categorized, collected, arranged*
> *averted: avoided*

8. E

Looking at the first blank first, if there were *internal power struggles [in] the government,* then it's likely that the government had something like *deep ideological* "differences" or "conflicts." For the second blank, we can predict that these conflicts and *power struggles* harmed or crippled *the government.* Although choice (C)'s first-blank choice, **distortions,** sounds negative, like "differences" or "conflicts," choices (A) and (E) make *more* sense. We can easily imagine *deep ideological* **disputes** or *deep ideological* **divisions** going hand in hand with *internal power struggles,* but it's hard to imagine *ideological* **distortions.**

Now we can turn to (A) and (E)'s second-blank choices. (A) doesn't make sense given the context of the sentence—why would *deep ideological* **disputes** *and internal power struggles* **facilitate** *the government?* (E) is the best choice—*deep ideological* **divisions** *and internal power struggles* **paralyzed** *the government.*

> *distortions: perversions, twisted versions*
> *facilitate: assist*
> *stymied: frustrated, impeded*

9. D

The terms *popular remedy* and *as yet* are key in this sentence. Large *doses of vitamins* are popularly thought to be good but their effectiveness has not been proven at this time. (D) **unproven** is the correct answer. Answer choices (A), (B), (C), and (E) are wrong because they imply that medical experts understand and approve of large doses, which clearly contradicts the sentence.

10. B

A **TROUT** is a type of **FISH,** just as a **human** is a type of **mammal.**

11. A

Bridge: If you **INHALE** something, it goes into your **LUNGS.** If you **swallow** something, it goes into your **stomach.**

12. A

A **BRAGGART** is, by definition, someone who **BOAST**s. A **laggard** is, by definition, someone who **tarries.** A speaker, not a **hypocrite,** is someone who, by definition, **speaks,** so (B) is wrong.

> *laggard: lingerer, one who lags behind*
> *extrovert: someone very outgoing*
> *tarry: to dawdle, be late, delay*
> *hypocrite: someone who pretends to be what he or she is not*

13. B

To **ALLEVIATE** is to reduce **PAIN,** just as to **depreciate** is to reduce **value.** In choice (D), to **deviate** is to move away from some set **standard.** That's not the same as lowering a **standard.**

14. C

Bridge: To **INFURIATE** someone is to **ANNOY** him or her a great deal. In correct choice (C), to **terrify** someone is to **frighten** him or her a great deal.

> *satiate: to satisfy*

15. D

By definition, someone **MISERLY** is not characterized by **MAGNANIMITY,** or generousness. Similarly, someone **innocent** is not characterized by **culpability.**

> *transient: wandering from place to place*
> *stupefaction: overwhelming amazement*
> *fastidiousness: the quality of being painstaking or particular*
> *avarice: greed*
> *magnanimity: generosity*
> *culpability: guilt*

The Time Passage

Next up is a fairly abstract science passage. This particular passage is perhaps a little bit harder than the ones you're going to encounter on Test Day—but don't be intimidated by the subject matter. Even if your passage is written by a Nobel Prize winner, it's going to contain ideas that you can relate to, and probably some ideas that you've seen before.

The topic of the passage is how difficult it is to comprehend long stretches of time. Paragraph two tells us that our minds aren't built to handle the idea of thousands of years passing. We have *some* conception of the past through the art, writing, and photography of previous generations, but the scale of longer time periods eludes us. Paragraphs four and five attempt to bridge this gap by providing a few everyday yardsticks; the time the human race has been around is compared to a few seconds in a week, or a few letters in a book. Essentially, that's all you need to take from your first reading of the passage; the details you can come back to later.

16. D

Here, in paragraph one, the author's talking about why we find it difficult to understand vast stretches of time. We're told that the *span* of what we can remember is limited because our lives are relatively short. So *span* in this context means the amount of time we're able to recollect—the (D) **extent.**

(A) **rate of increase,** (B) **value,** and (E) **accuracy** are all correct definitions of *span,* but they're not aspects of memory as discussed in the passage. And (C) **bridge,** the most common definition, doesn't fit at all.

HINT: *The golden rule about vocabulary questions on the Critical Reading section is that they test vocabulary IN CONTEXT. You're being asked how a particular word is used in the passage, not how it's usually defined.*

17. C

Before writing, we're told, the wisdom of generations was passed down in two ways—verbally, and "to a lesser extent," in pictures, carvings, and statues. This means that the wisdom of the past was transmitted less effectively by nonverbal means, and thus (C) **more effectively by the spoken word than by other means.**

Choices (A) and (B) distort this idea. Nowhere are we told that wisdom was **rejected.** And since spoken words *and* pictures were both used, it was obviously not an all or nothing proposition. (E) doesn't make much sense. How could there be an emphasis on **science** before writing existed? (D), finally, makes no sense at all—the author never says that all ancient wisdom was **fiction.**

18. B

This is a Little Picture question asking about the purpose of a detail. The question asks why the author discusses the impact of writing. Looking at the lines around the line reference given, we're told that writing has made the transmission of information about the past a lot more precise and extensive. Pictures and photography are also mentioned as ways in which the experience of the past has been passed down. So choice (B)'s correct here—writing is mentioned as an **example** of how cultures record knowledge about the past.

(A) is a distortion—the author is showing us something about the past, not why we remember hardly anything. He never implies any criticism of **preliterate cultures,** so choice (C) is out too. Choices (D) and (E) are wrong because the author never mentions them in the context referred to or in the whole passage.

19. C

Another Vocabulary-in-Context question. The word *ready* can mean several things—choices (A), (C), (D), and (E) are all possible meanings. In this context, however, it most nearly means **immediate,** choice (C). In

the sentence before the cited line, the author says "there is no simple way" to understand vast stretches of time. And in the sentence following the cited line, the author compares the way we understand time to the way a blind man "laboriously" constructs a picture of his surroundings. This implies that our understanding of time is a difficult and time-consuming task, not something we can do readily or **immediately.**

20. E

Another question asking about the purpose behind part of the author is argument. Give the context a quick scan. Once again, the author's talking about how difficult it is to understand vast stretches of time. We're told that it's like a blind man building up a sensory picture of his surroundings. This is an **indirect** process, so choice (E) is right.

Choice (C) is dealt with later in paragraph four, so you can eliminate it right away.

Choice (A) is too sweeping. The author never says that human beings are completely **unable to comprehend time.** (B) and (D) have nothing to do with the passage.

21. A

Inference skills are required here. What is the author's underlying point in mentioning *the Big Bang and the Cambrian Period*? The author introduces this discussion in the cited passage by saying that **a week** provides a better yardstick for **the age of the earth** than a day. The Big Bang and the Cambrian Period are used as examples to support this point. So (A) is right—it's the point about the time scale that the author's trying to demonstrate.

Choices (D) and (E) both distort the point in different ways. The author is not suggesting that the time scale of a day should be totally abandoned—just that the week is a better scale. The development of (B) **agriculture** is another supporting example like the Big Bang and the Cambrian Period, but it's not the author's central point here. Finally, **fossils** have nothing to do with the question at hand, so (C) is easily eliminated.

22. C

A more straightforward comprehension question this time. When we go back to the lines referred to, we're told about the problem with linear maps: When you produce one that's big enough to show us on it, the map becomes too big to study and reproduce conveniently. (C) gets the right paraphrase here. Notice especially the match up in synonyms for "convenient reproduction" and "examination."

(A), (B), and (E) aren't supported here—there's nothing about **scientific standards, overlapping** periods, or ignorance about **pre-Cambrian times** in the passage. (D) doesn't address the problem. The question is about getting our human experience on the map.

23. D

What's the overall point the author is trying to prove?

The Big Picture is that life started on earth so long ago that it is difficult for us to comprehend. Everything that follows is meant to illustrate this point, including the time scales. Don't let the material confuse you. The point is (D)—**the immensity of time** since the origin of **life.**

(C) is tricky to reject because it's an aspect of the larger argument, but it's not the whole point. The other wrong choices mention issues that the author hardly touches on. In paragraphs four to six, the author's not concerned with getting **dates** right (A), the question of how **life** actually began (B), or the (E) **development of communication.**

The Susan B. Anthony Passage

This humanities passage is from a speech by Susan B. Anthony, a 19th-century women's rights leader. Anthony admits at the outset that she was recently charged with the "crime" of voting. Her intention is to prove that her vote was no crime, but rather the exercise of her Constitutional rights, which no state should be allowed to impinge upon. This generates the passage's big idea: that Anthony—and by extension all women—should be allowed to vote. You may have found Anthony's style a little dated or confusing. Don't worry; the questions will help you focus on specific details.

24. C

The important thing here is to see what exactly Anthony is saying. The question stem is keyed to the

first paragraph. In the second sentence she states that she "not only committed no crime, but . . . simply exercised my citizen's rights, guaranteed me . . . by the National Constitution." The words *no crime* are the first important clue. You can immediately rule out (A) and (E) because they say she believes the act was **illegal.** The second part of the line discusses the **Constitution,** so (C) is clearly a restatement of her argument.

(B) and (D) both make sense, but she does not state these points in the first paragraph. Therefore, they are wrong.

25. A

The most common meaning of *promote* is "to move up"—to a higher position, rank, or job. This doesn't make sense, though, in the phrase "promote the general welfare." "General welfare" means the good of all people, so to (A) **further** it, makes the most sense.

(B) **organize** and (C) **publicize** both could apply to the general welfare, but not as well as (A). They refer more to promotion as you would do with a concert or sports event. (D) **commend** means "praise," which seems silly in the context given, as does (E) **motivate.**

HINT: *In Vocabulary-in-Context questions, the right answer is usually not the most common meaning of the given word. Be sure to reread the context.*

26. E

Anthony points out that no subgroup was excluded by the wording of the preamble of the Constitution. ". . . we formed it . . . to secure [the blessings of liberty,] not to the half of ourselves . . . but to . . . women as well as men." Therefore (E) is correct. **All people deserve to enjoy the rights** of **the Constitution.**

Anthony never claims that the Founding Fathers plotted to deny women their rights (A). (B) is incorrect because the author's concern is women's rights and not rights of any other group. Though **some male citizens** may **still be denied basic rights,** (B) goes against the gist of what is being said. (C) is like (A) in that it's a claim Anthony never makes. Finally, though (D) is a point that Anthony does make, she doesn't make it until the next paragraph.

27. B

We're still looking at the same part of the passage.

Look at the structure of the quoted sentence: "We didn't do it only for X, but for X *and* Y." "Posterity" means **future generations,** which would include men and women. So the X, the "half of our posterity," refers to the posterity of those who already enjoy the blessings of liberty. In other words, **males.** (B) is the right choice.

(A) has nothing to do with what Anthony is discussing. Since the construction of the sentence makes it clear that the "half of our posterity" is not the whole of those who want to vote, (C) is out. There's no way of saying that one-half of the people are and will be **opponents of women's rights,** so (D) is wrong. And (E) wrongly suggests that in the **future,** one half of the country's population will be members of government.

28. A

Reread the keyed paragraph. Anthony is saying that a state that prohibits women from voting violates federal law—the Constitution. Therefore it becomes "an odious aristocracy, a hateful oligarchy." Neither of these things is a **democracy.** (A) is the correct answer.

Anthony mentions **rebellion,** but she doesn't mean the kind of violent **rebellion** (B) talks about. (C) is wrong because of the word **remain.** The nation is not and never has been **an aristocracy.** (D) plays off the same sentence as (B) does, but instead of going too far, it doesn't go far enough. Anthony wants the laws against women voting repealed; she doesn't want them merely discussed. (E) is totally wrong because at no point is Anthony arguing that an **aristocracy** should be preserved.

29. C

You might readily associate *hardihood* with (A) **endurance** and (B) **vitality,** but a quick check back in context shows you these aren't correct. Anthony says she doesn't believe her opponents would have the ---- to say women aren't "persons." Saying such an offensive thing would take a lot of **nerve,** choice (C). It might also take a lot of **stupidity** (E), but that's too strong a word, considering Anthony's diplomatic tone.

30. D

The stem keys you to the second to last sentence of the passage. *Abridge* means "deprive," so Anthony is saying that no state can deprive citizens of their rights. (D) states exactly this.

In (A), **privilege** means "luxury," but voting is a basic right, not a luxury. (B) comes out of nowhere; there's no discussion of courts in this passage. (C) plays off Anthony's reference to "any old law." She's not talking about any **outdated laws** in this passage; she means any law that prohibits women from voting. Anthony never addresses how the laws will be changed, only that they must be changed, so (E) is out.

---

antagonism: hostility

SECTION 2

1. D

This is not a difficult question. The use of the word *and* tells us that we're looking for a word to fill the first blank which is consistent with scarcity of rain—a word like "dry." We can, therefore, eliminate (A) and (C) at once. Since farming conditions are bad, our second blank should express the idea that there's no point in trying to work there. By that criterion, choices (B) and (E) can be eliminated. This leaves us with (D) **future.** (D)'s first word, **infertile,** also fits perfectly, so (D) is the correct answer.

> *barren: not productive*

2. D

The structural clue in this sentence is *not only . . . but,* which suggests that the students were doing something even worse than **ignoring the rules.** The only word that fits here is **flouting,** choice (D).

> *flouting: mocking, treating with*
> *contempt*

3. A

The word *while* following the comma in the second part of the sentence tells us that there will be a contrast between what some critics believe about *dadaism* and what *others insist the movement was.* The best choice is (A)—*some critics believe that the* **zenith** *of modern art came with dadaism, while others insist the movement was a* **sham.** Other choices have single words that would make sense in one of the blanks, but none of the pairs except (A) expresses the contrast that is implied by the sentence.

> *zenith: highest point*
> *sham: hoax*

4. C

In this question you are asked to make a logical connection between two parts of a sentence. It is clear that the content of the journalist's article either had no impact, in which case there was little or no response from the public, or it attracted a great deal of attention and was followed by a lot of correspondence. (C) is the correct answer. The author would never have thought *her article was so* **controversial** *were it not for the* **spate** *of correspondence.* The other answer choices are wrong because they sound contradictory when plugged into the sentence. For example, in choice (A), if the article were **interesting,** one would expect it to be followed by a lot of correspondence—not by a **dearth,** or lack of it. In choice (D), if the article were **commonplace** (ordinary), why would an **influx** of letters follow its publication?

> *spate: a sudden flood or rush*
> *dearth: lack*
> *inflammatory: likely to arouse strong*
> *feeling or anger*
> *influx: flow coming in*

5. E

If many readers have difficulty following Descartes' *complex, intricately woven arguments,* then it's likely that his writings are something like "complicated," "esoteric," or "obscure." The best choice is (E) **abstruse.**

> *abstruse: difficult to understand*
> *generic: common, general*
> *trenchant: extremely perceptive,*
> *insightful*

6. B

The phrase *even though* indicates contrast. So, *even though* the prisoner *presented evidence clearly proving that he was nowhere near the scene of the crime,* he was (B) **indicted,** or formally charged with committing the crime.

exculpated: absolved, proved to be
innocent
exhumed: removed from a grave
rescinded: cancelled, taken back

7. C

A *premise* is a proposition which is used as the basis for an argument—or a story. If scientists are critical of the *premise* for a movie, we can infer that they are so because they consider it to be unscientific, without basis in fact, or **speculative.** (C) is therefore the correct answer. (A) is wrong, because if the *premise,* or underlying argument, were **scientific** then it would hardly be open to criticism by scientists. (B) is wrong because there's no reason to think that the theme of the return of the dinosaurs is **tacit,** or unexpressed, in the movie.

tacit: silent; understood but
unexpressed

8. B

Looking at the second blank first, if Mozart **left no rough drafts,** it's probably **because he was able to write out his compositions in** "a complete, unrevised" **form.** So, for the second blank, (B) **finished** looks best. (E) **concise** is also possible, so let's try (B) and (E) in the first blank. We've already seen that Mozart didn't need to revise his compositions—therefore, it makes sense to say that he "composed music with *exceptional* ease or **facility.**" (E) **independence** is just too ambiguous to fit in to the context of the sentence.

concise: using as few words as possible,
to the point

9. D

If dogs are *known for their devotion,* then it's likely that they *were often used as symbols of* "faithfulness, loyalty, or fidelity" *in Medieval and Renaissance paintings.* (A) **resistance** and (E) **antagonism** are not what we're

looking for, and choices (B) and (C), while positive, don't relate to the idea of *devotion.*

antagonism: hostility

10. C

In this sentence we find a description of two contradictory characteristics which exist in the same group of people. On the one hand, they are *brutal*; on the other, they are *heroic.* Such an occurrence is termed a paradox and therefore (C) **paradoxical** is the correct answer. Choices (A), (D), and (E) are wrong; it is **unfortunate, distressing,** and **appalling** that they are brutal—but not that they are heroic.

paradoxical: like a riddle; opposed to
common sense but true
explicable: able to be explained

11. E

A **CHARLATAN** is by definition not **SCRUPULOUS.** A **tyrant** is a ruler who uses power oppressively and unjustly. So a **tyrant** is, by definition, not **just.**

charlatan: a fraud or a quack, someone
who pretends to have more knowledge
or skill than he or she possesses

12. C

GREED is the desire to **ACQUIRE** large amounts of things. **Gluttony** is the desire to **eat** large amounts, so (C) is the best answer.

(A) won't work; someone who experiences **fear** may or may not want to **disguise** him- or herself. In (B), it may be hard to **persuade** someone characterized by **inertia,** but **inertia** isn't the desire to **persuade** large amounts.

inertia: apathy, inactivity

13. A

The word **BLOW** is being used to mean "a swipe or punch." To **PARRY** means "to deflect, ward off," so our bridge is *to* **PARRY** *a* **BLOW** *is to deflect it.* (A) shares the same bridge—to **counter** an **argument** is to deflect it.

In choice (B), you might **sidestep** or avoid an argument or issue, but there isn't really any clear connection between **sidestep** and **offense.** In (C), to **defer** isn't to deflect or ward off a **ruling.**

> *pitfall: a trap or hidden danger*
> *defer: put off or delay*

14. E

By definition, **SLURS** are words that **MALIGN,** just as **compliments** are words that **flatter.** The other choices don't fit this bridge. For instance, in (C), **whispers** aren't necessarily words that **torment.**

15. A

A **LENTIL** is classified as a **LEGUME,** a bean or pea, in the same way that **rice** is classified as a **cereal.**

Even if you didn't know that a **LENTIL** is a **LEGUME,** you might have been able to arrive at the answer by eliminating all choices with no good bridges. For example, in (B) **food** may or may not provide **nutrition,** or nourishment.

> *husk: the outer covering of a kernel or seed*

16. D

To **INDULGE** an **APPETITE** is to satisfy it. Similarly, to **humor** a **whim** is to satisfy it.

In (A), you can **filter** out an **impurity,** but it doesn't make sense to say that to **filter** out an **impurity** is to satisfy it. (C) might have been a tempting choice, since the word **coddle** is similar to **INDULGE.** But **coddle** doesn't have a necessary connection to **emotion.**

> *coddle: to overindulge, pamper*

17. B

Bridge: **MELLIFLUOUS** means "sweet **SOUND**ing." **Fragrant** means "sweet **smell**ing."

In (D), a **raucous discussion** would be a harsh-sounding, noisy debate.

> *mellifluous: sweet sounding, melodious*
> *fragrant: sweet smelling*
> *raucous: harsh or grating*

18. C

A **GUFFAW,** by definition, is loud, unrestrained **LAUGH**ing. In the same way, a **yell** is loud, unrestrained **talk**ing.

19. C

The word **CELESTIAL** means "having to do with the **HEAVENS.**" The word **nautical** means "having to do with **ships.**"

> *celestial: having to do with the heavens*
> *nautical: having to do with ships*
> *viscous: thick and gluey*

20. C

To **ENERVATE** is to lessen or decrease **VITALITY.** In (C), to **daunt** is to lessen **courage.**

You could have worked backwards by eliminating answer choices with inappropriate or weak bridges. For example, in (A), one can **consolidate power** by securing and strengthening one's position, but that bridge doesn't work with the stem words. Choice (B) has a weak bridge, too: To **energize** is to fill with energy, but that doesn't always result in **action.** If you plug the stem words into (D)'s bridge, you get, "To **ENERVATE** is to assess the **VITALITY** of something." It doesn't sound sensible, so (D) is out, too. In (E) to

admit guilt is to confess. That couldn't be true of the stem as well. By process of elimination, (C) is correct.

> *enervate: to lessen or decrease vitality*
> *daunt: to subdue or dismay*
> *energize: to fill with energy*
> *estimate: to assess the worth of*
> *something*

21. D

An **OLIGARCHY** is, by definition, a form of government in which power is held by a **FEW** people. Answer choice (D) is analogous to this: A **monarchy** is a form of government in which power is held by **one** person.

If the definition of **OLIGARCHY** posed a problem, you could again eliminate wrong answers. For instance, in choice (A), the terms **government** and **majority** are not always linked. Similarly, in (B), **authority** and **consent** don't necessarily go together. In (C), a **country** may or may not have a **constitution.**

> *oligarchy: a form of government in*
> *which power is held by a few people*
> *monarchy: a form of government in*
> *which power is held by one person*
> *constitution: a set of principles*
> *according to which a nation is*
> *governed*

22. A

Bridge: Someone who is **UNTRUTHFUL** is characterized by **MENDACIOUSNESS.** Choice (A) is correct: Someone who is **circumspect** is characterized by **caution.**

What if you don't know what mendaciousness or circumspect mean? You must try to eliminate wrong answers. Remember that the stem words and the correct answer choice will have the same strong bridge. Work backwards. Does (B) have a strong bridge? A person who is **timid** exhibits certain a type of **behavior**—that's not a strong connection. Similarly, (C)'s bridge is weak: Everyone has a **physique** of some kind,

not just **agile** people. Answer choices (D) and (E) can also be eliminated because they have weak bridges. That leaves us with (A).

> *mendaciousness: lying*
> *circumspect: cautious or watchful*

23. B

The bridge can be stated as: Something that is **INEXCUSABLE** is impossible to **JUSTIFY.** Likewise, in (B), something that is **unassailable** is impossible to **attack.**

> *unassailable: not open to attack or*
> *question*
> *affable: friendly and polite*
> *revere: to feel deep respect or awe for*

The Twain Passage

This excerpt from Mark Twain's *Life on the Mississippi* should be amusing and easy to read. All the humor comes from the same technique—using deadpan, matter-of-fact language to describe the exaggerated daydreams and jealousies of a boy's life.

The central point here is the author's envy of the engineer, and many of the questions focus on this. The author starts with his own glamorous ideas about steamboating, then spends most of the passage on the show-off engineer. The passage finishes with the author's own failure to find work as a pilot. The slightly old-fashioned style isn't hard to follow, but several questions focus on the author's figurative use of words.

24. B

The key word in the sentence is *supposed.* Of course, a justice of the peace doesn't possess unlimited power, but because of inexperience the author *supposed* he did. (B) accurately uses **naive** (inexperienced, gullible) to characterize the author's misconception. Three of the wrong choices assume that the father really did have unlimited powers and explain this in different ways—**frontier justice** (A, D), public support (C). (E) mistakenly views the boy's description of his father as an indication that the boy's childhood **environment** was **harsh.**

25. C

Distinction has several meanings, including those in (A), (B), (C), and (E). The key to its use here is context: In the previous sentence the author is talking about his naive ideas of his father's great power. (C) **prestige,** suggesting high status and honor, fits this context; the other three don't. (D) is not a meaning of *distinction* at all.

26. E

This question asks about the literal meaning of the sentence, but inference and context help, too. The sentence explains that the author wanted the job because a deck hand was "conspicuous," or easily seen. The previous sentence stresses standing "where all my old comrades could see me," so you can deduce that the author wants to be seen and admired in what he imagines is a glamorous profession (E).

(A) and (B) invent advantages that are not mentioned, and miss the humor by suggesting common-sense economic motivations. (C) assumes that if the author could be seen by his "old comrades" in the first job, he must want *not* to be seen by them in a different job; but this is false, since he'd be "conspicuous" in the second job, too. (D) brings in an ambition—becoming a pilot—that the author doesn't develop until the end of the passage.

27. B

Again, context helps. The *Sunday-school* reference is explained in the next sentence. The engineer had been "worldly"— which is what Sunday school probably taught students not to be—and the author had been "just the reverse." In other words, the author followed his *Sunday-school teachings,* the **engineer** didn't, yet the **engineer** gets the glory. The underlying idea is that this was **unjust** (B).

(A) is never mentioned. (C) takes the Sunday-school reference literally and misses the humorous tone. (D) invents an ambition that the author never mentions; his reaction is pure envy, not frustrated ambition. (E) misconstrues the reference to the engineer as "world-

ly"; it means he didn't take Sunday-school seriously, not that he was **unscrupulous** (dishonest or crooked).

28. C

To get this question, you need to read the sentence that follows. The engineer was not generous because he sat about where "we all could see him and envy him." The implication is that great people should be generous by not showing off or (C) **flaunting** their success.

(A) refers to the Sunday-school comment, but that was about undeserved greatness, not lack of generosity. (B) and (D) interpret *generous* in the literal sense of not caring for money, but the author is using the word figuratively. (E) relates to the author's unfulfilled desire to work on a steamboat, but the engineer is not thinking about the author, he is just showing off.

29. D

The engineer does everything for the purpose of showing off. He talks the jargon of the trade to make himself look knowledgeable, or (D) **sophisticated.**

Reading between the lines, we realize he's not an **expert** (A), and doesn't care about knowledge for its own sake (B). His (C) **ignorance** on other subjects is not mentioned; in fact, he has a working knowledge of St. Louis. (E) takes literally the phrase about how the engineer "forgot common people could not understand"—he couldn't **communicate effectively.** But the author says the engineer talked "as if" he forgot common people. In other words he didn't fail to communicate, he chose not to, to impress others.

30. E

The first four choices are all common meanings of *consideration,* but the context makes it clear that the figurative use in (E) is meant. The boys had *consideration* because they knew something about St. Louis, but their glory is over because the engineer knows much more. Prestige, respect, or (E) **reputation** supplies the meaning that fits. Boys are not likely to have the qualities of **generosity, deliberation, contemplation,** or **unselfishness** as a result of knowing a little about St. Louis.

31. A

The context makes it clear that the engineer had, or at least seemed to have, much more familiarity with St. Louis than the other boys with their "vague knowledge"; their "glory" is ended because he can talk rings around them about St. Louis (A).

There's no indication that (B) **St. Louis has changed,** or that the boys had been lying—their knowledge was "vague," not false (D). Reading between the lines, it's clear that travel to St. Louis was still rare enough to seem **enviable** (E). As for choice (C), the passage implies just the opposite.

32. A

With his "hair oil . . . showy brass watch chain, [and] leather belt," the engineer was obviously out to **impress** (A). The next sentence confirms that, telling us "no girl could withstand his charms."

The author never says the young man's dress is **typical** (B). (C) and (E) are both wrong; the emphasis here is on the engineer's charms, not the author's **wardrobe** or **fashion** ideas. (D) won't work because the engineer's behavior is as showy and superficial as his clothes.

33. D

As often in these questions, wrong choices give flat-footed, literal interpretations where the author is being humorous. (A) misunderstands the reference to Providence—the author is criticizing *providence,* not thanking it, because it has spared an "undeserving reptile," the engineer. So the author feels resentment, or (D) **outrage,** because the engineer's good luck seems **undeserved.**

Choice (B) sounds believable at first, but the passage doesn't emphasize the lucky **escape**—it focuses on people's sense that the engineer got better than he deserved. (C) and (E) are never mentioned.

34. C

The passage focuses on the author's ambition to work on a steamboat and his envy of the engineer. This makes (C) and (D) the strongest choices, so you need to decide between them. Looking at (D), the passage certainly emphasizes the engineer's **boastfulness,** but only within the framework of the author's dreams and ambitions (paragraphs one and five) and the author's reactions to the engineer. So (C) describes the whole passage whereas (D) describes only the long central paragraphs. In a major purpose/major focus question, the answer that sums up the whole passage will be correct.

The (A) **life** of the **town** is barely suggested. (B) is wrong because the passage's events don't end in **success**—although in reality, Mark Twain did go on to become a pilot. The author's (E) **conflict with his parents** is mentioned only briefly, toward the end of paragraph four.

35. E

The last paragraph discusses the author's failed attempts to become a pilot, and his daydreams that he will still become one, so (E) works best. Mates and clerks are mentioned as ignoring the author, but he never considers becoming either a (A) **mate or a clerk,** looking for some other job (B), giving up his aim of being a pilot (C), or asking his parents' forgiveness (D).

SECTION 3

The Shakespeare Pair

This paired passages present two opposing arguments on a single subject, the subject here being "Who Really Wrote Shakespeare's Plays?" The author of the first passage maintains that Francis Bacon actually wrote the plays, basing that conclusion on the assertion that Shakespeare didn't have the education and social experience necessary to create such sophisticated plays. The author of the second passage takes issue with that, claiming that Shakespeare's genius grew out of a deep understanding of human nature rather than any wide learning or arcane knowledge.

1. B

A Vocabulary-in-Context question. Here we're asked the definition of the word *entertain* in line 2, where it is used in the phrase "entertain some doubt." Well, when you entertain doubt, or entertain an idea, you are holding it in your head. You are **harboring** it, in the sense of **to harbor** as "to be host to." So choice (B) is correct.

The other choices are all acceptable dictionary definitions of the verb *entertain*, but none fits the context as well as choice (B) does. (A) **amuse** is a common synonym for *entertain*, but how does one amuse doubt? (C) **occupy** and (E) **engage** are closer, but they don't fit the sentence either. One's *mind* is occupied or engaged, but the doubt itself is not occupied or engaged. Meanwhile, (D) **cherish** adds a sense of valuing the entertained thing, as if it were something desirable.

2. D

The author claims that the person who actually wrote the plays must have had "intimate knowledge of life within royal courts and palaces," but that Shakespeare was just a commoner, without that kind of "firsthand experience" of the aristocracy. He wants to cast doubt on Shakespeare's **familiarity with the life of [aristocrats],** or choice (D).

Shakespeare's ability to (A) **write poetically** and his (C) **ability to support himself as a playwright** never come up in Passage 1. The **knowledge of foreign**

places mentioned in (B) does come up, but being a commoner is not necessarily related to Shakespeare's apparent lack of travel. Choice (E) is the closest wrong choice, since the aristocracy was the **government** in Elizabethan England, but the issue is his knowledge of all aspects of aristocratic life.

3. E

Two Shakespearian plays—*Coriolanus* and *Love's Labour's Lost*—are mentioned in lines 28–31 in connection with the allegedly specialized knowledge they contain. They support the point that the educated aristocrat Bacon was a more likely author than was the undereducated commoner Shakespeare. So (E) answers the question best.

Choice (A) is a clever wrong choice, but it's too extreme. The author's not trying to prove that *only* Bacon could have written these plays, just that Bacon was far more likely than Shakespeare to have written them. The **deep understanding of human nature** mentioned in (B) is something brought up in Passage 2, not Passage 1. The author is not comparing the two plays to **works written by Bacon,** as (C) claims. And (D) is wrong since nothing about society is mentioned with regard to *Coriolanus.* Also, it's not the **broad spectrum of society** the author alludes to with regard to *Love's Labour's Lost*, but rather the knowledge of just the upper range of society.

4. A

It's clear that Ms. Bacon is looking down on **actors,** of which Shakespeare was one, regarding them with the **disdain** expressed in correct choice (A).

She's not **resentful** of how the **characters are portrayed,** choice (B), since she's talking about the characters themselves and what they tell us about real-life actors. Given her opinion of actors, she certainly doesn't **regret that [their] conditions weren't better,** choice (C). (D) is closer, but it's a distortion. She never doubts that anyone could **create such characters;** she doubts that the author of the plays could be like such a character. And finally, in (E), there's no evidence in the quote that Ms. Bacon thinks the actors are inept at their art, just that they are vulgar and lowly persons.

5. B

This question sends you back to paragraph 4 of Passage 1, where Bacon's preference for anonymity is explained. The author claims that, because the plays were "controversial," Bacon felt that associating himself with them would have been "politically and personally damaging." So **he wished to protect himself from the effects of controversy,** choice (B).

(A) is wrong, since Bacon did publish a lot of **writing** under his own name. (C) is plausible, but it's not the reason given in paragraph 4 or anywhere else in the first passage. (D) tries to confuse us by introducing the subject of **lowly actors** from the preceding paragraph. And (E) is a fabrication since we know that Bacon was already **famous** from his other writings.

6. C

This question takes us to the first paragraph of Passage 2, where the emphasis is on language ability. The author doubts that Bacon, a writer primarily of academic Latin, would have had the ability to produce the exalted English in which the plays were written. That makes (C) the best answer.

(A) is a distortion. Just because Bacon wrote most of his own work in another language doesn't mean that he was **unfamiliar** with English. (B)'s emphasis on the difficult switch from **scientific writing** to **playwriting** is close, but language rather than the type of writing is the focus. There's no reason to surmise that the author doubts Bacon's ability to **cooperate** on a **committee,** choice (D). Finally, (E) is wrong because there is no evidence in the first paragraph that the author has doubts about Bacon's ability to produce that amount of work.

7. D

Back to Vocabulary-in-Context. This question asks about *premier* as it is used in the phrase "premier stylist in the English language." The author definitely wants to indicate the sublime language of the plays here, so *premier* is being used in the sense of "of the first rank," or, as choice (D) has it, **greatest.** (A), (C), and (E) all play on the sense of *premier* as "first in sequence," (**inaugural,** by the way, means "marking the commencement or beginning") but the author is not

referring here to when Shakespeare wrote. He's writing about how well Shakespeare wrote. On the other hand, (B) **influential** misses on two counts—first, it's not a definition of *premier* in any context, and second, the issue of influence on other writers is not brought up here.

8. B

The next Vocabulary-in-Context question concerns the adjective *encyclopedic* in line 75, where it's used to modify the noun "knowledge." The author says that Shakespeare's genius was one of common sense and perceptive intuition, not encyclopedic knowledge, which is related to great book-learning. So the knowledge described as *encyclopedic* is wide-ranging and in-depth—**comprehensive,** choice (B).

(A) **technical** is close to the sense of the context, but it's not a synonym of *encyclopedic,* so it really won't work here. (C) won't work either, since **abridged** (meaning "condensed") cannot describe the kind of exhaustive knowledge the author is describing here. And while it may take discipline to gain encyclopedic knowledge, *encyclopedic* itself cannot be defined as **disciplined,** so cut (D). Finally, (E) **specialized** isn't quite right, since it implies a narrowness of focus.

9. E

The reference to *Shakespeare's status as a landowner* comes in the third paragraph of Passage 2, where it is brought up to show that Shakespeare would have been "knowledgeable about legal matters related to . . . real estate." That makes (E) the best answer, "legal matters" being equivalent to **the law.**

(A) is interesting, since the author does say that owning land was quite an accomplishment for a **playwright,** but it has nothing to do with his knowledge of the law. (B) is off, since owning land doesn't make one automatically friendly with the highborn set. (C) is wrong, because Shakespeare's financial state is just a side issue; it's not the point of bringing up Shakespeare's landowning status. And (D) doesn't fit, since no one doubts that **Shakespeare was a commoner.**

10. A

This question directs us to lines 99–102, where the author claims that *literary genius* "can flower in any socioeconomic bracket." That implies that genius has little to do with a person's social and financial position—or, as correct choice (A) has it—genius doesn't depend **on a writer's external circumstances.**

(B) fails by bringing in the notion of **comprehension of human nature** from elsewhere in the passage. (C) is a common cliché, but there's no evidence here that the author felt that Shakespeare's genius was **enhanced by poverty.** In fact, this author implies that Shakespeare wasn't even all that poor. (D) may be a true statement, but **recognition** of genius isn't really under discussion here; it's the simple existence of genius. And (E) is a distortion; the author claims that at least one kind of genius does not stem from **book-learning and academic training,** but that doesn't mean that those things would **stifle** *literary genius.*

11. C

Go back to the fourth paragraph of Passage 1, where our first author claims that Bacon may have "hired a lowly actor" like Shakespeare to put his name to the plays and take the heat of controversy. How would our second author respond to this claim? The second author, remember, writes in the concluding paragraph of Passage 2 that "no elaborate theories of intrigue and secret identity are necessary to explain the accomplishment of William Shakespeare." Surely Author 2 would regard the **scenario** described in Passage 1 as just this kind of **unnecessary** theory, so (C) is the best guess for how Author 2 would react.

As for choice (A), Author 2 may or may not agree that the plays were **controversial** in their time, so (A) won't work. (B) gets the thrust of Author 2's argument wrong. Author 2 denigrates the notion that Bacon wrote the plays not by arguing that Bacon wasn't a great scholar, but by arguing that it didn't require a great scholar to write the plays. (D) tries to turn Author 1's argument on its head. A nice idea, perhaps, but Author 2 shows no hint of doing anything of the kind. And (E) brings up the notion of Shakespeare's social **respectability,** which really isn't of much concern to Author 2.

12. C

What would be Author 1's reaction to Author 2's *skepticism* that Bacon, the author of Latin treatises, could be the "premier stylist in the English language"? Well, Author 1's repeated assertions of Bacon's scholarly genius and Shakespeare's lack of education are both reflected in choice (C), which makes it a good bet as the correct answer.

(A)'s mention of the **similarities between Latin and English** is enough to kill this choice, since Author 1 mentions no such similarities in the passage. (B) is a true statement, perhaps, but it doesn't really address the issue. (D) is fairly nonsensical, since it would weaken Author 1's entire theory about why Bacon hired Shakespeare. Finally, (E) makes a good point, but again, there is no hint of this sentiment in Author 1's statements.

Compute Your Score

Step 1: Figure out your Verbal raw score. Refer to your answer sheet for the total number right and the total number wrong for all three Verbal sections in the practice test you're scoring. (If you haven't scored your results, do that now, using the answers that follow the test.) You can use the chart below to figure out your Verbal raw score. As the chart shows, your Verbal raw score is equal to the total right in the three Verbal sections minus one-fourth of the number wrong in those sections. Round the result to the nearest whole number.

PRACTICE TEST A

	NUMBER RIGHT	NUMBER WRONG	RAW SCORE
SECTION 1:	☐ −	(.25 x ☐)	= ☐
SECTION 2:	☐ −	(.25 x ☐)	= ☐
SECTION 3:	☐ −	(.25 x ☐)	= ☐
		VERBAL RAW SCORE =	☐ (ROUNDED)

PRACTICE TEST B

	NUMBER RIGHT	NUMBER WRONG	RAW SCORE
SECTION 1:	☐ −	(.25 x ☐)	= ☐
SECTION 2:	☐ −	(.25 x ☐)	= ☐
SECTION 3:	☐ −	(.25 x ☐)	= ☐
		VERBAL RAW SCORE =	☐ (ROUNDED)

Step 2: Find your practice test score. Use the table below to find your practice test score based on your Verbal raw score.

Find Your Practice Test Score

Raw	Scaled	Raw	Scaled	Raw	Scaled
−3 or		22	450	48	620
less	200	23	460	49	630
−2	230	24	470	50	640
−1	270	25	470	51	640
0	290	26	480	52	650
1	300	27	490	53	660
2	310	28	490	54	670
3	320	29	500	55	670
4	330	30	510	56	670
5	330	31	510	57	680
6	340	32	520	58	690
7	350	33	530	59	690
8	360	34	530	60	700
9	370	35	540	61	710
10	370	36	550	62	720
11	380	37	550	63	730
12	390	38	560	64	730
13	390	39	570	65	740
14	400	40	570	66	750
15	410	41	580	67	760
16	410	42	590	68	770
17	420	43	590	69	780
18	430	44	600	70	790
19	430	45	600	71 or	
20	440	46	610	more	800
21	450	47	610		

Don't take your practice test scores too literally. Practice test conditions cannot precisely mirror real test conditions. Your actual SAT Verbal score will almost certainly vary from your practice test scores. Your score on a practice test gives you a rough idea of your range on the actual exam.

If you don't like your score, it's not too late to do something about it. Work your way way through this book again, and turn to Kaplan's *SAT & PSAT*, our more comprehensive test prep and college admissions guide, for even more help.

How Did We Do? Grade Us.

Thank you for choosing a Kaplan book. Your comments and suggestions are very useful to us. Please answer the following questions to assist us in our continued development of high-quality resources to meet your needs.

The Kaplan book I read was: _____

My name is: _____

My address is: _____

_____

My e-mail address is: _____

What overall grade would you give this book? (A) (B) (C) (D) (F)

How relevant was the information to your goals? (A) (B) (C) (D) (F)

How comprehensive was the information in this book? (A) (B) (C) (D) (F)

How accurate was the information in this book? (A) (B) (C) (D) (F)

How easy was the book to use? (A) (B) (C) (D) (F)

How appealing was the book's design? (A) (B) (C) (D) (F)

What were the book's strong points? _____

How could this book be improved? _____

Is there anything that we left out that you wanted to know more about?

Would you recommend this book to others? ☐ YES   ☐ NO

Other comments: _____

_____

_____

Do we have permission to quote you? ☐ YES   ☐ NO

Thank you for your help. Please tear out this page and mail it to:

Dave Chipps, Managing Editor
Kaplan Educational Centers
888 Seventh Avenue
New York, NY 10106

Or, you can submit your comments electronically by using Kaplan's online feedback form at http://www.kaptest.com/customer-service/lvl5_comments.jhtml

Thanks!

SIXTY · YEARS · OF
KAPLAN
60
BUILDING · FUTURES

Just in case the rock star thing doesn't work out.

Kaplan gets you in.

For over 60 years, Kaplan has been helping students get into college. Whether you're facing the SAT, PSAT or ACT, take Kaplan and get the score you need to get into the schools you want.

1-800-KAP-TEST

kaptest.com AOL keyword: kaplan

*Test names are registered trademarks of their respective owners.

World Leader in Test Prep

About KAPLAN®

Kaplan, Inc. is one of the nation's leading providers of education and career services. Kaplan is a wholly owned subsidiary of The Washington Post Company.

KAPLAN TEST PREPARATION & ADMISSIONS

Kaplan's nationally recognized test prep courses cover more than 20 standardized tests, including secondary school, college and graduate school entrance exams, as well as foreign language and professional licensing exams. In addition, Kaplan offers a college admissions course, private tutoring, and a variety of free information and services for students applying to college and graduate programs. Kaplan also provides information and guidance on the financial aid process. Students can enroll in online test prep courses and admissions consulting services at www.kaptest.com.

Kaplan K12 Learning Services partners with schools, universities, and teachers to help students succeed, providing customized assessment, education, and professional development programs.

SCORE! EDUCATIONAL CENTERS

SCORE! after-school learning centers help K–10 students build confidence along with academic skills in a motivating, sports-oriented environment.

SCORE! Prep provides in-home, one-on-one tutoring for high school academic subjects and standardized tests.

eSCORE.com is the first educational services Web site to offer parents and kids newborn to age 18 personalized child development and educational resources online.

KAPLANCOLLEGE.COM

KaplanCollege.com, Kaplan's distance learning platform, offers an array of online educational programs for working professionals who want to advance their careers. Learners will find nearly 500 professional development, continuing education, certification, and degree courses and programs in Nursing, Education, Criminal Justice, Real Estate, Legal Professions, Law, Management, General Business, and Computing/Information Technology.

KAPLAN PUBLISHING

Kaplan Publishing produces retail books and software. Kaplan Books, published by Simon & Schuster, include titles in test preparation, admissions, education, career development, and life skills; Kaplan and Newsweek jointly publish guides on getting into college, finding the right career, and helping children succeed in school.

KAPLAN PROFESSIONAL

Kaplan Professional provides assessment, training, and certification services for corporate clients and individuals seeking to advance their careers. Member units include:

- Dearborn, a leading supplier of licensing training and continuing education for securities, real estate, and insurance professionals

- Perfect Access/CRN, which delivers software education and consultation for law firms and businesses

- Kaplan Professional Call Center Services, a total provider of services for the call center industry

- Self Test Software, a world leader in exam simulation software and preparation for technical certifications

- Schweser's Study Program/AIAF, which provides preparation services for the CFA examination

KAPLAN INTERNATIONAL PROGRAMS

Kaplan assists international students and professionals in the United States through a series of intensive English language and test preparation programs. These programs are offered at campus-based centers across the United States. Specialized services include housing, placement at top American universities, fellowship management, academic monitoring and reporting, and financial administration.

COMMUNITY OUTREACH

Kaplan provides educational career resources to thousands of financially disadvantaged students annually, working closely with educational institutions, not-for-profit groups, government agencies and grass roots organizations on a variety of national and local support programs. These programs help students and professionals from a variety of backgrounds achieve their educational and career goals.

BRASSRING

BrassRing Inc., the premier business-to-business hiring management and recruitment services company, offers employers a vertically integrated suite of online and offline solutions. BrassRing, created in September 1999, combined Kaplan Career Services, Terra-Starr, Crimson & Brown Associates, thepavement.com, and HireSystems. In March 2000, BrassRing acquired Career Service Inc./Westech. Kaplan is a shareholder in BrassRing, along with Tribune Company, Central Newspapers, and Accel Partners.